HAND IN HAND

Selected Reprints and Annotated Bibliography on Working with Students Who Are Deaf-Blind

Kathleen Mary Huebner
Jeanne Glidden Prickett
Therese Rafalowski Welch
Elga Joffee, Editors

AFB
PRESS
NEW YORK

MW00999607

Printed in the United States of America

Library of Congress Cataloging-in-Publication Data

Hand in hand : selected reprints and annotated bibliography on working
    with students who are deaf-blind / Kathleen Mary Huebner . . . [et
    al.], editors.
        p.   cm.
      ISBN 0-89128-938-0 (pbk. : acid-free paper)
      1. Blind-deaf--Education--Bibliography. 2. Blind-deaf children-
    -Education--Bibliography. 3. Blind-deaf children--Rehabilitation-
    -Bibliography.   4. Blind-deaf children--Means of communication-
    -Bibliography.   I. Huebner, Kathleen Mary. II. American Foundation
    for the Blind.
    Z5346.H36   1995
    [HV1597.2]
    016.37191 ' 1--dc20   94-32260
                                                                    CIP

Second printing, 1997

This publication was funded through Cooperative Agreement #H086A00005 from the U.S. Department of Education, Office of Special Education and Rehabilitative Services. The opinions or policies expressed herein do not necessarily reflect those of the U.S. Department of Education, and no official endorsement should be inferred. ∎

Functional Skills

Implications of Various Etiologies

Instructional Strategies and Intervention Issues

ANNOTATED BIBLIOGRAPHY

*T*his collection of reprints and annotated listings is one component of the materials produced by the AFB Deaf-Blind Project, a four-year federally funded effort established to fulfill the need for information and resources of educators who work with students who are deaf-blind. The other components include a self-study manual, *Hand in Hand: Essentials of Communication and Orientation and Mobility for Your Students Who Are Deaf-Blind;* an in-service training guide; and a videotape and accompanying discussion guide. Together, they present a constellation of information for service providers who need to know how to work effectively with deaf-blind students. They can be used alone or in combination to supplement each other to enhance educational efforts.

The articles reprinted in this volume were selected because of their particular value to classroom teachers working on their own as self-study students to seek more information on deaf-blind children. They were identified through a literature search, recommendations from AFB Deaf-Blind Project National Consortium members, and a survey of service providers throughout the nation; consortium representatives and project staff reviewed and verified the importance of each one. Articles were chosen because they are relevant to the project's focus on the topics of communication and orientation and mobility; because they contain useful information, regardless of prevailing educational trends, about effective practices in many settings and circumstances with students who are deaf-blind; and because they support other information in the project materials. The articles may provide more detailed information on particular topics than the *Hand in Hand* self-study manual or video, different or expanded perspectives, or concrete examples of the application of theory. We are indebted to the authors and publishers of the articles included in this volume for granting permission to reprint them here.

Although in recent years more literature has addressed the needs of students who are deaf-blind than in the past, comparatively less is written about this population than about other groups. This scarcity is in all likelihood related to the low incidence of the disability and the resulting shortage of specialized service providers and others working with these students who are able to conduct research and write about them. This set of materials is not exhaustive, but it includes in one convenient place articles on specific topics that are essential for teachers. Some of the information presented in these pieces is important because it will give *Hand in Hand*'s readers a background for understanding how services have evolved over time for students who are deaf-blind, which also influences how future services will be delivered. Other articles provide supplementary information about specific instructional topics or issues that teachers often identify. The entire collection is intended to add to the overall information a teacher has about how students who are deaf-blind learn and how these students can be assisted most effectively as they develop life skills.

Although the articles presented here represent a useful body of knowledge on their own, we recommend that you read these reprints as you work through the self-study manual to supplement the information provided there. The articles have been grouped into five broad categories: (1) Communication, (2) Orientation and Mobility, (3) Functional Skills, (4) Implications of Various Etiologies, and (5) Instructional Strategies and Intervention Issues, as indicated in the table of contents of this book. Within each category, the articles were arranged to flow whenever possible both from the general to the specific and chronologically in terms of the individual's development. Many of the articles have been written by leading authorities in the field of education of children who are deaf-blind. The references cited in the reprints will lead you to additional sources that you may find helpful. In this way, the reprint collection was designed to broaden readers' perspectives and strengthen their understanding of the unique needs of deaf-blind students.

The annotated listings presented in the second part of this book are brief descriptions of basic resources on deaf-blindness, deafness,

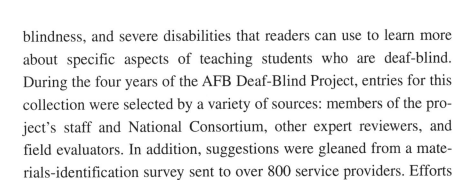

blindness, and severe disabilities that readers can use to learn more about specific aspects of teaching students who are deaf-blind. During the four years of the AFB Deaf-Blind Project, entries for this collection were selected by a variety of sources: members of the project's staff and National Consortium, other expert reviewers, and field evaluators. In addition, suggestions were gleaned from a materials-identification survey sent to over 800 service providers. Efforts were designed to identify materials considered "classic," essential, and of greatest value to readers.

The entries are presented in two sections: print materials and audiovisual materials. Within these sections, they are alphabetized by author. Each entry contains the following information:

- author
- title
- date of publication
- publisher or distributor (name and address)
- ISBN (International Standard Book Number, or catalog or other number assigned by the publisher or distributor)
- approximate cost at press time
- format (including number of pages for print media and running time in minutes for videotapes)
- subject or descriptors (listed in order of significance)
- summary of the content.

In cases in which authorship is not clearly indicated on the materials themselves, "NA," for "not applicable," is used for the author designation. The same designation is used when an ISBN is not assigned to materials, as is the case with many videotapes. With this knowledge, readers can locate books, videotapes, and other materials that they may wish to purchase for their own use directly from the sources or that they may borrow for review from libraries.

To help readers find information easily, a list of materials appears at the beginning of the annotated listings. Entries are divided again into print and audiovisual materials, but here they are alphabetized by title so they can be accessed another way.

This annotated bibliography contains basic materials and is not meant to be comprehensive; many other good reference materials exist that could not be included for space reasons. However, the entries in this collection are a sound starting point for ongoing self-study efforts and an effective supplement for work with students who are deaf-blind. Given the fast-moving progress now taking place regarding the availability of materials in electronic media, readers are also encouraged to explore the body of knowledge that may be obtainable in electronic formats. ■

Kathleen Mary Huebner, Ph.D., Director of the AFB Deaf-Blind Project, is the Chairperson of the Division of Graduate Studies in Visual Impairment and Director of Education and Rehabilitation Programs of the Institute for the Visually Impaired at the Pennsylvania College of Optometry in Philadelphia. Previously, she was Director of the National Program Associates Department and National Consultant in Education at the American Foundation for the Blind and directed the Graduate Teacher Training Program at the State University of New York at Geneseo. A former instructor of individuals with visual impairments and an orientation and mobility specialist, Dr. Huebner has co-authored and edited several books and written numerous articles on services for individuals who are visually impaired. She has given numerous presentations and consulted at schools, teacher training programs, and government agencies nationwide and abroad on topics related to blindness and multiple impairments.

Jeanne Glidden Prickett, Ed.D., is the Coordinator of Materials Development for the AFB Deaf-Blind Project. She was previously Assistant Professor and Coordinator of the Program in Visual Impairments at the Johns Hopkins University Division of Education in Baltimore, as well as Technical Assistance Consultant to the Maryland Deaf-Blind Project. Dr. Prickett was also the Coordinator of the National Information Center on Deaf-Blindness at Gallaudet University in Washington, DC. A former supervisor of special education services and teacher of children who are visually impaired, hearing impaired, and deaf-blind, she has published articles and given numerous presentations on the education of children and youths who are deaf-blind.

Therese Rafalowski Welch, M.Ed., the Coordinator of Consortium Activities for the AFB Deaf-Blind Project, is the former Director of Washington State Services for Children with Deaf-Blindness and a former teacher of children who are deaf-blind. She has given numerous presentations and provided in-service training at program sites throughout the United States and abroad on issues related to the education of children who are deaf-blind. Her publications include a guide on early intervention for families of children who are blind or visually impaired and articles on services for children who are deaf-blind and their families.

Elga Joffee, M.Ed., M.P.S., is National Program Associate at the American Foundation for the Blind (AFB) and Chairperson of AFB's National ADA (Americans with Disabilities Act) Initiative. A certified orientation and mobility specialist, she is the producer of *We Can Do It Together,* a videotape and companion curriculum for teaching orientation and mobility to students with severe visual and multiple impairments, used systemwide in New York City public schools. She has written and presented widely on orientation and mobility, the Americans with Disabilities Act, and other issues in the field of visual impairment. ■

Lou Johnson Alonso, M.A., is Professor in the Department of Counseling, Educational Psychology, and Special Education and Coordinator of the Program for Blind, Deaf-Blind, and Orientation and Mobility Teacher Education at Michigan State University in East Lansing.

Kevin D. Arnold, Ph.D., is a psychologist in private practice in Columbus, Ohio, and on the clinical faculty of the University of Dayton School of Education. Previously he was the Director of the Great Lakes Area Regional Center for Deaf-Blind Education at Ohio State University in Columbus.

Vic Baldwin, Ed.D., is Director of Teaching Research at Western Oregon State College in Monmouth, Oregon.

Chigee Jan Cloninger, Ph.D., is Director of the Vermont State Program for Students with Dual Sensory Impairments; Coordinator of the State of Vermont Interdisciplinary Team for Intensive Special Education; and Research Associate Professor at the University Affiliated Program of Vermont, Center for Developmental Disabilities, University of Vermont, Burlington.

Michael T. Collins, M.Ed., is Director of the Hilton/Perkins Program and previously Supervisor of the Deaf-Blind Program of the Perkins School for the Blind in Watertown, Massachusetts.

Joyce Ford, parent representative on the National Consortium, is President of the National Family Association for Deaf-Blind and lives in Boise, Idaho.

H. D. Bud Fredericks, Ed.D., is Research Professor at Teaching Research, TRACES Project (Teaching Research Assistance to Children and Youth Experiencing Sensory Impairments), Western Oregon State College in Monmouth, Oregon.

Charles W. Freeman, M.Ed., is Education Program Specialist with the U.S. Department of Education, Office of Special Education Programs, in Washington, DC.

Lori Goetz, Ph.D., is Director of the California Research Institute and Professor at San Francisco State University, Department of Special Education, in San Francisco, California.

Steven B. Johnson, M.S., is Assistant Director, Special Education Division, and Administrator, Management and Coordination, Deaf-Blind Services, California Department of Education in Sacramento.

Thomas W. Jones, Ph.D., is Professor of Education at Gallaudet University in Washington, DC.

Roderick J. Macdonald, M.A., is Management Analyst with the U.S. Department of Labor, Office of Information Resources Management, in Washington, DC, and Past President of the American Association of the Deaf-Blind in Silver Spring, Maryland.

Joseph J. McNulty, M.A., is Director of the Helen Keller National Center for Deaf-Blind Youths and Adults in Sands Point, NY.

Rosanne K. Silberman, Ed.D., is Professor in the Department of Special Education and Coordinator of the Teacher Preparation Program in Visual Impairment and Severe Disabilities Including Deaf-Blindness at Hunter College of the City University of New York in New York City.

Susan J. Spungin, Ed.D., is Vice President, National Programs and Initiatives, of the American Foundation for the Blind in New York City.

Louis M. Tutt, M.Ed., is President of the Maryland School for the Blind in Baltimore and Outgoing President of the Council of the Schools for the Blind. ■

*T*he AFB Deaf-Blind Project would like to thank the authors and publishers of the articles appearing in this volume for granting permission for their inclusion. A full listing of articles and credits follows, corresponding with the order in which the articles appear in this book.

"Prelanguage Communication of Students Who Are Deaf-Blind and Have Other Severe Impairments," by N. E. Tedder, K. Warden, and A. Sikka, *Journal of Visual Impairment & Blindness,* 87(8) October 1993, pp. 302-307. Copyright 1993 by the American Foundation for the Blind.

"Preverbal Communication of Blind Infants and Their Mothers," by Charity Rowland, *Journal of Visual Impairment & Blindness,* 78(7) September 1984, pp. 297-302. Copyright 1984 by the American Foundation for the Blind.

"Tactile Iconicity: Signs Rated for Use with Deaf-Blind Children," by Penny L. Griffith, Jacques H. Robinson, and John H. Panagos, *Journal of The Association of Persons with Severe Handicaps,* 8(2), Summer 1983, pp. 26-38. Reprinted with permission.

"Analytic Study of the Tadoma Method: Effects of Hand Position on Segmental Speech Perception," by Charlotte M. Reed, Nathaniel I. Durlach, Louis D. Braida, and Martin C. Schultz, *Journal of Speech and Hearing Research,* 32, December 1989, pp. 921-929. Reprinted with the permission of the American Speech-Language-Hearing Association.

"Interpreting for Deaf-Blind Students: Factors to Consider," by Karen Petronio, *American Annals of the Deaf,* 133(3), July 1988, pp. 226-229. Reprinted with permission.

"Providing O&M Services to Children and Youth with Severe Multiple Disabilities," by Brent R. Bailey and Daniel N. Head, *RE:view,* 25(2), Summer 1993, pp. 57-66. Reprinted with permission of the Helen Dwight Reid Educational Foundation. Published by Heldref Publications, 1319 18th Street, N.W., Washington, DC 20036-1802. Copyright 1993.

"Orientation and Mobility for Students with Severe Visual and Multiple Impairments: A New Perspective," by E. Joffee and C. H. Rikhye, *Journal of Visual Impairment & Blindness,* 85(5) May 1991, pp. 211-216. Copyright 1991 by the American Foundation for the Blind.

"Modifications of the Long Cane for Use by a Multiply Impaired Child," by Kathleen Ann Morse, *Journal of Visual Impairment & Blindness,* 74(1) January 1980, pp. 15-18. Copyright 1980 by the American Foundation for the Blind.

"Developing Vision Use Within Functional Daily Activities for Students with Visual and Multiple Disabilities," by June Downing and Brent Bailey, *RE:view,*

21(4), Winter 1990, pp.209-220. Reprinted with permission of the Helen Dwight Reid Educational Foundation. Published by Heldref Publications, 1319 18th Street, N.W., Washington, DC 20036-1802. Copyright 1990.

"Concepts and Issues Related to Choice-Making and Autonomy among Persons with Severe Disabilities," by Doug Guess, Holly Anne Benson, and Ellin Siegel-Causey, *Journal of The Association for Persons with Severe Handicaps,* 10(2), Summer 1985, pp. 79-86. Reprinted with permission.

"Teaching Students Who Are Deaf-Blind and Cognitively Disabled to Effectively Communicate Choices During Mealtime," by Carole R. Gothelf, Daniel B. Crimmins, Caren A. Mercer, and Patricia A. Finocchiaro, *Deaf-Blind Perspectives,* 1(1), Fall 1993, pp. 6-8. Reprinted with permission.

"An Approach to Teaching Self-Dressing to a Child with Dual Sensory Impairment," by Jenifer L. McKelvey, Lori A. Sisson, Vincent B. Van Hasselt, and Michel Hersen, *Teaching Exceptional Children,* 25(1), Fall 1992, pp. 12-15. Copyright 1992 by The Council for Exceptional Children. Reprinted with permission.

"The CHARGE Association: Implications for Teachers," by Thomas W. Jones and Michele T. Dunne, *American Annals of the Deaf,* 133(1), March 1988, pp. 36-39. Reprinted with permission.

"The Impact of Retinitis Pigmentosa on Young Adults: Psychological, Educational, Vocational, and Social Considerations," by L. A. Nemshick, McC. Vernon, and F. Ludman, *Journal of Visual Impairment & Blindness,* 80(7) September 1986, pp. 859-862. Copyright 1986 by the American Foundation for the Blind.

"The Usher's Syndrome Adolescent: Programming Implications for School Administrators, Teachers, and Residential Advisors," by Wanda M. Hicks and Doin E. Hicks, *American Annals of the Deaf,* 126(4), June 1981, pp. 422-431. Reprinted with permission.

"Services for Children and Youths Who Are Deaf-Blind: An Overview," by A. M. Zambone and K. M. Huebner, *Journal of Visual Impairment & Blindness,* 86(7), September 1992, pp. 287-290. Copyright 1992 by the American Foundation for the Blind.

"Perspectives of Parents Whose Children Have Dual Sensory Impairments," by Michael F. Giangreco, Chigee J. Cloninger, Patricia H. Mueller, Susan Yuan, and Susan Ashworth, *Journal of The Association for Persons with Severe Handicaps,* 16(1), Spring 1991, pp. 14-24. Reprinted with permission.

"Functional Vision Screening for Severely Handicapped Children," by Beth Langley and Rebecca F. DuBose, *New Outlook for the Blind,* 70(8), October 1976, pp. 346-350. Copyright 1976 by the American Foundation for the Blind.

"Developmental Scales versus Observational Measures for Deaf-Blind Children," by Martin H. Diebold, W. Scott Curtis, and Rebecca F. DuBose, *Exceptional Children,* 44(4), January 1978, pp. 275-278. Copyright 1978 by The Council for Exceptional Children. Reprinted with permission.

"Early Intervention for Infants with Deaf-Blindness," by Martha G. Michael and Peter V. Paul, *Exceptional Children,* 57(3) December/January 1991, pp. 200-210. Copyright 1991 by The Council for Exceptional Children. Reprinted with permission.

"Instructional Strategies for Learners with Dual Sensory Impairments in Integrated Settings," by June Downing and Joanne Eichinger, *Journal of The Association for Persons with Severe Handicaps,* 15(2), Summer 1990, pp. 98-105. Reprinted with permission.

"Strategies for Educating Learners with Severe Disabilities Within Their Local Home Schools and Communities," by Jacqueline S. Thousand and Richard A. Villa, *Focus on Exceptional Children,* 23(3), November 1990, pp. 1-24. Reprinted by permission of Love Publishing Company, Denver.

"A Classroom Environment Checklist for Students with Dual Sensory Impairments," by Catherine H. Rikhye, Carole R. Gothelf, and Madeline W. Appell, *Teaching Exceptional Children,* 22(1), Fall 1989, pp. 44-46. Copyright 1989 by The Council for Exceptional Children. Reprinted with permission.

"Clarifying the Role of Classroom Interpreters," by P. Lynn Hayes, *Perspectives in Education and Deafness,* 11(5), May/June 1993, pp. 8-10, 24. Reprinted with permission from *Perspectives in Education and Deafness,* a publication of Gallaudet University Pre-College Programs.

"Maximizing the Independence of Deaf-Blind Teenagers," by J. J. Venn and F. Wadler, *Journal of Visual Impairment & Blindness,* 84(3) March 1990, pp. 103-108. Copyright 1990 by the American Foundation for the Blind.

"A Local Team Approach," by Jane M. Everson, *Teaching Exceptional Children,* 23(1) Fall 1990, pp. 44-46. Copyright 1990 by The Council for Exceptional Children. Reprinted with permission.

"Supported Employment for Persons with Deaf-Blindness and Mental Retardation," by S. L. Griffin and J. Lowry, *Journal of Visual Impairment & Blindness,* 83(10) December 1989, pp. 495-499. Copyright 1989 by the American Foundation for the Blind. ■

Selected Reprints

Prelanguage Communication of Students Who Are Deaf-Blind and Have Other Severe Impairments

N.E. Tedder: K. Warden; A. Sikka

Abstract: Although instruments for assessing language have been useful for researchers and teachers of students with severe impairments, they have not provided a systematic way to observe or assess students who are deaf-blind, have other severe impairments, and function at the prelanguage level of communication or taken pragmatic competence into account. This article describes an instrument that is applicable to such students, provides many opportunities for recording interactions at the prelanguage level, and allows for the structured observation of pragmatic aspects of communication.

Although few people who are identified as deaf-blind are totally blind or totally deaf (Baldwin, 1991; Myers, 1981; Wolf, Delk, & Schein, 1982), the disability resulting from a deficit in both vision and hearing is substantially greater than the disability from either deafness or blindness alone because each new disability continuously magnifies the effect of the total. More than half the students who are deaf-blind have tertiary disabilities, most commonly mental retardation (Baldwin, 1991; Trybus, 1984). Whenever additional disabilities are combined with impaired vision and impaired hearing, the effect of the disabilities and their interaction on all the systems involved in human development defies simple description. The effects of such interactions are reflected in the definition of eligibility for services to children who are deaf-blind:

> [Children who are deaf-blind are those with] auditory and visual handicaps, the combination of which causes severe and other developmental and educational problems [so] that they cannot properly be accommodated in special education programs solely for the hearing handicapped child or for the visually handicapped child (U.S. Office of Education, 1975, p. 7415).

Development of communication

In contrast to Chomsky (1965), most modern language theorists believe that communication is not a single developmental function, but that it is complex, involving all domains. The development and use of symbols, proposed by Bates (1979) and others (Bloom & Lahey, 1978; Bruner, 1975; Piaget, 1954; Schaffer, 1977), suggest a model in which language develops as part of an interdependent and interactive system; physical, cognitive, and linguistic development occur at least somewhat concurrently; and progress in each system facilitates the development of the others. Bates (1979, p. 6) described this synergy as the "Great Borrowing." She stated: "Within the study of normal children, comparisons can be made between language development and parallel (perhaps yoked) developments in other domains" (p. 4). In other words, physical development facilitates cognitive development, which facilitates linguistic development, and vice versa.

Effects of deaf-blindness and other severe impairments

A similar development among domains is assumed among children who are deaf-blind and have multiple handicaps. That is, an impairment in one domain, such as the physical, influences the speed and efficiency of other domains, such as the cognitive and sensory. According to Orlansky (1981, p. 9),

> it is virtually impossible to identify the precise cause of [such] a child's functional limitations. We may observe, for example, that a certain child shows no response to loud sounds and bright lights, but we may not know whether his lack of response is due to specific auditory and visual impairments or to profound mental retardation.

The lack of motor ability that is not related to profound mental retardation may also prevent the child's response. Furthermore, reduced physical ability prevents the child from experiencing many objects and thus limits the opportunity for the increased cognitive and sensory stimulation that handling objects provides. If vision is reduced, the visual rewards for motor activity are also reduced, and motor activity decreases. If movement does not occur, there is a lack of kinesthetic or tactile sensation to stimulate further movement; as a result, fewer opportunities are provided for visual and auditory stimulation. All systems experience a delay caused by a deficit in one domain, and the delay is magnified by deficits in more than one domain. The child who is deaf-blind easily becomes totally dependent on the "programmed" experience provided by others. As Walsh (1981, p. 27) noted:

> Deaf-blind children generally do nothing with their environment other than exist within it. A deaf-blind child, because of the lack of vision and hearing, is not attracted to his environment and will not explore unless prompted and led.

The interaction-interdependence, or "Great Borrowing," is as effectively blocked across multiple systems in a child who is deaf-blind as it is synergistic in a normal child.

Prelanguage in the normal child

The prelanguage period of normal child development is generally considered to be age 9–13 months. During this linguistic period, which Siegel-Causey and Downing (1987, p. 16) termed "nonsymbolic," communication occurs through smiles, body language, eye contact, and vocalizations. Bates, (1979, pp. 4–5) defined "two critical moments in the dawning of human communication through symbols: (a) the onset of communicative intentions and conventional signals and (b) the emergence of symbols and the discovery that things have names."

Certainly, children communicate before 9 months, but the communication is dependent on the respondents' interpretation (Bates, 1976); that is, the sounds an infant makes, or some other behavior in which the infant engages, is consistently interpreted to have a specific goal by an adult. The infant, however, has neither a specific goal nor plans for the use of the adult as an agent. When the communication behavior becomes "intentional," the infant gains the adult's attention as a goal in itself or to get the adult to act as an agent to obtain something the infant wants (Bates, 1979). The purposeful interaction with another person for a specific reason constitutes communicative "intention."

A conventional signal is an infant's behavior that an adult interprets within a certain context to have a specific meaning. Thus, when an infant cries, the parent assumes that the infant is communicating that he or she is hungry, wet, or in pain. When the behavior occurs within a context and is accompanied by a gesture and enhanced by intonation, the parent often becomes a competent predictor of the meaning of the infant's sound. In addition, the infant's responses to the adult's communication are endowed with comprehension by the adult (Chapman & Miller, 1980). For example, when an infant smiles in response to "Smile for Mommy," the mother enthusiastically interprets the infant's response as understanding, when the truth is that the infant is already smiling or is smiling in response to the tone of the mother's voice or her smile. The apparent underlying purpose of this type of response is the infant's attempt to stimulate the adult to continue communicating to facilitate the infant's linguistic development. Any understanding by the infant is cued entirely by the context.

An infant is said to be using symbols when an adult and the infant use sounds and-or gestures that are systematized and mutually intelligible. Toward the end of the first year, conventional symbols begin to evolve. There is evidence that infants understand some words in context at this time (Chapman & Miller, 1980) and may begin to use "true words" near the end of this period. True words (vocal or signed) are those that are spontaneously produced in a consistent form with a consistent meaning (Nelson, 1973). The use of a true word carries with it the recognition that the object or activity has a name, the name is separate from the object or activity, and the object or activity exists independent of the context (Bates, 1979; Piaget, 1954).

Communication with people who are deaf-blind

The concern for people who are deaf-blind centers primarily on communication, whatever the stage of life (Maxson, Tedder, Lamb, Giesen, & Marmion, 1989; Siegel-Causey & Downing, 1987). This

concern is more intense than the concern for the development of communication in a person who is deaf because the array of communication media is even more restricted. Communication is achieved with great difficulty by the person who is deaf-blind and requires far greater effort by would-be communicators. Helen Keller (1903) once remarked that blindness separates one from things, but deafness separates one from people. The child who is deaf-blind and has other severe impairments and is dependent on others for the most minimal interaction has a difficult time interacting with the adults who will facilitate his or her development of language.

Communication with a person who is deaf-blind may be done using a formal method, such as American Sign Language (ASL) confined to a restricted visual field, note writing in large print or printed on palm, or braille (for a description of the "formal" methods of communication, see Kates & Schein, 1980). More often, communication may be a composite of made-up signs (or improperly made ASL), some signed English, gestures, pantomime, loud talking, physical contact, and anything else that comes to the "sender's" mind. The more disabled the person who is deaf-blind, the more likely that informal, prelanguage methods will be used. It is also likely that a person who is deaf-blind and has other severe impairments will remain at the prelanguage or nonsymbolic level throughout life (Siegel-Causey & Downing, 1987). In addition to a basic communicative disability, this person is called on to make communicative sense of a conglomeration of inconsistent communication styles, which adds confusion to the already difficult process.

Although some people who are adventitiously deaf-blind (such as Robert Smithdas and Helen Keller) are extremely articulate in formal systems, most children who have other severe impairments and are deaf-blind must have carefully structured, interactive prelanguage interventions (Siegel-Causey & Downing, 1987; Snow, 1984). Such interventions require caregivers who are skilled at recognizing the children's prelanguage attempts and potential communicators who can structure prelanguage to imitate the children's attempts and progress to more advanced interactions, rather than just anticipate the children's needs and thus eliminate the necessity of developing communication. A planned intervention program, such as that suggested by Siegel-Causey

and Guess (1989), should be based on careful observation and assessment.

Assessment-observation programs

Programs for children who are disabled and language delayed

Many language-assessment and intervention programs are used with children who are disabled and language delayed. The following are three of the most widely used and best regarded that are also used with children who are deaf-blind (Wilson, 1981).

The Language Acquisition Program. The Language Acquisition Program (LAP) for the Retarded or Multiply Handicapped (Kent, 1975) was developed for children aged 5–20 who are severely retarded and those who are nonverbal. It is a test-teach-retest model that depends on shaping, prompting, and reinforcing as teaching strategies to progress across three levels (preverbal, verbal-receptive, and verbal-expressive). The preverbal section addresses appropriate gross motor behaviors and imitative behaviors. The manuals have some information on sign language and total communication, but the preferred mode is oral (Wilson, 1981).

The Environmental Pre-language Battery (EPB). This battery is one portion of the more comprehensive Environmental Language Intervention Program (DeAnna, Horstmeier, & McDonald, 1975), which includes an assessment and teaching portion for parents and teachers. Based on Piagetian theory, it assesses the skills necessary for acquiring language before and during the single-word-utterance stage without specific recommendations for teaching, but the authors suggest that the natural environment should be used to communicate everyday social interactions (Wilson, 1981).

Language Intervention Program for Developmentally Young Children. Usually referred to as the Bricker Intervention Program (Bricker, Dennison, & Bricker, 1976), this language intervention program, based on the work of Piaget, also uses operant conditioning as a teaching approach. It designs a language repertoire specific to the student's context for maximum control over the environment (Coggins & Sandall, 1983).

Programs specific to deaf-blind children

Two examples of instruments created specifically to assess the communication of children who are deaf-blind are the *Sign Language Curricula,* (1978), developed by the Deaf-Blind Department at the Perkins School for the Blind and *Helping Kids Soar,* developed at the Alabama Institute for the Deaf and Blind (1989). Both instruments contain diagnostic and developmental units to be used by teachers. All the units require, however, that the teacher provide a stimulus and that the student respond. These instruments are beyond the prelanguage stage of language development—the level at which many students who are deaf-blind function. They look at expressive and receptive repertoires without respect to the environmental aspects of the communication process.

At least one instrument has been developed for the assessment of children who function at the prelanguage level. The *Communicative Intention Inventory* (Coggins & Carpenter, 1981) is a system for observing and coding communication at the early intentional level. It specifies eight intentional acts of communication and gives the child the opportunity to be an initiator, rather than just a responder.

Limitations of existing systems

Although the LAP, the EPB, the Bricker Intervention Program, and the Communicative Intention Inventory are appropriate for use with a child who is language delayed and-or mentally retarded, their users must meet four assumptions: 1) that the child has functional vision and can make eye contact, 2) that the child has functional hearing or uses sign language, 3) that the child has the gross motor ability to attend, and 4) that the child has enough fine motor control to imitate. The previous descriptions of children who are deaf-blind and have other severe impairments preclude the use of these instruments, often well into the adolescent years. Furthermore, although the development of communication in such adolescents has most often been described as occurring at the "language" level, even the "prelanguage" level identified in these instruments is too advanced for a majority of this population. That is, the cognitive and motor skills of many adolescent students who are deaf-blind and have other severe impairments are still not at the point of imitation, and many such students are not yet able to attend for significant periods.

In sum, the interactiveness and interdependence (Bates, 1979) of the social, cognitive, and physical development of children with multiple impairments,

including deaf-blindness, prevent the behaviors that permit the assessment of the most basic linguistic competence assumed in these programs. The intervention curricula designed by the Perkins School and the Alabama Institute for the Deaf and Blind reflect the multiple limitations of a child who is deaf-blind, but do not place enough emphasis on the prelanguage level and do not observe communication as a process within a specific context. None of these instruments pays significant attention to the pragmatics of communication.

Need for a different observation system

The authors suspect that more communication is present in situations involving students who are deaf-blind and have other severe impairments than can be noted by instruments of the types just mentioned. Available instruments allow a thorough analysis of the syntax (form) of an utterance and of the semantics (content) of an utterance, but not an observation of the pragmatics of the situation. There is some evidence (Coggins & Sandall, 1983) that children who are developmentally delayed use their language differently than do normal children. Thus, children who are deaf-blind and who have the most profound developmental delays may use language in much different ways.

Pragmatics is particularly important for assessing students who are language impaired and are functioning at the prelanguage level because the initial intentionality of the students' communication is highly dependent on the context. At this level, a broader description of the situation (the communicators, role taking, and efficacy as indicated by the appropriateness of the responses), and the various modes of communication reflect a more accurate picture of the ability of students who are deaf-blind and have other severe impairments. Observation at the prelanguage level can also provide a wealth of information about how, or if, the adult communicator facilitates communication in these students.

The Communication Observation Schedule

The Communication Observation Schedule (COS) (Tedder & Sikka, 1991) was designed to record systematically the pragmatics of communication with a child who has severe impairments including deaf-blindness and who is

functioning primarily at the prelanguage level. It allows for advancement in communication skills by continuing through the use of true words. (Details on the COS are available from the authors on request.)

An interaction involves at least two people and may involve several modes of communication. The COS provides the opportunity to observe and record the context (purpose) of an interaction, who initiates and who responds to it, the mode of response, and whether the response is appropriate. Its communication modes range from the most rudimentary prelanguage communication to the initial use of a formal language system. Materials required for rating include a pencil, a stopwatch, and two or three COS sheets; two observers do the rating in person or by watching a videotape of the interaction under observation. The next two sections describe the types of interactions and modes of communication that are recorded on the COS.

Types of interactions

The type of interaction that is observed usually fits into one of four categories in a school setting: 1) instruction-information, 2) praise, 3) discipline, or 4) teasing-joking. An interaction is categorized as *instruction-information* when the teacher interacts with the student specifically for the purpose of teaching a concept or lesson or a student attempts to initiate an interaction to obtain help or information from classmates or teachers. The *praise* category includes any interaction involving positive reinforcement. Praise is often a smile, but may include such concrete acts as giving rewards of food. *Discipline* includes attempts to control behavior through negative reinforcement or through punishment (for example, holding a finger on the student's lips and saying "shhh" or ignoring the behavior). The category of *teasing or joking* includes interactions in a social setting that may involve "picking on" the student in a friendly manner, tickling, joking, or making a "funny" comment. The visual or auditory aspects of these modes are dependent upon whether the student has remaining vision or hearing, a characteristic of most "deaf-blind" students.

Modes of communication
Physical mode
Physical contact (touching) is one nonverbal means of gaining or redirecting some-

one's attention or providing reassurance or guidance and is one of the most pervasive forms of communication with a person who is deaf-blind and has other severe impairments. Since it seems intuitive to touch another person for the purposes of communication, the physical mode is often used in conjunction with other modes of communication (such as hand-over-hand guidance with sign language and-or voice) by adults in a teaching environment or in other environments. Touching (placing a hand on a student's shoulder, tapping the student's hand, or nudging the student) is often used with a student who is deaf-blind to announce one's presence, to guide the student, or to indicate that it is the student's turn to do something. The student who is deaf-blind uses physical contact reflexively at the most basic level of communication and for a number of other purposes: to seek reassurance, to establish a position in space, to gain attention, or to indicate turn taking.

Instrumental communication

Instrumental communication uses an object as a means of communication. Five types of objects are identified in the COS.

1. *Mechanical and-or electronic equipment.* For example, computers have been adapted to allow deaf-blind persons to use a switch to control mechanical voice output; to display a yes-no response via a screen message; to indicate the user's choice by calling up a desirable screen display, by playing music, or by starting-stopping a mechanical toy; or to deliver a prerecorded message when the person presses one of several buttons. Other computer access equipment may translate Morse code into large-print words on a screen or input braille and be read by voice output equipment. These latter adaptations may be beyond the capabilities of the population under discussion, but the former adaptations are in use in many locations.

2. A *communication board* uses some symbol system (including specifically designed figures or symbols to fit the person's environment) that allows the student to point to one or a series of pictures to communicate an idea either as an initiator or as a respondent. It may also be used by the teacher, usually to initiate an interaction.

3. A *communication book* is an individually designed system involving a collection of pictures and-or "survival phrases" that correspond to specific aspects of the person's environment. Although similar to communication using pictures, these books are developed for a specific communicative purpose. For example, a person may have more than one communication book—a book for a work situation, a book for home, and a book for other social situations. Since the communication book is a collection specific to a situation and is commonly used, it constitutes a separate category. Communication books may be used to initiate or to respond in an interaction.

4. *Communication using pictures* involves the use of photographs or drawings of real objects, such as an apple, or the representation of an emotion, such as a "sad face." Pictures may include those of relatives, familiar buildings, the school bus, or types of people, such as police officers.

5. *Communication using an object* itself may be expressive or receptive and may be used to initiate or respond to an interaction. For instance, the teacher may hold up two objects (a ball and a block) to allow the student who is deaf-blind to choose, or the student may extend an empty glass to indicate the desire for more to drink. Responses may include touching the ball or block in response to the teacher's request, "Give me the ___."

Gestures

Gestures are any physical movements made by a person to indicate communicative intent that do not involve physical contact with another person. Examples are nodding the head, raising the eyebrows, flicking the hand, scowling, smiling, or waving good-bye. These movements are separate from sign language systems or approximations of signs. Gestures can indicate communicative intent, such as calling the adult's attention to an action, an object, or the student. Coggins and Carpenter (1981) noted that gestural or gestural-verbal activity is the initial mode of communicative intent, and Bates (1979) acknowledged that the use of gestures is the first acquisition of symbols. Because of the multiplicity and interaction of disabilities, a child who is deaf-blind and has other severe impairments may use idiosyncratic gestures. For instance, a child who has severe cerebral palsy and low vision may lurch away from something he finds interesting to place it in his best visual field. Therefore, a person who is familiar with the child's typical reactions should be consulted before any behavior is interpreted as being appropriate or inappropriate.

Sign language

Sign language may refer to ASL, used in the United States by people who belong to the deaf culture, or Signed English, another formal sign system, that is used in many schools and by people who are deaf as an interface with spoken English or a less formal system (such as "home signs"). As long as they are mutually intelligible to the people in an environment, such systems are considered language. A gesture that approximates the sign (a sign that is imperfect because of the person's lack of fine motor ability) is considered sign language for the use of the instrument. People who are familiar with a child's modes of communication should be consulted when the distinction between sign and gesture is questionable. Sign language systems that are used with people who are deaf-blind must be used with sensitivity to a child's visual fields and visual acuity or take a tactile form.

Voice

Voice may include both verbalizations (words) and vocalizations (nonwords). All infants babble, including those who are profoundly deaf. The use of voice does not correlate with the degree of hearing loss. Some people who do not, in theory, have enough hearing to talk, do so anyway. Thus, it is important to encourage all modes that may be used as communication by a person who is deaf-blind, has other severe impairments, and functions at the prelanguage level (Siegel-Causey & Guess, 1989; Snow, 1984). Certain vocalizations, whether or not they are approximations of words, may serve a communicative purpose as long as they are consistent and mutually intelligible. Again, the observer should check with the people who are most familiar with the student being observed to determine if a particular vocalization stands for a word. Just as some words are inappropriate responses, vocalizations may also be inappropriate.

Other behavior

This category allows the observer to record any other behavior (including clapping hands, tapping a pencil on a desk or starting or stopping some form of stereotypical behavior, such as rocking or eye poking) that may be interpreted as communicative in intent but that is not otherwise categorized and to note his or her intuitions regarding the interaction being observed that may be categorized more concretely at a later time. Any additional notes should be made in the Comments section of COS.

No response

This category provides a way to note no observable behavioral response by any communicator to an initiation. No response may be appropriate in some situations, indicating "I understand." Merely receiving information may be entirely cognitive, in which case no observable response is expected. Ignoring an initiation that calls for an answer would be noted as an inappropriate response.

Potential uses of the COS

The emphasis in the COS is on the prelanguage level of communication of students who are deaf-blind and have other severe impairments. The instrument provides for an analysis of the context of the communication, which is essential at this emerging intentional stage of communication. Within the context, the interaction between the student who is deaf-blind and another communicator may be examined for its purpose, initiation-response, appropriateness of the response, and mode or modes of communication. These factors constitute the "dynamic social interactions between a child and competent [communicators] in the environment" (Coggins & Sandall, 1983, p. 170) in which adults who are aware of the evolving nature of a child's communication and are responsive to providing opportunities for interaction encourage that child to become an active participant.

Because observations of interactions involve gathering information on two people, it is possible to examine the behavior of each person as well as the context of the interaction. The COS allows several observations of both the student's and the teacher's use of language or prelanguage. Since the instrument is complex, videotaped interactions permit the most accurate observations. Observations may focus on the *number of interactions within a specified time; duration of an interaction;* or *frequency of various modes,* which may be used to infer a preference for certain types of communication in various situations. The *proportion of appropriate-inappropriate* responses may also be indexed by the type of interaction, the communicator (teacher or student), or the mode of communication of the initiation. The *number of "no response" occasions* may be indicative of many types of problems (such as the inability to see the sign, the inability to recognize the sign, or acting-out behavior). Observation of *no response* by the caregiver or teacher may

indicate the need for increased sensitivity to particular aspects of the student's prelanguage abilities.

The COS may also be used over time to *assess* changes in the student's development. The use of information from several aspects of the instrument permits a more definitive description of the student's communication and can be designed to detect particular strengths and areas that require more specific interventions.

In addition, the COS may be adapted for a variety of situations in which communication is required, such as the work environment or social settings. Tedder and Sikka (1991) presented a variation of the COS that may be used for observing communication in the work environment.

Conclusion

The person who wishes to facilitate the development of communication with a student who is deaf-blind and has other severe impairments must be sensitive to communication at the prelanguage level and to the pragmatics of that communication. The facilitator of communication will wish to imitate and reinforce the student's current level and present the next developmental step (Siegel-Causey & Guess, 1989). The planning and frequency of communicative interaction, as well as the model or modes that best facilitate development, is even more crucial to students who are deaf-blind and have other severe impairments. The purpose of communication and the context of many interactions between these students and their teachers has been ignored or overlooked as a source of information for facilitating communication, and it is hoped that the COS will provide an efficient method of guiding purposeful interactions with such students.

References

Alabama Institute for the Deaf and Blind. (1989). *Helping kids soar.* Talladega, AL: Author.

Baldwin, V. (1991). Understanding the deaf-blind census. *TRACES Newsletter,* **1**(2), 1-4.

Bates, E. (1976). *Language and context.* New York: Academic Press.

Bates, E. (1979). *The emergence of symbols: Cognition and communication in infancy.* New York: Academic Press.

Bloom, L. & Lahey, M. (1978). *Language development and language disorders.* New York: John Wiley & Sons.

Bricker, D., Dennison, L., & Bricker, W. (1976).

A language intervention program for developmentally young children. Miami: University of Miami.

Bruner, J. (1975). The ontogenesis of speech acts. *Journal of Child Language,* **2**(1), 1-19.

Chapman, R. & Miller, J. (1980). Analyzing language and communication in the child. In R. Schiefelbusch (Ed.), *Nonspeech language and communication: Analysis and intervention* (pp. 159-196). Baltimore, MD: University Park Press.

Chomsky, N. (1965). *Aspects of a theory of syntax.* Cambridge, MA: MIT Press.

Coggins, T.E. & Sandall, S. (1983). The communicatively handicapped infant: Application of normal language and communication development. In S.G. Garwood & R.F. Fewell (Eds.), *Educating handicapped infants: Issues in development and intervention* (pp. 165-214). Rockville, MD: Aspen Systems Corp.

Coggins, T. & Carpenter, R. (1981). The communication intention inventory: A system for observing and coding children's early intentional communication. *Applied Psycholinguistics,* **2,** 235-251.

DeAnna, S., Horstmeier, D., & McDonald, J. (1975). *Environmental language intervention program.* Columbus: Ohio State University.

Kates, L. & Schein, J.D. (1980). *A complete guide to communication with deaf-blind persons.* Silver Spring, MD: National Association of the Deaf.

Keller, H. (1903). *The story of my life.* New York: Dell.

Kent, L. (1975). *Language acquisition program for the retarded or multiply handicapped.* Champaign, IL: Research Press.

Maxson, B.J., Tedder, N.T., Lamb, A.M., Giesen, J.M., & Marmion, S. (1989). The education of deaf-blind youth: Teacher characteristics and program issues. *RE:view,* **21**(1), 39-48.

Myers, S.O. (1981). A general overview of disabilities and handicaps. In S.R. Walsh & R. Holzberg (Eds.), *Understanding and educating the deaf-blind/severely and profoundly handicapped* (pp. 43-50). Springfield, IL: Charles C Thomas.

Nelson, K. (1973). Structure and strategy in learning to talk. *Monographs of the Society for Research in Child Development,* **38** (Serial No. 149).

Orlansky, M.D. (1981). The deaf-blind and the severely/profoundly handicapped: An emerging relationship. In S.R. Walsh & R. Holzberg (Eds.), *Understanding and educating the deaf-blind/severely profoundly handicapped* (pp. 5-24). Springfield, IL: Charles C Thomas.

Perkins School for the Blind. (1978). *Sign language curricula.* Watertown, MA: Author.

Piaget, J. (1954). *The construction of reality in the child.* New York: Ballantine.

Schaffer, H.R. (Ed.). (1977). *Studies in mother-infant interaction.* London: Academic Press.

Siegel-Causey, E. & Downing, J. (1987). Non-symbolic communication development. In L. Goetz, D. Guess, & K. Stremel-Campbell (Eds.) *Innovative program design for individuals with dual sensory impairment* (pp. 15-48). Baltimore, MD: Paul H. Brookes.

Siegel-Causey, E. & Guess, D. (1989). *Enhancing nonsymbolic communication interactions among learners with severe disabilities.* Baltimore, MD: Paul H. Brookes.

Snow, C.E. (1984). Parent-child interaction and the development of communicative ability. In R.L. Schiefelbush & J. Pickar (Eds.), *The acquisition of communicative competence* (pp. 69-107). Baltimore: University Park Press.

Tedder, N.E. & Sikka, A. (1991). *The communication observation schedule.* Mississippi State University, Rehabilitation Research & Training Center on Blindness and Low Vision, Starkville, MS.

Trybus, R.J. (1984). Demographics and population character research in deaf-blindness. In J.E. Stahlecker, L.E. Glass, & S. Machalow (Eds.), *State-of-the-art: Research priorities in deaf-blindness.* San Francisco: University of California, Center on Mental Health and Deafness.

U.S. Office of Education. (1975). Programs for education of the handicapped. *Federal Register, 40*(35), 7415.

Walsh, S.R. (1981). *Understanding and educating the deaf-blind/severely and profoundly handicapped.* In S.R. Walsh & R. Holzberg (Eds.), *Curriculum selection for the deaf-blind, severely/profoundly handicapped* (pp. 25-37). Springfield, IL: Charles C Thomas.

Wilson, A. (1981). Curriculum selection for the deaf-blind, severely/profoundly handicapped. In S.R. Walsh & R. Holzberg (Eds.), *Understanding and educating the deaf-blind/severely profoundly handicapped* (pp. 133-182). Springfield, IL: Charles C Thomas.

Wolf, E., Delk, M., & Schein, J. (1982). *Needs assessment of services to deaf-blind individuals.* Silver Spring, MD: REDEX.

Norma E. Tedder, Ph.D., research director, Division of Public Service Training, East Campus, University of New Orleans, New Orleans, LA 70148; Kathleen Warden, Ph.D., assistant professor, Department of Special Services Education, University of Tennessee, 121 Claxton Education Annex, Knoxville, TN 37996-3400; Anjoo Sikka, Ph.D., research scientist, Rehabilitation Research and Training Center on Blindness and Low Vision, P.O. Drawer 6189, Mississippi State University, Mississippi State, MS 39762.

Preverbal Communication of Blind Infants and Their Mothers

CHARITY ROWLAND, Ph.D.

Dr. Rowland is an assistant research professor, Teaching Research, Monmouth, Oregon.

Teaching Research, Communication Skills Center for Deaf-Blind Children, Oregon State System of Higher Education, Monmouth, OR 97361

Abstract: Films of interactions between five mothers and their blind infants, aged 11 months to 2 years, 8 months, made at regular intervals over six months, were analyzed to determine the development of communicative skills in each mother-infant dyad. It was found that, although the frequency of the infants' vocalizations was within normal limits, the vocalizations did not follow normal patterns of responsiveness, and the mothers' responses to them were weak and inconsistent. Suggestions are made for a highly structured program to enhance the communicative skills of parents and their blind infants.

The lack of research on the linguistic and communicative abilities of visually impaired persons reflects the fact that visual impairment *per se* does not seem to impede the eventual acquisition of adequate language skills. The apparent ease of language development in blind persons is surprising because visually impaired infants typically display significant (although not permanent) delays in most developmental areas (see Fraiberg, 1977).

The Literature

The purpose of the study was to examine in detail the beginning of language in blind infants. Basic to this study were the premises that prelinguistic communicative behaviors are critical precursors of linguistic behavior and that communication between parents and infants is bidirectional. Since the mid-1970s, research on sighted infants has confirmed the bidirectionality of early communication and revealed the sophisticated communicative abilities of infants (Lewis & Rosenblum, 1977; Schaffer, 1977). Much of the research in this area has been devoted to the analysis of vocal and visual exchanges between mothers and infants because

An earlier version of this article was delivered at the American Foundation for the Blind Research/Practice Seminar, Chicago, June 1981. The research on which the article was based was supported by a dissertation-aid grant from the Graduate College of the University of Oklahoma, Norman.

most early communication occurs within the mother-infant dyad. Mutual gaze and visual exchange are an important aspect of early communication between parents and their sighted infants (Collis & Schaffer, 1975). Bateson (1975) found that sighted infants under 3 months old engage in vocal exchanges with their mothers which are similar to normal adult patterns of conversation in that each partner takes turns — alternating between vocalizing and listening. Bateson stressed the importance of the interactional context in which the infant is studied and the rule-governed nature of mother-infant interactions. When mother-infant interactions are studied as if they were real conversations, it is found that many functions of language can be seen in the infants' preverbal behavior. For instance, an infant can request an object by showing excitement when the mother appears with it or by pointing and reaching for it. Conversely, an infant can effectively protest or refuse to do something by pushing away an unwanted item, by turning away from the mother, or by crying and fussing.

Bates et al. (1977) studied the relationship between these early communicative behaviors and language development in a longitudinal study of sighted infants, aged 9–13 months, in which their verbal and gestural communication, play behavior, and sensory-motor and cognitive development were assessed. The study was correlational and revealed a gestural complex (a network of relationships, appar-

ently based on a shared structure), that included pointing, giving, showing, and ritualized requests, as well as a single language complex. They found that such cognitive measures as imitation, the use of tools, symbolic play (pretending), and combinatorial play (the coordinated manipulation of two objects) were good predictors of gesture and language. However, the cognitive measures of object permanence and spatial relationships were poor predictors of gestural or verbal development. The authors interpreted their data as providing support for a common foundation for prelinguistic communication and language. This foundation can be described as the ability to communicate through conventional signals, such as gestures and vocalizations.

The study described in this article investigated the preverbal communicative abilities of blind infants. Because the contextual unit of the study was the mother-infant dyad, the behavior of both the infants and their mothers was examined. The author assumed that some of the preverbal communicative exchanges found in the research on sighted infant-mother dyads would be present in the blind infant-mother dyads. However, she anticipated that the absence of sight in the infants and the absence of certain types of feedback that mothers expect from sighted infants (such as visual exchanges) would affect the quality and patterning of their communicative exchanges.

Subjects

The five subjects of the study were enrolled in the preschool program of a university-affiliated child study center in Oklahoma City, Oklahoma. All were totally blind or had no more than minimal light perception at birth and had no concomitant sensory handicaps, although several had other types of handicaps.

It is important to note that the characteristics of the subjects varied considerably. That is, Amy, Maria, and Tanya, who were aged 11, 15, and 16 months, respectively, when the investigation began, were within six months of the same age and were totally blind. Donna and Jason (aged 30 and 32 months) were considerably older than the other three and their sight had begun to improve since birth. With the exception of Maria, all the subjects were severely developmentally delayed. Brief descriptions of each subject at the time of the initial observation follow, and Table 1 provides a profile of the subjects. Table 1 includes month-equivalences for the cognitive skills of each child at the start of the project. Cognitive skills were assessed using the cognitive subscale

Table 1. Profile of the Five Subjects

Data	Amy	Maria	Tanya	Donna	Jason
Birthdate	December 1977	July 1977	June 1977	May 1976	February 1976
Age when the research started	11 months	15 months	16 months	30 months	32 months
Family's income	Low-middle	Low	Low	Low-middle	Low
Area in which the home is situated	Urban	Urban	Rural	Urban	Rural
Ordinal position in the family	Second of two children	First and only child, but fourth of four under 21 years in a close extended family	Third of three children	First of three children	Second of two children
Others in the home	The mother, the father, and one sibling	The mother, two aunts, an uncle, a grandmother, and various other relatives who move in and out	The mother and two siblings	The mother, the father, and two siblings	The mother, the father, and one sibling
Current vision	Responds to bright lights	None	No visual response	Visual tracking; locates large items across the room	Visual tracking; locates small items up to 4 feet away
Visual diagnosis	Visual impairment, cortical basis	Congenital anophthalmia	Bilateral optical hypoplasia	Visual impairment, cortical basis	Cortical blindness
Age when the visual impairment was diagnosed	6 months	Birth	Before 9 months	15 months	6 months
Concomitant handicaps	Generalized hypotonia	None	None	Hypertonicity in all extremities; hypotonicity in the trunk; microcephaly	None
Age during the first evaluation by the child study center	10 months	3 months	9 months	7 months	13 months
Vision at the time of referral to the child study center	No consistent response; may see shadows	None	No visual response	Light perception	Occasional response to light
Age when therapy began	11 months	4 months	10 months	8 months	14 months
Cognitive level in month equivalences at the start of the research[a]	2–5 months	7–9 months	3–7 months	3 months	4–14 months

[a]Cognitive subscale of the Callier-Azusa scale. The lower number represents the base level; the higher number represents the highest splinter skill demonstrated. See R. S. Stillman (Ed.), *The Callier-Azusa Scale* (Dallas: Callier Center for Communication Disorders, 1978).

of the Callier-Azusa scale (Stillman, 1978).

Amy. At 11 months, Amy had no useful vision and suffered from generalized hypotonia. She sat only with support, had poor head control, and would hold objects passively and for no more than a few seconds. However, she demonstrated excellent head turning and eye orientation to auditory cues. She seemed happy to be left alone, playing with her hands and babbling. Amy lived with her parents and an older brother.

Maria. Because she was born without eyes, Maria's blindness was evident from the start, and her educational programming began at 4 months. At 11 months, she was by far the most advanced of the subjects in her social, motor, and language skills. During the first observation, she tried eagerly to stand up and walk (although she did not crawl yet) and would stand unassisted for a moment. A confident, insatiably sociable infant, Maria was

the only child of a young mother, a member of a large extended family.

Tanya. At 16 months, Tanya was developmentally delayed in all areas and had no visual response. She was a passive, contented baby who was able to sit unassisted but had only once sat up by herself. Once in a sitting position, she frequently engaged in self-stimulative behavior. She could push herself up into a crawling position and let herself down, and her tactile exploration was proceeding well. Tanya lived with her mother and two older siblings.

Donna. At 30 months, Donna's vision had improved over the previous two months from light perception alone to visual tracking of objects held at arm's length. She had the most severe concomitant handicaps of all the subjects: hypertonicity of all limbs, hypotonicity of the trunk, and microcephaly. She could neither sit unsupported nor put herself in-

to a crawling position. Donna lived with her parents and two younger siblings.

Jason. Jason's sight had also begun to improve. Although he had no diagnosed concomitant handicaps, at 32 months he was seriously delayed in all areas and demonstrated severe behavioral problems that did not improve over the course of the project. When held, he would often avert his head and refuse to make eye contact. He spent extended periods engaging in self-stimulative behavior. He could stand if supported but could not walk independently. Jason was the younger of two children and lived with both parents.

Procedures and Analysis

The initial information was obtained from a communicative skills interview, based on that of Bates et al. (1977), which the author administered to the mothers at the beginning of the study. This interview assessed the presence or absence of ges-

Table 2. Scores on the Communicative Skills Interviews at the Beginning and End of the Study

Behavior	Amy Beg. Score	Amy End Score	Maria Beg. Score	Maria End Score	Tanya Beg. Score	Tanya End Score	Donna Beg. Score	Donna End Score	Jason Beg. Score	Jason End Score
Gestural Communication										
Points										
Shows										
Gives				x						
Expresses desires:										
Cries or whines	x	x			x	x			x	x
Becomes agitated					x	x	x	x		
Reaches		x	x	x	x	x	x	x	x	x
Makes special sounds	x	x	x	x			x	x		x
Uses words				x						?a
Moves toward the object				x				x	x	x
Expresses dislike:										
Cries or fusses	x	x	x	x	x	x	x	x	x	x
Becomes agitated		x							x	x
Makes special sounds		x			x	x		x		x
Pushes away		x			x	x		x	x	x
Averts head		x			x	x	x	x	x	x
Shakes head				x						?a
Uses words				x						
Shows off			x	x		?a				
Laughs with others	x	x	x	x	x	x			x	x
Repeats behavior for laughter				x	x	x				
Number of non-conventional gestures made in the films[b]	9	24	13	18	4	47	5	44	5	14
Number of conventional gestures made in films[b]	0	0	2	12	0	0	0	0	0	0
Play and imitation										
Likes music			x	x	x	x	x	x	x	x
Dances to music				x						
Sings to music			x	x						
Combinatorial play				?a	?a	x				
Symbolic play (pretends)										
Imitates vocalizations		?a	x	x	x	x	x	x	x	x
Imitates gestures			x	x	?a	x				
Imitates activities			x	x	?a	x				
Number of games played	0	0	5	10	2	5	3	5	5	8
Language										
Understands "no"			x	x	x	x			x	x
Responds to "where is"			x	x		x				x
Responds to "go find"				x						?a
Responds with excitement to pleasant words			x	x	x	x	x	x	x	x
Negative response to unpleasant words				x		x				
Touches named item			x	x						
Number of words comprehended	0	3	10	60	5	9	4	6	8	?a
Number of words spontaneously produced	0	0	10	42	0	0	1	1	0	1

[a] A question mark indicates that the finding was uncertain.
[b] The prestudy score includes the number of different gestures produced in four films from the first observation; the poststudy score includes all the new gestures produced in subsequent films.

tural communicative behaviors, play, imitation, and language skills.

At regular intervals during the next six months, films of mother-infant interactions were made in the infants' homes to document the development of communicative skills in each dyad. Twenty-two films were made of each mother-infant dyad. The films were analyzed at two-second intervals for seven categories of infant behavior and three categories of maternal behavior, for a total of 42 subcategories. A minimum of 80-percent reliability was achieved between two observers for each behavioral category and for each subject. At the end of the study, the communicative skills interview was administered again.

Results and Discussion

In considering the results of the research, it is important to remember that four of the five infants suffered from additional disabilities that had not yet been completely diagnosed. Therefore, the observed difficulties in communicative development may not be solely attributable to their lack of vision. However, the infants represented a fairly typical sample of severely visually impaired children, since it is rare to find an infant who presents a severe visual loss without concomitant sensory or motor deficiencies.

Communicative repertoire. Table 2 presents the communicative skills of the five subjects at the beginning and end of the study, based on the two interviews. Clearly, the subjects displayed most of the normal mechanisms for expressing pleasure and displeasure (agitation, crying, some special vocalizations). They also engaged in some vocal imitation and devel-

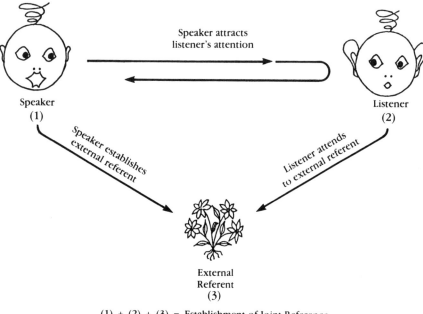

(1) + (2) + (3) = Establishment of Joint Reference

Figure 1. Completing the communicative circuit.

oped limited receptive vocabularies indicating that they comprehended some speech. In addition, all infants displayed repertoires of nonconventional idiosyncratic gestures (including batting their arms, throwing their bodies backward in their mothers' arms), most of which were associated with such affective states as excitement and aversion. However, only Maria began to produce words spontaneously and communicatively, and only Maria produced any conventional gestures (such as waving "bye-bye" or nodding her head "yes").

Bates et al. found that combinatorial play (e.g., stacking blocks, putting objects in and out of containers, and stringing beads) and symbolic play (pretending) were highly correlated with the gestural complex in sighted infants. However, only Tanya displayed true combinatorial play, and none of the infants engaged in symbolic play. The delay in symbolic play was not surprising, in light of the self-other confusion typical of visually impaired children (Fraiberg, 1977). Giving and showing—two conventional gestures that normally form the basis of early games and turn-taking rituals — also were absent (although Maria was just beginning to give objects to her mother at the end of the project). Furthermore, as expected, these infants did not engage in the traditional requesting gestures (looking, pointing, and reaching), which require visual reference.

Completing the communicative circuit. The absence of conventional gestures (such as pointing, showing, nodding, and waving) in these visually impaired infants

may reflect their delayed acquisition of the construct of external reference. External reference is part of a complete "communicative circuit," which may be described as follows: The participants in a communicative interaction are referred to as the speaker and the listener, whether or not vocal language is involved. First, a speaker establishes a topic of conversation, or "external referent." He or she may do so by looking at the referent, touching it, or manipulating it. Then, the speaker must attract the listener's attention. (An infant may fuss or vocalize to attract attention. An older child or adult may approach and touch the listener or say, "Hey, you!") Once the listener's attention is gained, the speaker must direct that attention to the external referent, thus establishing joint reference and completing the communicative circuit.

This communicative circuit is not easily completed by blind or visually impaired infants because they have difficulty determining where they end and another person or object (the potential external referent) begins. Thus, they may not realize that another entity exists if it is beyond arm's reach or is silent. This type of self-other confusion and delayed person-and-object permanence (the comprehension that a person or object exists even when it cannot be seen, heard, or touched), have a serious impact on the ability to establish external referents. Therefore, blind and visually impaired infants probably require more active exploratory experiences that, in turn, depend on an advanced level of locomotor ability, in order to experience

the concepts and relationships critical to the establishment of joint reference.

With neither language nor gestural referencing abilities, the infants in the study seemed to develop the means to obtain objects independently before they developed the means to communicate their desire for an object. Maria, Donna, and Jason were able to move toward a desired object or person. Thus, they began to fulfill their own needs before they began to communicate them. This stage of doing for oneself may bridge the gap between pre-referential communication and spoken language. Only Maria went beyond this stage to the regulation of adult behavior through verbally expressing her desires.

Observational Data

The discussion of the data from the filmed interactions will be limited to the behavioral categories of the infants' smiles, gestures, and vocalizations, and the mothers' touching and vocalizations. Frequency data for selected behavioral categories for each mother-infant dyad are presented in Table 3.

As discussed in earlier articles (Rowland, 1981, 1983), neither the vocalization rates nor the facial expression rates of the infants seemed low. Vocalizations occurred at a mean of 24 percent of all scored intervals across subjects, while facial expressions (positive and negative combined) occurred at a mean of 23 percent of intervals. It is significant to note that none of the mothers considered their infants to be particularly quiet, and all the mothers reported high rates of vocalization by their infants when they left them alone. Fraiberg (1977) speculated that the mothers of blind infants might, themselves, vocalize less frequently in response to their infants' reduced vocalizations. However, in this study, the mothers' vocalizations occurred at an average of about 40 percent of the measured intervals. This rate is comparable to the vocalization rate of 43 percent reported by Ling and Ling (1976) for mothers of sighted infants between one and 24 months of age.

After the frequency analysis, the temporal sequences of behaviors for each mother-infant pair were analyzed. A "lagged conditional probabilities" program (Sackett, 1979) was used to examine the interdependence of infant and maternal behaviors over time. This program allowed the author to analyze the average frequencies of behaviors to determine whether the occurrence of a given behavior affects the occurrence of a subsequent behavior. For instance, if Tanya's mother vocalized, did that change the probability

Table 3. A Comparison of the Mother-Infant Dyads on the Proportion of Intervals Containing Each Selected Behavior

Infants' Behavior	Amy	Maria	Tanya	Donna	Jason
Makes nonvocal sounds[a]	.17	.26	.25	.26	.45
Vocalizes	.30	.23	.19	.09	.39
Makes a positive facial expression	.08	.23	.30	.27	.12
Makes a negative facial expression	.07	.03	.00	.00	.04
Uses a spontaneous manual gesture	.01	.06	.09	.10	.00
Explores space	.03	.12	.00	.00	.01
Manipulates a toy[a]	.17	.31	.27	.33	.46
Explores a toy[a]	.06	.04	.10	.01	.01
Explores the mother	.00	.02	.05	.00	.00
Reaches for a toy[a]	.01	.20	.17	.40	.19
Touches self	.35	.03	.10	.06	.15
Engages in no manual activity	.46	.24	.33	.41	.27
Maternal Behavior					
Touches the infant	.87	.53	.67	.48	.47
Vocalizes to the infant	.44	.66	.56	.41	.57
Makes nonvocal sounds[a]	.56	.24	.30	.44	.17
Does vocal imitation of the infant	.01	.03	.00	.00	.01

[a]Proportions generated from sequences involving toys only.

that Tanya would vocalize or smile? If Jason smiled, did that increase or decrease the probability that his mother would touch him or perhaps vocalize? A first-order transitional probability is the likelihood that a specific behavior will follow another specific behavior at the immediately succeeding interval.

An examination of the first-order transitional probabilities of infant communicative behaviors following selected maternal behaviors revealed a striking lack of responsiveness in the infants. The expected probability of an infant's smiling was the most likely to be altered by an antecedent maternal behavior. However, neither the infants' vocalizations nor their gestures showed clear patterns of responsiveness across subjects. A mother talking to her infant or rattling a toy did not often prompt the infant into any observable change in behavior. With respect to the infants' behavior following their mothers' vocalizations, it was especially disappointing to find that the infants' vocalizations were less likely than were their smiles or gestures to increase after their mothers vocalized. The one exception to this observation was Jason, who vocalized stereotypically for extended periods, regardless of any antecedent behavior by his mother.

The lack of responsiveness of the infants' vocalizations was surprising, given the strong emphasis that was placed on the reinforcement of vocalization in the home programs recommended to the infants' mothers. Perhaps the deviation in vocal behavior, which Fraiberg suspected, reflects differences in temporal organization rather than in the rate of production. The infants did not seem to vocalize when they were expected to — in response to maternal behavior or stimulation. Indeed, the mothers' attempts to en-

courage them to vocalize often were met with silence.

When the first-order transitional probabilities of maternal behavior following specific infant behaviors were examined, it was clear that the mothers responded rapidly and frequently to their infants' communicative behavior. The most reliable changes in the expected probabilities of maternal behavior occurred in response to the infants' smiles. The mothers' responses to their infants' gestures and vocalizations were less reliable. However, the mothers were less likely to respond with a vocalization than with a touch or a nonvocal sound to their infants' behavior. Thus, they did not reinforce their infants vocally as often as they did in other ways.

Importance of Silence

The lack of vocal responsiveness by the mothers and infants contrasts sharply with the conversational quality of vocal exchanges in sighted mother-infant dyads. A carefully prescribed and consistent response to infant vocalizations seemed to be lacking in the environments observed in this study. Since vocal behavior probably will be the first recognizable referential behavior in blind or visually impaired children, a consistent pattern of maternal responses to infant vocalizations should be beneficial. But a vocal exchange is composed of more than vocalizations.

In a vocal exchange, each partner fills the pauses between vocalizations with listening, signified by silence. Even before vocalization patterns emerge, normal infants seem to be good listeners. Thus, Condon and Sander (1974) found that the motor behavior of newborn babies was synchronized with the sound segments of adult speech. In the words of Osofsky (1979, p. 528): "Listening, or attentive-

ness to auditory stimuli, provides a means through which infants can participate in vocal communication behaviorally before they can initiate meaningful speech." A silent or listening response to a vocalization may be as powerful as a vocal response. Constant vocal stimulation by a mother and her failure to pause and listen may be almost as damaging to patterns of mutual interaction as a lack of stimulation. Said behavior violates the pauses between vocalizations found in the normal conversational pattern of turn-taking mentioned earlier. Thus, the pauses between vocalizations, or the "listening" turns, in a conversation may be as important as the "speaking" or "vocalizing" turns.

Some of the mothers observed in the study provided almost constant vocal stimulation to their infants. This behavior was a natural consequence of their desire to prod their infants to respond. The result, however, was that a natural conversational pattern was impossible. Furthermore, silence, or listening, is an especially important behavior for blind or visually impaired infants because competing auditory stimuli are difficult to process simultaneously—and auditory information is virtually the only available information about the environment that is beyond arm's reach of these nonambulatory infants. Listening is so critical to interpreting the distal environment that it may be maladaptive for them to clutter the auditory environment with their vocalizations. Thus, when the mother vocalizes, the infant's undivided attention, reflected by silence, may be the safest response. When the infant is alone and the environment does not require close attention it will be "safer" for the infant to vocalize.

Clinical Suggestions

The poorly developed vocal patterns of the five infants in the study may reflect the lack of reliable vocal input from their mothers, as well as the mothers' weak responses to their infants' vocalizations. Given that actual speech, rather than gestures, probably will be the first recognizable referential behavior produced by these children, a tightly structured program of parental vocalizations and responses to the infants' vocalizations should be beneficial. Parents could be coached in the systematic alternation of vocalization and silence and in the consistent reinforcement of the early vocal behavior of their infants. A carefully engineered program of parental response may enhance the communicative use of vocalizations by their children.

Such a program should be structured according to the following principles:

- The vocalizations of infants should be reinforced as frequently and consistently as possible.

- Vocal reinforcement should be provided a short time *after* the infant stops vocalizing so the infant is not interrupted and the turn-taking pattern is reinforced.

- Vocal reinforcement by parents should include the imitation of the infant's sounds, both verbal (words) and preverbal (nonword vocalizations).

- The infant should be cued to the appropriate moments for vocalization by emphasizing the difference between periods of parental vocalization and silence. Such cues can be given in two steps. (1) Parents can place their mouth on the infant's cheek or place the infant's hand on their mouth when they are speaking so the infant can feel the speech act. (2) Parents can continue to hold their mouth against the child's cheek or hold the infant's hand on their mouth between vocalizations; then the infant can "feel" the silence—the cue that the parent is providing a safe space for a response.

- A constant barrage of verbal commentary by parents is not advisable. Although language stimulation is important, the quality of such stimulation would be improved by offering short bursts of commentary interspersed with short periods of silence.

Conclusions

The importance of early exchanges between mothers and infants as a starting point for preventive intervention cannot be overstressed, as the experience of the five infants in the study shows. For about six months after they were born, all but one of the five infants in the study were assumed to have sight, and hence were treated as sighted infants. Only Maria, who was born without eyes, began an educational program for blind babies shortly after birth. She was the only infant who was not seriously delayed in several areas of development as she approached her second year. The assumption that the other four infants had vision must have fostered inappropriate interaction patterns geared to the sensory abilities of sighted infants, causing the parents to be frustrated and the infants to be confused. The failure to establish mutually satisfying communicative interactions during these critical first months is difficult to remedy, and may affect social interaction negatively. The time required to undo ineffective interaction patterns and to forge new, effective ones may far exceed the time it took to establish the faulty patterns.

References

Bates, E., Benigni, L., Bretherton, I., Camaioni, L., & Volterra, V. (1977). *Cognition and communication from 9–13 months: A correlational study.* Program on Cognitive and Perceptual Factors in Human Development, Report No. 12. Boulder: Institute for the Study of Intellectual Behavior, University of Colorado.

Bateson, M. C. (1975). Mother-infant exchanges: The epigenesis of conversational interaction. *Annals of the New York Academy of Sciences,* **263,** 101–113.

Collis, G. M., & Schaffer, H. R. (1975). Synchronization of visual attention in mother-infant pairs. *Journal of Child Psychology & Psychiatry,* **4,** 315–320.

Condon, W. S., & Sander, L. W. (1974). Synchrony demonstrated between movements of the neonate and adult speech. *Child Development,* **45,** 456–462.

Fraiberg, S. (1977). *Insights from the blind.* New York: Basic Books.

Lewis, M., & Rosenblum, L. A. [Eds.]. (1977). *Interaction, conversation and the development of language.* New York: John Wiley & Sons.

Ling, D. & Ling, A. (1976). Communication development in the first three years of life. In Z. Jastrzembska (Ed.), *The effects of blindness on early development,* (pp. 160-172). New York: American Foundation for the Blind.

Osofsky, J. D. [Ed.]. (1979). *Handbook of infant development.* New York: John Wiley & Sons.

Rowland, C. (1981) Communicative strategies of visually impaired infants and their mothers: Descriptive data. In B. Urban [Ed.], *Proceedings of the 18th Congress of the International Association of Logopedics and Phoniatrics, Washington, D.C.* (pp. 87–92). American Speech-Language and Hearing Association.

Rowland, C. (1983). Patterns of interaction between three blind infants and their mothers. In A. E. Mills [Ed.], *Language acquisition in the blind child: Normal and deficient* (pp. 114–132). San Diego: College Hill Press.

Sackett, G. P. (1979). The lag sequential analysis of contingency and cyclicity in behavioral interaction research. In J. D. Osofsky [Ed.], *Handbook of infant development* (pp. 623–649). New York: John Wiley & Sons.

Schaffer, H. R. [Ed.]. (1977). *Studies in mother-infant interaction.* New York: Academic Press.

Stillman, R. S. [Ed.]. (1978). *The Callier-Azusa Scale.* Dallas: Callier Center for Communication Disorders.

Tactile Iconicity: Signs Rated for Use with Deaf-Blind Children

Penny L. Griffith, Jacques H. Robinson, and John H. Panagos

Author Information

Penny L. Griffith, Ph.D., Department of Special Education, Kent State University.

Jacques H. Robinson, Ph.D., Department of Special Education, Kent State University.

John H. Panagos, Ph.D., Department of Speech Pathology, Kent State University.

Article Descriptors

deaf-blind; iconicity; sign language; blind; language learning; tactile perception

Signs selected from lists used in studies with mentally retarded and autistic children and previously rated for visual iconicity were presented tactilely to 13 blind persons. Visual and tactile ratings were found to be very similar across blind, deaf, and hearing-sighted adults, and hearing-sighted children. Findings suggest that developmental language theory can account not only for the similarity in subjects' responses, but also for the particular signs that are most likely to be perceived as iconic. Sign rankings are provided, indicating the signs that should be most salient to deaf-blind children.

Iconicity, the visual resemblance between a sign and the object or action it represents, has been shown to be one factor contributing to the ease of sign acquisition by mentally retarded and autistic children (Fristoe & Lloyd, 1977; Griffith & Robinson, 1980; Konstantareas, Oxman, & Webster, 1978; Brown, Note 1). While American Sign Language (ASL) has been found to be no more iconic than spoken languages, based on the linguistic definition (Bellugi & Klima, 1976; Frishberg, 1975), several investigators have examined sign vocabularies used with mentally retarded children and found them to contain a large number of iconic signs relative to the entire ASL lexicon (Griffith & Robinson, 1981; Brown, Note 1; Lloyd & Fristoe, Note 2). A linguistic definition (Wescott, 1971) of an icon indicates that the sign should have a physical resemblance to its real world referent and should be guessable by persons naive of the language. However, a series of investigations regarding iconicity and learning (Griffith, Panagos, & Robinson, 1981; Griffith & Robinson, 1980; Griffith & Robinson, 1981; Griffith, Robinson & Panagos, 1981; Brown, Note 1; Mandel, Note 3) has led to a redefining of iconicity. Results of these studies suggest that iconicity be defined as the associations made by a learner between a sign and its meaning that help the learner recall the sign. The associations need not be based on physical resemblance between the sign and its meaning.

Brown (Note 1) suggested that the rating of signs by naive observers might be the most useful way to determine iconic values for signs to be taught. Using this technique, responses of three different groups of subjects (college students, first graders, and deaf adults) were compared and were found to be highly similar. In addition, the ratings were found to be valid predictors of which signs would be learned most easily by mentally retarded children (Griffith & Robinson, 1980). It was concluded that successful sign acquisition depends on both the degree of perceptual salience available to a learner in a sign and the learner's ability to make some association between the sign and its meaning. Learners tend to make similar associations for signs they rate as very iconic, although not identical ones (Griffith, Robinson, & Panagos, 1981). As suggested by Brown (Note 1), these investigations confirm that perceptions of iconicity are "time-, culture-, and experience-bound" (p.1), and also that nonverbal handicapped learners are able to perceive iconicity and use it in recalling a sign.

Up to this point, iconicity, the association value of signs for teaching nonverbal children, has been studied entirely through the visual channel. However, sign language, the major form of communication used by the deaf-blind community, is presented and perceived through the tactile-kinesthetic mode (Jensema, 1981). While sophistication with the use of any communication system goes beyond associations made between the symbol presented and its meaning, it seems that the study of tactile sign salience could provide useful information concerning initial sign teaching to deaf-blind children, similar to that available for mentally retarded and autistic learners.

A review of the literature provided very little information specific to the use of manual forms of communication with deaf-blind children or vocabulary selection based on any perceptual qualities of signs. Nineteen different methods of communication were reported in use with deaf-blind children in this country (Jensema, 1979). In a survey conducted by Jensema (1981), deaf-blind children were found to prefer using manual methods, including gestures, pantomimes, and signs, over any of the other methods used by their teachers. About 65% of the teachers who responded to the survey indicated that they used manual systems with their students. In general, though, overall communication abilities of deaf-blind youngsters were reported as very limited. Communication abilities were affected by such factors as degrees of hearing and vision losses, age of onset, additional handicaps, and educational training.

Jensema's report suggested that while deaf-blind children should be provided with external auditory and visual stimuli, stress should be placed upon the tactile channel, which appears most useful to the learner in receiving and sending information and from which the disposition to communicate arises.

Sign Selection for Deaf-Blind Children

Only one set of authors offered specific signs and a rationale for the selection of those signs to be taught to deaf-blind persons (Gold & Rittenhouse, 1978). Eight practical signs were selected: *toilet, enough, more, sit, stand, eat, drink,* and *stay,* with the rationale that these signs communicate basic needs in the environment. Gold and Rittenhouse (1978) indicated that *enough, more, sit,* and *stand* should be taught last, and *toilet* could be taught independently of the other signs. The rationale for this arrangement of presentation was unclear, although the authors stated that the handshape for *eat* could be repeated later in teaching *more.* A task analysis focused on the steps in forming the handshapes of the signs with the learner and the presentation of these signs during the appropriate situation.

A large number of sign manuals are available for use with severely handicapped learners (Fristoe & Lloyd, 1977), but until very recently no systematic approach had been applied toward the development of a first sign vocabulary to be used with any population (Fristoe & Lloyd, 1980). Fristoe and Lloyd (1980) used two main criteria for developing their initial teaching

sign lexicon: (a) developmental data from normal children, adapted from Holland (1975) and Lahey and Bloom (1977), and (b) the frequency of occurrence of a sign in 20 manuals for the mentally retarded. Holland's (1975) core lexicon for teaching spoken language to disordered children focused on (a) what is important to the child, (b) objects that are present and events that are happening and stressed, and (c) communication rather than language skills. Lahey and Bloom (1977) added that words should be related to (a) the ease with which a concept can be demonstrated, (b) the eventual usefulness of certain words to the child, and (c) the organization of lexical items into content categories.

Dealing with formational aspects of signs, other authors have suggested that first signs be selected or adapted on the basis of (a) ease of formation (Lloyd & Fristoe, Note 2; Robbins, Note 4; Wilson, Note 5; Creedon, Note 6); (b) their concreteness (Bonvillian & Nelson, 1978; Baron & Isensee, Note 7, Note 8); and (c) their iconicity (Griffith & Robinson, 1980; Konstantareas et al., 1978; Brown, Note 1). Brown (Note 1) hypothesized that the first 50 words acquired in normal language are the most concrete and that the signs representing these words should be highly iconic.

Finally, some attention has been given to sign selection on the basis of form class. Several authors have suggested that verb or action signs might be more salient to learners than nouns. Konstantareas et al. (1978) found the ease of learning sequence with autistic children to be verb, adjective, and then noun signs.

The present investigation was designed as the first in a series to study various aspects of the tactile perceptual qualities of signs. The purpose included (a) a comparison between sign ratings based on tactile-kinesthetic perceptions by blind subjects and visual perceptions by sighted subjects, (b) a test of Brown's (Note 1) hypothesis concerning the iconicity of the first 50 words/signs, using Fristoe and Lloyd's (1980) initial sign lexicon, and (c) a ranking of Fristoe and Lloyd's (1980) sign lexicon according to form class.

Method

Subjects

Eleven blind adults (CA = 21 years to 77 years, mean = 40.6 years) and two blind adolescents (CAs = 14/15 years) served as subjects for this study. Participants volunteered while attending a summer recreational program sponsored by the Cleveland (Ohio) Society for the Blind. An interview was held with each subject, during which personal data were obtained and the study was explained. Subject characteristics are shown in Table 1. The group included both men and women and an approximately equal number of congenitally and adventitiously blind persons. A major criterion for participation was that each subject had no previous experience with sign language. All subjects reported that they had no additional handicapping conditions.

& Croneberg, 1965). Fristoe's list contained 50 initial and 40 additional signs, including nouns, adjectives,

Table 1
Subject Variables

Subject	Age	Visual Acuity	Etiology	Age of Onset
1. Male	59	R 20/400 L removed	Cataracts	Congenital
2. Male	37	R 20/400 L 20/400 No macular vision	Macular degeneration	Congenital
3. Male	77	Light perception only	Retinitis pigmetosa	44
4. Female	75	Legally blind	Nerve paralysis	24
5. Male	58	Light perception	Glaucoma	28
6. Male	23	No vision	Retrofibroplasia	Congenital
7. Female	60	No vision	Unknown	Congenital
8. Female	21	No vision	Glaucoma	Partial until age 16
9. Male	45	Light perception	Cataracts	Congenital
10. Male	15	None	Unknown	Congenital
11. Female	25	None	Accidental fall	13
12. Female	22	Eyes removed	Glaucoma	20
13. Female	14	None	Unknown	Congenital

Visual ratings used for comparison in this study were obtained previously (Griffith & Robinson, 1980) from three groups of sighted subjects. These groups consisted of (a) 20 first graders (CA = 6.6 years to 7.0 years, mean = 6.8 years); (b) 20 college students (CA = 19.8 years to 21.0 years, mean = 19.11 years); and 12 deaf adults (CA = 32.2 years to 68.4 years, mean = 47 years). Groups 1 and 2 were recruited on a volunteer basis. All had normal hearing (as established by school records and interview) and had no previous exposure to sign language. All deaf subjects in Group 3 stated that they had used sign language as their main mode of communication for at least 25 years.

Subject variables for analysis in the present study, then, included the following: (a) blind or sighted, (b) adult or child, (c) hearing or deaf, and (d) familiarity or unfamiliarity with signs.

Selection of Signs to be Rated

Two lists of signs were presented for rating: Fristoe and Lloyd's (1980) initial teaching sign lexicon, and Griffith and Robinson's (1980) list previously rated for visual iconicity. Griffith's list contained 100 noun signs selected from three manuals for the mentally retarded and also listed in the *Dictionary of American Sign Language on Linguistic Principles* (Stokoe, Casterline,

and verbs. Color signs from Fristoe's list were not included in this study, and a number of noun signs were common to both lists, so the final number of signs presented to the blind subjects totaled 166. Six of the eight practical signs suggested by Gold and Rittenhouse (1978) for deaf-blind persons were found on either the Fristoe or the Griffith list, and so ratings were obtained for these. All signs are listed in Appendices A and B.

Procedure

Each subject was seen individually for two 1-hour sessions. Each sign and its spoken equivalent were made by the experimenter while the subject felt the sign with his/her hands. Several examples were presented initially so that subjects learned to search for the sign (since location changed from the neutral position to the chest, face, to head positions, etc.). To ensure that subjects understood the rating task, five practice signs were presented. Subjects were asked to rate the signs from one to five: one if there seemed to be no connection between the sign and its meaning, and five if the connection was very obvious. Once the experimenter was sure the subjects understood the task, presentation and rating of signs proceeded.

Responses were made verbally and recorded on response sheets by the experimenter. Anecdotal information was also recorded.

Results

Mean ratings were obtained for each sign across the 13 subjects. Signs were then rank ordered from most iconic to least iconic. These data are shown in Appendix A for the blind subjects. A Hoyt reliability score was obtained (alpha = .901) and indicated that congenitally and adventitiously blind persons rated signs similarly. The mean ratings were compared to those obtained from sighted groups for the 100 noun signs (Griffith & Robinson, 1980) using a Pearson product-moment correlation. Moderate to high positive correlations were found for all groups. The correleation coefficients are shown in Table 2.

lower scores in general than did either handicapped group. Deaf subjects, the only group familiar with signs, rated most signs in the medium range, and very few in the low range. Blind subjects rated most of the signs as high, and very few as low. It can be speculated that deaf subjects based their judgments on the entire repertoire of ASL signs available to them or that their judgments were based on factors other than iconicity, such as formational (phonological) characteristics or linguistic meaningfulness. Also speculatively, the hearing-sighted groups may have based their judgments of signs on their entire visual repertoire of objects and actions, resulting in lower ratings due to the large number of alternatives available. Blind subjects may have considered the rating scale in a binary fashion,

	Children	College	Deaf	Blind
Children		.74	.69	.58
College			.73	.60
Deaf				.62
Blind				

Table 2
Pearson Correlation Coefficients
for Ratings of Iconicity of 100 Noun Signs

Note: p <.001 for all coefficients.

Next, each subject group's rank-ordered list was divided into thirds of high, medium, and low iconic signs, to determine which signs were commonly rated. Agreement across groups as to which signs were very iconic versus medium or noniconic is shown in Table 3. For high and low iconic categories there was over 50% agreement across groups (high iconic = blind 19/34 signs, children 19/36, deaf 19/35, college 19/36; low iconic = blind 19/33, children 19/32, deaf 19/35, college 19/32). The medium category represented "fuzzy" signs, about which subjects tended to disagree most often. Overall, blind subjects rated signs similarly to sighted subjects. Data for all four groups are shown in Appendix B.

Table 4 shows the number of signs rated high, medium, or low using numerical ranges. The groups, at first, appear to be much more idiosyncratic than indicated by either the correlation or the item analysis. Inspection of the data, however, showed that group differences were minimal in relation to the potency of the sign stimuli. For instance, children seemed to use a binary scale to rate, although they were trained to use a three-point scale. The hearing-sighted groups gave

more common to processing auditory stimuli, than as a visual linear scale, or may have rated signs so highly because they had a smaller repertoire of interfering alternatives than did sighted subjects. Whatever the subject differences inherent in the modes of getting information, the similarity of the ranked hierarchy of signs across groups stands out as the significant result of the study and suggests that salient features of signs are very potent and are perceivable regardless of mode of presentation.

Ratings of Fristoe and Lloyd's Initial
Sign Teaching Lexicon

Tactile ratings obtained for Fristoe and Lloyd's list are shown in Appendix C, and the ratings for Gold and Rittenhouse's practical signs are in Appendix D. The items chosen by Fristoe and Lloyd were judged as very iconic by the blind subjects. About three-fouths of these signs were rated highly iconic, and only six signs were rated low in iconicity. Four of Gold and Rittenhouse's practical signs were rated high, two were rated medium, and two signs (*stay* and *enough*) were not included.

Using tactile ratings of the blind subjects, content

Table 3
Agreement on Level of Iconicity by Blind and Sighted Subjects by Ranked Order of Signs

Agreement: With Three Sighted Groups			Agreement: With Two Sighted Groups			Agreement: With One Sighted Group		
High	Medium	Low	High	Medium	Low	High	Medium	Low
*telephone	*tea	*shoes		*Child/Deaf*			*Child*	
*snow	fork	*bread	body	*hospital	pie	hot dog	rain	nurse
*baby	*morning	*girl	*tree	*candy	gym	skates	*night	egg
*eyes	*coffee	*store	bird	*butter	*peach	pop	fire	*boy
*door	chair	*father	dress	medicine		hamburger	salt	*nickel
*toothbrush	*flower	rest room	bath	trampoline			mother	*cow
*iron		*meat	coat	*cookie			pepper	doctor
*nose		*Coke		dog			orange	sandwich
*mouth		*potato					fish	
*ball		*color		*Child/College*			toast	
*house		*restaurant	*key	*police	*school		bicycle	
bed		*farm	monkey	*onion	*water		apple	
*book		*number	*car	head			food	
*airplane		*pig	*banana	*candle				
*bowl		*name	clock	*gift			*Deaf Adults*	
*cup		*paper	milk	*knife		police	*clock	night
*winter		*woman		money		*head	banana	onion
*box		*cheese				knife	car	candle
*handkerchief		*men		*Deaf/College*			key	gift
*napkin		*home	*fire	*skates	*salt		water	*money
monkey			*fish	cow	*orange		school	
			*bicycle	*egg	*pepper		nickel	
			*food	*doctor	*mother		*milk	
			*rain	*nurse	*apple		*skates	
				*hot dog	*toast			
				*pop	cookie		*College*	
				*hamburger		hospital	*bird	*medicine
				boy		nickel	*tree	butter
				sandwich		*trampoline	*gym	candy
						*dog	*body	
						night	*pie	
							peach	
							*bath	
							*coat	
							*dress	
							Blind Only	
						fork	rest room	
						chair, slt	bed	
						sandwich	monkey	

*Agreement by blind and sighted subjects.

Table 4
Number of Signs Rated High, Medium, and Low Iconic
Based on Numerical Ratings

		High Iconic	Medium Iconic	Low Iconic
Children (n = 20)	Mean rating score range	2 – 3	1 – 1.99	0 – .99
	Number of signs (n = 100)	1	44	55
College students (n = 20)	Mean rating score range	3.4 – 5	1.8 – 3.39	0 – 1.79
	Number of signs (n = 100)	26	26	48
Deaf adults (n = 12)	Mean rating score range	3.4 – 5	1.8 – 3.39	0 – 1.79
	Number of signs (n = 100)	26	58	16
Blind (n = 13)	Mean rating score range	3.68 – 5	2.34 – 3.67	1 – 2.33
	Number of signs (n = 100)	54	31	15
Across group totals		107	159	134

Note. N = 400 signs

category signs from Fristoe's list were found to have the following iconic ranks: prepositions (n = 5), mean = 4.72; verbs (n = 22), mean = 4.29; nouns (n = 35), mean = 3.85; and adjectives (n = 13), mean = 3.73. These findings support (although tentatively, since the number of signs tested was very small) the notion that verb signs are more salient than noun signs and that prepositions may be the most salient of all form class signs.

Discussion

The results of this study indicate not only that information about the iconic qualities of signs is available and perceivable through the tactile mode, but that blind subjects interpret the information similarly to sighted persons. Thus signs thought to be highly iconic to learners through the visual mode should also be iconic through the tactile mode.

What are the qualities of signs that make them iconic? Evidence from an earlier study (Griffith, Panagos, & Robinson, 1981) showed that particular aspects of signs are most salient in subject associations. Mandel (Note 3) described devices by which iconic signs are presented by the signer. His presentation devices included (a) miming an action, (b) pointing to the referent, (c) substituting the hands for the referent, and (d) two means of drawing the referent in the air. His devices included direct representation (the thing itself) and indirect representation (something else to represent the referent). Griffith, Panagos, and Robinson (1981) found that observers' association responses included three main categories across Mandel's (Note 3) devices: (a) motion of or done to the referent or its representative, (b) attributes of the referent, and (c) the name of the thing. The most frequent associations, however, motion done to the referent and function/purpose of the referent, represented the most salient and closely associated qualities of signs.

Developmental language theory can account for similarity in subjects' responses across modalities, even in signing, based on these qualities. Nelson (1974) proposed a conceptual model to account for normal children's initial translation of meaning into words that contained a whole-to-part hierarchy: (a) concepts, (b) instances, and (c) attributes. First concepts emerge from *actions* with objects and interactions with people. Experiences become a function *core* that contains relational information. Within this relational information (associations), first identifications are based on functions—and later identifications are based on attributes. Finally, labels are given in the form of names. Although these do not necessarily occur in a developmental sequence, Nelson (1974) pointed out that function represented by action is the most highly salient quality of concepts mapped by children.

Highly iconic signs, then, are more likely to be early signs reflecting early concepts as hypothesized by Brown (Note 1). Highly iconic signs are easier to learn because they look like the action or object they represent; but they are also likely representations of highly salient, dynamic concepts, and these concepts are easy to acquire.

Implications for Teaching Deaf-Blind Children

The fact that highly iconic signs represent highly salient concepts, which are reflected in a child's early expressions, suggests that what may be most obvious to a new learner of any age will be concepts (signs/words) that can be associated by him/her. This means that what is functional to the teacher (toilet, sit, stand, wait) may not be most functional or meaningful to the learner.

The criteria suggested by Lahey and Bloom (1977) and Holland (1975) for selection of first vocabularies, and used by Fristoe and Lloyd (1980) in developing their initial sign vocabulary, are most appropriate for vocabulary selection for deaf-blind clients, regardless of age. Initial sign teaching should focus on what appears to be highly familiar to a client—on manipulatives, whose whole design can be perceived tactilely (spoon, drink, cup), and on actions meaningful to the person (eat, swing, rock). In most cases these items will be iconic; however, those that are most iconic and meet other criteria should be the easiest to learn. The ratings provided in this study can be referred to in selecting some first signs. Once deaf-blind children are able to associate sign and meaning for highly salient concepts, communication training can proceed in a more successful and purposeful manner.

Appendix A
Rank Order of Signs Rated by Blind Subjects

Sign	Rating	Sign	Rating	Sign	Rating
*up	5	trampoline	4.4	morning	3.27
eye	5	tree	4.4	candle	3.27
nose	5	*come	4.36	dress	3.2
toothbrush	5	*table	4.36	flower	3.18
baby	5	bowl	4.36	butter	3.18
*cry	5	*help	4.36	*work	3.18
*drink	5	*pants	4.36	*bathroom/toilet	3.18
door	5	*afraid	4.36	*happy	3.1
*big	4.9	hamburger	4.36	nurse	3.1
rain	4.9	tea	4.3	pie	3.1
*open	4.9	*walk	4.27	*good	3.0
*comb	4.9	*run	4.27	water	3.0
head	4.9	*spoon	4.27	*angry	3.0
key	4.81	*put	4.27	boy	3.0
mouth	4.81	gym	4.27	apple	3.0
food	4.81	*wash	4.18	cow	2.9
napkin	4.81	bed/sleep	4.18	meat	2.9
*down	4.81	candy	4.18	salt	2.9
*give	4.81	*play	4.18	home	2.9
cold/winter	4.81	bird	4.1	*have	2.9
book	4.81	*finished	4.09	*dirty	2.9
snow	4.8	*hat	4.09	*how	2.81
telephone	4.8	bath	4.09	money	2.72
bicycle	4.8	*this/that	4.09	bread	2.72
*you	4.73	gift	4.0	*t.v.	2.7
airplane	4.72	police	4.0	pepper	2.7
*stand	4.72	*hot	4.0	*no	2.68
fire	4.72	monkey	3.9	cheese	2.54
fish	4.72	coat	3.9	pig	2.5
iron	4.72	hot dog	3.9	toast	2.5
*in	4.72	pop	3.85	restaurant	2.5
*go	4.63	*stop	3.85	paper	2.4
house	4.63	*make	3.81	school	2.36
*heavy	4.63	body	3.81	girl	2.36
eat/food	4.63	clock	3.81	peach	2.33
dog	4.63	skates	3.8	shoes	2.27
chair/sit	4.63	*bring	3.72	man	2.2
*kiss	4.63	rest room	3.72	mother	2.18
*throw	4.54	knife	3.63	orange	2.12
banana	4.54	*cat	3.63	woman	2.1
ball	4.54	*bad	3.63	potato	2.0
box	4.54	coffee	3.54	medicine	1.90
cup	4.54	*more	3.54	*what	1.72
*shirt	4.54	cookie	3.45	store	1.7
*under	4.54	doctor	3.45	father	1.54
*on	4.54	*get	3.45	*who	1.36
car	4.54	milk	3.45	*do	1.27
*fall	4.54	onion	3.4	color	1.27
*clean	4.54	hospital	3.36	number	1.22
fork	4.45	egg	3.36	farm	1.2
handkerchief	4.45	*might	3.3	nickel	1.1
sandwich	4.4	*sad	3.3	Coke	1.0

*Sign occurred only on Fristoe and Lloyd list; not used in comparison with sighted groups.

	Children			College Students			Deaf Adults			Blind Adults		
	Rank Order	X̄	Classi-fication*	Rank Order	X̄	Classi-fication	Rank Order	X̄	Classi-fication	Rank Order	X̄	Classi-fication
airplane	22	1.55	H	18	4.13	H	13.5	3.91	H	18.5	4.72	H
apple	69.5	.70	M	95.5	.04	L	72	2.0	L	69	3.0	L
baby	4.5	1.80	H	2	5.	H	3	4.16	H	3	5	H
ball	16	1.65	H	6	4.77	H	29.5	3.25	M	27	4.54	H
banana	16	1.25	H	60	1.54	M	37	3.08	H	27	4.09	M
bath	33	1.25	H	5	5.	H	13.5	3.91	H	42	4.18	M
bed	19.5	1.60	H	12.5	4.54	H	23.5	3.58	H	39.5	4.18	H
bicycle	63.5	.80	M	15	4.36	H	23.5	3.58	H	15	4.8	M
bird	30.5	1.30	H	37.5	2.77	M	25	3.5	H	41	4.1	M
body	24.5	1.50	H	50	1.95	M	27.5	3.33	H	49.5	3.81	H
book	22	1.55	H	12.5	4.45	H	8	3.16	H	10.5	4.81	H
bowl	26.5	1.45	H	16	4.13	H	13.5	3.91	H	35.5	4.36	H
box	24.5	1.55	H	7	4.72	H	33	3.16	H	27	4.54	H
boy	88	.45	L	60	1.59	M	63	2.25	M	69	3.0	L
bread	73.5	.65	M	78	.50	L	72	2.0	L	75.5	2.72	M
butter	52	.95	M	78	.50	L	59	2.33	M	64.5	3.18	M
candle	66	.75	M	44	2.36	M	72	2.0	L	61.5	3.27	L
candy	46.5	1.0	H	87	.22	L	59	2.33	M	39.5	4.18	M
car	11	1.7	H	12.5	4.54	H	37	3.08	H	27	4.54	H
chair	52	.95	M	62	1.50	M	51	2.58	M	18.5	4.63	H
cheese	69.5	.70	H	95.5	.04	L	81.5	1.91	L	78	2.54	M
clock	2	1.95	H	10	4.60	H	49	2.66	M	49.5	3.81	M
coat	35.5	1.2	H	52	1.8	M	10	4.0	H	46	3.9	M
coffee	46.5	1.0	M	51	1.90	M	37	3.08	H	54	3.54	L
Coke	82.5	.50	L	78	.5	L	87	1.66	M	99	1.0	L
color	88	.45	M	93	.09	L	97.5	1.0	L	95	1.27	L
cookie	60.5	.55	M	74	.63	L	67	2.08	L	56	3.45	M
cow	82.5	.55	M	63	1.5	M	45	2.83	L	72.5	2.9	H
cup	30.5	1.30	H	23.5	3.77	H	17.5	3.83	M	27	4.54	H
doctor	95	.35	L	48.5	2.09	M	46.5	2.75	H	56	3.45	M
dog	52	.95	M	33.5	2.95	M	53	2.50	M	22.5	4.63	M
door	7	1.75	H	26	3.59	H	21.5	3.66	H	3	5	H
dress	33	1.25	H	66	1.27	M	29.5	3.25	H	63	3.2	H
egg	77	.60	L	56.5	1.68	M	46.5	2.75	M	60	3.36	M
eye	4.5	1.8	H	12.5	4.54	H	17.5	3.83	H	3	5	H
farm	92	.40	L	99	0	L	99	0	L	97	1.2	L
father	82.5	.55	M	85.5	.27	L	72	2.0	M	94	1.54	L
fire	38	1.15	M	31	3.13	H	10	4.0	H	18.5	4.72	H
fish	60.5	.85	M	20	4.04	H	10	4.0	H	18.5	4.72	H
flower	60.5	.85	M	67.5	1.23	M	39.5	3.0	M	64.5	3.18	M
fork	42	1.05	M	54.5	1.72	M	53	2.5	M	30.5	4.45	M
food	56	.90	M	35.5	2.81	H	4	4.16	H	10.5	4.81	H
gift	66	.75	M	40	2.54	M	85	1.75	L	43.5	4.0	H
girl	77	.60	L	78	.5	L	94	1.41	L	83.5	2.36	H
gym	92	.40	L	44	2.36	M	94	1.41	L	38	4.27	L
hamburger	28	1.40	H	67.5	1.23	M	53	2.5	M	37	4.36	M
handkerchief	26.5	1.45	H	22	3.86	H	33	3.16	H	30.5	4.45	H
head	46.5	1.0	M	37.5	2.77	M	13.5	3.91	H	6.5	4.9	H
home	82.5	.50	L	99	0	L	67	2.08	L	72.5	2.9	H
hospital	46.5	1.0	M	29.5	3.18	H	39.5	3.0	M	60	3.36	M

*H = high iconic, M = medium iconic, L = low iconic

TACTILE ICONICITY

23

Appendix B (Continued)
Ratings by Group

	Children			College Students			Deaf Adults			Blind Adults		
	Rank Order	X̄	Classification*	Rank Order	X̄	Classification	Rank Order	X̄	Classification	Rank Order	X̄	Classification
hot dog	16	1.65	H	60	1.52	M	27.5	2.33	M	46	3.9	M
house	16	1.65	H	18	4.13	H	1	4.5	H	22.5	4.63	H
iron	11	1.7	H	31	3.18	M	27.5	3.33	H	18.5	4.72	H
key	7	1.75	H	21	3.95	H	42	2.91	M	10.5	4.81	H
knife	52	.95	M	56.5	1.68	M	33	3.16	H	53	3.63	M
man	69.5	.70	L	92	.13	L	67	2.08	L	87	2.2	L
meat	82.5	.50	L	83	.36	L	78	1.91	L	72.5	2.9	L
medicine	56.5	.90	M	73	.72	L	55.5	2.41	M	92	1.90	M
milk	35.5	1.20	H	28	3.22	H	42	2.91	M	56	3.45	M
money	66	.75	L	65	1.36	M	72	2.0	M	75.5	2.72	L
monkey	11	1.70	H	5	4.86	H	33	3.16	H	46	3.9	L
morning	46.5	1.0	M	46.5	2.09	M	49	2.66	M	61.5	3.27	M
mother	60.5	.85	M	95.5	66	L	89	1.60	M	88	2.18	M
mouth	11	1.70	H	9	4.68	H	6.5	4.08	H	10.5	4.81	H
name	95	.35	L	95.5	66	L	83.5	1.83	L	90.5	2.10	L
napkin	19.5	1.60	H	32	3.0	M	33	3.16	H	10.5	4.81	H
nickel	98	.30	L	16	4.19	H	28	2.25	M	98	1.1	L
night	40	1.10	M	33.5	2.95	H	81.5	1.91	L	60	3.36	H
nose	11	1.70	H	2	5	H	17.5	3.83	H	3	5	H
number	99	.20	L	99	0	L	78	1.91	L	96	1.22	M
nurse	73.5	.65	L	46	2.36	M	42	2.91	M	66	3.1	M
onion	52	.95	M	41	2.5	M	91	1.58	L	58	3.45	M
orange	56.5	.90	M	81.5	.45	L	72	2.0	L	89	2.12	L
paper	95	.35	L	85.5	.27	L	98	.83	L	82	2.4	L
peach	77	.60	L	58	1.59	M	91	1.58	L	85	2.3	L
pepper	46.5	1.0	M	69	1.04	L	86	1.66	L	77	2.7	L
pie	73.5	.65	L	53	1.77	M	78	1.91	L	66	3.1	M
pig	98	.30	L	75	.54	L	78	1.91	L	80	2.5	L
police	42	1.05	M	39	2.68	M	6.5	4.08	H	43.5	4.0	M
pop	24.5	1.5	H	64	1.4	M	59	2.33	M	48	3.85	M
potato	82	.50	L	89	.18	L	78	1.91	L	91	2.0	L
rain	38	1.15	M	35.5	2.81	H	21.5	3.66	H	6.5	4.9	H
restaurant	90	.50	L	91	.14	L	94	1.41	L	80	2.5	L
rest room	82.5	.50	L	89	.18	L	91	1.58	L	52	3.72	L
salt	42	1.05	M	81.5	.45	M	72	2.0	L	72.5	2.9	L
sandwich	69.5	.70	L	54.5	1.72	M	59	2.33	M	33	4.4	M
school	92	.40	L	70	1.0	L	63	2.25	M	83.5	2.36	M
shoes	73.5	.65	H	78	.5	L	83.5	1.83	L	86	2.27	L
skates	19.5	1.65	H	44	2.36	M	44	2.8	M	51	3.80	M
snow	3	1.85	H	23.5	3.77	H	4	4.16	H	15	4.8	H
store	82.5	.55	L	89	.18	L	88	1.66	M	93	1.7	M
tea	38	1.15	M	47	2.22	M	65	2.16	M	37	4.3	M
telephone	1	2.05	H	4	4.9	H	2	4.29	H	15	4.8	H
toast	63.5	.80	M	72	.77	L	97.5	1.0	L	80	2.5	L
toothbrush	7	1.75	H	8	4.72	H	17.5	3.83	M	3	5	H
trampoline	56.5	.90	M	25	3.6	H	49	2.66	M	33	4.4	M
tree	29	1.35	M	42	2.40	M	26	3.41	H	33	4.4	M
water	88	.45	L	84	.32	L	55.5	2.41	M	69	3.0	L
winter	33	1.25	H	27	3.27	H	20	3.75	H	10.5	4.81	H
woman	98	.30	L	71	.86	L	95	1.33	L	90.5	2.10	L

*H = high iconic, M = medium iconic, L = low iconic

Appendix C
Tactile Ratings Obtained for Items Included in Fristoe and Lloyd's (1980) Initial Teaching Sign Lexicon

Nouns		Verbs		Adjectives		Prepositions	
1. baby	5.0	1. cry	5.0	1. big	4.9	1. up	5.0
2. door	5.0	2. drink	5.0	2. heavy	4.63	2. down	4.81
3. comb	4.9	3. open	4.9	3. open	4.9	3. in	4.72
4. book	4.81	4. give	4.81	4. clean	4.54	4. under	4.54
5. winter/cold	4.80	5. stand	4.72	5. afraid	4.36	5. on	4.54
6. you	4.73	6. go	4.63	6. bad	3.63		
7. chair	4.63	7. kiss	4.63	7. more	3.54		
8. dog	4.63	8. throw	4.54	8. sad	3.3		
9. eat/food	4.63	9. fall	4.54	9. happy	3.1		
10. house	4.63	10. clean	4.54	10. good	3.0		
11. ball	4.54	11. come	4.54	11. angry	3.0		
12. boy	4.54	12. help	4.36	12. dirty	2.9		
13. cup	4.54	13. walk	4.27	13. no	2.68		
14. shirt	4.5	14. run	4.27				
15. car	4.45	15. put	4.27				
16. table	4.36	16. wash	4.18				
17. pants	4.36	17. finished	4.09				
18. spoon	4.27	18. make	3.81				
19. bed	4.18	19. bring	3.72				
20. candy	4.18	20. get	3.54				
21. bird	4.10	21. work	3.18				
22. hat	4.0	22. have	2.9				
23. coat	3.9						
24. cat	3.63						
25. coffee	3.54						
26. milk	3.45						
27. cookie	3.45						
28. bathroom	3.1						
29. water	3.09						
30. apple	3.0						
31. t.v.	2.7						
32. girl,	2.36						
33. shoe	2.27						
34. mother	2.18						
35. father	1.54						

Appendix D
Tactile Ratings Obtained for
Gold and Rittenhouse's (1979) Practical Signs

1.	drink	5.0
2.	eat	4.81
3.	stand	4.72
4.	sit	4.63
5.	more	3.54
6.	toilet	3.18
7.	enough	(not rated)
8.	stay	(not rated)

Reference Notes

1. Brown, R. *Why are signed languages easier to learn than spoken language?* Keynote address, National Symposium on Sign Language Research and Training, Chicago, May 30, 1977.
2. Lloyd, L., & Fristoe, M. *Transparency of manual signs used with individuals having severe communication impairment.* Paper presented at the Eleventh Gatlinburg Conference on Research in Mental Retardation, Gatlinburg, TN, March 8, 1978.
3. Mandel, M. *Iconicity of signs and their learnability by non-signers.* Paper presented at the National Symposium on Sign Language Research and Teaching, Chicago, May 30–June 3, 1977.
4. Robbins, N. *Selecting sign systems for multi-handicapped students.* Paper presented before the American Speech and Hearing Association, Houston, TX, November 1976.
5. Wilson, P. S. *Sign language as a means of communication for the mentally retarded.* Paper presented at Eastern Psychological Association, New York, 1974.
6. Creedon, M. P. *Language development in nonverbal autistic children using a simultaneous communication system.* Paper presented at the biennial meeting of the Society for Research in Child Development, Philadelphia, 1973.
7. Baron, N. D., & Isensee, L. M. *Effectiveness of manual versus spoken language with an autistic child.* Unpublished paper, Brown University, Providence, RI, 1976.
8. Baron, N., & Isensee, L. M. *Iconicity and learnability.* Paper presented at the Second Annual Boston University Conference on Language Development, Cambridge, MA, September 30–October 1, 1977.

References

Bellugi, U., & Klima, E. S. Two faces of sign: Iconic and abstract. In S. Harnard, D. Horst, & J. Lancaster (Eds.), *Origins and evolution of language and speech.* New York: New York Academy of Science, 1976.

Bonvillian, J., & Nelson, K. Development of sign language in autistic children and other language handicapped individuals. In P. Siple (Ed.), *Understanding language through sign language research.* New York: Academic Press, 1978.

Frishberg, N. Arbitrariness and iconicity: Historical change in American Sign Language. *Language,* 1975, *51*(3), 696–719.

Fristoe, M., & Lloyd, L. Manual communication for the retarded and others with severe communication impairment: A resource list. *Mental Retardation,* 1977, *15*(5), 18–21.

Fristoe, M., & Lloyd, L. Planning an initial expressive sign lexicon for persons with severe communication impairment. *Journal of Speech and Hearing Disorders,* 1980, *45*(2), 170–180.

Gold, M., & Rittenhouse, R. Task analysis for teaching eight practical signs to deaf-blind individuals. *Teaching Exceptional Children,* 1978, *10*(2), 34–37.

Griffith, P., Panagos, J., & Robinson, J. H. A three-dimensional approach to iconicity. *Perceptual Motor Skills,* 1981, *52*, 665–666.

Griffith, P., & Robinson, J. H. The influence of iconicity and phonological similarity on sign learning in mentally retarded subjects. *American Journal of Mental Deficiency,* 1980, *85*(4), 291–299.

Griffith, P., & Robinson, J. H. A comparative and normative

study of the iconicity of signs rated by three groups. *American Annals of the Deaf*, 1981, *126*(4), 440–449.

Griffith, P., Robinson, J. H., & Panagos, J. Perception of iconicity in American Sign Language by three groups of observers. *Journal of Speech and Hearing Disorders*, 1981, *46*(4), 388–397.

Holland, A. Language therapy for children: Some thoughts on context and content. *Journal of Speech and Hearing Disorders*, 1975, *40*, 514–523.

Jensema, C. A review of communication systems used by deaf-blind people—Part I. *American Annals of the Deaf*, 1979, *124*(6), 720–725.

Jensema, C. Report of communication method usage by teachers of deaf-blind children—Part II. *American Annals of the Deaf*, 1981, *126*(4), 392–394.

Konstantareas, M. M., Oxman, J., & Webster, C. D. Iconici-ty: Effects on the acquisition of sign language by autistic and other severely dysfunctional children. In P. Siple (Ed.), *Understanding language through sign language research*. New York: Academic Press, 1978, 213–235.

Lahey, M., & Bloom, L. Planning a first lexicon: Which words to teach first. *Journal of Speech and Hearing Disorders*, 1977, *42*, 340–349.

Nelson, K. Concept, word, and sentence: Interrelations in acquisition and development. *Psychological Review*, 1974, *81*(4), 267–285.

Stokoe, W. C., Casterline, D., & Croneberg, C. *A dictionary of American Sign Language on linguistic principles*. Washington, D.C.: Gallaudet College Press, 1965.

Westcott, R. Linguistic iconism. *Language*, 1971, *47*, 416–428.

ANALYTIC STUDY OF THE TADOMA METHOD: EFFECTS OF HAND POSITION ON SEGMENTAL SPEECH PERCEPTION

CHARLOTTE M. REED   NATHANIEL I. DURLACH   LOUIS D. BRAIDA
Research Laboratory of Electronics, Massachusetts Institute of Technology

MARTIN C. SCHULTZ
Southern Illinois University

In the Tadoma method of communication, deaf-blind individuals receive speech by placing a hand on the face and neck of the talker and monitoring actions associated with speech production. Previous research has documented the speech perception, speech production, and linguistic abilities of highly experienced users of the Tadoma method. The current study was performed to gain further insight into the cues involved in the perception of speech segments through Tadoma. Small-set segmental identification experiments were conducted in which the subjects' access to various types of articulatory information was systematically varied by imposing limitations on the contact of the hand with the face. Results obtained on 3 deaf-blind, highly experienced users of Tadoma were examined in terms of percent-correct scores, information transfer, and reception of speech features for each of sixteen experimental conditions. The results were generally consistent with expectations based on the speech cues assumed to be available in the various hand positions.

KEY WORDS: Tadoma, deaf-blind, tactile speech communication, segmental identification

The Tadoma method is a means of tactile speech communication that evolved within the deaf-blind community. In this method, the hand of the Tadoma user is placed over the face and neck of the talker to monitor actions of the face associated with speech production (including lip movements, jaw movements, laryngeal vibration, and airflow at the lips). Previous research on Tadoma has documented the receptive speech-communication abilities of highly experienced, deaf-blind Tadoma users (see Norton et al., 1977; Reed, Durlach, Braida, & Schultz, 1982; Reed et al., 1985). The results of this research indicate average Tadoma scores of roughly 60% correct for consonant identification, 45% for vowel identification, 40% for identification of open-set monosyllabic words, and 65% for key words in CID sentences. These scores are roughly comparable to those obtained by normal subjects listening to speech in white noise at signal-to-noise ratios in the range of 0–6 dB (Miller, Heise, & Lichten, 1951).

The performance achieved by experienced Tadoma users is superior to that obtained with any artificial tactile system to date (see Reed, Durlach, & Braida, 1982, and Sherrick, 1984, for a review of this literature). Among the reasons hypothesized for the success of the Tadoma method are (1) the extensive training received by these Tadoma users as students in deaf-blind educational programs compared to the training provided to experimental subjects with artificial tactile displays; (2) the use of the hand for receiving tactile input, with the associated rich innervation of tactile receptors and the extensive representation in the somatosensory cortex compared to other body sites; and (3) the multidimensional, articulatory nature of the "talking face" display used in Tadoma compared to the typically unidimensional, spectral displays employed in most artificial tactile systems.

The goal of the current study was to explore further the characteristics of the Tadoma display. A series of experiments concerned with identification of small sets of speech segments was conducted in which the subjects' access to various types of articulatory information was systematically varied by imposing limitations on the contact of the hand with the face. The results of such tests are capable of providing insight into the relationship between the physical cues available through the Tadoma display and the perception of features used to distinguish among speech segments. Ultimately, such experimentation should lead to improved understanding of the Tadoma method and of tactile speech perception in general.

METHODS

Subjects

The subjects for these experiments were three highly experienced, deaf-blind users of the Tadoma method (LD, RB, and JC). Subjects LD and RB were males whose ages were 50 and 42 years, respectively; subject JC was a female whose age was 50 years. The onset of deafness and blindness was simultaneous as a result of meningitis at age 19 months for LD, 20 months for RB, and 7 years for JC. The results of audiometric testing on these subjects indicated essentially no response to auditory stimulation (with the exception of minimal unilateral low-frequency response for LD and RB, most likely as a result of vibrotactile stimulation). Similarly, tests of vision revealed no measurable visual acuity in any of the three subjects. Each of these subjects received extensive speech and language training through Tadoma following the onset of deafness and blindness, and they all use Tadoma as one of their major means of communication. The receptive speech-communication and linguistic abilities of LD, RB, and JC are documented in Reed et al. (1985) and Chomsky (1986). Additional studies of LD are available in Norton et al. (1977) and in Reed, Durlach, Braida, & Schultz et al. (1982). Further biographical details of each of these subjects are available in Chomsky. These 3 subjects were selected for the study on the basis of their willingness to make repeated trips to our laboratory for data collection as well as on their Tadoma skills. Compared to the six other Tadoma users whose speech-reception data are reported in Reed et al. (1985), the performance of LD, RB, and JC was superior on tests of connected-speech reception and linguistic ability and was slightly above average on tests of isolated-word and segmental reception.

Stimuli

The stimuli for these experiments were a set of eight initial consonants in C-/ɑ/ syllables and a set of eight vowels and diphthongs in /h/-V-/d/ syllables. A classification of each of these sets of sounds in terms of traditional articulatory speech features is provided in Table 1. The sets of sounds were selected to provide relatively high performance under normal Tadoma reception as well as to contrast a variety of speech features. The set of eight consonants contrasts the features of voicing (4 voiced vs. 4 unvoiced sounds), manner (4 plosives vs. 4 fricatives), and place (4 sounds produced in the front of the mouth vs. 4 sounds produced medially). The set of eight vowels and diphthongs contrasts the features of rounding (3 rounded vs. 5 unrounded stimuli), tense (5 tense vs. 3 lax stimuli), high (4 high vowels vs. 2 nonhigh vowels vs. 2 diphthongs whose initial and final components have different values on this feature), back (5 back vs. 3 nonback stimuli), and low (1 low vs. 6 nonlow stimuli vs. 1

TABLE 1a. Classification of the eight consonant stimuli on three articulatory features.

Features	/p/	/t/	/f/	/s/	/b/	/d/	/v/	/z/
Voicing	1	1	1	1	2	2	2	2
Manner	1	1	2	2	1	1	2	2
Place	1	2	1	2	1	2	1	2

TABLE 1b. Classification of the eight vowel and diphthong stimuli on three articulatory features.

Features	/i/	/ɪ/	/ʌ/	/ɑ/	/ʊ/	/u/	/eɪ/	/aʊ/
Round	−	−	−	−	+	+	−	+
Tense	+	−	−	+	−	+	+	+
High	+	+	−	−	+	+	c*	c*
Back	−	−	+	+	+	+	−	+
Low	−	−	−	+	−	−	−	c*

*The symbol "c" denotes a change in value on a given feature from the initial to the final component of a diphthong.

diphthong whose initial and final components have different values on this feature).

Experimental Design

The identification of each set of stimuli (consonants or vowels) was studied for a set of 15 conditions that varied in the contact allowed between the hand and the face. Based on analysis of previous segmental confusion data from Tadoma users, as well as on our own observations as native subjects attempting to learn Tadoma (Reed, Rubin, Braida, & Durlach, 1978; Reed, Doherty, Braida, & Durlach, 1982), and on the basis of physical measurements made by Hansen (1964), we have hypothesized that there are four major components to the Tadoma display: (1) breath flow at the mouth (B); (2) in-out and up-down movements of the upper and lower lips (L); (3) up-down movements of the jaw (J); and (4) laryngeal vibration present on the neck (N). In addition to a condition employing the normal Tadoma hand placement, 14 other experimental conditions were devised to present each of these four major cues alone (to the extent possible), in combination with every other major cue, and in all possible three-cue groupings. Precise isolation of the individual cues is difficult for a variety of reasons (e.g., the strong coupling of the lip and jaw movements, the spread of vibration from the larynx to the jaw and lips, etc.); however, an attempt was made to devise a hand placement for each condition that maximized the presence of information from the desired source or sources.

A list of the conditions and a description of the hand position associated with each is provided in Table 2. To achieve the condition where the major cue was breath flow (B), the thumb was placed in the breath stream in front of the mouth and no hand-face contact was made. For the condition where the major cue was lip movements (L), the thumb was covered with a rubber glove (to allow perception of lip movements without breath cues) and placed on the lips, while the fingers were curled into the hand and made no contact with the face. For the condition where the major cue was jaw movement (J), the hand was placed along the ridge of the jaw. Finally, for the condition where the major cue was laryngeal vibration at the neck (N), the hand was placed over the neck in the region of the larynx. Hand placements for the two-cue and three-cue conditions are described in Table 2. A number of conditions required the placement of the individual fingers, the thumb, or the palm of the hand in locations different from those used in normal Tadoma. For example, to achieve the two-cue condition of Breath and Neck cues, the thumb was placed in front of rather than on the lips, and the fingers were placed entirely over the larynx rather than fanning out over the face and neck. It is our impression that the subjects did not have great difficulty attending to a specific type of facial action or vibration with a part of the hand different from that employed in normal Tadoma.

Finally, a 16th condition was included in which normal Tadoma hand placement was used but the speech was

TABLE 2. Experimental conditions.

Conditions	Description of hand position
One-cue conditions	
Breath (B)	Thumb placed in breath stream in front of mouth; fingers and hand off face.
Lip movements (L)	Gloved thumb placed over lips; fingers and hand off face.
Jaw movements (J)	Hand placed over mandibular ridge.
Vibration on neck (N)	Hand placed over larynx.
Two-cue conditions	
B,L	Thumb placed on lips; fingers and hand off face.
B,J	Fingers on mandibular ridge; thumb in breath stream in front of mouth.
B,N	Thumb in breath stream in front of mouth; fingers on neck over larynx.
L,J	Gloved thumb on lips; fingers on mandibular ridge.
L,N	Gloved thumb on lips; fingers on neck over larynx.
J,N	Fingers on mandibular ridge; thumb on neck over larynx.
Three-cue conditions	
B,L,J	Thumb placed on lips; fingers on mandibular ridge.
B,J,N	Thumb in breath stream in front of lips; fingers fan out over cheek and neck.
L,J,N	Gloved thumb on lips; fingers fan out over cheek and neck.
B,L,N	Thumb on lips; fingers on neck over larynx.
Full-hand conditions	
Normal Tadoma	Thumb placed over lips; fingers fan out over face and neck.
Whispered speech	Same as above.

whispered. In whispered speech, the vocal cords are held close together, causing frication when breath passes between them for voiced sounds, while the movements of the articulators remain roughly normal (O'Connor, 1973, p. 29). Thus, whispering provides a condition involving normal Tadoma hand placement in the absence of laryngeal vibration and in the presence of roughly normal articulatory movements.

Procedure

The Tadoma user sat facing the talker with the preferred hand in the position described for a given experimental condition. On a table in front of the subject was a Braille-embossed card listing the eight possible consonant responses or the eight possible vowel responses. One stimulus set (either consonants or vowels) was selected and the 16 conditions were presented in random order (with different orders used for different subjects). Data for normal Tadoma were always obtained first to ensure that a relatively high level of performance could be achieved before introducing alterations in hand position. Randomized lists of the eight stimuli in each set were constructed and a 100-trial list was presented under each condition. On a given trial, the speaker read the stimulus syllable with the subject's hand positioned appropriately. The subject then scanned the Braille card and selected a response which was recorded by the experimenter before the next trial was presented. No trial-by-trial correct-answer feedback was provided.

Subjects RB and JC were tested first on consonants followed by vowels; the reverse order was used for LD. For JC, all consonant conditions were presented by 1 male speaker (MS) and all vowel conditions were presented by a different male speaker (ND). For RB, the consonant conditions were divided between 2 male speakers (ND and MS) and the vowel conditions were presented by another male speaker (PZ). For LD, the consonant conditions were divided among four male speakers (MS, ND, PP, and SR), and two of these speakers (MS and ND) presented the vowel conditions. Ideally, 1 speaker would have presented all 16 conditions for a given stimulus set to one subject; however, this was not always possible. Data obtained in 100-trial runs for different speakers on the same condition (including normal Tadoma and several conditions with altered hand placements) indicated that scores were similar across speakers. For example, on the two-cue condition of Breath and Lip, subject LD's vowel scores ranged from 40%–56% correct for 3 different speakers, and normal Tadoma scores for different speakers were generally within five percentage points of each other.

Data Analysis

For each subject and stimulus set, an 8 × 8 stimulus-response confusion matrix was compiled from the 100 trials collected on each of the 16 experimental conditions. Percent-correct scores and information transfer were calculated from these matrices. In addition, the information transfer associated with each of the features described in Table 1a for consonants and in Table 1b for vowels was calculated.

RESULTS AND DISCUSSION

The percent-correct scores and the information transfer in bits for each subject under each of the 16 experimental conditions are provided in Appendix A for consonants and in Appendix B for vowels. The maximum amount of information in each of the 8-item stimulus sets is 3 bits. The amount of information available on each consonant feature (voicing, manner, and place) is 1 bit. The amount of information available on the vowel features is roughly 1 bit for the features round, tense, back, and low and 1.4 bits for the feature high.

The percent-correct scores for individual subjects averaged over the one-cue, two-cue, and three-cue conditions are plotted in the upper half of Figure 1 for consonants and the lower half of Figure 1 for vowels. For both stimulus sets, percent-correct scores, which were similar across the 3 subjects, increased uniformly with the number of cues provided by the hand placement. The normal Tadoma score, which averaged roughly 90% correct on both stimulus sets, was somewhat higher than the average three-cue score. Given the high degree of similarity across subjects, further presentation of results provided below is based on averages across subjects.

In Figure 2, information transfer (IT) in bits, averaged across subjects, is plotted as a function of hand position. For consonants (shown in the upper half of Figure 2), IT for the one-cue conditions averaged 1.2 bits and ranged from 1.0 bit for B alone to 1.4 bits for L alone. For the two-cue conditions, IT averaged roughly 1.7 bits and ranged from 1.4 bits for (B,N) to 2.0 bits for (L,N). For the three-cue conditions, IT averaged roughly 2.2 bits compared to 2.6 bits obtained with the normal Tadoma hand position. For vowels (shown in the lower half of Figure 2), a somewhat larger degree of variation was observed among the one-cue conditions than was seen for consonants. Performance for B alone (0.7 bits) and L alone (1.1 bits) was lower than for N alone (1.6 bits) and J alone (1.4 bits). For the two-cue conditions, IT averaged 1.6 bits and ranged from 1.2 for (B,L) to 1.8 bits for (L,N). For the three-cue conditions, IT averaged roughly 2.1 bits compared to 2.5 bits for normal Tadoma.

For both the consonants and vowels, the IT obtained in the multiple-cue conditions (including the normal Tadoma condition) was always substantially less than the sum of the ITs for the individual cues that made up the multiple-cue conditions. Thus, for example, with the consonants, the sum of the ITs for the 4 one-cue conditions is 4.8 bits, whereas the IT for the normal Tadoma condition is only 2.6 bits. To a large extent, this result is forced by the small size of the stimulus set; no IT can exceed 3 bits, the amount of self-information in the stimulus set. It should be noted, however, that the same result is likely to occur even with a much larger stimulus set (because the information carried by one cue is degraded when the other cues are activated, or the information in the various cues is partially redundant, etc.). That

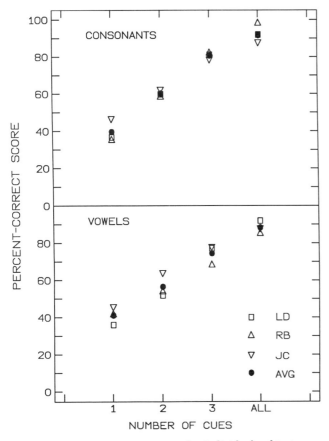

FIGURE 1. Percent-correct scores for individual subjects as a function of the number of cues contained in the hand position. Consonant performance is shown in the upper half and vowel performance in the lower half of the Figure. Four conditions are averaged into the 1-cue score, six conditions into the 2-cue score, and four conditions into the 3-cue score. The score for normal Tadoma is represented by ALL.

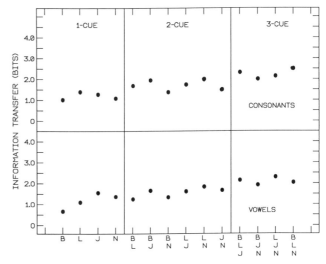

FIGURE 2. Information transfer (IT) in bits averaged across subjects as a function of hand position.

such would be the case is suggested, for example, by the tendency of the ITs for the 2-cue conditions to be both less than the sum of the component 1-cue ITs and substantially less than 3 bits.

Feature analyses of the confusion matrices obtained for different conditions indicated that performance on individual features was affected by the particular cues available. In Figure 3, percentage IT on individual features is plotted for each of the four single-cue conditions and for normal Tadoma.

For consonants, different profiles of performance on the features voicing, manner, and place were observed for the four different one-cue conditions (see upper half of Figure 3). For the B-alone condition, some information on manner of consonant production was provided with essentially no transmission of voicing or place information. The characteristics of the breath stream felt by the thumb in front of the lips provided information that helped the subjects distinguish plosive from fricative sounds. Generally, a stronger, more concentrated burst of air is associated with plosive production compared to a more diffuse air stream for fricatives. For the L-alone condition, transmission of both place and manner information was relatively high, with basically no information provided on

voicing. With a gloved thumb placed over the lips (to allow perception of lip movements without breath cues), the distinction of front versus mid consonants was easily perceived. Information for distinguishing plosives from fricatives was also available under this condition. For example, the lip closure for the bilabial plosives /p/ and /b/ is distinct from that which occurs for the labiodental fricatives /f/ and /v/. The manner information obtained from the B-alone and L-alone conditions may be somewhat distinct, because the percent IT on manner for the two-cue condition (B,L) was nearly double that obtained on either single-cue condition. For the J-alone condition, some information was transmitted on each of the three features, with the highest percent IT observed for voicing. This same general pattern was observed for the N-alone condition; however, the percent IT on each feature was substantially less for N-alone compared to J-alone. The better perception of voicing on the jaw compared to the neck may be related to the fact that in the N-alone condition, laryngeal vibration is perceived basically independently of other events in the production of the speech stimulus, whereas with the hand placed on the jaw, vibration is perceived in relation to jaw height. The perception of vibration relative to jaw movement proba-

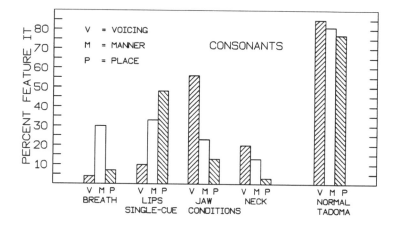

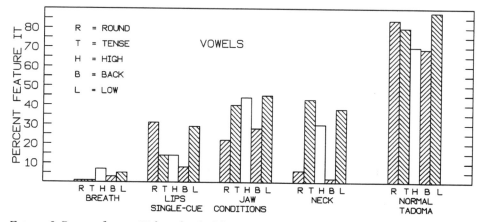

FIGURE 3. Percent feature IT for individual features averaged across subjects for each of the four single-cue conditions (Breath, Lips, Jaw, and Neck) and for normal Tadoma. For consonants, percent feature IT is shown for voicing (V), manner (M), and place (P). For vowels, percent feature IT is shown for round (R), tense (T), high (H), back (B), and low (L).

bly aids in the distinction between voiced and voiceless sounds, given that voicing distinctions rely heavily on relative timing cues. Of the four single-cue conditions, L-alone and J-alone appear to provide useful information on a larger number of features than do B-alone and N-alone.

For vowels, different profiles of performance were observed on the five features round, tense, high, back, and low for each of the four single-cue conditions (shown in the lower half of Figure 3). For the B-alone condition, virtually no information was transmitted on any of the features. For L-alone, performance was highest for the features round and low. The lip-rounding present on three of the vowels in the set (/u, ʊ, aʊ/) is easily felt with the thumb placed over the lips. The presence of the feature low, which relates to a lowering of the body of the tongue in the mouth relative to its neutral position, may be associated with movements of the lower lip. For both the J-alone and N-alone conditions, tense, high, and low were the best perceived features. The features high and low are related to the raising and lowering of the body of the tongue in the mouth and are accomplished in part by movements of the jaw, which are perceptible both with the hand placed on the jaw and on the neck. The feature tense is associated with a tightening of the musculature of the neck, which likewise, can be felt with the hand placed either on the jaw or neck. The major difference between the J-alone and N-alone conditions lies in the perception of the features round and back. Although

moderate amounts of percent IT were observed on these features under the J-alone condition, essentially no information about these features was conveyed through the N-alone condition. It should be pointed out that the highest performance on the feature back, which is associated with sounds in which the body of the tongue is retracted towards the back of the mouth, was observed on the J-alone condition.

For both consonants and vowels, the percent IT on any given feature for the single-cue conditions was always less than that obtained in the normal Tadoma condition. This result suggests that information from different cues is combined in the perception of a given feature through normal Tadoma. Note, however, that the subjects were not provided correct-answer feedback in this study. Although the subjects had extensive previous experience with the normal Tadoma hand position, it is unlikely that they had previous experience with speech reception under the altered conditions. Thus, it is likely that the subjects used the reduced information available in the one-, two-, and three-cue conditions similarly to how they would have used this information as part of the normal Tadoma display (rather than having had the opportunity to relearn to use this information in a more optimal way).

Differential perception of features for different types of cues was assessed further by analyses that are summarized in Figure 4. Performance on each feature is shown averaged across all one-, two-, or three-cue conditions that contain a given cue versus those conditions in which

CONSONANTS

VOWELS

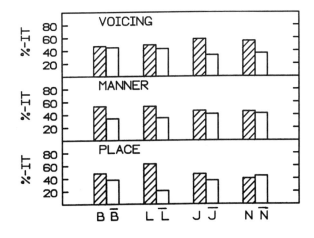

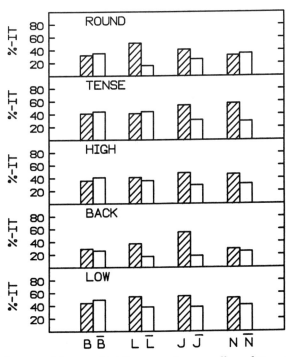

FIGURE 4. Percent feature IT for three consonant features (left) and for five vowel features (right), averaged across all conditions that contained a given cue [Breath (B), Lips (L), Jaw (J), and Neck (N)], compared to the average across all conditions in which that cue was absent (B̄, L̄, J̄, and N̄).

THE TADOMA METHOD

that cue was absent. For example, for Breath (B) the conditions averaged were B, BL, BJ, BN, BLJ, BJN, and BLN, while the remaining conditions were averaged to obtain the B̄ score. The score represented by each bar is based on the average across seven conditions. The results were computed on individual subjects and then averaged to obtain the scores reported in the figure.

Consonant data are shown for the features of voicing, manner, and place (on left). The perception of voicing was the same whether or not breath or lip cues were available; however, voicing performance was superior for those conditions in which jaw or neck cues were present compared to conditions in which these cues were absent. The perception of manner was unaffected by the presence or absence of jaw or neck cues; however, manner performance was superior for those conditions which contain breath or lip cues compared to those which do not. Finally, the transmission of place information was most highly affected by the presence or absence of lip movements and basically unaffected by the presence or absence of the other cues.

Vowel data are shown on the right for the features round, tense, high, back, and low. Perception of the feature round was affected only by the presence or absence of lip and jaw information. Perception of the features tense and high was affected only by the presence or absence of cues from the jaw and neck. The feature back was differentially affected by the presence or absence of jaw and lip cues. Finally, perception of the feature low appears to be affected by three of the four cues: lips, jaw, and neck.

The effects of the removal of one cue from the normal Tadoma display, as occurs in the three-cue conditions, support the notion that redundant information is provided by the cues in normal Tadoma. Generally, removal of one cue did not have a large differential effect on performance across the various consonant or vowel features. For example, when only the breath cue was eliminated in the consonant tests, the percent feature IT was virtually identical (roughly 60%) for voicing, manner, and place. One exception to this general finding was noted: The perception of place in consonants and of lip-rounding in vowels suffered when lip cues were absent.

A final condition was concerned with the effects of whispering on the perception of speech through Tadoma. Whispering affected both overall percent-correct scores (resulting in average scores of 54% for consonants and 56% for vowels) and overall IT (1.7 bits for consonants and 1.6 bits for vowels). Individual feature reception for consonants indicated extremely poor reception of voicing (10% feature IT), modest reception of manner (60% feature IT), and good reception of place (80% feature IT). The poor reception of voicing reflects the fact that laryngeal vibration does not occur in whispered speech; thus, a major distinction between voiced and voiceless consonants is no longer available to the Tadoma reader. The reduction of the manner score is most likely due to alterations in airflow that occur as a result of the laryngeal posture for whispering. Finally, the good reception of the place feature reflects the fact that articulatory movements

remain relatively normal for whispering. For vowels, round and low were the best-perceived features (with %-feature IT ranging from 50%–60%), and tense, high, and back were roughly equally well perceived (with %-feature IT ranging from 30%–40%). The details of the feature scores are less easily explained for the whispered vowels than for consonants; however, the features round and low may be interpreted as reflecting aspects of vowel production that are closely related to the external articulatory movements most easily felt through Tadoma (i.e., liprounding and jaw lowering). In general, the results obtained with whispered speech emphasize the role of laryngeal vibration in the perception of speech through Tadoma.

CONCLUDING REMARKS

Systematic variations in the positioning of the hand on the speaker's face for Tadoma produced systematic effects on percent-correct scores, information transfer, and perception of individual features in a small-set segmental identification task. Furthermore, different patterns of performance on individual speech features were observed as a function of hand position.

The information-bearing capacity of each of the single-cue conditions for the stimulus sets employed here was roughly one bit. This result is in line with that observed for unidimensional tactile stimulation using artificial devices (see Rabinowitz, Houtsma, Durlach, & Delhorne, 1987). Detailed comparisons of the data from the current study with models of information transfer is difficult, however, because of imperfect cue control. Thus, for example, although voicing information can be reduced by moving the hand away from the larynx, it cannot be eliminated completely without moving the hand away from the head entirely. Similarly, although airflow information can be reduced by use of a thumb glove, such an alteration may also reduce sensitivity to lip movement. Despite imperfections in control of the cues available to the subjects and the limited amount of self-information in the stimulus sets, the results lend support to the notion that the various cues available to the Tadoma reader provide differential information concerning speech sounds while at the same time being partially redundant.

The synthetic Tadoma system currently under development and testing in our laboratory (Leotta, Rabinowitz, Durlach, & Reed, 1988; Reed et al., 1985) provides a valuable research tool for conducting better controlled versions of these hand-restriction experiments. The "artificial face" incorporates up-down and in-out movements of the jaw, air flow at the lips, and vibration on the neck. With the synthetic system, cues can be independently and completely eliminated merely by disabling the appropriate channels. Such experiments can provide further testing of our hypotheses about how the various cues are employed in Tadoma and can also offer insight into issues concerning the minimum input information required for speech reception. In addition, various transformations of both the signals used to activate the display and of the device itself can be used to explore issues concerning the success of the Tadoma method.

ACKNOWLEDGMENTS

This work was supported by a grant from the National Institutes of Health (Grant No. 5 R01 NS14092). We wish to thank subjects LD, JC, and RB for their enthusiastic cooperation. We are grateful to W. M. Rabinowitz for his comments on the original manuscript.

REFERENCES

CHOMSKY, C. (1986). Analytic study of the Tadoma method: Language abilities of three deaf-blind subjects. *Journal of Speech and Hearing Research, 29,* 332–347.

HANSEN, R. J. (1964). *Characterization of speech by external articulatory cues as the basis for a speech-to-tactile communication system for use by the deaf-blind.* Unpublished master's thesis, Massachusetts Institute of Technology, Cambridge, MA.

LEOTTA, D., RABINOWITZ, W. M., DURLACH, N. I., & REED, C. M. (1988). Preliminary speech-reception results obtained with the synthetic Tadoma system. *Journal of Rehabilitation Research and Development, 25,* 45–52.

MILLER, G. A., HEISE, G. A., & LICHTEN, W. (1951). The intelligibility of speech as a function of the context of the test materials. *Journal of Experimental Psychology, 41,* 329–335.

MILLER, G. A., & NICELY, P. E. (1955). An analysis of perceptual confusions among some English consonants. *Journal of the Acoustical Society of America, 27,* 338–352.

NORTON, S. J., SCHULTZ, M. C., REED, C. M., BRAIDA, L. D., DURLACH, N. I., RABINOWITZ, W. M., & CHOMSKY, C. (1977). Analytic study of the Tadoma method: Background and pre-liminary results. *Journal of Speech and Hearing Research, 20,* 574–595.

O'CONNOR, J. D. (1973). *Phonetics.* Baltimore, MD: Penguin Books.

RABINOWITZ, W. M., HOUTSMA, A. J. M., DURLACH, N. I., & DELHORNE, L. A. (1987). Multidimensional tactile displays: Identification of vibratory intensity, frequency, and contactor area. *Journal of the Acoustical Society of America, 82,* 1243–1252.

REED, C. M., DOHERTY, M. J., BRAIDA, L. D., & DURLACH, N. I. (1982). Analytic study of the Tadoma method: Further experiments with inexperienced observers. *Journal of Speech and Hearing Research, 25,* 216–223.

REED, C. M., DURLACH, N. I., & BRAIDA, L. D. (1982). Research on tactile communication of speech: A review. *ASHA Monographs, 20.*

REED, C. M., DURLACH, N. I., BRAIDA, L. D., & SCHULTZ, M. C. (1982). Analytic study of the Tadoma method: Identification of consonants and vowels by an experienced Tadoma user. *Journal of Speech and Hearing Research, 25,* 108–116.

REED, C. M., RABINOWITZ, W. M., DURLACH, N. I., BRAIDA, L. D., CONWAY-FITHIAN, S., & SCHULTZ, M. C. (1985). Research on the Tadoma method of speech communication. *Journal of the Acoustical Society of America, 77,* 247–257.

REED, C. M., RUBIN, S. I., BRAIDA, L. D., & DURLACH, N. I. (1978). Analytic study of the Tadoma method: Discrimination ability of untrained observers. *Journal of Speech and Hearing Research, 21,* 625–637.

SHERRICK, C. E. (1984). Basic and applied research on tactile aids for deaf people: Progress and prospects. *Journal of the Acoustical Society of America, 75,* 1325–1342.

APPENDIX A

PERCENT CORRECT SCORES AND INFORMATION TRANSFER IN BITS FOR CONSONANTS
FOR EACH SUBJECT UNDER EACH CONDITION.

Subject	Percent Correct Score			Information Transfer (Bits)		
	LD	RB	JC	LD	RB	JC
Single-cue conditions						
Breath (B)	30	18	35	1.03	1.25	0.79
Lips (L)	44	38	58	1.42	1.16	1.63
Jaw (J)	36	44	66	1.04	1.13	1.66
Neck (N)	37	41	28	1.09	1.42	0.76
Two-cue conditions						
B,L	50	63	62	1.35	1.93	1.79
B,J	50	81	86	1.42	2.20	2.24
B,N	54	27	41	1.40	1.45	1.30
L,J	80	55	57	2.16	1.34	1.74
L,N	86	60	70	2.57	1.59	1.85
J,N	39	64	59	1.36	1.53	1.62
Three-cue conditions						
B,L,J	76	91	71	2.17	2.67	2.14
B,J,N	69	59	89	2.00	1.43	2.57
L,J,N	88	86	67	2.44	2.06	1.92
B,L,N	92	92	88	2.66	2.37	2.50
Full-hand conditions						
Normal Tadoma	94	93	88	2.63	2.61	2.46
Whispered Tadoma	37	58	66	1.40	1.79	2.00

APPENDIX B

PERCENT CORRECT SCORES AND INFORMATION TRANSFER IN BITS FOR VOWELS
FOR EACH SUBJECT UNDER EACH CONDITION.

Subject	Percent Correct Score			Information Transfer (Bits)		
	LD	RB	JC	LD	RB	JC
Single-cue conditions						
Breath (B)	27	20	11	0.52	0.77	0.71
Lips (L)	25	53	53	0.51	1.31	1.47
Jaw (J)	54	52	65	1.44	1.67	1.57
Neck (N)	38	41	54	1.05	1.31	1.75
Two-cue conditions						
B,L	46	40	61	1.19	0.99	1.56
B,J	49	43	77	1.23	1.63	2.11
B,N	39	47	55	1.03	1.49	1.51
L,J	63	63	54	1.59	1.75	1.53
L,N	62	79	65	1.54	2.26	1.73
J,N	52	50	73	1.50	1.57	1.95
Three-cue conditions						
B,L,J	77	77	79	2.10	2.19	2.16
B,J,N	71	50	86	1.98	1.45	2.33
L,J,N	90	76	82	2.57	2.06	2.26
B,L,N	71	70	66	1.93	2.30	1.93
Full-hand conditions						
Normal Tadoma	92	85	88	2.70	2.39	2.45
Whispered Tadoma	47	46	74	1.32	1.23	2.26

Interpreting for Deaf-Blind Students: Factors to Consider

Karen Petronio

Ten deaf-blind college students were interviewed to find out what they need and want from sign language interpreters. This information was combined with findings from observations of many deaf-blind interpreting situations. The focus of this article includes the following four areas: 1) types of signing; 2) modifications to the signing; 3) visual information that needs to be conveyed; and 4) other factors that will influence deaf-blind interpreting situations.

L̶ack of information and training opportunites relating to sign language interpretation for deaf-blind persons causes many problems for both the deaf-blind person and the interpreter. Most interpreters have to learn their skills through trial and error while on the job. This usually results in misunderstandings for the deaf-blind person and frustration for the interpreters. If interpreters and deaf-blind people were aware, beforehand, of what factors needed to be considered, problems could be alleviated and better services could be provided.

To find out what deaf-blind people want and need from interpreters, the author interviewed 10 deaf-blind college students. This data was combined with additional information obtained from observations of a variety of deaf-blind interpreting situations. Both the interviews and observations focused on considerations for signing preferences; determining the needs for signing modifications necessary to accommodate persons having different visual impairments; the responsibility for conveying environmental information in addition to spoken and/or signed information; and other influential factors.

The 10 interviewed students ranged from freshmen, some using interpreters for the first time, to upperclassmen and graduate students, who have used interpreters at least three years. Although all were classified legally blind, they all dif-

Karen Petronio has an M.A. in linguistics. She is a certified member of the Registry of the Interpreters of the Deaf and currently a free-lance interpreter in Seattle, Washington.

fered in what they could or could not see. Their degrees of hearing loss also varied; some had moderate losses while others were profoundly deaf.

Findings

In general, the findings show that deaf-blind students expected their interpreters to follow the basic philosophy, principles and code of ethics of the Registry of Interpreters for the Deaf (RID). Although the students expected the ethics of interpreting for deaf consumers and deaf-blind consumers to be the same, the interviews and observations made it obvious that additional strategies and techniques often have to be used when interpreting for deaf-blind people because of their visual impairment.

The information points to four areas that interpreters need to consider: (1) signing preferences; (2) signing modifications; (3) visual information; and (4) related factors. These four major areas will be the focus of this article.

Signing Preference

Of the four areas being discussed, signing preference is most familiar to interpreters for the deaf. The third section of the RID code of ethics states: " . . . the message should be conveyed in the language most readily understood by the client." When interpreting for deaf consumers, interpreters are accustomed to using the type of signing the deaf person prefers, i.e. ASL or signing using a more English-like syntax. When interpreting for deaf-blind clients the interpreter also may shadow (or copy) a presenter who is signing.

The deaf-blind students interviewed for the current article were accustomed to one or several of the following kinds of interpreting situations:

1. Interpreting from a spoken message—a hearing interpreter listens and signs using ASL;
2. Interpreting from a signed message—a deaf or hearing interpreter watches ASL and changes it to more English-like signing or vice-versa;
3. Transliterating from a spoken message—a hearing interpreter listens and signs using an English-like work order or manual system;
4. Shadowing—a deaf or hearing interpreter watches someone signing and copies the signing.

Sign Modification

When using ASL the signer confines his or her signs to the front of the body, usually extending from the top of the head to the waist, with the side parameters being the area the arms can reach with the elbow bent. Sometimes modification of this space, as well as modifications of some signs, occurs when interpreting for deaf-blind people. Even the small sample of students in this study needed a wide range of sign and space modifications.

Deaf-blind persons who had tunnel vision often needed interpreting within a smaller signing space. Instead of the customary two-feet square, they might need signs constructed within, say, a 10-inch square. Distance, moreover, can affect how much a person with tunnel vision can see. One student in the study was able to see signs in the normal signing space when the interpreter stood 15 or more feet away. If the interpreter stood closer, she needed signs restricted within a smaller space. (The setting and lighting determined where she wanted the interpreter to be positioned).

Another student had tunnel vision in addition to being very near-sighted. He needed the interpreter to sit two or three feet away and sign in a restricted space, approximately a nine-inch inch square near the interpreter's mouth. He depended heavily on lipreading; therefore, it was important that he could clearly see the interpreter's face. If signing was restricted to a small area, he was able to see both the interpreter's signs and face. When an interpreter is signing in a restricted space, attention must be paid to signs that normally occur outside this area. Signs such as *RUSSIA*, which normally occur at the waist, have to be modified or fingerspelled so the deaf-blind consumer won't miss them. Any indexing, pointing or setting-up must also occur within the restricted space, again, so the deaf-blind person can see it.

Students with very restricted tunnel vision often hold the interpreters wrist so they know where to look. One student, who uses this method arranges the desk tops or chair backs so she can rest her elbow on them and prevent her arms from tiring. Occasionally, especially when the lighting is poor, she uses tactual interpreting, i.e., she puts her hand or hands on top of the interpreter's and understands signs primarily through touch instead of vision.

Several of the students had visual impairments that require the interpreter to consider several factors. For example, two students had difficulty seeing at a distance as well as seeing any small movements. This made it difficult for them to distinguish the various handshapes in fingerspelling. They needed very slow, clear fingerspelling and preferred signs whenever possible. One of these students gave up on

several interpreters, who either could not or would not slow their fingerspelling. Both students wanted the interpreter to sit about three feet away and sign in the normal signing space. Many interpreters erroneously thought they had to sign in a restricted space for these two students; however, this made it difficult for them to understand because the signs were too small and close together.

Three students reported difficulty seeing at a distance, but easily understood when the interpreter sat close. They wanted the interpreter to sit three to five feet away, sign in the normal space, and use clear fingerspelling at a normal speed.

Many deaf-blind people who use sign language but are unable to see the signs clearly use tactual interpreting. These people usually are unable to clearly see the interpreter's face and receive most (usually all), information manually by placing a hand on top of the interpreter's. Problems can arise because in ASL, negation, adverbs, grammatical structures and many other features of the language are expressed with specific facial expressions (Baker, Cokely, and Liddell, 1980;). Interpreters must ensure they convey such information manually. One student reported confusion over negated verbs, such as *DON'T UNDERSTAND*, whenever the interpreter used the appropriate head movement and facial expression, but omitted the sign *NOT*. The student thought *UNDERSTAND* was signed, instead of *DON'T UNDERSTAND*.

When deaf-blind people use one-hand tactual sign language, the interpreter must be conscious of what signs might be misunderstood and make accommodations. Some signs require information from both hands, i.e., *FRESHMAN, CANDLE*. If the deaf-blind person is only aware of what is occurring with one hand, he misses the sign. Misunderstandings can be avoided by modifying the sign, fingerspelling, or by substituting other conceptually correct signs.

Visual Information

Interpreters often have to convey visual environmental information in addition to the spoken/signed message when interpreting for deaf-blind people. Often, visual information has to be conveyed for the interpreted message to make sense. Deaf-blind consumers are usually unaware of what is occurring in the visual environment, either because they can't see it, or because their usable vision is focused on the interpreter. In her guidelines for interpreters, Theresa Smith stated: "You must report the visual environment as well as the auditory environment. This does not mean you must tell him everything you see (e.g. height of the ceiling, color of the walls) any more than you tell a deaf person everything you hear. But it does mean that you do tell him everything of significance (e.g. someone entering the room, expression and mood of the speaker, size of the group, whose hand is raised) . . . '' (Smith, 1977). The necessary visual environmental information often can make the difference between the deaf-blind person fully understanding the message or only getting a vague ideal of what occurred.

Several students reported difficulty following class discussions when the interpreter did not indicate who was speaking. On several occasions students reported understanding the signs but not being able to make sense of the total message. Later they discovered the reason: more than one person had been speaking. Therefore, it is important that the interpreter indicate when a speaker changes and, if possible, who the person is.

Another student was often frustrated during class discussions; she would want to respond to someone's comment, but didn't know who made it, or which direction to face when responding. In a small class, the interpreter can learn the students' names, then identify them by name and point in their direction before interpreting what they said, e.g., T–O–M, (point). In larger classes the interpreter can point in the person's direction and give a short description, e.g., (point), *GIRL, END SEAT*. This way, the deaf-blind person has an idea who commented and will know if that person comments again. One student, who has usable vision, wanted her interpreter to identify the speaker, by name if possible, then with a short description of their clothes, e.g., *MARY*, (point), *GREEN SHIRT*; this enabled her to look over and find the person.

Many students reported frustration and embarrassment when a teacher or classmate asked a question and waited for a response while the deaf-blind person remained unaware the question was directed to him or her. This problem arose in many of the observed situations; the deaf-blind person did not know someone was expecting a response because he or she was unable to see the speaker's facial expressions and the interpreter had not conveyed this information. In addition to facial expression providing grammatical information in ASL (such as if the sentence is a question or statement), expressions also provide conversation-regulating information (Baker, 1978). In particular, eye contact signals that a speaker has finished and awaits response. Because the deaf-blind person cannot see the speaker's face, it is extremely important that the interpreter convey this information. For clarity, the interpreter can add manual signs, i.e. question marks directed from the speaker to the student. One student wanted the interpreter to use her name sign, followed by a directional *QUESTION* every time someone directed a question to her. She then knew the question was specifically for her.

Most students wanted everything the teacher and other students said to be interpreted. Two students with usable vision were able to see students sitting on either side of them and the teacher, when the teacher was near. In those cases (if time-lag permitted) the interpreter could point to the signer, the student would watch the signer, then shift back to watching the interpreter.

One consumer said that his vision varied; thus, his interpreting would vary. Some days he might be able to see the teacher's signs and other days he would watch the interpreter. While watching the teacher, he wanted the interpreter ready to repeat any fingerspelled words he might miss, or take over when the teacher moved too far from him to see. The interpreter would continue to interpret any comments from other students. Another student, who had tunnel vision, was usually able to see the teacher but needed all classroom discussion interpreted because he had difficulty following turntaking.

Because the deaf-blind students were unable to read what was written on the board or overheads, interpreters had to transmit this information. A few students with usable vision asked the teacher to provide a large print or dark print copy of overheads; when the teacher pointed on the overhead, the interpreter pointed on the student's copy. If a teacher wrote a complicated diagram or wrote a complex math formula, some students wanted their interpreters to copy it on paper. Although copying was helpful for the student, particularly when the teacher repeatedly referred to the material, the interpreter usually could not both copy material and interpret without missing information. It was beneficial when the teacher understood the situation and had materials prepared beforehand.

When teachers pointed to something in the room or on the board, the interpreter had to identify or describe the point of reference. If the teacher said, "this is bigger than that" the interpreter had to identify the objects or the statement would make little sense to the deaf-blind person.

Other Factors

The interpreter's general interpreting skill is crucial, but cannot alone guarantee a successful experience with a deaf-blind client. Other factors can prevent the deaf-blind person from fully understanding the message.

Because interpreting for deaf-blind people is still a new field, many referral services and interpreters do not request or receive adequate information prior to service delivery. Deaf-blind consumers reported that occasionally their interpreters were unable to understand the presenters. At times a deaf interpreter, skilled at shadowing or interpreting from a signed message, would be assigned to interpret for an unskilled signer or a presenter who used only voice. Some hearing interpreters arrived were likewise unable to interpret the signed messages of deaf presenters. This problem could be alleviated if the interpreters knew the presenter's mode and type of communication before accepting a job.

In the present study, bad seating choices often left interpreters unable to see and/or hear everything they needed. Unless the interpreters carefully positioned themselves so they could see and/or hear everything necessary (including the presenter, participants and any visual displays), they missed information.

A positive correlation appeared between the deaf-blind students' experience with and knowledge of using interpreters and their satisfaction. Those who were satisfied and said they felt they were getting the same information as their classmates were the same students who had used interpreters for three or more years. Many students new to using interpreters, said they felt frustrated; some didn't understand enough sign language, some didn't know what to tell interpreters and some didn't know what to expect from interpreters. Effective interpreting is unlikely when the interpreter does not correctly assess the consumers' needs, expecially they type of signing they want (e.g. ASL, English-like), what they need interpreted and whether they need the signing modified.

Summary and Implications

It is apparent that deaf-blind consumers have specific needs that interpreters must consider for successful interpreting to occur. It is also apparent that these needs vary from one individual to another and sometimes from day to day with a single person. Thus interpreters must be flexible and aware of many different factors, specifically: (1) what kind of signing they should use; (2) what modifications they must make to their signing; (3) what visual information they should convey; and (4) what other factors will influence their interpreting. Although these four areas have been artificially separated in this paper, in real life they all occur together, making the interpreter's job complex.

This study points to some suggestions to help provide better interpreting services:

For Interpreters. Interpreters, both deaf and hearing, need training. Training should include theory and strategies and techniques for interpreting for deaf-blind consumers. Interpreters also need training to develop skills in: a) shadowing and interpreting from ASL to another form of signing and vice versa; b) interpreting using different modifications and methods, such as tactual communication or signing in a restricted space; and c) conveying important visual information.

For Deaf-Blind Consumers. Deaf-blind people need training on how to use interpreters, what information they should give the interpreter and what they can expect the interpreter to do or not do. Students with the most experience were the most satisfied. It would be beneficial if deaf-blind people new to using interpreters were aware of techniques and strategies successfully used by other deaf-blind people.

For Teachers and Others. If teachers and others who worked with deaf-blind people were aware of the role, duties and limitations of the interpreter, and of the communication needs of the deaf-blind person, better services would result.

While this study involved only a small number of deaf-blind students in a very specific setting, it is a beginning for understanding what is involved with deaf-blind interpreting. Clearly, more research is needed. For example, what linguistic adaptations are made when a visual language uses a tactual mode? What is involved in deaf-blind interpreting outside of academic settings? As interpreters and deaf-blind consumers become more aware of what is involved, and what strategies and techniques can address them, the quality of interpreting services provided to deaf-blind people will be improved.

Bibliography

Baker, C. (1978). Regulators and turn-taking in American Sign Language discourse. In L. Friedman (Ed.), *On the other hand: New perspectives on American Sign Language.* New York: Academic Press, 215–236.

Baker, C., & Cokely D. (1980). *American Sign Language: A teacher's resource test on grammar and culture.* Silver Spring, MD: T. J. Publishers.

Liddell, S. (1980). *American Sign Language syntax.* Great Britain: Mouton Publishers.

Smith, T. (1977). *Guidelines for working/playing with deaf-blind people.* Unpublished paper. Seattle, Washington: Seattle Community College.

Providing O&M Services to Children and Youth With Severe Multiple Disabilities

BRENT R. BAILEY and DANIEL N. HEAD

Students with severe multiple disabilities often have difficulties in a number of developmental areas, including motor skills, communication and language abilities, vision, hearing, and behavioral and intellectual functioning. They require services from a team of specialists, each of whom is responsible for a different area of need. An orientation and mobility (O&M) instructor may be part of such a team if the student has a visual impairment or is handicapped in travel situations and is able to benefit from O&M training.

O&M instructors are certified "specialists" trained to deal with the challenges of travel for students without effective visual input (Gee, Harrell, & Rosenberg, 1987; Wiener & Welsh, 1980). Traditionally, O&M instruction is part of a medical model of service delivery, a model that typically uses individual disciplines (speech and language, physical therapy, occupational therapy, psychology, sensory impairments) to address each specific area of need (Pugach, 1988). This medical model tends to divide the child with multiple disabilities into separate problem areas (Campbell, 1987; Rainforth & York, 1987).

In both the educational and rehabilitation setting, the medical approach often defines how team members carry out their responsibilities. Each specialist assesses the student and then provides isolated instruction in his or her area of expertise based on two broad assumptions: (a) that certain skills must be mastered before other skills are introduced and (b) that any skill learned can be transferred to other contexts.

However, students with severe multiple disabilities do not always master skills in the usual developmental sequence. They also have difficulty generalizing skills learned in one setting to different settings where the new skill must be integrated with other behaviors (Rainforth & York, 1987; York, Long, Caldwell, Brown, Fanella-Albright, Rogan, Shiraga, & Marks, 1985). These students frequently cannot progress sequentially through a complete learning hierarchy. Therefore, the education program designed to teach only the unlearned skills fails to capitalize on the strengths the students have acquired (York et al., 1985). The result is that the basic skill areas such as communication, decision making, gross and fine motor, and vision never actually become incorporated into real-life activities. Current initiatives in special education are stressing instructional models that occur in natural settings. Model programs for students with multiple disabilities include age-appropriate activities and materials, functional and meaningful skills, adaptive techniques and devices, varying levels of support and assistance to provide opportunities for partial participation, and social contact with nondisabled peers (Falvey, 1989; Horner, Meyer, & Fredricks, 1986; Snell, 1987; Stainback & Stainback, 1985). Although more and more school districts are serving students with multiple disabilities in integrated settings, this model is not easy to implement (Arick, Brazeau, & Falco, 1989). In part, this is caused by difficulty in training staff and in securing effective, coordinated efforts from all education personnel (Brown, Long, Advari-Solner, Schwarz, VanDeventer, Ahlgren, Johnson, Gruenewald, & Jorgensen, 1989).

In this article we will explain why O&M training for children and youth with severe multiple disabilities should be part of functional and meaningful activities. We will also outline a new role for the O&M instructor who works with these students, using specific examples of teaching travel skills in the context of an activity.

Current Role of O&M Instructors

O&M instruction teaches safe, successful, and efficient travel strategies that compensate for a lack of vision (Hill & Ponder, 1976). An O&M instructor usually provides training on a one-to-one basis and builds on previously acquired skills (Harley & Merbler, 1980; Hart, 1980; Primrose, 1981). He or she introduces specific travel procedures, gauges the student's progress in acquiring various strategies and techniques, and designs lessons that support generalization across travel environments.

In general, O&M services are difficult to obtain. Appropriately trained instructors remain scarce (Head, 1989; Stewart & Zimmerman, 1990). Therefore, those instructors working with young people with visual impairments and severe multiple disabilities need to develop workable models that will allow them to provide O&M services despite shortages of personnel.

Transdisciplinary Teaming

In other disciplines the need to coordinate hard-to-secure services has resulted in the recommendation that specialists use a cooperative approach (Campbell, 1987;

Cipani, 1989; Hutchinson, 1978; MacDonald & York, 1989; Rainforth & York, 1987; Szymanski, Hanley-Maxwell, & Parker, 1990; Woodruff, 1980). Transdisciplinary teams are particularly appropriate for a student with severe multiple disabilities, principally because they promote location-based intervention to support the integrated curriculum used with this population (Baumgart & VanWallegham, 1986; Erhardt, 1987) and stress communication across disciplines that focuses all instructional goals into real-life settings for the child or youth (Bailey & Murray-Branch, 1993; Orelove & Sobsey, 1987). This approach encourages finding ways to teach necessary skills when and where students need to use them. Specific skills are presented together as the child performs an activity (i.e., a functional skill cluster). Collaborative teaming includes (a) consultation with teachers, instructional assistants, parents (direct services providers); (b) conducting interventions in the presence of other professional staff; (c) team determination of necessary skills; (d) integrated therapy and instruction by specialists in communication and motor and sensory impairments; and (5) assessment of the student's needs in relation to functional performance (i.e., task and discrepancy analysis) rather than in relation to deficits in specific disciplines.

Central to the transdisciplinary model of service delivery is the concept of "role release" (Lyon & Lyon, 1980; York et al., 1985). Each team member exchanges information and responsibilities about his or her primary role area. This sharing allows other members to perform specific functions associated with another member's traditional role.

Role release should not result in an indirect service approach. Rather, the opposite is true. Discipline-specific team members including O&M instructors need to maintain direct "hands-on" contact with these students during actual learning activities.

Students With Severe Multiple Disabilities Including a Visual Impairment

Professionals trained to work with children with visual impairments often feel inadequately prepared to teach students whose learning style is affected by more than a vision loss (Erin, Daugherty, Dignan, & Pearson, 1990). Traditional vision programs tend to center around enhancing the student's visual functioning, activating the student's existing visual capabilities, or stimulating alternative sensory areas (Downing & Bailey, 1990). This "therapy" approach is not appropriate to meet the broad needs of students with additional severe multiple disabilities (Downing & Bailey, 1990). These students learn best in integrated classroom and community environments where they can practice skills as a meaningful and functional part of a whole activity (Brown et al., 1989; Brown, Nisbet, Ford, Sweet, Shiraga, York, & Loomis, 1983).

In programs for individuals with severe multiple disabilities, O&M intervention would be furnished in ways more similar to the goal of support services such as occupational therapy, physical therapy, or speech-language pathology. The focus would be on helping the student to benefit from the special education programming provided in his or her primary placement. Although O&M training usually takes place in a functional setting, the lessons often rely on a pull-out service model and are not part of a meaningful activity. Thus, students with severe multiple disabilities, including a visual impairment, continue to have difficulty recognizing when and where O&M skills are necessary in natural contexts.

These students need to practice skills within typical activities, and O&M services need to help them acquire travel skills at the time and in the places where they are required. Students could then benefit from instruction that improves both their participation in activities and their learning of skills. O&M training should seek to increase their level of involvement within the existing learning environments.

The overall problem has been what to do with those who cannot generalize or synthesize skills to new settings and activity sequences (Brown, Zanella-Albright, Rogar, York, Udvari-Solner, Johnson, VanDeventer, & Loomis, 1988). These young people have difficulty attaining skills not practiced within the context of real experiences.

Other disciplines are addressing these problems with teaching strategies that specify regular practice in the actual settings where skills and behaviors will be used (Brown et al., 1983; Brown et al., 1988; Horner & McDonnell, 1982; McDonnell, Horner, & Williams, 1984). The distinction between traditional teaching and the newer approach is the difference between learning through participation in actual activities in real settings and being taught a system of adaptive techniques to be applied across any new situation. In the past, these students have been considered incapable of benefiting from O&M services because they have been unable to build from prerequisites to more advanced techniques. By contrast, a curriculum based on a particular student's life needs will motivate and reinforce the learning of whatever specific travel skills are called for in existing and typical activities.

The Role of O&M in Support of Children and Youth Who Are Visually Impaired With Severe Multiple Disabilities

Only by reviewing each student's real-life environments can the O&M instructor provide effective program support for a student. Rather than address skill development apart from where skills will be used, O&M instructors need to help students develop their travel capabilities during times that create real demands on their ability to participate. A switch to learning actual travel routes within activities is, therefore, critical.

Students with severe multiple disabilities need to concentrate on improving their ability to function in a meaningful way (Brown et al., 1983). For many students, a new skill will be a valid objective only if it will be functionally useful. In addition, learning new skills should increase or maintain opportunities for these students to have experiences with people without disabilities (Brown et al., 1989).

The O&M instructor must evaluate the student to find out what specific compensatory skills he or she needs to participate in actual activities at school and in the community. In their collaborative goal setting, the team, including the O&M instructor, should focus on the demands of specific travel situations. Practicing techniques must facilitate the student's skill development and also reinforce the usefulness of the skill in a purposeful, real-life context.

Learning to trail along a wall that is never traveled is of no real value. Instructing a student to trail along the route to the bathroom when it is necessary to do so is functional and meaningful. Teaching a student to trail without a purposeful or necessary objective provides the instructor with no basis from which to infer if the student can trail successfully when the skill is required in a real context. The only way to determine whether a student with severe multiple disabilities has a skill is to test performance against the demands of an actual situation. Thus, the task analysis of travel steps within activities becomes mandatory.

An example of an activity divided into necessary and meaningful skill areas might include being taught to trail along a wall in the kitchen to find the refrigerator. At the refrigerator, the student might learn to search for the handle, open the door, locate a soft drink can, and close the door. Next, the student might square-off against the refrigerator door in order to cross an open space to a table. At the table, the student would locate a chair, sit down, open the can, pour the drink into a glass, and finish the beverage. Upon finishing the drink, the student would stand and trail to the trash container and dispose of the empty can. The skills needed for the activity would not be taught in isolation but within this identified skill cluster (Helmstetter & Guess, 1987). The required O&M skills in this sequence are trailing (to the refrigerator and the trash container) and squaring-off (to cross the open space). The other skills needed to accomplish the sequence occur, as they should, between the travel components. The activity is completed in the right order, and the student practices the skills as they are needed. Parts of the activity, or the whole activity, might be considered a skill cluster (i.e., the critical actions necessary to complete a functional task or to increase participation in a meaningful activity).

Parents, educational staff, and student preferences help decide what skill clusters are appropriate for a particular individual. Decisions about teaching an O&M technique should be made by the same process as is used to determine whether to teach any critical skill: by the actual travel demands the student encounters in typical school and community activities. An analysis of the student's performance at each step of the real-life activity or task will determine the instructional content. Techniques or skills the student is unable to complete are targeted for intervention if they would allow the student to participate more fully in the activities.

Decisions to teach specific movement skills, modify the teaching sequence, or eliminate certain travel steps require identifying areas in which the student is discrepant. First, the activity is broken into the component steps that usually are performed by people without disabilities. The young person with severe multiple disabilities is then evaluated at each step of the analyzed task; those parts of a task that he or she cannot accomplish are labeled discrepant. All O&M instructors are trained to identify which discrepant steps will require O&M training and to evaluate the degree to which other skills are present in the student's repertoire. However, completing a task-and-discrepancy analysis of O&M skills or movements within a real activity is not typically part of an instructor's training.

Task-and-Discrepancy Analysis Defined

Programs serving students with severe multiple disabilities commonly use a functional task and discrepancy analysis (Brown, Shiraga, York, Zanella, & Rogan, 1984; Hanley-Maxwell, 1986). Evaluation determines which new skills must be taught and how to arrange optimal support in the functional location where the behavior must occur. Based on a top-down orientation to assessment, the team organizes a student's program around the skills that nondisabled peers must master. Once the appropriate integrated environment has been selected, a list of needed travel skills and activities is completed. Each skill or activity is broken into steps, and the discrepancies between the student's current performance abilities and the demands of the activity are identified. The O&M instructor then develops the appropriate interventions, including procedures to teach the discrepant or missing skills. Specific integrated environments are always selected, based on the student's current placement and where he or she is ultimately expected to function. Once actual settings and activities are determined, the student's progress toward skill acquisition is assessed regularly. Overcoming the discrepancies that exist between the demands of an activity and the student's ability to perform the steps becomes the focus and responsibility of the whole educational team.

An appropriate application of this procedure would be similar to a model used in indirect therapy and advocated by Sternat, Messina, Nietupski, Lyon, and Brown (1977). Assessment is conducted in natural environments; travel demands are reviewed within functional activities; strategies applied to improve travel efficiency are targeted throughout the day and across all settings; and the decision to teach or adapt a travel step is determined by the demands encountered within the context of the natural setting, for example a community vocational site.

A student might use a lower hand-and-forearm technique to move from a desk in the middle of a work room to a nearby wall. Once in contact with the wall, the student would trail the wall surface with one hand and might position the other arm and hand in front of the upper body if protection is necessary. A long cane kept next to the door might be used to travel to a break room on another floor. The student would use a diagonal cane technique while walking down the hallway and switch the cane's placement at the end of the hall to descend a set of stairs. The student's performance of all the O&M skills needed to complete the route are evaluated to determine which ones he or she can do at a functionally appropriate level, which ones need modification, and which ones must be adapted (e.g., the student learns to take a different route using an elevator because detection of the stairs with a cane is unsuccessful, unsafe, *and* unteachable).

In the past, an O&M instructor might have taught this range of skills separately, and the student would have practiced them without an actual travel objective (i.e., out of context). Techniques of self-protection (upper hand-and-forearm placement) and trailing might be taught first; the diagonal cane technique and touch technique might be introduced later. The use of a particular destination preferred by a student reinforces learning the skills to traverse that travel route. Systematically reducing the support required to assist a student through a route (prompting and fading techniques) are typical of all programs for students with severe disabilities. Successful programs will increase students' opportunities to participate in activities as well as teach skills. Instructors teach knowing that a student may always need some level of support to participate and that not all skills taught will be learned. For example, learning a route between home and a neighborhood grocery store frequently used by his family is important to one student. His special education teacher arranges to use the student's home as a teaching site. Once a week, the student is instructed at home in daily hygiene, housekeeping, and food preparation. Making a snack is the final activity and is preceded by a trip to the grocery store. The route, in a residential area with light traffic, involves walking two blocks and making one turn and one street crossing. Applying a task-and-discrepancy analysis to the route and to the student's ability to make the trip, the O&M instructor identifies two important areas of discrepant functioning: the student does not consistently turn in the correct direction, and he does not cross the street safely. To determine what modifications will be necessary, the O&M instructor breaks these two discrepant areas down further and identifies prompts and strategies to help the student succeed. The student practices these each time he makes a trip to the store. Whether he will ever complete the route independently is not known. However, the route is an important objective for a number of reasons:

1. His parents have identified it as a goal.
2. The student is naturally motivated to go because the family shops at this store.
3. The student can learn this route without being required to generalize any of the skills from another context.
4. Regardless of whether the student becomes independent, practicing the route will not interrupt other programming.
5. Practicing the travel skills will occur in the correct sequence of the whole activity (first the domestic task of making a shopping list occurs at home, followed by the actual shopping for items at the grocery store).
6. The student can practice the route at other times when he goes to the store with his family.
7. The student can practice other critical O&M skills once in the grocery store (e.g., orientation in the store aisles).

8. The impact of on-site instruction by the O&M teacher wil be maximized because other persons present at the same time (e.g., family members, teachers) can observe procedures and be trained to implement them.

9. Should the student not be successful in learning the whole route, there is still a greater likelihood that his overall functioning during the whole learning experience will improve. He will have remained within an integrated community setting where there are increasing opportunities to practice other meaningful skills and to interact with people without disabilities. Partial participation in such environments remains a more valued and beneficial goal than independent completion of tasks in non-functional, isolated, or out-of-context situations.

The intervention procedures outlined above require on-going evaluation within the context of typical and natural settings. This approach targets the immediate and actual travel needs of the student during functional activities and tasks. All travel-related steps a student is unable to complete remain viable for teaching the appropriate O&M technique as a possible adaptive option. Enhanced participation in activities is the overall goal of instruction.

Conclusion

In this article we have offered an alternative approach to O&M services for children and youth with severe cognitive, motor, and sensory impairments. Instruction emphasizes interventions that occur within natural settings, routines, and activities. Out-of-context instruction that teaches skills by following a particular progression of graduated lessons has not dealt effectively with the learning needs of these young people.

O&M instruction will have a greater impact for these students if all support personnel and care givers, including qualified O&M teachers, implement activity-based interventions. A student with severe multiple disabilities learns best when viewed as a *whole person* whose learning needs are interrelated with his or her typical daily life.

REFERENCES

Arick, J., Brazeau, K., & Falco, R. (1989). Prioritizing inservice needs for educators of students with severe handicaps in heterogeneous integrated settings. *Education and Training in Mental Retardation, 24*(4), 371–380.

Bailey, B. R., and Murray-Branch, J. (1993). Collaborative communication programming: Providing a meaning-based curriculum to students with severe multiple disabilities. *Journal of Educational and Psychological Consultation, 4*(1), 29–47.

Baumgart, D., & VanWallegham, J. (1986). Staffing strategies for implementing community-based instruction. *Journal of the Association for People with Severe Handicaps, 11*(2), 92–102.

Brown, L., Long, E., Udvari-Solner, A., Schwarz, P., VanDeventer, P., Ahlgren, C., Johnson, F., Gruenewald, L., & Jorgensen, J. (1989). Should students with severe intellectual disabilities be based in regular or special education classrooms in home schools? *Jour-*

nal of the Association for Persons with Severe Handicaps, 14(1), 8-12.

Brown, L., Nisbet, J., Ford, A., Sweet, M., Shiraga, B., York, J., & Loomis, R. (1983). The critical need for nonschool instruction in education programs for severely handicapped students. *Journal of the Association for Persons with Severe Handicaps, 8*(3): 71-77.

Brown, L., Shiraga, B., York, J., Zanella, K., & Rogan, P. (1984). Ecological inventory strategies for students with severe intellectual disabilities. *Educational programs for students with severe intellectual disabilities.* University of Wisconsin at Madison and Madison Metropolitan School District, Vol. 14, 45-47.

Brown, L., Zanella-Albright, K., Rogan, P., York, J., Udvari-Solner, A., Johnson, F., VanDeventer, P., & Loomis, R. (1988). An integrated curriculum model for transition. In B. Ludlow, A. Turnbull, & R. Luckasson (Eds.), *Transitions to adult life for people with mental retardation—Principles and practices* (pp. 67-81). Baltimore: Paul H. Brookes.

Campbell, P. H. (1987). The integrated programming team: An approach for coordinating professionals of various disciplines in programs for students with severe and multiple handicaps. *Journal of the Association for Persons with Severe Handicaps, 12*(2), 107-116.

Cipani, E. (1989). Providing language consultation in the natural context: A model for delivery of services. *American Association on Mental Retardation, 27*(3), 317-324.

Downing, J., & Bailey, B. (1990). Developing vision use within functional daily activities for students with visual and multiple disabilities. *RE:view, 24*(4), 209-220.

Erhardt, R. (1987). Visual function in the student with multiple handicaps: An integrative transdisciplinary model for assessment and intervention. *Education of the Visually Handicapped, 19*(3), 87-98.

Erin, J., Daugherty, W., Dignan, K., & Pearson, N. (1990). Teaching visually handicapped students with multiple disabilities: Perceptions of adequacy. *Journal of Visual Impairment & Blindness, 84*(1), 16-20.

Falvey, M. A. (Ed.). (1989). *Community-based curriculum: Instructional strategies for students with severe handicaps.* Baltimore: Paul H. Brookes.

Gee, K., Harrell, K., & Rosenberg, R. (1987). Teaching orientation and mobility skills within and across natural opportunities for travel. In L. Goetz, D. Guess, & K. Stremel-Campbell (Eds.), *Innovative program design for individuals with dual sensory impairments* (pp. 127-157). Baltimore: Paul H. Brookes.

Hanley, Maxwell, C. (1986). Curriculum development. In F. R. Rusch (Ed.), *Competitive employment: Issues and strategies* (pp. 187-198). Baltimore: Paul H. Brookes.

Harley, R. K., & Merbler, K. B. (1980). Development of an orientation and mobility program for the blind multiply impaired low vision children. *Journal of Visual Impairment & Blindness, 74*(1), 9-14.

Hart, V. (1980). Environmental orientation and human mobility. In R. Welsh & B. Blasch (Eds.), *Foundations of orientation and mobility* (pp. 9-36). New York; American Foundation for the Blind.

Head, D. N. (1989). The future of low incidence training programs: A national problem. *RE:view, 21*(3), 145-152.

Head, D. N. (1990). Educational deficit: An inappropriate service criterion for children with visual impairments. *Journal of Visual Impairment & Blindness, 84*(3), 207-210.

Helmstetter, E., & Guess, D. (1987). Application of the individualized curriculum sequencing model to learners with severe sensory impairments. In L. Goetz, D. Guess, & K. Stremel-Campbell (Eds.), *Innovative program design for individuals with dual sensory impairments* (pp. 255-282). Baltimore: Paul H. Brookes.

Hill, E., & Ponder, P. (1976). *Orientation and mobility techniques: A guide for the practitioner.* New York: American Foundation for the Blind.

Horner, R. H., & McDonnell, R. S. (1982). Comparison of single instance and general case instruction in teaching a generalized vocational skill. *Journal of the Association for Per-*

sons with Severe Handicaps, 7(3), 7–20.

Horner, R. H., Meyer, L., & Fredricks, B. (Eds.). (1986). *Education of learners with severe handicaps: Exemplary service strategies.* Baltimore: Paul H. Brookes.

Hutchinson, D. J. (1978). The transdisciplinary approach. In J. B. Curry & K. K. Peppe (Eds.), *Mental retardation: Nursing approaches to care* (pp. 62–74). St. Louis: C. V. Mosby.

Lyon, S., & Lyon, G. (1980). Team functioning and staff development: A role release approach to providing integrated educational services for severely handicapped students. *Journal of the Association for Persons with Severe Handicaps, 5*(3), 250–253.

MacDonald, C., & York, J. (1989). *Instruction in regular education classes for students with severe disabilities: Assessment, objectives and instructional programs.* Minneapolis: University of Minnesota, Institute on Community Integration.

McDonnell, J. J., Horner, R. H., & Williams, J. A. (1984). Comparison of three strategies for teaching generalized grocery purchasing to high school students with severe handicaps. *Journal of the Association for Persons with Severe Handicaps, 9*(2), 123–133.

Orelove, F. P., & Sobsey, D. (1987). Designing transdisciplinary services. In F. P. Orelove & D. Sobsey (Eds.), *Educating children with multiple disabilities: A transdisciplinary approach* (pp. 1–24). Baltimore: Paul H. Brookes.

Primrose, M. (1981). Orientation and mobility training for deaf-blind adults. *Journal of Visual Impairment & Blindness, 75*(3), 147–194.

Pugach, M. (1988). Special education as a constraint on teacher education reform. *Journal of Teacher Education, 39*(3), 52–59.

Rainforth, B., & York, J. (1987). Integrating related services in community instruction. *Journal of the Association for Persons with Severe Handicaps, 12*(3), 193–198.

Snell, M. (1987). *Systematic instruction for persons with severe handicaps.* Columbus: Merrill.

Stainback, S., & Stainback, W. (1985). *Integration of students with severe handicaps into regular schools.* Reston, VA: Council for Exceptional Children.

Sternat, J., Messina, R., Nietupski, J., Lyon, S., & Brown, L. (1977). Occupational and physical therapy services for severely handicapped students: Toward a naturalized public school service delivery model. In E. Sontag, J. Smith, & N. Certo (Eds.), *Educational programming for severely and profoundly handicapped* (pp. 263–266). Reston, VA: Council for Exceptional Children.

Stewart, I., & Zimmerman, G. J. (1990). Orientation and mobility services to students with visual impairments enrolled in Iowa public schools. *RE:view, 12*(1) [printed cover incorrect, should be *22*], 23–30.

Szymanski, E. M., Hanley-Maxwell, C., & Parker, R. (1990). Habilitation and rehabilitation: An ecological framework for transdisciplinary service delivery. In F. R. Rusch (Ed.), *Supportive employment: Models, methods and issues* (pp. 199–214). Sycamore, IL: Sycamore.

Weiner, W. R., and Welsh, R. L. (1980). The profession of orientation and mobility. In R. Welsh & B. Blasch (Eds.), *Foundations of orientation and mobility* (pp. 625–651). New York: American Foundation for the Blind.

Woodruff, G. (1980). Transdisciplinary approach for preschool children and parents. *Exceptional Child, 20*(1), 13–16.

York, J., Long, E., Caldwell, N., Brown, L., Zanella-Albright, K., Rogan, P., Shiraga, B., & Marks, J. (1985). Teamwork strategies for school and community instruction. in L. Brown, B. Shiraga, J. York, A. Udvari-Solner, K. Zanella-Albright, P. Rogan, E. McCarthy, & R. Loomis (Eds.), *Education program for students with severe intellectual disabilities*, Vol. 15, pp. 229–276. Madison: University of Wisconsin-Madison and the Madison Metropolitan School District.

Orientation and Mobility for Students with Severe Visual and Multiple Impairments: A New Perspective

E. Joffee; C.H. Rikhye

Abstract: An innovative program for teaching orientation and mobility (O&M) to students with severe sensory and cognitive impairments in the New York City public schools was developed on the premise that these students do not have to master prerequisite concepts and techniques to learn O&M. It incorporated tactile and tangible communication systems to teach O&M and was structured so mobility education was embedded in the students' daily activities in school and at home. This article examines the traditional model of O&M and the assumptions about how such students learn to be mobile, describes the evolution of this innovative program, and presents guidelines for planning and implementing similar programs in other educational and rehabilitation settings.

Many orientation and mobility (O&M) specialists in practice today received their education during the 1960s, 1970s, and early 1980s (Uslan, Hill, & Peck, 1989). At that time, O&M services were founded on methods and strategies for teaching that were developed to meet the needs of soldiers who were blinded during World War II.

As a result of a succession of public health crises, changes in medical technology, and legislation, the demands on O&M specialists changed radically. Diverse groups with visual impairments emerged: infants, toddlers, children, youths, and elderly persons, many of whom experienced mild to severe multiple impairments in addition to their visual impairment.

The OSERS-funded project, a Field-Based Multi-site In-Service Training Model for Teaching and Related Services Staff Working with Students with Deaf-Blindness, Grant No. G008730425, under the direction of Madeleine W. Appell, provided partial support for this program. The information presented in this article does not necessarily reflect the policy of the U.S. Office of Special Education and Rehabilitation Services, and no official endorsement should be inferred. The authors thank the administrators, staff, students, and parents at Public Schools 138, 233, and 396, New York, New York, and Educational Vision Programs and Services, New York City Board of Education, for their cooperation and willingness to explore innovative approaches to teaching O&M.

Advances in O&M techniques, as well as an understanding of some of the underlying processes of independent travel, were achieved primarily in relation to adults whose only disability was visual impairment (Gee, Harrell, & Rosenberg, 1987). Therefore, as the profession grew, O&M specialists often were providing services to a wide range of people with complex and multiple needs based on the techniques and programs developed in the late 1940s and early 1950s.

It is reasonable to expect that many O&M specialists may have been confused and frustrated when using these original techniques and programs to evaluate and teach students with severe visual and multiple impairments. Although their experience was apparently not documented in the O&M literature, Gates (1985) reported a similar phenomenon for teachers of the visually impaired.

It is understandable, therefore, that many O&M practitioners, academicians, special education administrators, and teachers may have questioned the relevance and value of teaching O&M to students who have severe visual and multiple impairments. It is also understandable that initial efforts to teach O&M to these students ultimately resulted in a reexamination of the O&M program model and of mobility techniques for this population (Gee et al., 1987) and heralded a search for alternative solutions.

This article presents a field-based program that effectively utilized innovative alternative methods for teaching O&M to students with severe visual and cognitive impairments. The program used individualized communication systems that were developed to meet the students' needs and included concrete object cues, touch cues, structured environments, repetitive route travel, and involvement of a transdisciplinary team.

Historical perspective

In the 1950s, many premature babies who were treated with oxygen administered in incubators developed retinal disorders that resulted in severe visual impairments. The rubella epidemic of the 1960s created another group of individuals with visual impairments who often had additional sensory, cognitive, and medical problems (Lyon, 1985). Increased longevity, a phenomenon of the late twentieth century (Sternlieb, Hughes, & Hughes, 1982), has resulted in a growing number of adults who experience the complications associated with aging, including adult-onset diabetes and visual impairments. Visual impairment also has been associated with the later stages of AIDS (Kiester, 1990). Therefore, with the rising incidence of AIDS, the development of advanced methods for its treatment, and continued research for treatment to prolong the lives of patients with AIDS, the profile of persons with visual impairments can be expected to change once again.

The most recent, and possibly the most challenging, population of individuals with visual impairments emerged during the 1970s and 1980s when an increasing number of infants with severe and multiple congenital disabilities, in addition to visual impairments, were born and survived (Gallagher, 1989). Powerful social forces associated with poverty, child and substance abuse, limited access to health care, and environmental factors, combined with advanced medical technology, have produced this growing population of children.

Today, the original O&M program model is supplemented by O&M curricula and programs based on this model that have been modified for those who are congenitally blind, preschool children, school-age children, and the elderly, as well as those who have low vision (Uslan et al., 1989). In the next decade, however, both the model and curricula used by O&M specialists to teach individuals with severe visual and multiple impairments

and other newly emerging populations are likely to evolve.

Although O&M practitioners have been and are providing instruction to individuals who have severe visual and multiple impairments, programs and adapted technology are not widely reported in the literature. The majority of O&M programs that were documented during the 1970s and early 1980s focused on assessments and interventions that stressed the development of prerequisite sensory, motor, and conceptual skills (Gee et al., 1987). Hill and Ponder (1976) wrote that the acquisition of travel skills was dependent on the mastery of a hierarchy of cognitive and technical skills according to a set, ordered sequence. Students were expected to progress through a continuum of skills only after they had mastered the assumed prerequisites. Most individuals with severe multiple handicaps were believed not to have the prerequisite cognitive, psychomotor, communication, social, and behavioral skills essential for independent mobility (Gee et al., 1987) and, in many instances, were considered unsuited for O&M services.

A new model

Reports of changes in the traditional sequential O&M model were published only in the late 1980s. For example, Gee et al. (1987) reexamined the assumptions about how O&M skills can be learned as well as taught. They revealed that because the traditional O&M curriculum relies on prerequisites, it lacks the perspectives, framework, and tools that O&M specialists need to work with students who have severe cognitive, sensory, and physical impairments.

Gee and Goetz (1985) reported teaching O&M to students with severe visual and multiple impairments who failed to demonstrate conceptual and sensory prerequisites when evaluated according to the Peabody Mobility Scale. Nevertheless, the students succeeded in learning and generalizing mobility tasks because, according to Gee et al. (1985), they were taught O&M tasks using a modified mobility model.

Characteristic modifications were made in the traditional O&M model. Rather than learning the assumed prerequisite skills according to the traditional sequence of lessons (Hill & Ponder, 1976), students were taught the actual indoor mobility techniques they needed to move about in specific environments. Changes in activities during the school day were

considered to be motivators for travel, and rote learning of several functional travel routes was emphasized. Specific skills (such as trailing and crossing open areas) were taught for negotiating the actual environment. This functional model also included a system of physical prompts and positioning used to teach mobility techniques and a team approach for teaching and reinforcing O&M skills.

Compelling needs

Students with severe visual and multiple impairments have the same need to move safely and independently about their environment as does everyone else. They need to move from one location to another, to recognize when such movement should be initiated, to know where they want to or must go, and to know when to stop. Furthermore, they experience the same lack of security, safety, and information because of their visual impairments as do students with milder or no concomitant disabilities. They require mobility education to allay their fears, secure their safety, and learn techniques that enable them to travel as independently as possible.

Legal mandate

The legal mandates of P.L. 94-142 and P.L. 99-457 have underscored the requirement and professional obligation to teach O&M skills to children and youths with severe visual and multiple impairments.

Because there were no appropriate models and strategies for teaching O&M to individuals with severe visual and multiple impairments, many special education and rehabilitation programs either omitted O&M services or used strategies that were ineffective. Thus, programs that were otherwise appropriate but lacked relevant O&M instruction, hindered their ability to achieve the ultimate goal—teaching the skills for maximum independence during the school years and beyond.

Gee et al.'s (1987) innovative model for teaching O&M seems to be a sound foundation for developing a range of mobility programs to address the specific needs of diverse groups with severe visual and multiple impairments, including those with dual sensory impairments, those who are not ambulatory, and those with no apparent expressive or receptive language skills.

Motivation of students

Gee et al.'s (1987) functional approach to teaching mobility to students with severe visual and multiple impairments assumed that travel skills would be taught when natural opportunities for travel occurred in daily routines. It also assumed that motivation for travel would automatically occur as a result of changes in activity that took place according to the daily schedule. For example, it was expected that a student would be motivated to initiate travel along a route to the cafeteria at lunchtime. In teaching mobility skills, Joffee (1989) found that although this model was applicable to students with multiple disabilities who had symbolic communication skills (the ability to form abstract ideas that represent environmental entities), students who did not have these skills could not anticipate forthcoming events. Consequently, these students did not respond to motivators that were built into natural opportunities for travel during the school day. Therefore, a reliance on changes in activities during the school day was not an adequate motivation for all such students to move.

An implication of Joffee's (1989) findings is that a student's individual level of receptive communication ability is significant for determining how to teach O&M skills. Students whose communication skills enable them to form and retain symbolic representations associated with specific destinations can be motivated to travel either by language or changes in activity. Those who cannot form these symbolic representations require teaching methods that are adapted to their needs.

Innovative project
In 1987, a project to develop and implement improved instructional programs for students with severe visual, auditory, and multiple impairments was initiated in the New York City public schools under a grant coordinated by the St. Luke's–Roosevelt Hospital Developmental Disabilities Center. One of the project's objectives was to train consultant teachers to serve as resources to the students, their instructors, their parents, and related service personnel.

Early on, the school and project staff recognized that it was crucial to add O&M instruction to the educational programs of students with sensory and multiple impairments. To meet the project's objectives of enabling staff to teach functional life skills, O&M instruction had to be incorporated from the outset of the students' educational experience through the transition to adult life and beyond.

The acquisition of independent O&M skills, such as walking to the rest room, moving about the classroom to participate in activities, and traveling to the cafeteria, requires ongoing and consistent intervention to teach safe, purposeful mobility. Addressing transitional skills like going shopping in the community, doing laundry at a laundromat, eating in a restaurant, going to the post office, or traveling to a supported employment site, also require O&M education. A school-based university-trained and certified O&M specialist was assigned to develop an effective O&M program that included specific methodologies for teaching students with dual sensory and severe multiple impairments.

This recognition of the need to include O&M instruction was especially significant because O&M services had not initially been regarded as a priority. However, it required the development of approaches, strategies, and a curriculum to create the framework for nurturing the students' participation in daily living, educational, social, and vocational activities.

The adapted O&M program
Six students with severe visual and multiple impairments who received weekly half-hour individualized O&M instruction for 1½ school years succeeded in learning specific O&M skills. These skills included the sighted guide technique, a modified trailing technique, moving around obstacles, and crossing short open areas with no trailing surface (Joffee, in press). One student learned modified diagonal and touch cane techniques. These students were able to travel familiar routes (from their classroom to the cafeteria, from the classroom to the rest room, and from the classroom to the gym, for example) using modified mobility techniques and appeared to have acquired basic mobility skills that they could use to travel along most routes in a variety of environments.

A new program included the following five interrelated elements: 1) environmental structure, 2) functional communication systems, 3) use of conventional O&M techniques, 4) consistent and repetitive use of route travel, and 5) the collaboration of a multidisciplinary team. This program integrated and applied the "most promising practices" for teaching individuals with dual sensory and multiple impairments from numerous disciplines. The principles of educating individuals with severe multiple handicaps (Falvey, 1989; Snell, 1983), communication strategies used with people who have dual sensory impairments (Rowland & Schweigert, 1990; Rowland & Stremel-Campbell, 1987; Siegel-Causey & Guess, 1989; Stillman & Battle, 1984), and conventional indoor O&M techniques (Hill & Ponder, 1976) were studied, in some instances prior to publication. Some of these materials required modifications, but others did not. They were infused into the program and curriculum.

Environmental structure
The indoor school and home environments used with this population of students while teaching and reinforcing O&M skills must be structured for "easy access" and safe movement. "Easy access" pathways are those that allow for simple and unobstructed routes of travel through the environment. They are established by the thoughtful placement of classroom or household furniture, shelving, and activity centers. Access for safe movement means that travel pathways are free of clutter, unprotected drop-offs, and obstacles. Once the environment is satisfactorily structured, furniture and other points of reference must remain in place (Rikhye, Gothelf, & Appell, 1989).

Functional communication system
Effective communication with students is a critical component of this O&M program. The students' impaired receptive and expressive speech, hearing disabilities, and limited cognitive abilities interfere with teaching approaches that rely on conventional verbal communication. Alternative strategies have to be used to indicate when a student wishes to or is expected to move about and what the intended destination is to be. Physical prompts and tactile signing, paired with verbal messages, are used to communicate with students about body movements. For example, a tug upward under the arms signals a student to stand, and a pat on the lower back signals that the student should sit.

Students use concrete objects, associated with specific activity areas in the classroom, school, or home, as *anticipation cues* (Rowland & Schweigert, 1990). In this O&M program, concrete object cues are used for two purposes: 1) motivation for movement, and 2) identification of landmarks and destinations. Cues used for the latter purpose are called destination markers. For example, a roll of toilet paper or a diaper would indicate that a trip to the rest room was intended; a bean bag or a small ball could convey that gym is to be the next destination. These concrete cues, affixed to door jambs and other landmarks with velcro fasteners, inform students about points of orientation and indicate when a destination has been reached.

Communication systems are individualized. They are developed by the O&M specialist in close consultation with communications specialists, other instructional staff, and parents and are based on the students' interests, daily schedule, cognitive ability, and level of communication skills. A strategy for fading prompts and anticipation cues is integrated into the communication strategy, so that students have the opportunity to develop increasingly greater symbolic communication skills and do not become dependent on prompts and artifacts for communication associated with movement.

Table 1 lists the physical prompts that have been used to convey body movement. It is important to note that prompts are simple, clear, and pertain only to a limited number of selected body movements. Table 2 lists the anticipation cues that have been used successfully by this project. Note that the destinations included in Table 2 are associated with a clear change of activity and place. It is recommended that the instructor select cues that are associated with activity areas that are physically distinct from one another. Anticipation cues should be concrete objects that are easy to handle and carry, simple, and clearly associated with the destinations they signify. Illustrations and photographs do not make satisfactory anticipation cues at the outset of a program, but they can be introduced gradually if symbolic skills develop. Pictographs, raised-line drawings, and thermoform images of tangible objects should be avoided for students who are totally blind because these items are not easily recognized.

Anticipation cues may be placed in sequentially ordered boxes on an anticipation shelf or calendar (Writer, 1987). Anticipation boxes contain the anticipation cues included in a student's schedule, which are set out daily in the order that they will be used by the students.

Use of conventional O&M techniques

Safe movement is taught using modifications of conventional indoor and outdoor O&M techniques (Joffee, in press). Students are positioned to move using the sighted-guide technique, trailing, direction-taking procedures, and long cane techniques. Electronic travel devices, including the Polaron, Mowat Sensor, or Russell Pathsounder, may signal students to attend to visual information (Joffee, 1987) or be used as a secondary travel tool for students using wheelchairs and ortho-

Table 1. Physical prompts to convey body movements.

Body movement	Prompt
Stand up	Gentle upward tug on either side of the student's rib cage just beneath the armpit.
Sit down	Gentle pat (1) on the student's small of the back and/or a gentle downward pressure on both shoulders.
Turn right	Gentle pat (1) on the student's right shoulder, followed by a gentle push to begin the turn and, if necessary, to complete the turn.
Turn left	Gentle pat (1) on the student's left shoulder, followed by a gentle push to begin the turn, and, if necessary, to complete the turn.
Turn around	Two gentle taps (2) on the student's both shoulders, followed by a gentle push to begin the turn, and, if necessary, to complete the turn.
Start moving	Positioning for mobility techniques used for travel, such as sighted guide, trailing.
Stop	Firm but gentle tap below the student's collar bone.

pedic devices (Warren, Horn, & Hill, 1987).

Physical positioning and prompts accompany or replace verbal explanations when O&M techniques are introduced. Thus, an instructor may position a student alongside a wall, help the student to place his or her hand on the wall in the correct trailing position, and physically prompt the student forward to initiate or sustain travel. Likewise, an instructor may place a cane in a student's hand, position the student correctly to use the diagonal cane technique, and move along with the student to achieve travel along a route. If the

Table 2. Examples of anticipation cues associated with specific destinations/activities.

Cue	Destination	Activity
Spoon	Cafeteria	Mealtime
Bean bag	Gymnasium	Physical education
Diaper/ Toilet paper roll	Rest room	Toileting
Washcloth	Sink	Grooming
Backpack	School bus	Dismissal

student independently initiates and sustains travel, prompts are gradually reduced and eventually eliminated.

Since students are taught the mobility skills and routes they require to reach specific destinations associated with daily routine activities, skills are presented as they relate to the students' immediate and functional daily needs. The traditional sequence of presenting indoor mobility techniques does not have to be followed. The students may respond more positively if they are permitted to use a cane before they cross open areas without one. Thus, a student may use the diagonal cane technique to walk across a large classroom before he or she learns to walk to a sound source using protective techniques. As was noted, the instructor uses physical positioning and prompts to accompany or replace verbal explanations when introducing O&M techniques. The mastery of skills may be inconsistent and slow; therefore, repetition, consistency, and encouragement are key factors for success.

In this program, conventional familiarization, orientation, and self-familiarization methods or techniques that require abstractions about the layout and nature of environments, as well as the interpretation of auditory information, are not applied. Rather, orientation is achieved by the rote mastery of specific routes in familiar, controlled environments.

Consistent and repetitive route travel
The O&M specialist plans routes for students to use in all environments and for travel that is guided or assisted as well as travel that is eventually achieved independently. Routes are simple and direct, beginning at a clearly marked point of orientation and ending at a destination marked by a destination marker.

Route travel integrates functional communication in the following manner. At the initiation of a route, the student grasps an anticipation cue from an anticipation box or schedule board. The student carries the cue or holds it in his or her pocket for the duration of the trip. The student travels a specified route using mobility skills and techniques until he or she arrives at a destination. The destination is identified by matching the anticipation cue to the destination marker. The anticipation cue is deposited in a "closure box," located at the end of the route. Depositing an anticipation cue in the closure box signals the student that a desired destination has been located and the trip is completed. Reverse routes are treated as new entities, requiring the use of an anticipation cue associated with the point of orientation for the original route. For example, a classroom may have been a student's starting point. The classroom would be marked with a soft cloth, a textured block, or a rubber pad posted on the door jamb. When returning to the classroom, the student would select or receive the anticipation cue identical to the classroom marker and follow the prescribed route to the classroom destination.

Collaboration by the transdisciplinary team

For students who have visual impairments and severe multiple disabilities to benefit from the O&M program, it is necessary for the entire educational or rehabilitation team, including parents or caregivers, to cooperate in planning and implementing the program. The effective teaching of O&M skills requires input from many disciplines; it cannot be accomplished by the O&M instructor alone. To ensure the consistent and effective integration of O&M skills, every member of the team must utilize a uniform functional communication system, reinforce the correct body positions, and follow the prescribed mobility routes every time a student moves or is guided from one place to another. The team also works together to review and update the goals and tasks of the program at regular intervals.

Implementing the program

Responsibilities of administrators

The program described in this article was developed and introduced in a school setting. The methods for implementing the program, however, appear to be relevant to transition and rehabilitation programs as well.

The introduction of an innovative O&M program in educational and rehabilitation settings requires the support and cooperation of administrators at several levels, the involvement of professional staff and parents, and the cooperation of custodial staff. The overall school administrator, as well as the administrator of O&M services, must first acknowledge the value and responsibility of teaching O&M skills to students with severe visual and multiple impairments. The special education director or administrator of a state or private vocational rehabilitation program must become aware of the adapted curriculum and techniques required to teach these

skills. Making this information available to the administrators is the responsibility of O&M specialists.

Administrators become active program builders by disseminating information, sharing the program's objectives, and organizing the mechanisms for implementing O&M services. It is their responsibility to communicate the program's objectives and methods to the network of service providers who are involved in educating or rehabilitating these students: members of local Committees on Special Education, school principals or program directors, directors of transition programs, managers at vocational training sites, related service providers, and parents.

The special education or rehabilitation administrator is also responsible for sensitizing and educating O&M specialists in the unique perspectives and skills required to teach students who have severe multiple disabilities. The O&M specialists and teachers of the visually impaired will often need to attend workshops and training sessions about the special nature of this population. In-service education may include consideration of the impact of the disabilities on cognitive, physical, communication, and behavioral abilities. The compounded effects on students with severe sensory and multiple impairments should be addressed, as should such issues as the continuum of services from early childhood through transitional and vocational placement.

The on-site administrator or coordinator of the special education or rehabilitation program has the ongoing responsibility to ensure high-quality services and to update the program's objectives and methods, when necessary. It is recommended that the entire instructional or rehabilitation team (social worker, vocational rehabilitation counselor, rehabilitation teacher, job coach, and so on) and the parents plan the details of introducing the program. A mechanism for the ongoing supervision and coordination of the program must be established from the outset. In a small facility, the classroom teacher or work supervisor can assume this role. However, in a large program with several classrooms or work sites, a coordinating or consultant teacher should be responsible for monitoring the program to ensure the consistency of such elements as tangible communication systems, implementation of route travel, and the involvement of parents or caregivers.

Involving custodial staff

The on-site special education or rehabilitation administrator must gain the cooperation of the custodial staff to assure that furniture and other environmental features remain stable. The O&M instructor must select the most appropriate placement of materials used by the mobility program, considering the need to leave sufficient room for all students in the group who may use wheelchairs or other orthopedic devices.

The custodial staff must also be consulted regarding the placement of anticipation cues throughout the facility to ensure the program's compliance with sanitary, safety, and fire codes. The project described here was successful in gaining the custodial staff's assistance and support when the staff were told about the program's objectives and participated in deciding how to affix anticipation cues to walls, door jambs, stairwells, and so on.

Using video technology

Brief video presentations, produced while the program was being developed, were useful in educating participants at all levels. The program's objectives and simple implementation techniques could be easily communicated on videotape to administrators, O&M specialists, vision teachers, classroom staff, related services personnel, and parents. Videotapes were also useful to administrators and instructional staff in evaluating both the program and their own performance. The regularly scheduled videotaping of staff working with individual students is an excellent vehicle for monitoring progress, gauging the program's impact over time, and maintaining communication between the school and the parents.

Future directions

Innovations in O&M models and services for students with severe visual and multiple impairments are in an early phase of development and implementation. The administrators, instructional staff, providers of related services, and parents who participated in this project agree that O&M services that are geared to this special population of students have significantly improved overall management and outcomes of the educational program. The students' skills in mobility and their independence and awareness of the environment were enhanced.

Gee et al.'s (1987) challenge of the universal relevance of the assumptions made by the traditional sequential O&M teaching model appears to have been validated by this project. The modifications they proposed provided the framework for developing an effective mobility program tailored to meet the needs of students with severe visual and multiple impairments.

As alternative models and programs for teaching O&M skills are introduced to a wide spectrum of students in various types of facilities, further modifications may be made. The anticipated increase in the population of students with severe multiple impairments and concomitant sensory disabilities and the mandates for their education and rehabilitation compel service providers to cooperate in developing and implementing innovative approaches and programs.

References

Falvey, M.A. (1989). *Community-based curriculum: Instructional strategies for students with severe handicaps.* Baltimore, MD: Paul H. Brookes.

Gallagher, W.F. (1989). Foreword. In J.N. Erin (Ed.), *Dimensions: Selected papers from the* Journal of Visual Impairment & Blindness *on visually impaired persons with multiple disabilities* (p. v). New York: American Foundation for the Blind.

Gates, C.F. (1985). Survey of multiply handicapped, visually impaired children in the Rocky Mountain/Great Plains Region. *Journal of Visual Impairment & Blindness,* **79**, 385–391.

Gee, K. & Goetz, L. (1985). *Outcomes of instructing orientation and mobility across purposeful travel routes in natural environments.* Unpublished manuscript, San Francisco State University, Department of Special Education.

Gee, K., Harrell, R., & Rosenberg, R. (1987). Teaching orientation and mobility skills within and across natural opportunities for travel: A model designed for learners with multiple severe disabilities. In L. Goetz, D. Guess, & K. Stremel-Campbell (Eds.), *Innovative program design for individuals with dual sensory impairments* (pp. 127–157). Baltimore, MD: Paul H. Brookes.

Hill, E. & Ponder, P. (1976). *Orientation and mobility techniques: A guide for the practitioner.* New York: American Foundation for the Blind.

Joffee, E. (1987). The role of electronic travel aids. *Journal of Visual Impairment & Blindness,* **81**, 389–390.

Joffee, E. (1989). Developing O&M services for severely and profoundly retarded students in the New York City public schools. *Long Cane News,* **8**(1), 3–4.

Joffee, E. (in press). Orientation and mobility for students with dual sensory impairments. In C.H. Rikhye (Ed.), *Functional life skills for students with dual sensory impairments: A handbook for parents and instructional staff.* Albany, NY: New York State Education Department, Title VI-C Project.

Keister, E. (1990). *AIDS & vision loss.* New York: American Foundation for the Blind.

Lyon, J. (1985). *Playing God in the nursery.* New York: W.W. Norton.

Rikhye, C., Gothelf, C., & Appell, M. (1989). A classroom environment checklist for students with dual sensory impairments. *Teaching Exceptional Children,* **22**, 44–46.

Rowland, C. & Schweigert, P. (1990). *Tangible symbol systems: Symbolic communication for individuals with multi-sensory impairments.* Tucson, AZ: Communication Skill Builders.

Rowland, C. & Stremel-Campbell, K. (1987). Share and share alike: Conventional gestures to emergent language for learners with sensory impairments. In L. Goetz, D. Guess, & K. Stremel-Campbell (Eds.), *Innovative program design for individuals with dual sensory impairments* (pp. 49–76). Baltimore, MD: Paul H. Brookes.

Siegel-Causey, E. & Guess, D. (1989). *Enhancing nonsymbolic communications among learners with severe disabilities.* Baltimore, MD: Paul H. Brooks.

Snell, M.E. (1983). *Systematic instruction of the moderately and severely handicapped* (2nd ed.). Columbus, OH: Charles E. Merrill.

Sternlieb, G., Hughes, J.W., & Hughes, C.O. *Demographic trends and economic reality: Planning and markets in the 80's.* New Jersey: Center for Urban Policy Research.

Stillman, R.D. & Battle, C.W. (1984). Developing prelanguage communication in the severely handicapped: An interpretation of the Van Dijk method. *Seminars in Speech and Language,* **5**(3), 159–170.

Uslan, M.M., Hill, E.W., & Peck, A.F. (1989). *The profession of orientation and mobility in the 1980s: The AFB competency study.* New York: American Foundation for the Blind.

Warren, S.F., Horn, E.H., & Hill, E.W. (1987). Applications of advanced technologies. In L. Goetz, D. Guess, & K. Stremel-Campbell (Eds.), *Innovative program design for individuals with dual sensory impairments* (pp. 283–309). Baltimore, MD: Paul H. Brookes.

Writer, J. (1987). A movement-based approach to the education of students who are sensory impaired/multihandicapped. In L. Goetz, D. Guess, & K. Stremel-Campbell (Eds.), *Innovative program design for individuals with dual sensory impairments* (pp. 191–224). Baltimore, MD: Paul H. Brookes.

Elga Joffee, M.Ed., M.P.S., national orientation and mobility consultant, American Foundation for the Blind, 15 West 16th Street, New York, NY 10011, was, at the time of the project's initiation, orientation and mobility specialist, Educational Vision Programs and Services; Catherine Hall Rikhye, Ed.D., staff developer, P.S. 138 at PS 130, 144–178 East 128th Street, New York, NY 10035, was, at the time of the project, program coordinator, St. Luke's–Roosevelt Hospital Developmental Disabilities Center.

Modifications of the Long Cane for Use by a Multiply Impaired Child

KATHLEEN ANN MORSE

Ms. Morse is an itinerant mobility instructor in the Seacoast region of New Hampshire.

The intent of all mobility techniques is to provide protection or information when a visually impaired person is moving within various environments. Whether we consider forearm or upper arm protective techniques, trailing, diagonal cane, or touch technique, whether we refer to hallways or sidewalks, safety and effectiveness while gaining independence of movement are of utmost importance. Yet students who are aware of their location and show readiness to travel independently to often-used areas have often been unable to master any protective or information-gathering technique to ensure safe passage. Each of the basic mobility techniques requires an ability to recognize, duplicate, and sustain a particular arm and hand position and, in the case of touch technique, perform fine motor movements with hand and wrist. Related to maintaining positions are component requirements of body image on a level that allows recognition and use of major body parts, spatial awareness that allows forward movement and front locations to be distinguished from those to the back and side, and physical strength adequate to perform and sustain techniques long enough to reach the desired destination.

It is a rare student who executes techniques precisely, but as long as adequate coverage is not compromised, effective safety and information-gathering can be maintained. However, for many students, the basic requirements of body image, spatial awareness, and especially physical ability, are not present and may, in fact, be unattainable. As a result, safety levels and effectiveness are neither satisfactory nor acceptable.

With the student's need to move about independently and his or her basic familiarity with the environment, the challenge to be met is the discovery of an alternative mobility technique which will provide safety and information and yet be within the capabilities of this type of student. The modification of a long cane and techniques described below were designed for a particular deaf-blind child. However, any student experiencing similar difficulties with the usual mobility techniques might possibly profit from similar variations in approach.

Deaf-Blind Girl

CY was a fourteen year old girl when first seen by me. She had several visual problems, including surgical aphakia, retinopathy, and glaucoma, which resulted in functional vision that fluctuated from shadow and occasional color perception to minimal light perception. She also had a profound sensori-neural hearing loss and did not appear to respond to sound even while wearing a hearing aid. She had received mobility instruction during the previous two years, with emphasis on following directions, walking on the right side of halls and stairs, forearm technique, and pushing a cane in front of her for detection of stairs. Although often able to follow one- and two-step directions, she did not travel school routes independently. Within buildings she moved about alone, but often at the risk of hitting her head or body on walls, open doors, and corners. The cane had been previously discontinued as of little use because she had been watching the cane and not where she was going. However, in the interim, she began to lose the vision upon which her safety relied.

CY was unable to learn and perform forearm technique adequately to protect herself. Her arm was rarely positioned far enough across her body but rather protected only half of her, and her hand was often angled closer to her body than her elbow, with fingers facing downward and curled. Resistance and tactual feedback applied to her raised forearm during walking resulted in only temporary improvement of one minute or less. She did not voluntarily attempt to use forearm

Abstract: *One alternative is proposed for meeting the primary goals of all mobility techniques, those of safety and information, for those students whose orientation establishes them as ready to travel independently, but whose body image, concepts, or physical abilities preclude the use of standard mobility methods. Modification of the long cane and variations in technique are described.*

technique when traveling around the building outside of mobility class.

When it was observed that CY did hold her arm straight forward in an effort to protect the head of a toy she enjoyed riding, an attempt was made to have her carry a favorite doll in the hope that she would be motivated to protect a special toy more than herself when walking. While holding the doll against her chest with her free hand assured that her forearm would be out and away from her body, no improvement in coverage across body was seen.

Rudimentary Touch Technique Too Difficult

Touch technique with a long cane was attempted as a possible solution to allow for safe travel, since she had demonstrated knowledge of and basic orientation to the school buildings. Although lacking the basic preparation for touch technique, it was the method which would provide the most protection and environmental information, and would be the best technique to choose if substantial effort were to be invested in only one method. After several months of little consistent progress, even with food and praise rewards throughout lessons as motivators to stimulate learning and attention, it became obvious that even rudimentary touch technique was also much too difficult. She was not physically capable of moving the cane right and left, or of lifting it or sliding it on the floor, even for a short period of time. She constantly changed hands, even after only one or two minutes of use. She could not remember to move the cane and would often stop any arc motion with it after a few steps, or stop walking completely until reminded to continue moving both herself and the cane.

Endeavoring to teach diagonal cane technique would have met with similar results, since its requirement of retaining a particular arm position away from the body and a hand position resulting in diagonal placement of the cane, was beyond her physical capabilities at that time and it would have been actually more difficult to hold a position than to control cane movement.

A Modified Cane

It was observed that if left to her own devices, this student naturally held her arm next to her body with the cane pointing somewhat straight ahead of her, a position which was obviously most comfortable for her. What was needed was a modified cane which required no movement left to right but which would passively provide coverage and protection when grasped with her arm at her side. Since the cane would most often be extended straight forward from her right hand, the thought was to attach a diagonal piece that would touch the floor on the left, where cane arc would normally bring the tip, thus clearing a body-wide path when she pushed the cane forward. Attaching the diagonal section to intersect the primary cane less than half-way up would allow adequate time to stop for poles, corners, or other vertical objects entering between the two pieces. A section angled from the primary cane was chosen over a "Y" shape because of the student's natural inclination to keep her arm at her side and her already demonstrated inability to maintain an arm position with her hand centered.

The idea, along with the long cane, proposed specifications, and an old cane that would provide parts, were all brought to an instructor in the metal shop. The shop instructor, who made the cane, suggested the addition of a brace between the two sections to make the structure stronger. This brace had a secondary advantage of blocking narrow obstacles even sooner, thus allowing more time for the student to react to them.

Construction of the Modified Cane

Total cane height was 41 inches [102.5 cm]. The diagonal piece was attached to the cane at a point just less than half-way (17 inches [42.5 cm] from the floor). Total coverage tip to tip was 18 inches [45 cm], a distance adequate to provide protection across her, and corresponding to the area that would have been covered by conventional touch technique. In order to decrease resistance on the cane while being pushed forward, especially during the early stages of practice, well-worn nylon tips were fastened on the ends of each cane segment and angled to slide smoothly across flat surfaces.

The process of crush bending was used to mold the ends of each piece of tubing to the cane. It involved:

(1) Heating the end of a piece of aluminum tubing from an old cane; (2) placing it inside a mold—an old pipe of slightly larger diameter than was needed to fit around the cane, cut in half lengthwise; (3) crushing the tubing against the pipe mold with a steel rod (or pipe) of slightly smaller diameter than was needed to fit around the cane; (4) continued heating while crushing slowly; (5) bending the crushed end of the aluminum piece to the appropriate angle, while heating to prevent breaking. This process minimized the possibility of splitting the aluminum during bending, and provided for two thicknesses of metal rather than one at each juncture. Ordinary one-inch [2.5 cm] hose clamps were used to fasten pieces together, one clamp at each end of the brace and two attaching the diagonal sections to the primary cane (see Fig. 1).

Addition of an angled segment as well as a brace between sections contributed a substantial increase in weight when compared to a long cane. However, since this cane would only be pushed along a floor or sidewalk rather than lifted and tapped with each step, the effect was a decrease in amount of hand and arm strength necessary to employ the cane. Pushing the cane, establishing constant friction with a variety of sur-

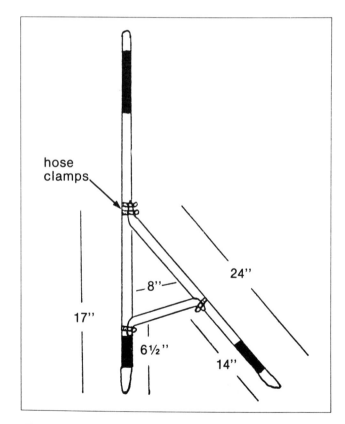

Figure 1. Modified cane for use by a deaf-blind girl.

faces, would be expected to wear down cane tips much more quickly than conventional touch technique. More frequent tip replacements would be necessary especially after traveling along cement surfaces and rough pavement.

Techniques with the Modified Cane

Initially, CY was taken on a conducted exploration of her new cane as the instructor gently guided her hands over all sections of the cane, which was labeled "new" cane ("new" being a sign familiar to her). At the beginning of subsequent lessons she checked the cane herself as reassurance she was still the possessor of this different device. By means of demonstration she learned to hold the cane tips in front of her by merely grasping the cane with her arm at her side, and pushing it along the floor. She hd no difficulty recognizing which cane tip had lodged against an obstacle and usually retrieved the cane and launched it forward in the appropriate direction away from any object. In the beginning, her retrieval and subsequent exploration in another direction was accomplished with two hands holding the cane owing to its awkwardness, uncertain spatial dimensions, and weight. However, as she gained familiarity through frequent practice, her use of the device became smoother and it was more often controlled with one hand.

After a few well-timed comments from her teachers along the lines of: "You didn't bump your head. Wonderful!" and after hitting herself on a corner when she was without the cane, she began to make the connection between cane use and ease of walking and really understand the function and purpose of the cane in her own unique way. On her own initiative she began to trail with the appropriate hand, switching the cane to the other hand when necessary. She started to search with the cane for doorways, stairs, and openings. And she found it important to reach forward in order to tactually explore obstacles to check her location, an interest she had not previously shown.

The modified cane cleared a path equal to that of touch technique but no wider. It was no more of an obstacle to other pedestrians than a long cane nor was it a hindrance in ordinarily furnished classrooms and living areas which normally have ample walking space. Although it occasionally needed to be lifted over door sills and edges of rugs, the cane moved smoothly even over carpeted surfaces.

Negotiating Stairs

Continuing her travel indoors, CY needed a method to negotiate stairs safely. Since she used only familiar stairways with railings, she learned to grasp the right-hand railing and carry her cane vertically in her left hand while ascending. However, some modifications were made to accommodate the cane's extra width. As she moved to the right side of stairs she turned the cane 180° so the crook curved away from her. The resultant position placed the diagonal section across in front of her, warning of any pedestrians she might bump into, rather than across the unused portion of the stairway. Without this method she occupied the space of an entire stairway which made it difficult for others to use the stairs at the same time.

For descending stairs, CY approached the stairs, allowing the cane to locate the top stair by dropping over the edge. She then moved to the right side of the stairway and, holding the railing, proceeded downstairs, cane held in the normal position in front of her. Usually she held the cane just above the stairs. Occasionally she touched each subsequent stair edge with the cane using a tapping motion. After experimenting with various cane positions it became apparent that this was the easiest and least dangerous method of descending. She naturally angled the cane in front of her so she was not blocking the other half of the stairway with the risk of tripping someone else. When held in this way with the primary, straight part of the cane positioned across in front of her, the diagonal section was angled slightly away from her and posed no danger of her tripping over it. If changed 180°, as in ascending, she risked stepping over the diagonal piece and falling if she did not keep the cane far enough ahead.

Despite its extra weight, CY had no difficulty carrying it up or down stairs. Holding it vertically appeared to require less wrist strength than moving a cane back and forth. In addition, although she generally used hand railings when available, she did occasionally ascend and descend several steps outside the building without moving to the railing. Her balance was sufficient to require no extra support.

Outdoor Travel

While the cane became stuck in sidewalk cracks and irregularities as well as grass when it was first used outside, CY quickly adapted to it and perhaps improved her hand, wrist, and arm strength at the same time. She soon was having little difficulty pushing the cane along sidewalks and pavement and was able to rescue the cane from grass which had captured the tip(s).

Two trailing methods were attempted:

1. Moving the cane right or left in the direction of the appropriate grassline, a method similar to the usual two-point trailing technique, except that the distance to be covered is much smaller because of the cane's width.
2. Trailing with one tip on the pavement and one tip on the grass, which required a certain amount of lifting up on the grass side to minimize sticking and catching.

CY was much more proficient using the first method. It took some time for her to realize the need for a specific route and to search for, and recognize, landmarks—especially intersecting sidewalks. The fact that her vision fluctuated made it very difficult to teach trailing and exact routes. If she was seeing well enough to locate intersecting sidewalks visually, she had no idea why she was being taught trailing. She was functioning on a level where she learned only from immediate situations and needs. Like many other students, she could not understand the connection between learning now and a future need, even if it was tomorrow. Therefore, trailing and exact routes had to be taught on those days when she actually needed those techniques. This also meant very close cooperation with her classroom teachers in order to keep abreast of her daily visual status as well as close observation to evaluate her visual level at each class time.

During this period CY was seen for mobility every day for classes ranging from 15 minutes to 30 minutes. After several weeks she was given the cane to use within the school building and soon outside. The classroom teachers and child care worker reinforced the skills she learned in class and provided the continuity necessary to establish long-lasting skills and learning. They also provided supervision and guidance during the time she was still learning particular routes and practicing techniques.

Results

The cane proved itself to be a marvelous success both for traveling and for her own self-confidence. She began to walk more swiftly and demonstrated increased interest in her surroundings. She was no longer fearful of moving about. When using the cane, she had no major physical contacts with furniture, walls, or doors, whereas without it she continued to bruise her head and arms. She no longer needed to receive rewards to remain alert when walking.

Since using the modified cane was more suited to her capabilities, CY was able to begin traveling and learning without the frustration she must have felt before. Along with safer travel, other changes began to appear in her behavior, especially within the classroom, that would lead to the conclusion that as moving around became easier for her she began to feel better about herself and her school work. This very passive girl who always waited to be told what to do and who needed frequent encouragement to persist with just about any task, began asking for materials when she needed more at her desk. She began to search the classroom for her teachers in order to request things. She started conversations more often. It was obvious from her frequent smiles that she

was happier and that her confidence had increased.

Even though this long cane was modified to meet the particular needs of CY, many students and clients demonstrate similar difficulties and needs. Modifications along these lines—keeping in mind the primary goals of safety and information—and tailoring them to suit the particular strengths and weaknesses of each person, might prove useful in several situations, for example, for those who intellectually cannot master the idea of continual arc motion with a conventional long cane, and for those who physically cannot perform adequate cane movement, whether because of age (young or old), muscle weakness, or physical handicap.

A modified cane may be considered as a temporary measure until sufficient development, intellectually or physically, has occurred, or it may be the only method that can provide safe travel for someone whose condition does not change. Either way, safe, independent travel may be brought within reach of previously restricted populations. ∎

Developing Vision Use Within Functional Daily Activities for Students With Visual and Multiple Disabilities

JUNE DOWNING and BRENT BAILEY

ABSTRACT: This paper offers an alternative strategy to out-of-context visual stimulation training for students with concomitant visual and multiple disabilities. The emphasis is on visual assessment and intervention within meaningful, functional activities. Instruction in vision use for students with severe disabilities in addition to visual ones occurs only if the activity requires improved visual skills. A decision-making strategy is provided so that the vision specialist can maximize effective intervention. A case study of a student with severe, multiple disabilities outlines decision-making steps for intervention.

Vision is the primary mode through which we receive information about the world (Barraga, 1986; Piaget & Inhelder, 1969). Children and adults who have severe multiple disabilities including a visual impairment may not be able to gain access to visual information because of the combined effects of their disabilities.

These individuals often must *learn* to apply their remaining vision to become more efficient and competent in daily activities.

Visual and other severe multiple disabilities limit the number and complexity of skills performed. Individuals with severe disabilities require more opportunities to attain skills, and transferring their acquired skills to other activities and environments is difficult (Brown, Nisbet, Ford, Sweet, Shiraga, York, & Loomis, 1983; Horner, McDonnell, & Bellamy, 1986). In overall functioning, these individuals place within the lowest 1% of the population (Brown, et al., 1983).

A number of teachers of students with visual handicaps are unprepared to provide effective instruction for students with severe and multiple disabilities. Though skilled in teaching students who are visually impaired and have normal to above normal intelligence, vision teachers may have minimal training or experience in the area of multiple handicaps. Students with visual and multiple handicaps typically have severe to profound mental retardation, a mild to severe physical and/or behavioral disability, and often a label of legal or functional blindness. Teaching these students to use their residual vision and assisting the classroom teacher to make programmatic changes may challenge the expertise of many vision specialists.

This paper offers a decision-making process for determining the need to intervene in the area of vision use. It suggests an instructional format that incorporates interventions within functional, age-appropriate activities and emphasizes assisting the student to achieve efficient use of vision within natural contexts.

Problems With the Traditional Role of the Vision Specialist

Traditionally, individuals with multiple handicaps, including a visual handicap, have received special visual training in isolated contexts (Ficociello, 1976; Jose, Smith, & Shane, 1980; Potenski, 1983). The vision specialist or paraprofessional under this specialist's direction usually implemented this "pull-out" model of intervention. The training consisted of vision stimulation activities derived directly from developmental assessment tools that targeted the area of need (Ficociello, 1976; Langley & DuBose, 1976). Instructional sessions were controlled to reduce distractors, to highlight visual input, and to structure the learning environment. Consequently, the visual training focused on visual behaviors (i.e., gaze, localization, tracking) but might not address context or practicality. Materials used for such intervention followed the assessment guidelines (i.e., lights; large, colorful balls; shiny objects). These materials might be visually stimulating, but might not motivate the individual to respond because of age and/or inability to recognize the purpose of responding. (Although out-of-context intervention is not recommended by the authors, it may be necessary to perform very basic and out-of-context assessments to initially determine whether the student has any response to visual stimuli and what those responses are.)

On the Individualized Educational Plan (IEP), objectives that target visual skills often were written in a manner that isolated the skill from any specific activity. As a result, the student could make progress on an objective, without being able to demonstrate that progress within meaningful activities. For example, John might improve his ability to look at a bright flashing light but might not look at people when speaking to them or at his food while eating.

Like any basic skill, the effective use of vision may need to be taught. The absence of data to support the transfer of visual skills from isolated training sessions to actual environments (Goetz & Gee, 1987a; Hatlen & Goetz, 1981; Lunderwold, Lewin, & Irwin, 1987) makes it essential that goals for vision use be integrated into a natural routine of functional activities. As with any skill that is determined to be meaningful to an individual with severe disabilities, use of vision should be taught when it is needed. This instruction will be most effective during meaningful activities, across a variety of natural settings, and if taught by many different instructors (Horner et al., 1986). The typical instructional responsibilities for a vision specialist have revolved around adapting materials, providing sensory stimulation, and teaching compensatory skills such as Braille, abacus, and orientation and mobility (Spungin & Taylor, 1986). In general, the specialists support the student's adaptation to classroom demands and expectations.

This traditional role may not meet the special instructional needs of students with severe multiple disabilities. Because students with severe multiple disabilities are typically engaged in activities different from their more academic peers, vision specialists may feel ill-prepared to address their visual needs. Therefore, these students may not benefit from expertise that is crucial to their development.

Contextual Use of Vision

To address the problems stated above, some researchers have incorporated the teaching of vision use within daily activities (Goetz & Gee, 1987a; Utley, Duncan, Strain, & Scanlon, 1983). Their research has identified specific steps that target the use of vision within functional activities. These steps involve determining if vision is required to perform an activity, determining what visual skills are needed, identifying critical moments to use vision within tasks, and developing intervention strategies to teach the desired visual skills (Goetz & Gee, 1987a).

Because the act of seeing occurs at all times and because the vision specialist cannot provide continual direct service to any one student, the vision specialist may be more effective and efficient as a consultant to the educational team. Vision specialists can apply their knowledge within the classroom and all other natural learning environments (e.g., school, home, and community facilities). They can help the teacher identify which parts of functional activities require, or would benefit from, improved visual skills. To be a successful consultant the vision specialist will need to establish rapport with team members, demonstrate solid consulting techniques (Erin, 1988; Idol, Paolucci, Whitcomb, & Nevin, 1986), and possess clear communication skills to instruct direct service providers who will furnish the necessary daily intervention.

Guidelines for Intervention

Assess Visual Skills Within Context

Identifying appropriate vision objectives must first be a part of an overall discrepancy analysis, which compares an individual's current behaviors with the specific skills needed to perform an identified task (Brown, Shiraga, York, Zanella, & Rogan, 1984). A decision then is made to teach the missing skill or to adapt the situation. Skills are targeted for intervention if the student does not demonstrate them to a sufficient degree to ensure task completion. The basic visual skills of attending, localizing, tracking, shifting gaze, scanning, and reaching (moving) toward an object (Jose, 1983; Langley & DuBose, 1976) are taught within functional activities for the individual as part of the sequence of a given activity. Table 1 shows the basic visual skills that are used in making a fruit and ice cream drink: attending in all steps; localizing in Steps 1, 2b, 4b, 6, 7a, 8, and 9; shifting gaze in Steps 2a and 4a, and scanning in Step 7a.

Determine the Need for Intervention

The vision specialist analyzes the possible strategies such as personal assistance (sighted guide), adapted devices, aids and/or materials, a change in the sequence of steps, alteration of the activity expectation, or modification or elimination of the step to help the student complete the visual tasks within an activity. One strategy may be the decision to teach the student the visual skill needed to complete the step.

The decision to intervene by teaching a necessary visual skill is not a foregone conclusion. Because efficient use of vision is not required for all activities, the vision specialist first must determine if intervention is actually necessary. Some individuals, who may not attend to objects or people, are capable of performing a given activity. For some individuals, visual information may be so vague and unreliable that performing the activity without using vision is actually more efficient. Vision specialists must apply their unique knowledge and experience to determine if helping individuals use vision will improve the ability of those people to perform certain tasks. If not, then teaching the visual skill is either not warranted or not the correct intervention for that situation. Observing how the student performs a given activity *without* using vision will help decide whether or not to teach vision skills. The vision specialist may gain considerable insight into the need for or benefit of vision by performing the same activity with and without sight. Such insight is especially critical when the student is unable to verbalize what is or is not problematic.

The overall objective is to increase the individual's involvement and competence in the activity. The specialist will need to consider a number of variables, including age of student, number of years without using vision, conditions under which the activity is performed (e.g., available lighting, size of materials, and contrast), student motivation, other limiting cognitive and physical disabilities, and the complex-

Table 1. Discrepancy Analysis of Visual Skills with Intervention Strategies: Making a Fruit and Ice Cream Drink

Task	Student performance	Intervention strategy
1. Obtain necessary materials	$-^a$	Provide sibling or parental assistance
2. Choose preferred fruit	−	Substitute a foil for one fruit
a. Shift gaze between two types of fruit	−	(use auditory cues, change proximity, exaggerate contrast, present in different fields)
b. Reach for and pick up one of the fruits to indicate choice	$+^b$	
3. Put fruit in blender	+	
4. Choose preferred flavor of ice cream	−	Substitute foil for one flavor of ice cream (see 2a for presentation strategies)
a. Shift gaze between two flavors of ice cream	−	
b. Reach for and pick up one of the cartons of ice cream to indicate choice	+	
5. Put ice cream in blender	−	Have sibling assist or use soft ice cream
6. Put top on blender	−	Provide auditory cues to top (by tapping top) to serve as auditory and visual reminder; withdraw cues.
7. Turn on blender	−	Add colored tab to correct button (fluorescent yellow or red); add high contrast key guard around buttons to allow only depression of correct key; use flashlight if needed
a. Scan buttons on blender to locate correct one	−	
b. Press button	+	
8. Take off top	+	
9. Pour drink into cup	−	Provide sibling/parental assistance or use adaptive stand to help peer

^{a}Student does not perform skill. ^{b}Student performs skill independently.

ity of the overall task, to determine if or how intervention will be beneficial. Decisions about strategies made during the initial evaluation must be reviewed and improved on a regular basis.

Identify Specific Visual Behaviors

A task analysis of the selected activity will determine the critical visual behaviors needed to perform the activity. The task analysis should review the necessary steps and state them in terms of specific visual behaviors (i.e., enter restaurant and *scan* for an empty seat, rather than enter restaurant and *find* an empty seat). Once the specific step(s) and skill(s) and the discrepancies between the student's abilities and the demands of the step have been identified, the vision specialist can determine how to intervene within the activity (i.e., what changes, instruction, and/or adaptations need to occur to enhance the individual's ability to successfully complete the activity).

Develop Techniques to Teach the Behavior(s)

Intervention requires a systematic strategy that provides specific guidelines to the teacher and directly relates to the correct or incorrect response of the student. To ensure consistent responding, the vision specialist will need to consider the motivation of the student. Activities should be selected that are age-appropriate, meaningful, and encourage student participation. Physically manipulating the student's head is intrusive and may not produce the desired response. Accentuating the visual characteristics of the task is the preferable way to draw visual attention to it. Illuminating the object requiring visual attention with a flashlight or penlight or a shift of gaze may be effective (Goetz & Gee, 1987b). A flashlight beam directed at a reflective spoon may help draw the child's visual attention to the spoon and enhance eye-hand coordination and purposeful use of vision while eating. Highlighting materials by colored borders, contrasting backgrounds, enlarged materials, or fluorescent paints can increase the probability that a student's visual attention will be drawn to the task. Auditory references (e.g., tapping a cup on the table to orient attending) may elicit the desired visual behavior also. Moving the object or person closer to the student is one option. Presenting the stimuli within different visual fields and planes is also another possible strategy. Providing partial assistance with the step until visual responses are consistent will help the student learn the sequence of the behaviors involved in the task. Requiring a particular response before an activity can be continued (e.g., making a choice by a shift of gaze) would make the activity contingent on the visual behavior. Whatever option(s) is chosen, gradually discontinuing the intervention as soon as possible should always be part of the overall goal.

Teach Other Direct Service Providers to Implement the Program

Direct service providers (teachers, parents, paraprofessionals) need to be aware of the visual components, how they are incorporated into the student's educational program, and what techniques are being used to assist the student in acquiring the skill. Large caseloads make it impossible for vision specialists to provide constant direct intervention; therefore, the consultative aspect of their role becomes imperative. As a member of the educational team, the vision specialist develops the necessary specific intervention strategies and instructs direct service providers in how to implement the strategies.

Monitor the Effectiveness

The vision specialist monitors the effectiveness of implementation. Monitoring includes providing information on which to base revision of the prescribed interventions and adjusting the procedures to enhance the student's skills.

Lack of progress signals the need to alter the strategies. Data are needed to determine if the program is effective or if changes are needed (Snell & Zirpoli, 1987; White, 1985). Collecting data on progress in the acquisition and use of visual skills and on the effectiveness of intervention strategies is an integral component of any adaptive or alternative instructional program.

An Example of Integrated and Contextual Training of Vision Use

The following case study is an example of structuring integrated and contextual vision use training. The vision specialist assumes primary responsibility for ensuring that the program is incorporated into the student's functional program.

No absolute rule exists for determining when a visual skill should be taught, as opposed to developing an adaptation or eliminating a specific visual step in the sequence. The decision-making process itself requires that each individual student, activity, and environment be evaluated on a situational basis.

Student. Kelly is a seventeen-year-old female with profound mental disabilities. She is nonverbal and nonambulatory and has limited behavioral responses. Her teacher reports that she is motivated by objects that vibrate, music, and eating certain foods. An opthalmologist diagnosed Kelly as cortically blind with no visual responses observed. Kelly has attended a public high school for approximately one year and receives her education in a self-contained classroom, the general school environment, and integrated community settings. Previously, Kelly had lived in a state institution since birth.

Based on institutional records, her program initially was designed under the assumption that she was totally blind. Because Kelly appeared to have some peripheral vision, indicated by her occasionally turning her head in response to visual stimuli, a decision was made to explore the possibility of improving her visual skills. An out-of-context assessment of Kelly's visual responses supported the assumption that Kelly had specific, though limited, visual skills.

Assuming functional peripheral vision, the critical visual steps in Kelly's scheduled activities were analyzed. Effective use of her remaining vision might allow Kelly to participate more independently in certain tasks and activities. The vision specialist identified steps involving visual skills and edited her program accordingly.

The following examples from Kelly's daily schedule are provided to demonstrate the decision making process:

Recreational skill: Playing the autoharp. Kelly will play the autoharp without assistance and apparently enjoys playing when she is alone or in the company of her nondisabled peers. If the harp is placed directly in front of her, Kelly will independently reach out to touch its surface. If on the initial try she does not come in contact with the strings, she stops trying to find them. To play the autoharp, Kelly must search (either tactually or visually) until she successfully finds the strings and produces sounds. If she is unsuccessful in touching the strings, she needs to search tactually. This requires physical assistance by a person, yet Kelly resists this type of intervention. The educational team decided that teaching Kelly to visually search the harp's surface would enable her to locate the strings without the physical intervention that she seemed to find aversive. Because Kelly had not demonstrated the ability to orientate visually in the past, an intervention to hold and direct Kelly's attention was necessary. An 8-inch fluorescent yellow and black bull's eye was placed beneath the strings of the harp to encourge Kelly to look at the harp. Initially, a flashlight beam was focused on this pattern to direct Kelly's attention to the strings. On the first trial, Kelly visually directed her attention to the target, but still required a slight physical prompt to her elbow before she would reach out and play the harp. Currently, a peer uses the flashlight to draw Kelly's attention to the target, and no physical prompting is necessary.

The size of the bull's eye is now being reduced. The vision objective is to have Kelly use her remaining sight to orient and reach independently for the strings of her harp. The intervention strategy to teach these skills requires the use of a bull's eye and flashlight as props to assist Kelly to use her vision more effectively. The degree and speed with which the instructional materials can be withdrawn depend on the level of success that Kelly is able to achieve and maintain. The overall goal is to help Kelly use the harp without the continual support of an assisting person. For Kelly, learning to use her remaining vision to achieve the critical step of locating the harp's strings increased her independent participation in this recreational activity. Had Kelly been successful at tactually locating the harp's strings, the decision to teach the visual skill of locating would probably not have been made.

While vision use might allow her to locate the harp strings more efficiently, it is not essential to playing the harp. Determining whether a vision skill should be taught needs to be based on more than the actual existence of a deficit in a skill area. Activities are chosen because they are meaningful, functional, and purposeful. Visual skills are taught if they are necessary to attain the desired goal. The individual's performance of a given activity will determine if teaching vision use would be beneficial for that individual.

Domestic skill: Making a fruit drink. At home, Kelly is not required to use her vision to transfer fruit slices from a bowl to a blender because she completes the task successfully and independently without visually orienting. She is sufficiently motivated by the task to keep her attention on it. Vision use *is* required to choose the fruits to be added to the blender (shift of gaze) and to press the necessary button on the blender (visually localize).

In both cases instructional materials (i.e., colored borders outlining available choices, yellow paint on blender buttons) highlight and direct Kelly's visual attention to materials crucial to the overall completion of the activity. If possible, these materials should be removed; but for some individuals their use may become a necessary and permanent adaptation.

Vocational skill: Sealing packages. At her job training site (a community hospital), an adaptation was constructed that incorporated a bright yellow surface to gain her visual attention and a vibrator for tactile feedback that activated a switch used to seal packages of surgical equipment. The only visual skill required to participate successfully in this particular job is visually locating the switch and coordinating eye-hand movements. Kelly is not motivated by the job, but the activity is essential for vocational placement. The visual and tactile adaptations are necessary to motivate Kelly to perform successfully and independently.

Community skill: Eating at a restaurant. As part of her community programming, Kelly selects food items at a fast-food restaurant before making a purchase. Food choice requires the visual skill of shifting gaze and is similar to the procedure used to select a fruit while making a snack. The decision was made to teach Kelly to visually orient to her drink selection so that she can independently reach for and grasp a container holding a preferred drink.

The instructional intervention in this sequence targets the development of basic visual skills required to locate and coordinate eye-hand movements to successfully attain a desired item. The milkshake is held at eye level and then slowly lowered to her tray until she visually locates, reaches for, and grasps the cup.

Summary

This paper has emphasized the consulting role for the vision specialist to integrate the training in visual skills into functional activities for the student with visual and multiple disabilities. Because these students may not transfer skills to activities where the skills are required (Horner et al., 1986; Stokes & Baer, 1977), specialists need to incorporate their specific intervention strategies within activity sequences that occur in natural environments. The team analyzes and determines the critical activities for the student. Steps are then isolated based on the behaviors required. Teaching the needed skill or adapting the step will change the student's inability to perform the step independently. The unique needs and abilities of each student require an individualized and functional approach to the teaching of vision use rather than the more traditional stimulation of vision in isolated activities and environments.

For the vision specialist this approach involves identifying the steps within activities that require vision, assessing the student's present level of vision use within context, targeting specific visual behaviors for intervention, developing teaching techniques and/or adaptations to help the student complete the step within the activity, teaching these techniques to other direct service providers, and collecting data to evaluate the strategies for teaching the skills. The vision specialist does not assume full responsibility for the direct teaching of each visual skill. Rather, the principal role for this specialist is in evaluating visual behaviors, developing teaching strategies, suggesting adaptations to enhance visual functioning, and monitoring the intervention program.

By incorporating the use of visual skills into individualized functional daily activities, the vision specialist ensures ample opportunities for practice, reduces the need to rely on the transfer of skills, and contributes to a more holistic educational program for the student. Such an approach to service delivery also makes efficient use of a limited number of certified vision teachers while ensuring practical support to individual students in need of such intervention.

REFERENCES

Barraga, N. (1986). Sensory perceptual development. In G. Scholl (Ed.), *Foundations of education for blind and visually handicapped children and youth* (pp. 83–98). New York: American Foundation for the Blind.

Brown, L., Nisbet, J., Ford, A., Sweet, M., Shiraga, B., York, J., & Loomis, R. (1983). The critical need for nonschool instruction in education programs for severely handicapped students. *Journal of the Association for the Severely Handicapped, 8*(3), 71–77.

Brown, L., Shiraga, B., York, J., Zanella, K., & Rogan, P. (1984). Ecological inventory strategies for students with severe intellectual disabilities. *Educational Programs for Students with Severe Intellectual Disabilities.* University of Wisconsin at Madison and Madison Metropolitan School District, Vol. XIV, 45–47.

Erin, J. (1988). The teacher-consultant. *Education of the Visually Handicapped, 20*(2), 57–64.

Ficociello, C. (1976). *Observing visual functioning in deaf-blind children.* Visual Assessment Kit. South Central Regional Center for Deaf-Blind, Dallas, TX.

Goetz, L., & Gee, K. (1987a). Functional vision programming: A model for teaching visual behaviors in natural contexts. In L. Goetz, D. Guess, & K. Stremel-Campbell (Eds.), *Innovative program design for individuals with dual sensory impairments* (pp. 77–98). Baltimore: Paul H. Brookes.

Goetz, L., & Gee, K. (1987b). Teaching visual attention in functional contexts: Acquisition and generalization of complex visual motor skills. *Journal of Visual Impairment & Blindness, 81*(3), 115–117.

Hatlen, P., & Goetz, L. (1981). Establishing generalized visual functioning in severely handicapped students (USOE Grant #G00830032). Field initiated research proposal.

Horner, R., McDonnell, J., & Bellamy, T. (1986). Teaching generalized skills: General case instruction in simulation and community settings. In R. Horner, L. Meyer, & H. D. Fredericks (Eds.), *Education of learners with severe handicaps: Exemplary service strategies* (pp. 289–314). Baltimore: Paul H. Brookes.

Idol, L., Paolucci-Whitcomb, P., & Nevin, A. (1986). *Collaborative Consultation.* Rockville, MD: Aspen.

Jose, R. (1983). *Understanding low vision.* New York: American Foundation for the Blind.

Jose, R., Smith, A., & Shane, K. (1980). Evaluating and stimulating vision in the multiply impaired. *Journal of Visual Impairment & Blindness, 74*(1), 2–8.

Langley, B., & DuBose, R. (1976). Functional vision screening for severely handicapped children. *New Outlook, 70*(8), 346–350.

Lunderwold, D., Lewin, L., & Irwin, L. (1987). Rehabilitation of visual impairments: A critical review. *Clinical Psychology, 7,* 169–185.

Piaget, J., & Inhelder, B. (1969). *The psychology of the child.* New York: Basic Books.

Potenski, D. (1983). Use of black light in training retarded, multiply handicapped, deaf-blind children, *Journal of Visual Impairment & Blindness, 77*(7), 347–348.

Snell, M., & Zirpoli, T. (1987). Intervention strategies. In M. Snell (Ed.), *Systematic instruction of persons with severe handicaps* (3rd ed.) (pp. 110–150). Columbus, OH: Charles E. Merrill.

Spungin, S., & Taylor, J. (1986). The teacher. In G. Scholl (Ed.), *Foundations of education for blind and visually handicapped children and youth* (pp. 255–264). New York: American Foundation for the Blind.

Stokes, T. F., & Baer, D. M. (1977). An implicit technology of generalization. *Journal of Applied Behavior Analysis, 10,* 349–367.

Utley, B., Duncan, D., Strain, P., & Scanlon, L. (1983). Effects of contingent and noncontingent vision stimulation on visual fixation in multiply handicapped children. *Journal of the Association for Persons with Severe Handicaps, 8,* 29–42.

White, O. (1985). The evaluation of severely mentally retarded population. In D. Bricker & J. Filler (Eds.), *Severe mental retardation: From theory to practice.* (pp. 161–184). Reston, VA: Council for Exceptional Children.

June Downing is director of the teacher training program in multiple handicaps at the University of Arizona in Tucson. *Brent Bailey* is an orientation and mobility specialist working with children with multiple and visual handicaps in the Madison Metropolitan School District in Madison, Wisconsin.

Concepts and Issues Related to Choice-Making and Autonomy Among Persons with Severe Disabilities[1]

Doug Guess, Holly Anne Benson, and Ellin Siegel-Causey

Author Information
Doug Guess, Professor, Department of Special Education, University of Kansas.

Holly Anne Benson, Doctoral Student, Department of Special Education, University of Kansas.

Ellin Siegel-Causey, Doctoral Student, Department of Special Education, University of Kansas.

Article Descriptors
preference; choice; decision-making; autonomy.

This paper discusses issues related to concepts of preferences and choice-making among persons with severe disabilities. Included are suggestions for acknowledging preferences, teaching choice as a decision-making process, and the broader implications of choice-making among persons with severe handicaps as an expression of personal autonomy and dignity. Directions for future research are discussed.

For most persons the ability and opportunity to make choices and decisions is an important and cherished component of their lives. The opportunity to make choices reflects favorably on one's perceived independence, dignity, and self-worth. Expressions of free choice are not only highly valued by our society, but are also protected and encouraged. According to the published literature, however, opportunities to make choices, decisions, and express preferences are conspicuously absent from educational programs for persons who are handicapped (Holvoet et al., 1983), particularly for those who experience severe handicaps. Despite this fact, choice-making among learners with severe disabilities continues to be an area that receives relatively little attention from practitioners and researchers in the field of special education (Guess & Siegel-Causey, 1985; Guess & Helmstetter, in press).

The purpose of this article is to first discuss, briefly, some reasons why choice-making has received relatively little attention in the education and treatment of persons with severe handicaps and, second, to provide a conceptual approach that will direct attention to this area as an important component of future practices. The conceptual approach will include some practical suggestions for teachers of learners with severe handicaps, and will identify areas of analysis for researchers who may be interested in teaching choice-making skills.

Turnbull and Turnbull (in press) point out that independent functioning among persons with handicapping conditions requires access to opportunities in life as well as the capacity to participate in those opportunities. They suggest that the act of choosing how to live one's life is the "catalytic trigger" of independence.

The position of Turnbull and Turnbull is shared by others (Shevin & Klein, 1984; Zeph, 1984) who acknowledge the importance of choice-making among persons with severe disabilities. Nevertheless, there exists among many practitioners and professionals the belief that persons with severe disabilities are not capable of making choices or decisions—or at least the kinds of choices that attending adults would perceive to be in the best interest of the person with a handicapping condition. Indeed, the educational and instructional technology used with learners who have severe handicaps has historically been predicated on a deviancy model wherein educators and other service providers assume to know what will enable the recipients of these efforts to better function in our society. Guess (1984) has referred to current educational approaches with learners who have severe handicaps as the "Let's-fix-it" model, which is primarily oriented toward identifying and teaching deficit skills or remediating perceived deviant behavior.

In the "Let's-fix-it" model instructional objectives are selected for the learner by caregivers, educators, and other service providers. The instructional format is highly structured, carefully controlled, and systematically implemented. Allowing the learner some exercise of choice over lesson content or instructional methodology is not consistent with the model. As pointed out by Guess and Siegel-Causey (1985), "Our perceptions of severely handicapped students, partly as a result of the controlling technology we use in their education and treatment, have diminished our ability to see them as individuals capable of even making a choice, let alone the right choice" (p. 236).

Another issue that mitigates against teaching or allowing choice- and decision-making is the use by some persons of "worst scenario" examples. Following a recent presentation on the topic of choice, one of the authors was confronted by a highly respected professional person in the field of special education who argued that choice-making among persons with severe handicaps is not a viable option. His position centered on an aggressive client who, given the opportunity, would "choose to hit him (the professional person) in the face." It is, of course, easy to identify one or more persons with severe handicaps who, given the opportunity, would make poor choices that might well jeopardize the safety and well-being of themselves or others. It is equally easy, however, to similarly identify nonhandicapped members of our society who have chosen to behave in less than desirable ways. Choice- and decision-making involve responsible actions and the capacity to evaluate one's decisions, as pointed out by Turnbull and Turnbull (in press). Necessarily, the act of choosing, and allowing persons with handicaps to make choices and to express preferences, carries with it a certain element of risk. Yet, this is what personal autonomy is all about, and persons with handicapping conditions have the same right as others to acquire autonomy. They need to learn, as do persons who are not handicapped, that wrong choices can sometimes have unpleasant consequences.

Importantly, persons with severe handicaps must also learn to take individual responsibility when their actions place others at risk. They need to experience the consequences imposed by society when one's behavior jeopardizes the well-being of other members of the community. To deny persons with mentally handicapping conditions the opportunity to make choices based upon the possibility of future inappropriate actions is inconsistent with their rights to be fully participating members of our society. This latter issue is complicated further by the possibility that denial of the opportunity to choose might, itself, precipitate inappropriate behavior towards others. (This will be discussed more fully in a later section.)

Definitions and Attributes

For persons with severe handicaps, variations in developmental achievements and chronological ages indicate a continuum of abilities to understand and express preferences and the decision-making processes required for choice-making. For purposes of practical application, it is useful to categorize levels of preference and choice that may be identified as educational objectives and which are amenable to intervention efforts. It is recognized that attempts to categorize various levels of choice are somewhat arbitrary and reflect, to a great extent, an effort to combine suggestions for instruction with some broader philosophical issues that pertain to personal autonomy. The three categories presented include: a) preferences; b) choice as a decision-making process; and c) choice as an expression of autonomy and dignity.

Preferences

Webster's New Collegiate Dictionary (1981) defines preference as including the "power or opportunity of choosing." Displaying a preference includes three important variables: one's propensity (liking) towards something; one's say (choice) about that item or occurrence; and/or a recognition that options exist. For example, one exhibits preference by turning off the morning alarm and sleeping 5 minutes more (choice); by having toast with peanut butter rather than jelly (liking); or choosing to have breakfast at home rather than stopping at the local fast food restaurant (options). Preferences are exerted by most persons within the composition of one's culture, family background, education, and lifestyle. Displaying preferences is an important aspect of being human, and should be acknowledged among persons with severe handicaps. As discussed by Bogdan and Taylor (1982), however, the use of labels tends to focus attention on the disability rather than recognizing that the person with a disability is simply another person with the same emotions, needs, and interests as other persons. "It (labeling) prevents us from seeing and treating the people so defined as human beings with feelings, understandings, and needs. . .we lose the ability. . .to see the world from their point of view" (p. 222).

Responsiveness to Preferences.

Many children with severe handicaps may be nonverbal and display abnormal reflex patterns and muscle tone that frequently interferes with their ability to communicate clearly with others. Two important aspects of their communication are the opportunity for utilizing nonverbal signals to display preferences and the responsiveness of others to the potential communicative nature of nonverbal behaviors. These conditions are similar to the normal development of communication in infancy which is characterized by nonverbal and primarily reflexive motor behaviors. A brief description of early infant interaction may aid the discussion.

What are the variables that contribute to the recognition of nonverbal behaviors as communicative in nature? How might nonverbal behaviors be incorporated into preference (and choice) responses?

During exchanges with caregivers, infants can initiate, maintain, terminate, and avoid interactions (Stern, 1977; Trevarthen, 1977). These early interactions are essentially based on the infant's eye movements, facial expression, vocal sounds, and body movements. These nonverbal behaviors are often accepted by the caregiver as the infant's expression of preferences and form an integral part of communication development. How does this interaction pattern develop into communication?

When interacting with infants, caregivers ". . .make the assumption that the infant is attempting some form of meaningful dialogue, and out of this assumption the communication of shared meanings begins to take place" (Newson, 1979, p. 208). From birth, caregivers interpret the behavior of infants as containing wishes, intentions, and feelings. Through constant monitoring, the caregiver interprets the infant's nonverbal signals as communicative in nature. In normal infant interaction, "over and over again, events which are quite accidental and beyond the control of either mother or child, are endowed with significance because of either the way the mother reacts towards the child in light of the event or its effect upon him" (Newson, 1979, p. 212).

Those working with children displaying severe handicaps may need to encourage the use of early prelinguistic behaviors. The communication mode that the child with severe handicaps displays must be recognized, expanded, and integrated into interactions. Service providers interacting with children having severe handicaps must be sensitive to the signals expressed in the same manner that caregivers recognize and respond to similar signals displayed by infants during interactions.

How might nonverbal signals of the child with severe handicaps develop into a mode for communicating preference? The child with severe handicaps may exhibit preferences from the first days of life. He or she may be very active in a dimly lit room and very passive when the same room is very bright. When put in a seated position, the child's arms may pull back towards the chest and a grimace appear on his or her face. This may be an indication of tight muscle tone and a special need to be positioned differently—all building into a preference for one type of position over another. Other nonverbal behaviors may indicate preferences for kinds of food, speed of being fed, temperature of foods, and so forth. It is common for caregivers and service providers to be sensitive to the basic needs of food, comfort, shelter, and the like, and to respond to nonverbal displays as indications of the child's preference behavior within these basic contexts of daily living.

However, it is uncommon that such basic preferences are considered in the context of other communicative exchanges.

As stated previously, the communication mode displayed by the child with severe disabilities must be incorporated into interactions. The mode may be speech, but often is sign language, a communication device, gesturing, eye gazing, and so forth. In the initial stages of assisting a child in building a communication mode, one should seek to incorporate personal preferences. For example, this might involve allowing the child to select what bite of food to receive next, whether to wear jeans or cords, and whether to look at a book or play outside. Initially the child may not fully comprehend that his or her nonverbal signals can control the responses of caregivers and can communicate preferences. This is similar to the way that accidental movement patterns of infants can be interpreted with significance by the caregiver and later recognized and intentionally repeated by the infant. By providing consistent responses to the child's nonverbal behaviors and opportunities for utilizing these behaviors in many interactions and environments, a systematic mode for communication of preferences may become meaningful for the child. At some point in time the child may realize "when I look at the item presented, that is the one Mom keeps giving me" or "when I close my mouth Sara takes that scratchy toy away from me but when I smile she brings it back out again."

From an educational perspective, it is important that caregivers and service providers are sensitive to, and recognize, the exhibition of preferences through modes of communication that may or may not include talking. The ability to exhibit preferences begins at the early nonverbal levels of development as caregivers recognize the communication modes of body movements, facial expression, gestures, and the like. These preferences can be built into patterns of interaction that incorporate choice across a variety of daily routines and interactions.

Choice as a Decision-Making Process

The previous sections discussed the importance of identifying and using preferences in the educational programming of individuals with severe disabilities. This process is especially useful with individuals who have limited response repertoires and/or who have not yet developed the ability to make choices.

Choice, as a decision-making process, involves the expression of preferences. It also, however, implies the ability to actively select among two or more alternative conditions. Choosing thus becomes an act, in and of itself, and an indication of the ability to make a decision based upon prior experiences, present needs, and future goals.

Research on choice-making among nonhandicapped persons has shown that grade school students learned sight vocabulary words better when allowed to choose between group or individual instruction (Berk, 1976); and higher rates of working and equivalent learning rates were obtained among elementary age students when they were allowed to choose reinforcers (Hockstra, 1979), or decide how many problems would have to be completed correctly before being reinforced (Felixbrod & O'Leary, 1973).

A series of investigations were conducted at Virginia Polytechnical Institute (Monty & Perlmuter, 1975; Monty, Rosenberger, & Perlmuter, 1973; Perlmuter & Monty, 1973, 1977) to measure the effects of choice on the learning of adults. Among the results it was found that choosing either stimulus or response items enhanced learning, and allowing even limited choices was as effective in enhancing learning as was allowing the individual to choose all the stimuli or responses, if choice was provided early in the session.

Studies that have investigated choice-making among persons with handicapping conditions are limited in number. A study by Lovitt and Curtis (1969) showed that a 12-year-old child with severe emotional problems improved performance on academic tasks when allowed to determine his own criterion level. However, Alexander (1974) found that allowing adolescents with moderate mental retardation to choose their reinforcers, either for the entire session or for each trial, did not lead to higher levels of performance on discrimination or perseverance tasks.

An investigation by Holvoet et al. (1983) indicated a slight facilitative effect on the rate of learning and on correct performance when adolescents with severe disabilities were allowed limited choices of educational activities. It was also found that variation in task choice sometimes did not occur until later sessions. This latter observation supports research (Newhard, 1984) that even some adolescent age students with severe handicaps do not comprehend the concept of choice-making, and that this skill might need to be taught (cf. Wuerch & Voeltz, 1982).

From a practical perspective, choice-making opportunities for persons with severe disabilities have typically involved the selection of reinforcers by students, which are then used by attending adults to further control the instructional environment and the performance of the learner. This limited choice opportunity thus serves as the means for furthering the development of other educational goals (ends). This, of course, is compatible with the controlling technology that is often used extensively with learners who have severe handicaps and is consistent with older "efficiency" arguments to promote higher levels of task performance. There are, however, other opportunities in educational programming that would allow learners to make decisions that lead to a more personal level of choice-making skills and, hopefully, more independent functioning in the environment. This would include, for example, opportunities for learners to choose materials to work (or play) with, settings where learning is to take place, persons to be with, activities to engage in, and so on. These types of opportunities would allow the learner to become a more active participant in the educational process, while at the same time developing personal autonomy and dignity as separate educational goals (to be discussed in the next section).

In the absence of extensive data and research, one can only speculate on the development of decision-making skills among learners with severe disabilities. It seems likely, however, that teaching learners with severe disabilities to make decisions and choices will require extensive programming that should start at the preschool level, and extend throughout (and possibly beyond) the public school years.

The actual procedures for teaching choice- and decision-making skills offer a unique challenge to both curriculum designers and researchers. Considerations for teaching these skills include selection of response modes to express choices, the identification of age-appropriate areas where choices and decisions should be made, and the instructional procedures that could most effectively teach this concept. Wuerch and Voeltz (1982), for example, have included instruction on choice-making as an important component of their leisure skills training program for persons with severe disabilities. More recently, Guess and Helmstetter (in press) have included the teaching of choice as a basic instructional component of the Individualized Curriculum Sequencing model for students with severely handicapping conditions. In this model, choice-making is taught within the context of other naturally occurring activities during classroom educational programs and is perceived as an important IEP objective for students in the development of personal autonomy.

Zeph (1984) has presented a model that allows teachers of students with handicaps to incorporate choice-making as a process for arriving at curriculum decisions. Shevin (1984) has provided guidelines and suggestions for teaching choice-making in the classroom to students with severe handicaps. He also discusses the role of applied behavior analysis in fostering choice-making skills.

Choice as an Expression of Autonomy and Dignity

In the course of a day, most of us make hundreds, if not thousands, of choices. Some may be as insignificant as whether we will have yogurt or cereal for breakfast, while others may have broader implications such as whether or not to quit our job, buy a new car, or move to another city. Each choice we make is an expression of our personal autonomy—our freedom to define who we are and what we value. The opportunity to make choices provides us with power to determine, to a great extent, what happens to us on a moment-by-moment basis as well as over the span of our lives. To have the power to make choices taken away would, for many of us, be devastating if not unbearable.

The importance of experiencing a sense of control over one's environment is particularly emphasized in the literature dealing with the phenomenon of *learned helplessness*. Learned helplessness is thought to result from a belief that nothing that one does makes a difference (Seligman, 1975). Persons who experience helplessness characteristically see no relationship between actions and outcomes; their perception of their ability to change life circumstances is severely distorted; and they frequently manifest passivity, negative expectations, and tendencies to self-deprecation (Hooker, 1976). According to Seligman (1975), persons who are particularly susceptible to learned helplessness are those who are most prone to denial, or loss, of control. Included in Seligman's list of susceptible populations are: the elderly, the institutionalized (medical hospitals, mental hospitals, prisons, concentration camps), minorities such as Native Americans, blacks, and Mexican-Americans, and persons who suffer from extreme poverty, abuse, and overcrowding. Among other symptoms, persons who suffer from learned helplessness may experience a variety of debilitating effects including: loss of self-esteem, decreased ambition, emotional disturbance, chronic reactive depression, and even psychogenic death (Frankl, 1963; Hooker, 1976; Seligman, 1975).

What has all this to do with persons who experience severe handicaps? Persons with severe handicaps are probably one of the most vulnerable groups of persons at risk for having their choices limited by others and for experiencing learned helplessness. Persons who are unable to mobilize, bathe, toilet, dress themselves, and communicate their needs are dependent upon others for assistance and, in some cases, survival. Unfortunately, it is not uncommon for caregivers (e.g., parents, teachers, guardians, siblings, personal care attendants) who are attending to a person's physical needs to overlook some less obvious, but very important, personal and emotional needs. These needs may include: to learn to perform a task independently or semi-independently, to experience a sense of accomplishment, to feel in control of the situation by providing input and feedback, and to try (despite the risk of failure), and lastly to fail. Some caregivers might feel that to complete tasks for persons with disabilities is easier and faster than allowing them to do it for themselves; while others may have the attitude that the person already has enough problems coping with his or her disability. Regardless of what the underlying intention is, the result can be to overprotect, to encourage learned helplessness, and to deprive the individual of potentially valuable life experiences. The opportunity to experience the feelings of pride, pleasure, and self-esteem that accompany successful attempts at performing tasks is extremely important to the growth and development of all individuals. Perske (1981) comments on the effect that overprotection of persons with handicaps may have:

> Overprotection may appear on the surface to be kind, but it can really be evil. An oversupply can really smother people emotionally and strip them of their dignity. Overprotection can keep people from becoming all that they can become. Many of our best achievements came the hard way: we took risks, fell flat, suffered, picked ourselves up and tried again. Sometimes we made it and sometimes we did not. Even so, we were given the chance to try. Persons with handicaps need these chances, too. (p. 51)

The goal of treatment for learned helplessness, according to Seligman (1975), should be to expose the person to multiple experiences of control over, and predictability of, environmental events. For instance, Seligman believes that the helpless person should be given maximum control over all aspects of his or her daily life including: "...choice of omelets or scrambled eggs for breakfast, blue or red curtains, going to the movies on Wednesdays or Thursdays, whether to wake up early or sleep late" (p. 183). According to Seligman, this level of control may result in longer life spans and greater happiness. Another suggested therapeutic intervention strategy for treating persons with learned helplessness entails assisting the person to realistically assess the parameters of a situation, generate alternatives for action, and determine probable outcomes of these actions (Aguilera & Messick, 1974; Hooker, 1976). Compare the above mentioned approaches with the approaches that are commonly taken with persons with severe handicaps who manifest very similar symptoms.

When persons with severe disabilities become nonresponsive, the assumption is generally made that the reinforcer is no longer salient. At that point teachers or other professionals begin the search for different, effective rewards that will consistently bring and maintain the individual's behavior under control. Seldom, if ever, is the person with the handicapping condition involved in the process of determining how their behavior, or the behavior of those around them, will be modified. The end result is more control for the caregivers and less control for the person being cared for. Ironically persons with handicaps are being treated with the very same "medicine" that made them "ill" in the first place—lack of control over their lives and circumstances.

As much as possible, persons with severe handicaps need to have the events in their day arranged to maximize contingent experiences. Contingent experiences refer to environmental events, both positive and negative, that are directly affected and controlled by the individual. A number of studies in the early 1970s examined the effects of contingent experiences upon learning in infants (Finkelstein & Ramey, 1976; Watson, 1971; Watson & Ramey, 1972). It was concluded in each of these studies that contingent experiences produce a "learning-to-learn" phenomenon and that infants who are exposed to contingent experiences may become more efficient and competent learners than infants who are not (Snell, 1978). Persons with severe handicaps need exposure to contingent experiences so as to enhance their learning potential as well as to prevent, or in some cases overcome, depression and helplessness. This means building independence, choice, and control into daily activities and routines that are largely characterized by dependence on others. Every available opportunity to express preference, choice, and dominance needs to be identified and capitalized on. Elizabeth Boggs (1978), a mother of a son with severe handicaps, recognizes how important this is:

> . . .rather than trying to create a normal environment for my son, I try to think of how the world must look from his point of view, and what kind of environment would not only minimize his boredom and loneliness but enhance his sense of dominance. . . (p. 62)

Outcome Measures and Research Directions

As noted earlier in this article, the issues of preferences, choices, and personal autonomy have received little attention in the field of special education, and especially in the area of severe handicaps. Ideologically, attention to these issues represents a departure from existing practices and is likely to be perceived by some persons as threatening to current state-of-the-art technology. Our position is that the ability and opportunity to express preferences, make decisions, and exercise choices are, in themselves, invaluable contributions to adaptive behavior and should be an integral component of the education of persons with severe handicaps. Moreover, it is our position that consistent opportunities to choose and express preferences might well have a positive impact on the learning process (as a means) as well as on the more long term personal development of persons with severe handicaps (as an end result).

As part of the educational process with learners who have severe disabilities, the options to express choice need to be researched as a possible catalyst to classroom (and home) instructional endeavors. Within this context, choice in instructional environments is perceived as an independent variable with diverse manifestations: e.g., choice of instructional materials, place of instruction, tasks to be learned, and so forth. Dependent or outcome measures are identified as consistent with existing practices such as rate of acquisi-

tion, generalization, and maintenance of the learned skill over time. The latter two measures (generalization and maintenance) would appear to be especially deserving of investigation given their limited occurrences in existing instructional endeavors. The central question is whether or not providing learners with severe handicaps the opportunity to participate more fully in their educational program (via choice-making) will increase the acquisition and long term use of functional skills in multiple environments.

A second, and certainly more difficult, outcome measure for researchers pertains to the impact of choice- and decision-making on the personal growth and development of persons with severe handicaps. The previous section on personal autonomy and dignity has pointed to some devastating outcomes when opportunities for individuals to choose are severely restricted. For persons with severe handicaps, the opportunities to choose and make decisions are often limited due to perceptions by others of their incompetence, assumptions of the technology used in their educational programming, and the environments in which many of them reside. Thus, the appropriate research questions center on what happens to a special population of individuals (persons with severe handicaps) when their opportunities to express preferences and choices are first acknowledged, and then provided (or taught).

Independent variables for this type of research would include a number of complex and interrelated factors such as: assessments of the extent to which choices and decision-making opportunities are provided across and within environments (and settings in those environments); the nature and conceptual bases of training programs and curricula used with persons who are severely handicapped; and the personal attitudes towards choice-making (and autonomy) by those caregivers and instructors who provide the training. Preliminary findings from an ongoing project at the University of Kansas, for example, have shown that few parents of adolescent students labeled severely or moderately handicapped have even considered choice- and decision-making as viable options for their children. Does this finding reflect the disability level of their children? Or, is this also an outcome of professional attitudes and practices that, over the years, have failed to acknowledge choice- and decision-making as important educational outcomes for persons who have severe disabilities?

Dependent or outcome measures of the impact of allowing choice- and decision-making on the personal growth and development of persons with severe handicaps provides an even greater challenge to researchers. This is due to the more qualitative types of variables that might be measured, such as indices of self-satisfaction, perceived competence by others, self-initiated behavior, and success in community living.

All of these indices relate directly, or indirectly, to concepts of self-esteem, autonomy, and other quality of life factors. The use of qualitative analytic techniques would be useful for investigations of this nature. As discussed by Switzky and Haywood (1985), "qualitative analytic techniques focus on the perceived world views of the retarded persons themselves in the context of their past and present situations" (p. 270).

Qualitative research techniques have been used to study the perception of persons with mental retardation in the areas of sexuality (Heshusius, 1982) and community adjustment (Taylor & Bogdan, 1981). The use of these research techniques to investigate choice- and decision-making opportunities would appear to be a viable extension of the methodology.

References

Aguilera, D., & Messick, J. (1974). *Crisis intervention: Theory and methodology.* St. Louis, MO: C. V. Mosby.

Alexander, D. (1974). Comparison for mental retardates of non-choice, initial-choice, and idiosyncratic-choice reward strategies. *Psychological Reports, 35,* 135–145.

Berk, R. A. (1976). Effects of choice of instructional methods on verbal learning tasks. *Psychological Reports, 38,* 867–870.

Bogdan, R., & Taylor, S. (1982). *Inside out. The social meaning of mental retardation.* Toronto: University of Toronto Press.

Boggs, E. M. (1978). Who is putting whose head in the sand or in the clouds as the case may be? In A. P. Turnbull & H. R. Turnbull (Eds.), *Parents speak out* (pp. 50–68). Columbus, OH: Charles E. Merrill.

Felixbrod, J. J., & O'Leary, K. D. (1973). Effects of reinforcement on children's academic behavior as a function of self-determined and externally imposed contingencies. *Journal of Applied Behavior Analysis, 6,* 241–250.

Finkelstein, N. W., & Ramey, C. T. (1976). *Learning to control the environment in infancy.* Unpublished manuscript, University of North Carolina, Chapel Hill.

Frankl, V. (1963). *Man's search for meaning: An introduction to logotherapy.* Boston: Beacon.

Guess, D. (1984, April). *Allowing the child greater participation in the educational process.* Paper presented at the Fifth Annual Montana Symposium, Early Childhood and the Exceptional Child, Billings, MT.

Guess, D., & Helmstetter, E. (in press). Skill cluster instruction and the Individualized Curriculum Sequencing model. In R. Horner, L. Meyer, & H. D. Fredericks (Eds.), *Education of learners with severe handicaps: Exemplary service strategies.* Baltimore: Paul H. Brookes.

Guess, D., & Siegel-Causey, E. (1985). Behavioral control and education of severely handicapped students: Who's doing what to whom? And why? In D. Bricker & J. Filler (Eds.) *Severe mental retardation: From theory to practice* (pp. 230–244). Reston, VA: The Council for Exceptional Children.

Heshusius, L. (1982). Sexuality, intimacy, and persons we label mentally retarded: What they think—what we think. *Mental Retardation, 20,* 164–168.

Hockstra, C. M. (1979). The effects of choice of consequences and procedures on preschool children's rate of working arithmetic problems. (Doctoral dissertation, Washington State University, 1978). *Dissertation Abstracts International, 39*(8-B), 4033–4034.

Holvoet, J., Brewer, M., Mulligan, M., Guess, D., Helmstetter, E., & Riggs, P. (1983). *Influence of activity choice on learning among adolescent students with severe handicaps.* Unpublished manuscript, University of Kansas, Lawrence.

Hooker, C. E. (1976). Learned helplessness. *Social Work, 21*(3), 194–198.

Lovitt, T. C., & Curtis, K. (1969). Academic response rate as a function of teacher and self-imposed contingencies. *Journal of Applied Behavior Analysis, 2,* 49–53.

Monty, R. A., & Perlmuter, L. C. (1975). Persistence of the effects of choice on paired associate learning. *Memory and Cognition, 3,* 183–187.

Monty, R. A., Rosenberger, M. A., & Perlmuter, L. C. (1973). Amount and locus of choice as sources of motivation in paired-associate learning. *Journal of Experimental Psychology, 97,* 16–21.

Newhard, M. (1984). *Effect of student choice of materials on learning and stereotypic and affective behavior.* Unpublished master's thesis, University of Kansas, Lawrence, KS.

Newson, J. (1979). The growth of shared understanding between infant and caregiver. In M. Bullowa (Ed.), *Before speech: The beginning of interpersonal communication* (pp. 207–222). London: Cambridge University Press.

Perlmuter, L. C., & Monty, R. A. (1973). Effect of choice of stimulus on paired-associate learning. *Journal of Experimental Psychology, 99,* 120–123.

Perlmuter, L. C., & Monty, R. A. (1977). The importance of perceived control: Fact or fantasy. *American Scientist, 65,* 759–765.

Perske, R. (1981). *Hope for the families: New directions for parents of persons with retardation or other disabilities.* Nashville, TN: Abingdon.

Seligman, M. (1975). *Helplessness: On depression, development, and death.* San Francisco: W. H. Freeman.

Shevin, M. (1984, Nov.), *Choice-making in the classroom.* Paper presented at the Eleventh Annual Conference of the Association for Persons with Severe Handicaps, Chicago.

Shevin, M., & Klein, N. K. (1984). The importance of choice-making skills for students with severe disabilities. *Journal of the Association for Persons with Severe Handicaps, 9*(3), 159–166.

Snell, M. E. (1978). *Systematic instruction of the moderately and severely handicapped.* Columbus: Charles E. Merrill.

Stern, D. (1977). *The first relationship: Infant and mother.* Cambridge, MA: Harvard University Press.

Switzky, H., & Haywood, H. E. (1985). Perspectives on methodological and research issues concerning severely mentally retarded persons. In D. Bricker & J. Filler (Eds.) *Severe mental retardation: From theory to practice* (pp. 264–284). Reston, VA: Division on Mental Retardation, Council for Exceptional Children.

Taylor, S., & Bogdan, R. (1981). A qualitative approach to the study of community adjustment. In R. Bruininks, C. Meyers, B. Sigford, & K. C. Lakin (Eds.), *Deinstitutionalization and community adjustment of mentally retarded people* (pp. 71–81). Monograph Number 4. Washington, D.C.: American Association on Mental Deficiency.

Trevarthen, C. (1977). Descriptive analysis of infant communicative behavior. In H. R. Schaffer (Ed.), *Studies in mother infant interaction* (pp. 227–270). London: Academic Press.

Turnbull, A. P., & Turnbull, R. (in press). Developing independence. *The Journal of Adolescent Health Care* (Symposium Edition on "Youth with Disabilities: The Transition Years").

Watson, J. S. (1971). Cognitive-perceptual development in infancy. Settings for the seventies. *Merrill-Palmer Quarterly, 17,* 139–152.

Watson, J. S., & Ramey, C. T. (1972). Reactions to response contingent stimulation in early infancy. *Merrill-Palmer Quarterly, 18,* 219–227.

Wuerch, B., & Voeltz, L. (1982). *Longitudinal leisure skills for severely handicapped learners.* Baltimore: Paul H. Brookes.

Zeph, L. (1984, Nov.). *The model of C.H.O.I.C.E.: A curriculum framework for incorporating choice making into programs serving students with severe handicaps.* Paper presented at the Eleventh Annual Conference of the Association for Persons with Severe Handicaps, Chicago.

Footnote

[1]Preparation of this manuscript was supported, in part, by a grant from the U.S. Office of Education, "Innovative Programs for Severely Handicapped Children: Parental Involvement—Severely Handicapped" (Grant #G008302983).

Teaching Students Who Are Deaf-Blind and Cognitively Disabled To Effectively Communicate Choices During Mealtime

by

Carole R. Gothelf
Director, Education Services
The Jewish Guild for the Blind

Daniel B. Crimmins
Director, Department of Psychology
Westchester Institute for Human Development
and New York Medical College Cedarwood Hall

Caren A. Mercer
Principal, Guild School
The Jewish Guild for the Blind

Patricia A. Finocchiaro
Coordinator, Day Treatment Program
The Jewish Guild for the Blind

Individuals who are deaf-blind and have a cognitive disability may not effectively communicate their desires and choices even when provided with the opportunity to do so, in part because of their frequently limited communication skills. The ability of these individuals to make choices may be further constrained by instructional staff and caregivers, who anticipate their wishes and make choices for them. These caregivers and instructional staff may be acting with only the best intentions for these individuals, perhaps in the belief that they are unable to make a meaningful choice. Often, however, these individuals have not been taught how to make a choice. For students who are deaf-blind and cognitively disabled to achieve valued life outcomes, it is essential that they are able to effectively communicate personal choices.

Given the essential nature of the ability to communicate choice and the potential barriers to choice-making, it is necessary to focus on teaching students who are deaf-blind and cognitively disabled the process of making meaningful choices and to develop a flexible curriculum in which they have opportunities to practice making choices within the context of their daily routines. Mealtime is ideal for this instruction. It naturally occurs on a consistent, daily basis, in school, at home and in community environments. The act of communicating what one wants to eat or drink and receiving what one has chosen results in natural consequences that are highly motivating, thus reinforcing the power of clear communication.

The table that follows offers a set of practical guidelines for teaching students who are deaf-blind and cognitively disabled to make choices during mealtimes. It is offered as an aid to instructional staff and caregivers to illustrate the ways in which a typical daily activity can be utilized to teach choice-making within the context of a natural routine. In addition, it has implications for how the skill can be increased in complexity as the student progresses. We offer this as an example that can be applied in other settings and activities, which include selecting something to do, choosing with whom to do it, choosing where to do it, choosing when to do i,t or choosing whether to do it at all (Brown & Gothelf, in preparation; Crimmins & Gothelf, in press).

Table 1

Choice-making Instruction		
Guiding Principle	**Example**	**Considerations**
People typically make choices in the environments in which the outcomes of their choice are available.	Choosing what to eat should take place where the student normally eats. Teaching choice-making in an artificial environment removes many of the naturally-occurring cues to the event.	Administrative policies and procedures should ensure that the choice-making process can take place. This may involve working with the cafeteria staff or revising lunch-time schedules.
The boundaries in which the choice-making activity takes place should be defined through the use of appropriate aids and cues. Providing boundaries minimizes the visual/motor and cognitive requirements of orienting and reaching.	A dycem placemat can be used to secure a cafeteria tray on a table, or on the lap tray of a student's wheel chair. A second dycem mat can be used to secure the plates and glasses on the tray. (Dycem is a non-slip plastic that is helpful in stabilizing objects on surfaces. It comes in reels or sheets that can be cut to size. It is portable, easily cleaned, inexpensive and available from adaptive aids catalogs).	If cafeteria trays are not available or necessary, the plates of food can be placed on a dycem mat directly on a table. For students with vision, the color of the dycem should be selected to provide contrast with the tray or table and the plates.
Individual preferences play an important role in enhancing motivation for the activity.	The student is presented with two entree samples, one at a time. The items from which a student is choosing should be two things which he or she is likely to want to eat.	Administrators should work with cafeteria staff to ensure that appropriate alternatives are made available. (E.g., if two hot meals are not available, a choice between a hot meal and sandwich, or between two sandwiches should be substituted.) Be aware that food preferences are influenced by a student's cultural and family background.
The student is made aware of the food through tactile/kinesthetic cues (guided or paired movements between the teacher and the student), visual, verbal, gestural and object cues. The teacher must assess the conditions that facilitate comprehension (e.g., with gestures, without gestures, etc.).	For each sample of food, the student is moved through touching the plate, touching the food, smelling the food, and tasting the food. A staff member will say the name of the food, sign it, and shape the student's hands to sign the name of the food.	The student's receptive vocabulary may be limited. Natural routines should be maintained within the normal context of mealtime in order to help the student comprehend the expectancies for his or her behavior.
Choices should be presented consistently in order to reinforce the physical structure within which choosing occurs. Placing the choices in the same locations in relation to the student's body each time they are presented helps the student to anticipate where the sample is likely to be.	The first sample is presented on the student's left, tasted with the left hand, and then removed. The second sample is then presented on the student's right, tasted with the right hand, and then removed. Care must be taken to ensure that the individual is not always choosing the sample on the right or the sample on the left.	The student's ability to reach, grasp, and manipulate utensils or the food itself, may be influenced by poor muscle tone, stability, or coordination, as well as limited visual functioning. Generally, proper postural alignment can be attained through the use of adaptive positioning equipment. Grasping and manipulating utensils can be assisted through the use of adaptive aids such as special spoons, plates with lips, or slant trays. (Campbell, 1987).

Continued

| Table 1 continued | Choice-making Instruction | |

Guiding Principle	Example	Considerations
Establishing routines within instructional sequences enables the student to anticipate the next step and encourages self-initiated choice-making. A pause or time-delay in a sequence (hands in the lap) may serve as a prompt to the student to initiate an interaction or make a selection (Siegel-Causey & Ernst, 1989).	Both samples are then presented to the student. The student touches the left plate with the left hand, and the right plate with the right hand. As the student touches each sample, he or she is reminded of its name. The student is then directed to place both hands in his or her lap (using verbal and/or physical prompt as needed). The student is then instructed: *"It is time to pick what you want for lunch."* Language input should be provided at a level and in a mode that the student can comprehend.	If a student does not respond when the question is repeated, the teacher communicates: *"That's OK, if you don't want the meat or the rice, I'll ask you again soon."* Language input should be provided at a level and in a mode that the student can comprehend. The teacher should always return and provide the student with another opportunity and additional prompting if necessary.
Reliable communication of preference depends upon a foundation of consistent responses to the student's non-verbal behaviors. Non-verbal behaviors need to be acknowledged by the teacher on the assumption that the individual is attempting to communicate meaningful dialog. This provides a basis for communicating shared meanings (Guess, Benson, & Siegel-Causey, 1985; Williams, 1991).	The student chooses the desired food by touching one of the samples, by looking or facial gesture, by starting to eat, by vocal sounds and/or body movements, by signing or in any way indicating his or her preference.	If the student reaches for both, or neither, the teacher must repeat the previous procedure, and reinforce that the student must choose one sample. The teacher must acknowledge any form of communication. If the student repeatedly reaches for both, he should be given some of each for lunch.
Components of everyday routines should be utilized to establish correspondence between words and their meanings. Routines enable students to take an active part in the activity and to communicate with the teacher.	The staff signs *"finished"* for the undesired plate and moves the student through the sign *"finished"* and prompts the student to move the plate away.	Initially, the student may require the teacher to move his hands for him. Subsequently, the teacher and the student should cooperatively move their hands together, the student's hands riding on top of the teacher's. The teacher should pause in the pushing action, and allow the student to communicate a desire to continue by moving the teacher's hands.
In addition to establishing correspondence between words and their meanings, the process of systematically using routines in the choice-making process must be established.	The teacher signs *"eat"* and the name of the desired food, and prompts the student to do the same. This procedure must follow the previous one.	The teacher may choose other ways to communicate the same message, such as signing the student's name followed by the signs for *"wants to eat"* and the name of the food. Language input should be provided at a level and in a mode that the student can comprehend.
Contingent communicative behavior is reinforced by getting the requested item. The student communicates through an action or a signal to indicate his preference.	The student is served a full portion of the food that was selected.	The student must join the cafeteria line to obtain the full portion of food.

Table adapted from Gothelf, C.R., Crimmins, D.B., Mercer, C.A., & Finocchiaro, P.A., (in press). Teaching choice-making skills to students with dual sensory impairments. TEACHING Exceptional Children; reprinted by permission of the editor.

References

Brown, F., & Gothelf, C.R. (in preparation). Teaching Choice Diversity: A Curriculum For Individuals With Severe Disabilities.

Campbell, Philippa H. (1987). Integrated Programming for Students with Multiple Handicaps. In L. Goetz, D. Guess, & K. Stremel-Campbell (Eds.), Innovative Program Design for Individuals with Dual Sensory Impairments (pp. 159-188). Baltimore: Paul H. Brookes.

Crimmins, D.B., & Gothelf, C.R. (in press). Examining The Communicative Purposes Of Behavior. American Foundation for the Blind: Deaf-Blind Project. New York: American Foundation for the Blind.

Guess, D., Benson, H.A. & Siegel-Causey, E. (1985). Concepts and Issues Related To Choice-making and Autonomy Among Persons With Severe Disabilities. The Journal of the Association for Persons with Severe Handicaps, 10, 79-86.

Siegel-Causey, E. & Ernst, B. (1989). Theoretical Orientation And Research In Nonsymbolic Development. In E. Siegel-Causey & D. Guess (Eds.), Enhancing Nonsymbolic Communication Interactions Among Learners With Severe Disabilities (pp. 17-51). Baltimore: Paul H. Brookes.

Williams, R.K. (1991). Choices, communication, and control: A call for expanding them in the lives of people with severe disabilities. In L. Meyer, C. Peck, & L. Brown (Eds.), Critical Issues In The Lives Of People With Severe Disabilities (pp. 543-544). Baltimore: Paul H. Brookes.

An Approach to Teaching Self-Dressing to a Child with Dual Sensory Impairment

Jenifer L. McKelvey • Lori A. Sisson • Vincent B. Van Hasselt • Michel Hersen

Instruction in toileting, dressing, and feeding received much attention in the 1960s and 1970s. During those years, behavioral principles first were applied to change levels of responding by individuals with mental and physical disabilities who were living in institutions (Van Hasselt, Ammerman, & Sisson, 1990). This focus was based on a desire to improve the quality of life of individuals with severe disabilities by increasing their independence and improving their social acceptability. One group that could benefit from instruction in self-help skills includes those individuals with dual sensory impairment. Most who are deaf and blind function in the severe to profound ranges of mental retardation due to their inability to perform basic skills (Orlansky, 1981). Instruction for this population is hindered by (a) the presence of interfering, maladaptive behaviors; (b) problems with adaptation of materials and techniques; and (c) difficulty in identifying reinforcers to use in skills instruction programs (Sisson, Van Hasselt, & Hersen, 1987).

Luiselli (1987, 1988a, 1988b) recently published several reports that described self-help skills interventions with children and adolescents who were deaf and blind and suffered from moderate to severe mental retardation. In one study (Luiselli, 1987), toilet training was conducted with a 19-year-old woman who sporadically wet her pants and refused to use the bathroom when requested. The program consisted of verbal cues to use the toilet and token reinforcement for voiding in the toilet. Monitoring revealed that the young woman's pants-wetting decreased after treatment began. When she was given reinforcement only after initiating toileting on her own, she began to use the bathroom more often, and her pants-wetting episodes did not increase. These improvements were maintained over 7 months.

Two other investigations (Luiselli, 1988a; 1988b) evaluated various prompting procedures to increase independent eating in children and youth who did not initiate eating on their own or who ate too slowly. In all, four individuals, ages 6 to 18, were instructed. Prompts to begin eating included manual touch (Luiselli, 1988b), placing one bit of food on the plate (Luiselli, 1988a), and graduated manual guidance (Luiselli, 1988a). In addition, prompts were combined with social praise (Luiselli, 1988a) or favorite foods (Luiselli, 1988b) for appropriate behavior and/or interruption for interfering self-stimulatory behavior (Luiselli, 1988b). Research showed the interventions to be effective.

The self-help skills instruction program described in this article used graduated guidance as a method of teaching independent dressing to a girl with profound mental retardation, seizure disorder, deafness, and blindness. Graduated guidance involves the use of full manual guidance with subsequent fading to light touch and, ultimately, to no teacher assistance. Other distinguishing aspects of the procedure include (a) teaching the entire sequence of dressing actions rather than chaining successive steps and (b) delivering instructions and praise continuously, while administering tangible reinforcement only when the student is completely dressed. The effectiveness of variations of this procedure has been demonstrated with adults with mental retardation (Azrin, Schaeffer, & Wesolowski, 1976) and children with mental retardation and blindness (Sisson, Kilwein, & Van Hasselt, 1988). The program described here was the first systematic application of graduated guidance to teach dressing skills to a child who suffered from multiple disabilities including both deafness and blindness.

Program Description

Cybill was an 11-year-old girl who attended a residential school for children with visual impairments. She was one of 10 participants in a federally funded program designed to promote behavioral improvement and social and vocational skills in youths with deafness and blindness. This student was selected for instruction in dressing skills based on her inability to pull on her socks, pants, and shirt.

Cybill suffered from severe sensorineural hearing loss and cortical blindness. She did not respond to auditory stimuli and had limited light perception. Reports from Cybill's teacher and the school psychologist indicated that she functioned in the severely to profoundly mentally retarded range of intellectual abilities. She also had a seizure disorder that was controlled with phenobarbital. Since her muscle tone, strength, range of motion, and motor coordination were within normal limits, Cybill's inability to perform basic self-help activities such as dressing, grooming, and toileting appeared to result from her dependence on others, noncompliance, communication barriers, and interfering stereotypic behaviors (e.g., mouthing, rocking, repetitive vocalizations) that were secondary to her numerous disabling conditions.

Table 1

Task Analyses for Socks, Shorts, and Shirt

SOCKS	SHORTS	SHIRT
Holds sock at opening with two hands, thumb inside and fingers outside, stretching garment open.	Holds shorts at waistband with two hands, thumb inside and fingers outside, stretching garment open.	Holds shirt at bottom with two hands, thumb inside and fingers outside, stretching garment open.
Puts toes into sock.	Puts one foot into shorts.	Puts shirt over head.
Pulls sock over ball of foot.	Pulls shorts over ankle.	Pulls head through opening.
Pulls sock over arch of foot.	Pulls shorts over calf.	Searches for left armhole.
Pulls sock over heel of foot.	Puts second foot into shorts.	Puts left hand through armhole.
Pulls sock over ankle.	Pulls shorts over second ankle.	Pulls shirt past wrist.
	Pulls shorts over second calf.	Pulls shirt past elbow.
	Pulls shorts over knees.	Pulls shirt past upper arm.
	Stands up.	Pulls shirt over shoulder.
	Pulls shorts over thighs.	Searches for right armhole.
	Pulls shorts over hips.	Pulls shirt past wrist.
	Pulls shorts up to waist.	Pulls shirt past elbow.
		Pulls shirt past upper arm.
		Pulls shirt over shoulder.
		Pulls shirt down to waist.

Setting and Materials

Instruction was carried out in Cybill's bedroom, which was furnished with a single bed and a cupboard for clothing. Her clothing included crew socks, shorts with an elastic waistband, and a short-sleeved pullover shirt.

Oyster crackers were used as Cybill's reinforcer after a variety of items were presented systematically to her in a pretest and her approach to each was monitored. She consistently consumed or handled several stimuli, including a cracker, juice, a heating pad, and a vibrator. The oyster cracker was chosen for its ease of presentation.

Procedure

Target Behaviors. To facilitate instruction and behavioral recording of responses, detailed task analyses were developed for putting on socks, shorts, and a shirt. These are shown in Table 1.

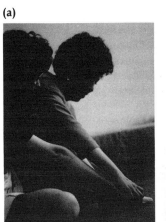  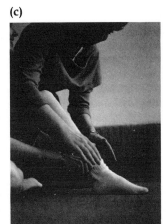 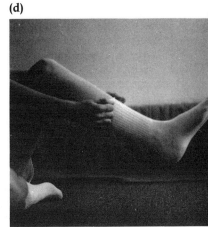

(a) (b) (c) (d)

An important aspect of this intervention is the gradual, systematic feeling of guidance. The beginning step is hand-over-hand manual guidance (a) which is later followed by guidance with two fingers (b). Eventually no assistance is needed (c) and independent performance is achieved (d).

Teaching Self-Dressing

Instruction. Instructional sessions were held in the morning, five times a week, and lasted for 10 minutes. Cybill and the instructor sat on the floor to begin each session, which simulated Cybill's usual morning routine. The instructor handed the garment to her in the proper orientation (front of the garment away from the child, back of the garment closest to the child). This served as the prompt to begin dressing.

Instruction consisted of guidance through all steps in the task analysis for each garment and social reinforcement as well as an oyster cracker after Cybill completed all steps in the task analysis. An instructional trial was ended when Cybill performed all steps in the task analysis or when she made errors or displayed physical resistance. The number of trials in each session varied due to inconsistency in her behavior and the complexity of the task demands (e.g., pulling on a sock vs. putting on a shirt).

The gradual, systematic fading of guidance was an important aspect of the intervention. This approach minimized errors while Cybill developed greater independence in dressing. Guidance was faded according to the following hierarchy, in which each successive step represented less therapist assistance in dressing:

1. Hand-over-hand manual guidance.
2. Guidance with thumb and two fingers.
3. Guidance with thumb and one finger.
4. Guidance with four fingers.
5. Guidance with two fingers.
6. Guidance with one finger.
7. No assistance.

A minimum of 10 trials was carried out at each level of the graduated guidance hierarchy. When 10 consecutive trials at one level were completed successfully, instruction advanced to the next level. If Cybill resisted guidance or was unable to complete the dressing task successfully, reinforcement was withheld, and the next 10 trials were conducted at the preceding level of assistance.

Instruction began with socks. Cybill was taught to put on her left sock. Instruction continued until the entire hierarchy of instructor assistance was completed and she demonstrated 100% mastery on three consecutive independent trials across 3 days. When Cybill met this criterion, the instructor implemented a maintenance procedure for putting on the sock. The maintenance procedure involved one to three trials per session in which Cybill was required to put on her sock without assistance. The instructor gave her an oyster cracker each time she completed the task successfully. Then, the remainder of the session was devoted to instruction in putting on shorts. Shorts and shirt instruction followed the same sequence as the sock instruction. Instruction ended when Cybill independently put on *all* garments on three independent trials across 3 days.

Assessment. Three assessment trials for each garment were conducted following the instructional sessions each day. In these trials, the instructor presented the garment but offered no assistance. A trial began when the garment was handed to Cybill; it ended when she completed all steps in the task analysis or when she made no response during a period of 30 seconds after the garment was presented. Three additional assessment trials were conducted 7 weeks and 15 weeks after instruction was completed to check on maintenance of the dressing skills.

Results

Before instruction began, Cybill was unable to complete any part of the dressing sequence for any of the clothing articles. However, her dressing skills improved gradually with instruction. Cybill could put on her sock independently after 27 sessions. To achieve 100% mastery of the dressing skill for her shorts, 38 sessions were necessary. Only 13 sessions were required for Cybill to demonstrate independence in putting on her shirt.

Follow-up probes showed that Cybill's self-dressing skills were maintained at posttreatment levels for up to 15 weeks. Although she was given no formal instruction during this follow-up period, she was encouraged by her caregivers to dress independently each morning. Anecdotal reports indicated that she was able to put on her socks, both short and long pants, and both short- and long-sleeved shirts following instruction, despite the fact that only one garment from each category had been used for instruction.

Conclusion

The success of the approach used with Cybill may be attributable to several factors. First, she experienced the entire sequence of steps involved in each dressing action on each instructional trial. This is in contrast to previous work that emphasized the acquisition of component parts of the dressing sequence and subsequent chaining of these parts to achieve the skill (e.g., Inglesfield & Crisp, 1985). Additional research is needed to determine the relative effectiveness of these two approaches with persons who have multiple disabilities.

Second, skills acquisition may have been facilitated by the systematic use of manual guidance. This strategy was particularly appropriate due to Cybill's auditory and visual impairments, which precluded use of verbal instructions and modeling. Also, gradual fading of assistance provided Cybill with many opportunities for positive reinforcement and minimized errors. Thus, intructor-student interactions were focused primarily on appropriate responding, and the sessions were pleasant.

Third, the enthusiastic participation of Cybill's parents, teacher, and child-care workers no doubt facilitated maintenance of appropriate dressing behaviors. They expressed considerable satisfaction with the results of instruction. When Cybill became more independent in putting on her clothing, time became available to work on more advanced self-help and social behaviors such as grooming and simple communication responses.

To date, very little controlled research has examined methods of combining individual self-help skills into longer behavioral chains (see Jarman, Iwata, & Lorentzson, 1983). Optimal performance in everyday situations calls for the execution of a series of self-help behaviors that are closely linked in time. This is an important area for future work with Cybill, as well as for continued efforts in self-help skills instruction with other individuals who have mental, physical, and sensory disabilities.

References

Azrin, N. H., Schaeffer, R. M., & Wesolowski, M. D. (1976). A rapid method of teaching profoundly retarded persons to dress by a reinforcement-guidance method. *Mental Retardation, 14,* 29-33.

Inglesfield, E., & Crisp, A. (1985). Teaching dressing skills to the severely mentally handicapped: A comparison of intensive and nonintensive strategies. *British Journal of Mental Subnormality, 31,* 46-53.

Jarman, P. H., Iwata, B. A., & Lorentzson, A. M. (1983). Development of morning self-care routines in multiply handicapped persons. *Applied Research in Mental Retardation, 4,* 113-122.

Luiselli, J. K. (1987). Secondary diurnal enuresis: Evaluation of cueing and reinforcement interventions with a sensory-impaired youth. *Journal of Mental Deficiency Research, 31,* 287-292.

Luiselli, J. K. (1988a). Improvement of feeding skills in multihandicapped students through paced-prompting interventions. *Journal of the Multihandicapped Person, 1,* 17-30.

Luiselli, J. K. (1988b). Behavioral feeding intervention with deaf-blind, multihandicapped children. *Child and Family Behavior Therapy, 10,* 49-62.

Orlansky, M. C. (1981). The deaf-blind and the severely/profoundly handicapped: An emerging relationship. In S. R. Walsh & R. Holzberg (Eds.), *Understanding and educating the deaf-blind/severely and profoundly handicapped* (pp. 5-23). Springfield, IL: Charles C Thomas.

Sisson, L. A., Kilwein, M. L., & Van Hasselt, V. B. (1988). A graduated guidance procedure for teaching self-dressing skills to multihandicapped children. *Research in Developmental Disabilities, 9,* 419-432.

Sisson, L. A., Van Hasselt, V. B., & Hersen, M. (1987). Psychological approaches with deaf-blind persons: Strategies and issues in research and treatment. *Clinical Psychology Review, 7,* 303-328.

Van Hasselt, V. B., Ammerman, R. T., & Sisson, L. A. (1990). Physically disabled. In A. S. Bellack, M. Hersen, & A. E. Kazdin (Eds.), *International handbook of behavior modification and therapy (2nd Ed., pp. 831-855).* New York: Plenum.

Jenifer L. McKelvey *is a Behavior Specialist and* **Lori A. Sisson** *(CEC Pennsylvania Federation) is a Research Clinical Psychologist, Western Pennsylvania School for Blind Children, Pittsburgh, Pennsylvania, where the study was conducted.* **Vincent B. Van Hasselt** *is an Associate Professor of Psychiatry and* **Michel Hersen** *is a Professor of Psychiatry and Psychology, University of Pittsburgh School of Medicine, Pittsburgh, Pennsylvania.*

This project was supported by grant number G008530258 from Special Education Programs of the U.S. Department of Education and MH18269 from the National Institute of Mental Health. The authors wish to extend thanks to Deb Faskow, Claudia Velverde, and Mary Jo Horgan for their varied contributions to the project.

The CHARGE Association: Implications for Teachers

Thomas W. Jones and Michele T. Dunne

CHARGE association is a diagnostic label for a group of congenital malformations, including hearing impairment and mental retardation, which frequently occur together. In the past several years, schools for hearing-impaired children, particularly those with programs for multihandicapped hearing-impaired students, have enrolled students with this diagnosis. A review of the literature concerning the CHARGE association yielded information concerning etiology and characteristics. From this review, generalizations are drawn for teachers of the hearing impaired working with students with the diagnosis of CHARGE association.

In the past several years, schools for hearing-impaired children, particularly those with programs for multihandicapped hearing-impaired children, have enrolled students with a new diagnostic label, "CHARGE association." This label derives from a number of recent medical studies which have linked some specific congenital malformations to each other. This grouping of anomalies may prove extremely beneficial to clinicians by enabling them both to identify malformations which may be ameliorated through therapy or early education and to determine prognosis (Hittner, Hirsch, Kreh, & Rudolph, 1979). Because of the educational implications of some of the specific anomalies, teachers of hearing-impaired children also should know about the CHARGE association and how to meet the special educational needs of children with that diagnosis.

Background

Hall (1981) first noted a cluster of non-randomly associated anomalies that occurred with choanal atresia, a blockage of nasal passages. Hall listed this group of anomalies as one of the 25 most common multiple anomaly syndromes. This initial report led to the identification of a rather consistent constellation of anomalies occurring in conjunction with one another. This constellation was assigned the acronym "CHARGE" with each letter representing one of the abnormalities generally associated with it.

Whether CHARGE is a syndrome or association is somewhat controversial. In genetics, a syndrome is a group of symptoms which appear simultaneously and constitute a specific pattern. In contrast, an association is the occurance together of two or more characteristics at a frequency greater than would be predicted on the basis of chance (Dobrowski, Grundfast, Rosenbaum & Zajtchuk, 1985). Although Davenport, Hefner and Mitchell (1986) made a strong case for treating CHARGE as a syndrome, most authorities treat it as an association because it is unclear exactly how many clinical entities with diverse etiologies it might represent (Pagon, Zonana, & Graham, 1982). Because of the possible multiple etiologies of the CHARGE association, its variable characteristics, and its newness as a diagnostic category, precise incidence statistics have not yet been derived. Hall (1981) listed it among the 25 most common multiple congenital anomaly syndromes. Kaplan (1985) estimated that choanal atresia, one of the primary diagnostic indicators in the CHARGE association, occurs once in every 8,000 births. Pagon et al. (1982) "believe the CHARGE association is common (p. 828)."

Pagon, Graham, Zonana and Yong (1981) proposed the acronym, CHARGE, as a means of helping physicians and other health care professionals to identify affected individuals. Each letter refers to a separate anomaly, as shown in Table 1. Following is a description of each of the anomalies:

Dr. Jones is an associate professor in the Gallaudet University Department of Education, Washington, D.C. Ms. Dunne is coordinator of Family Education at the New York School for the Deaf.

TABLE 1

Features of the CHARGE Association

Letter	Condition	Description
C	Coloboma	Missing parts of the iris or retina
H	Heart defects	Septal defects, patent ductus arteriosus, heart murmur
A	Atresia Choanae	Blockage of the postnasal passages
R	Retardation	Mental retardation or retarded physical growth
G	Genital Hypoplasia	Incomplete genital development
E	Ear deformities	Ear malformation, often accompanied by significant hearing loss

C - Coloboma. A coloboma is an absence or defect of the eye usually resulting from a failure of some part of the fetal fissure to close. Depending on the type of coloboma, visual impairments may or may not be present (Pagon et al., 1981). For example, part of the iris is missing in a coloboma of the iris, giving the pupil a keyhole-shaped appearance and reducing the child's ability to adjust to a brightly lighted area. Another frequent site of a coloboma is the retina, a result of which is a blank area in the child's visual field.

H - Heart Defects. The associated heart anomalies may include septal effects, patent ductus arteriosus, heart murmur or any number of other heart malformations (Dobrowski, Grundfast, Rosenbaum & Zajtchuk, 1985).

A - Atresia Choanae. Choanal atresia, a blockage of the paired passages between the nasal cavity and the nasopharynx, is one of the major criteria for diagnosis (Kaplan, 1985; Koletzko & Majewski, 1984). The blockage may be in either a bony or membranous form (Bergstrom & Owens, 1984).

R - Retarded Postnatal Growth and/or Central Nervous System Defects. Mental retardation has been evidenced in the majority of the children with the CHARGE association. Intelligence may range from nearly normal to profoundly mentally retarded (Dobrowski et al., 1985). Inadequate oxygen in the lungs and the blood may be the major cause of the mental retardation. According to Koletzko and Majewski (1984), 80 percent of the mentally retarded children with CHARGE association had choanal atresia which might have led to asphyxia shortly after birth. Retarded physical development also occurs with the CHARGE association. The majority of the children with CHARGE association are below the third percentile of physical growth norms (Pagon et al., 1981).

G - Genital hypoplasia. Genital hypoplasia, the incomplete development or underdevelopment of the genitals, is yet another associated anomaly. Pardo and Chua (1985) described the successful treatment of a newborn male infant with CHARGE association hormonal deficiency and undeveloped genitals.

E - Ear Deformities. Ear deformities in the CHARGE association are often accompanied by significant hearing impairment. Ear deformities have been noted that range from small ears without formation of the pinna to cup-shaped lop ears. Deafness has been predominantly sensorineural and ranges from mild to profound (Pagon et al., 1981).

Evidence has also been offered to support the inclusion of various other anomalies within the spectrum of CHARGE association. These include abnormal tongue size (Siebert, 1985) cleft lip and/or palate and hypopituarism (August, Rosenbaum, Friendly & Hung, 1983). Curatolo, Libutti and Brinchi (1983) suggested that patients with infantile spasms and ocular malformations should be evaluated with regard to CHARGE association. The occurrence of these disorders has not been frequent enough to warrant definitive inclusion in the CHARGE association.

In the period immediately following birth, the child with CHARGE association may have life-threatening physical anomalies such as choanal atresia, severe congenital heart disease and tracheoesophageal atresia. These problems must be addressed immediately. Approximately 30 percent of the CHARGE association patients die in early infancy (Primack & Feingold, 1983). Surgery may correct many of the anomalies.

Etiology

The cause of the CHARGE association is unknown. The specific defects seen in this disorder can for the most part be attributed to arrest in various aspects of normal embryologic development. The development of all of the involved organs takes place in the third to seventh week of gestation (Hennekam, Muis, Bloem, de Vries & Beemer, 1984). A teratogenic agent that influences the pregnancy during this critical period might lead to the malformations of the characteristic CHARGE association structures. Eye, ear, heart and nasal passage defects may occur prenatally following the use of drugs such as thalidomide, heart and eye, defects from the use of diphenylhydantoin (Bartoshesky, Bhan, Nagpaul & Pashayan, 1982) and heart defects from prenatal exposure to ethanol (Daft, Johnston & Sulik, 1986). The effects of ethanol suggest a relationship to Fetal Alcohol Syndrome (FAS) and, in fact, some studies show an overlap between FAS and heart anomalies found in CHARGE association and DiGeorge syndrome (absence of the thymus and parathyroid glands). Siebert, Graham and MacDonald (1985) used this information to support the suggestion that the subtle facial anomalies accompanied by heart defects in CHARGE, FAS and DiGeorge syndrome could have a similar origin.

In addition to the possibility of a teratogenic cause of CHARGE association, cases have been cited that support the belief in both recessive and dominant forms of inherited CHARGE association (Ho, Kaufman & Podos, 1975; Hittner et al., 1979).

Case Study

Goldson, Smith and Stewart (1986) described two cases of diagnosed CHARGE syndrome and discussed the developmental functioning of the two patients. Of particular interest is the second patient who at the writing of their article was 19 years of age. She was unique in that she provided a long-term perspective on a child with CHARGE association. The ninth child born to a 43-year-old mother and a 45-year-old father, she was the product of a difficult pregnancy complicated by nausea in the second trimester. During the latter part of the pregnancy, there was a marked decrease in fetal movement. At birth, she was underweight and had nasal congestion and discharge. Right choanal atresia was diagnosed as were colobomata of the retina, choroid and optic nerve. There was concern regarding overall development from the very beginning. Developmental milestones were achieved quite late. Hearing impairment was not diagnosed until approximately 4 1/2 years of age. Test results varied, however, a severe mixed loss was confirmed. Developmental scores at age 16 years on the Wechsler Adult Intelligence Scale - Revised were as follows: performance, 86; verbal, 70; combined score, 76. The girl attended a public school which provided speech and physical therapy. A diagnosis of CHARGE association was not made until the student was 16 years of age. At that time, she transferred to a state school for the deaf and blind to participate in a vocational program and for social reasons. Recent test results revealed an IQ in the low-normal range. She continued her vocational training and developed good independent-living and social skills.

Implications for Teachers

Vision Impairments. As described above, children with the CHARGE association may have colobomata (missing parts) of the iris, retina or other parts of the eye. Coloboma of the iris may make it difficult for the child to adjust to brightly lighted areas and to bright glare. Sometimes the use of sunglasses is recommended by the child's physician. The teacher should be aware of the child's difficulty in brightly lighted areas and ensure that sunglasses are used if they have been recommended. With a coloboma of the retina, part of the child's visual field may be missing. In these cases, the best angle for approaching the child, presenting materials and communicating with the child may not be from the direct front. The angle at which the child sees best should be determined. If the central part of the visual field is damaged, the child's visual acuity may be severely damaged and the student may require special materials such as large print or Braille books (Cross, 1975).

Early Intervention. For both medical and educational reasons, early identification and intervention are very important for any child who has the CHARGE association or any other syndrome or disorder. Thorough diagnosis and treatment of the association's medical problems can improve the prognosis. For example, endocrine evaluation should be conducted as early as possible to ensure early detection and treatment of potentially life-threatening hormonal deficiency (Pardo & Chua, 1985). Karyotyping is also recommended. Full audiologic evaluation including Auditory Brainstem Evoked Response, pure tone testing and tympanometry also should be completed as soon as possible.

In addition to the early diagnosis and treatment of medical conditions, early diagnosis should lead to the optimal educational placement for enabling the children to develop and use all abilities. Participation in an educationally-oriented early intervention or parent-infant program would be extremely beneficial. Early education may prevent potential subsequent secondary disabilities from developing, may enable the children to overcome or to compensate for many of their disabilities, and may help the family to adjust to the child's disabilities and provide a supportive environment for development (Garwood & Fewell, 1983).

Transdisciplinary Services. Like other multihandicapped hearing-impaired children, those with CHARGE association may have a variety of disabilities which require the cooperation of professionals from various disciplines. For example, the classroom teacher should work closely with the physical therapist to incorporate developmental principles of movement into the child's activities during the entire school day (Connor, Williamson & Siepp, 1978).

As children with CHARGE association grow and mature, new medical problems may present themselves. Some of these have been described earlier and include hypopituitarism and hormone deficiency and may have behavioral as well as physical manifestations. These should be dealt with as they arise. The teacher may be the first professional to notice such problems and should bring it to the parents' attention or make a referral to the appropriate person so that intervention may begin.

Intellectual Functioning. As mentioned above, the intellectual level of students with the CHARGE association is highly variable. Educational programming should be based on the children's level of functioning and should include modifications for intellectual deficiencies when appropriate. Such modifications include breaking objectives down into small steps, teaching the children to use skills in the actual settings in which they are to be applied, focusing instruction on functional skills rather than traditional academics, developing the children's strengths rather than focusing on their deficiencies and individualizing instruction so that different children may be working on different objectives at different rates at the same time (Snell, 1978).

Multiple Handicaps. With any child who has multiple handicaps, including those with the CHARGE association, the disabilities interact with each other to create characteristics and needs that do not occur in children with single disabilities (Jones, 1984). These additional characteristics and needs vary greatly and the teacher may need a great deal of creativity and resourcefulness to meet them. Children with multiple handicaps may require special instructional objectives and environments, instructional rates and methodology, and staffing arrangements (Jones, 1984).

Conclusion

The CHARGE association is a unique constellation of physical characteristics that have been associated with mental retardation and hearing impairment. While information describing the manifestations of this association is available, little has been published regarding the clinical or educational course that individuals with the CHARGE association follow.

The education of a child with CHARGE association should begin early and involve a true interdisciplinary approach. Cooperation between the family, medical facilities and educational personnel can serve only to benefit the child. Teachers of children with the CHARGE association should be able to meet the needs implied by their students' visual, mental and physical handicaps in addition to their hearing impairment, and should understand how these disabilities interact with one another to produce a child with truly unique educational needs.

References

August, G. P., Rosenbaum, K.N., Friendly, D., & Hung, W. (1983).Hypopituitarism and the CHARGE association. *The Journal of Pediatrics, 103*(3), 424-425.

Bartoshesky, L.E., Bhan, I., Nagpaul, K., & Pashayan, H. (1982). Severe cardiac and ophthalmologic malformations in an infant exposed to diphenylhydantoin in utero. *Pediatrics, 69* (2), 202-203.

Bergstrom, L., & Owens, O. (1984). Posterior choanal atresia: A syndromal disorder. *Laryngoscope, 95*, 393-398.

Connor, F. P., Williamson, G. G., & Siepp, J. M. (1978). *Program guide for infants and toddlers with neuromotor and other developmental disabilities.* New York: Teachers College Press.

Cross, H. E. (1975). Educational implications of visual disorders. In R. H. A. Haslam & P. J. Valletutti (Eds.), *Medical problems in the classroom: The teacher's role in diagnosis and management.* Baltimore: University Park Press.

Curatolo, P., Libutti, G., & Brinchi, V. (1983). Infantile spasm and the CHARGE association. *Developmental Medicine and Child Neurology, 25*, 367-373.

Daft, P. A., Johnston, M.C., & Sulik, K. K. (1986). Abnormal heart and great vessel development following acute ethanol exposure in mice. *Teratology, 33*, 93-104.

Davenport, S. L., Hefner, M. A., & Mitchell, J.A. (1986). The spectrum of clinical features in CHARGE syndrome. *Clinical Genetics, 29*, 298-310

Dobrowski, J. M., Grundfast, K. M., Rosenbaum, K. N., & Zajtchuk, J. T. (1985). Otorhinolaryngic manifestations of CHARGE association. *Otolaryngology - Head and Neck Surgery, 93* (6), 798-802.

Garwood, S. G., & Fewell, R. R. (1983). *Educating handicapped infants: Issues in development and intervention.* Rockville, MD: Aspen Publications.

Goldson, E., Smith, A. C., & Stewart, J. M. (1986). The CHARGE association. *American Journal of Diseases in Children, 140*, 918-921.

Hall, B. D. (1981). The twenty-five most common multiple congenital anomaly syndromes. In M. M. Kaback (Ed.), *Genetic issues in pediatric and obstetric practice.* Chicago: Yearbook Medical Publishers.

Hall, J. G. (1981). Editorial comment: Kaufman Syndrome. *American Journal of Medical Genetics, 8*, 395-396.

Hennekam, R. C. M., Muis, N., Bloem, G. W. D., de Vries, L. S., & Beemer, F. A. (1984). De CHARGE-associatie; een combinatie can congenitale afwijkingen [The CHARGE association: A combination of congenital anomalies]. *Ned Tijdschr Geneeskd, 128* (22), 1050-1053.

Hittner, H. M., Hirsch, N. J., Kreh, G.M., & Rudolph A.J. (1979). Colobomatous microphthalmia, heart disease, hearing loss, and mental retardation—A syndrome. *Journal of Pediatric Ophthalmology and Strabismus, 16* (2), 122-128.

Ho, C. K., Kaufman, R. L., & Podos, S. M. (1975). Ocular colobomata, cardiac defect, and other anomalies: A study of seven cases including two sibs. *Journal of Medical Genetics, 12*, 289-293.

Jones, T. W. (1984). A framework of identification, classification, and placement of multihandicapped hearing-impaired students. *Volta Review, 86*, 142-151.

Kaplan, L. C. (1985). Choanal atresia and its associated anomalies. Further support for the CHARGE association. *International Journal of Pediatric Otorhinolaryngology, 8*, 237-242.

Koletzko, B., & Majewski, F. (1984). Congenital anomalies in patients with choanal atresia: CHARGE association. *European Journal of Pediatrics, 142*, 271-275.

Pagon, R. A., Graham, J. M., Zonana, V. & Yong, S. (1981). Coloboma, congenital heart disease, and choanal atresia with multiple anomalies: CHARGE association. *The Journal of Pediatrics, 99* (2), 223-227.

Pagon, R. A., Zonana, J., & Graham, J. M. (1982). Letter to the editor: CHARGE association. *Pediatrics, 70* (5), 827-828.

Pardo, J. M., & Chua, C. (1985). The CHARGE association in a male newborn infant: Diagnostic and therapeutic considerations. *Clinical Pediatrics, 24* (9), 531-533.

Primack, W., & Feingold, M. (1983). Picture of the month. *American Journal of Disabilities in Children, 137*, 1117-1118.

Siebert, J. R. (1985). A morphometric study of normal and abnormal fetal to childhood tongue size. *Archives of Oral Biology, 30* (5), 433-440.

Siebert, J. R., Graham, J. M., & MacDonald, C. (1985). Pathologic features of the CHARGE association: Support for the involvement of the neural crest. *Teratology, 31*, 331-336.

Snell, M. E. (Ed.). (1978). *Systematic instruction of the moderately and severely handicapped.* Columbus, OH: Charles E. Merrill.

The Impact of Retinitis Pigmentosa on Young Adults: Psychological, Educational, Vocational and Social Considerations

L.A. Nemshick; McC. Vernon; F. Ludman

Abstract: Retinitis pigmentosa (RP) refers to a group of inherited retinal degenerative disorders in which night and peripheral vision are gradually lost. A national sample of young adults with RP reveals that a significant number feel that RP adversely affects their education, employment, mobility and socialization. Participants feel that special counseling is needed to accept and adjust to their condition, and that sharing with peers would be beneficial.

The period of greatest crisis in most persons who become blind as adults is during diagnosis. For those with progressive visual loss, the period of gradual degeneration prolongs the crisis. With young adults affected by retinitis pigmentosa (RP), the stress is intensified by the additional pressures of adolescence, school, choosing a career, maintaining a social life, and starting a family.

To determine how their needs can be better served, the RP Foundation Fighting Blindness asked young adults across the country to describe how they are coping with their eye condition and how it affects various aspects of their lives. These young adults identified special needs and concerns in the areas of education, employment, adjustment, socialization, visual aids and genetic issues.

Method

Early in 1981, a short questionnaire was mailed to more than 15,000 persons listed in the registry of the RP Foundation Fighting Blindness. A second, in-depth questionnaire was then mailed to those of this group (N = 800) between the ages of 13 and 30, with RP or with another allied retinal disorder. This 12-page questionnaire for Young Adults with Retinal Degenerations (YARD study) consisted of 55 questions—on education, vocational training, employment, counseling, adjustment, medical aspects, mobility, and special needs.

This research was funded by a grant from the RP Foundation Fighting Blindness, Baltimore, Maryland. The authors gratefully acknowledge the contributions made by Mindy Berman and Joann Boughman, Ph.D. to this study.

Results and Discussion

Demographics

At the close of this study, 307 or 38 percent of the questionnaires were returned with answers. The distribution of the responses, coming from 42 states, closely parallels the regional distribution of the total U.S. population. Most of the respondents are between 16 and 24 years of age, single, and have siblings. Over 90 percent indicate that they have RP, including about 11 percent who report Usher's syndrome (US). Other reported disorders are listed in Table 1. The abbreviation RP will be used to refer to RP and the other retinal degenerations mentioned in Table 1. Also, respondents (39%) who have ever received any type of counseling related to their condition will be referred to as "those who have received counseling" (see Table 2, p. 860).

Medical aspects

Early diagnosis affords young people affected with retinal degenerations an opportunity to take advantage of career and educational counseling before choosing a career. In this study, two-thirds of the sample report that they were diagnosed and told of their condition between the ages of 6 and 19, a time when most were

Table 1. Selected characteristics of respondents to YARD study[1] and selected comparisons with 1980 U.S. Population.

	YARD Study N = 307*	*1980 U.S. Total Population[2]* N = 226.5 mil.*
1. Type of Retinal Degeneration		
RP (incl. Usher's Synd., and RP with MD)	92%	
Usher's Syndrome	11	
RP with Macular Degn.	2	
Macular Degeneration (MD)	4	
Lawrence-Moon-Biedl Syndr.	2	
Batten's Disease	1	
Not Specified	1	
2. Other Long Term Health Problems (Besides RP)		
Nearsightedness	44%	
Loss of color vision	16	
Farsightedness	10	
Cataracts	9	1.7%[3]
Hearing loss	18	6.6[4]
Poor balance	11	
Ringing or buzzing in ears	5	
Epilepsy or seizures	4	0.9[5]
Fainting spells	1	
Other[6]	17	
3. Occupation of Employed	N = 147	N = 34.9m. (Ages 16-29)
Prof., tech., managerial	27%	20%
Sales	12	11
Clerical	17	19
Crafts & kindred	7	12
Operatives	7	14
Laborers	10	9
Service workers	12	15
Not specified	8	—

* Unless otherwise indicated
[1] Survey period was 7/81 to 7/84.
[2] 1980 U.S. Census of Population, Bureau of the Census.
[3] Nat'l. Center for Health Statistics, DHHS Publication No. (PHS) 81-1562, Feb. 1981.
[4] The Deaf Population of the U.S., Schein and Delk, 1974. This rate is for all ages combined. Related studies cited in this source suggest that the rate for ages 14-30 is less than two percent.
[5] Natl. Institute of Health Publication No. 80-1683, 11/79.
[6] Includes various conditions such as asthma, cysts, cerebral palsy, obesity, diabetes, allergies, high blood pressure, ataxia, astigmatism, mental retardation.

Table 2. Diagnosis, counseling and adjustment of YARD study respondents.[1]

N = 307, unless otherwise indicated

1. Age of Diagnosis of Retinal Degeneration		
	0- 5 yrs.	14%
	6-13	34
	14-19	35
	20 or older	17
2. Age First Told of Eye Condition		
	2- 5 yrs.	6%
	6-13	34
	14-19	36
	20 or older	24
3. Genetics		
	Percent of respondents who:	
	a. Were aware at TOS[2] that RP is inherited	88%
	b. Have relatives with retinal degeneration	52
	c. Felt genetic counseling is important	78
	d. Ever had genetic counseling	19
	e. Are interested in genetic counseling	83
4. Percent of respondents who felt their eye condition affected their[3]		
	a. School work (N = 187 students)	42%
	b. Employment (N = 147 employed)	39
	c. Mobility or physical ability	74
	d. Social and recreational activities	72
5. Others aware of respondent's eye condition		
	a. Close friend (N = 307)	90%
	b. Brother or sister (N = 293)	94
	c. Teachers (N = 187 students)	60
	d. Job supervisor (N = 147 employed)	58
6. Nonfamily members with whom respondents feel they can talk about their eye condition		
	a. None (N = 307)	22%
	b. Close friend (N = 307)	71
	c. Teachers (N = 187 students)	32
	d. Job supervisor (N = 147 employed)	23
	e. Counselor (N = 60 receiving counseling)	51
7. Counseling and adjustment (related to eye condition) (N = 307)		
	a. Ever received such counseling	39%
	b. Receiving counseling at time surveyed	20
	c. Aware of state DVR or similar agency	45
	d. Ever received services of state DVR or similar agency	45
	e. Feels special counseling needed for adjustment to eye condition	72
	f. Feels sharing with peers is or will be helpful	66
8. Career change for those employed		
	a. Those expecting a change (N = 147)	42%
	b. Those prepared for change (N = 62)	22

[1] Survey period was 7/81 to 7/84.
[2] Time of survey.
[3] Respondents who indicated their eye condition affected their school work, employment (job or job prospects), household chores, social or recreational activity, or mobility were asked to explain how each of these activities was affected. Problems reported which were *common to all or nearly all types of activities were:* work, classwork or homework taking longer than usual; difficulty with reading and paperwork; mobility or transportation problems; difficulty in seeing at night or in dimly lit areas; difficulty in seeing small objects. Other problems, *in social activities,* especially, were dependence on others; feeling embarrassed or awkward; *in employment,* were limited occupational choice; discrimination; job hazards.

still in school and had not yet chosen a career (see Table 2). A significant number in the sample were not diagnosed (17%) and/or informed (24%) of their condition until after 20 years of age. By this time, most had invested some time in a career and were starting families, without knowing the implications of RP.

When should parents tell their children?
The decision of when to tell a child that he or she has RP can be intensely traumatic and frightening for parents. Still, many young adults want to have this information as early as possible. One young man who was diagnosed at 19 comments:

I think it is important for young adults afflicted with RP to get a complete diagnosis of their condition and rate of regression, inform themselves as much as possible about RP and research being done, and plan their lives according to this information.

Yet, even though a large percentage of the participants were informed of their con-

dition prior to age 20, very few considered themselves prepared for an occupational or lifestyle change as their condition worsened (see Table 2).

Therefore, it is not enough merely to inform the person of the diagnosis at an early age, since young adults may adapt to a certain stage of their progressive loss and base long-term career and family decisions on this level of vision. Schein (1976) concurs, remarking that many points along the progressive path of RP can cause strains on one's personality and social identification. Perhaps periodic counseling as the RP progresses would aid in making the most effective use of early diagnosis.

Genetic counseling
Among the respondents, more than half report having relatives with RP or a similiar retinal disorder, and yet there is a marked discrepancy between those who think genetic counseling is important or who are interested in receiving it, and those who actually obtain such counseling (see Table 2). More information regarding genetic counseling should be made available to young adults with RP, including identification of places that can provide the service.

RP and hearing loss
The sample population's high incidence of hearing loss and related problems, such as poor balance and tinnitus (see Table 1), tends to coincide with recent findings reported by others (Boughman, Conneally, and Nance, 1980; Fishman, G., Vasquez, Fishman, M., and Berger, 1979; Karp, 1985; Vernon, Boughman and Annala, 1982). Despite the relatively high levels of reported hearing loss among those with RP, many ophthalmologists and other professionals do not know that RP and hearing loss are related and fail to make the diagnosis of Usher's syndrome or of the compounded loss.

Adjustment problems are severely compounded when the person has some hearing loss or is deaf at the time of diagnosis. A major problem reported by respondents with both hearing and vision impairment is severe difficulty with communication. As a result, this double loss of hearing and vision generates unique problems which require the attention of professionals knowledgeable about Usher's syndrome. For these reasons, it is recommended that those diagnosed with RP receive a complete hearing examination as soon after the RP diagnosis as possible, and that they thereafter obtain hearing examinations on a regular basis.

Eighty percent of the participants report having additional long-term problems, with nearsightedness being the most common. Other long-term health problems reported are listed in Table 1.

Visual and mobility aids
Slightly less than half (44%) report using visual and mobility aids and equipment, e.g., large print, braille, Noir sunglasses, a cane or a magnifier. Less frequently used devices are the Visualtek, recorded materials, the ITT Night Vision Aid, guide dog and Optacon. The fact that many respondents report using visual or mobility aids indicates that a need for such aids exists among the RP population. The development of new aids needs emphasis as well. Most of those surveyed (88%) express a desire to receive information on visual and mobility aids available.

Education

Over two-thirds of the participants completed high school at least; slightly less than half of the sample have some college education. One-fifth of the sample have completed at least four years of college while seven percent report participation in vocational training programs.

Impact of RP on education. It is quite significant that two-fifths of the students in the sample feel that their condition affects their school work, since in most cases their condition is still in the early stages (see Table 2). This suggests a need to examine the effects of RP more directly on education. For now, educators at least need to be aware of the student's eye condition and of some relatively easy and inexpensive ways with which they can help the student minimize the effects of RP in an effort to provide improved or equal access to their materials and curriculum. Following are some tips provided by students themselves:
• Allow the student to sit near the blackboard.
• Allow the student more time for tasks that involve reading.
• Use large print if possible.
• Avoid using computer-printed answer sheets and poorly printed mimeograph sheets.
• Avoid films, filmstrips and transparencies. They are difficult to see, and it is difficult for students with RP to take notes during such visual displays. When these situations cannot be avoided, a note taker should be provided.
• Be sure the classroom is well lit, even in daytime.
• Understand that some students with RP have difficulty adjusting from daylight to artificial light in hallways. Good lighting in hallways and on campus at night is necessary for good mobility.

Employment

Occupations of those with RP
Just under half of the participants were employed at full- or part-time jobs at the time surveyed. Thirteen percent were unemployed; i.e., were not students and were actively seeking work. This figure is high, considering the educational level of these persons. A wide variety of occupations was reported by the employed participants— engineer, secretary, artist, teacher, registered nurse, construction worker, sales clerk, machinist, social worker, and custodian, to name a few (see Table 1).

Effect of RP on employment
Almost two-fifths of those employed at the time surveyed report that their RP affects their job. The most common employment problems reported are difficulty with paperwork, reading, nightwork, assignments in dimly lit areas, mobility, and transportation.

In addition to the problems RP creates on the job, a third of the respondents feel their eye condition is an obstacle in obtaining employment. Transportation difficulties, perceived discrimination, restricted occupational choice, real or imagined safety hazards, night work limitations, and taking more time to perform tasks, are cited as reasons.

The decision to tell one's employer
Only a small percentage of those employed at the time surveyed believe that their employer's knowledge of their condition adversely affects their job. However, this percentage may be very misleading. Many employed respondents (44%) state that they did not tell their employer about their condition precisely because they believed that such knowledge would adversely affect their job status. One man who works as a meat cutter admits, "I feel I might not be hired if I were to honestly tell an employer about RP. I just say I'm night blind." Further study is necessary to clarify the rights of the employer and the affected employee on this matter.

Underemployment
Some participants report underemployment. That is to say, they are capable of functioning in higher level jobs but, because of perceived discrimination, are not successful in obtaining or maintaining such positions. For example, one young man explains:

I was turned down from several banking jobs because the employers felt that my vision was too high of a risk for them. I was hired as a cashier [but] I was let go because I was considered too great of a risk. I found this very discouraging because I felt I would not have had any problems at any of these jobs. As it is now, I have a dual degree, one in business administration, and presently I am working as a mechanic.

Career change and vocational counseling
Almost half of the employed participants anticipate a job change when their condition worsens. Yet, only one-fifth of those who expect this change are prepared for it (see Table 2). It is disconcerting that so few are prepared to choose an alternate career. Making such a change can be stressful and difficult. Not only may the person need vocational counseling, but he or she may also need personal counseling. A career change may easily rekindle some unsettled problems in adjusting to and accepting the condition, since this kind of move is a very concrete result of the disorder's progression. One woman recalls, "I was not ready to quit my job when my doctor said I should. It was the hardest thing I ever had to do." Ideally, with early vocational counseling such a situation can be avoided; however, it is more often the case that one is eventually forced to make some sort of job change.

The fact that less than half of those surveyed are aware of or receive Division of Vocational Rehabilitation (DVR) services suggests that there is a great need to inform persons with RP across the country of the various services available that would help them adapt their job environment to their condition (see Table 2). Ophthalmologists and optometrists should inform their patients of these services.

Much work remains to be done in adapting the work place to the needs of the visually impaired. The fact of the matter is that the choices of jobs for blind persons are currently limited. However, with increases in computer technology, low vision aids, and public awareness about RP, many of those with RP may find that certain adjustments and adaptations make career changes unnecessary even as their vision deteriorates.

Counseling, Adjustment and Psychological Aspects

Family
A large majority of the sample (82%) feel they receive support from their family

regarding their retinal disorder. However, 12 percent say they receive the wrong kind of "support," i.e., their families overprotect them, do not understand their condition or deny the existence of the problem. A few respondents request that family counseling be provided to help the entire family cope with the affected member's condition. Considering the genetic factors involved with RP, other non-affected family members who may be carriers could also benefit from such counseling. This service could also help family members work through the stages of coping that Vernon (1983) notes.

Socialization
A large majority (72%) report that their retinal degeneration interferes with their social activities (see Table 2). Difficulty in dark places such as bars, theaters, and in night activities pose the most frequently cited problems.

The social implications of RP can have just as much influence over one's quality of life as the vocational or psychological implications. Most of the respondents are at ages when social life, friends and dating are very important. Several describe the anxiety they experience in dark places, where sighted young adults frequently interact. As Barron (1974) suggests, many choose to avoid such risky situations altogether. One youth writes, "Most young people meet in bars where I can't see. I'm too shy to join other groups. I do not know anyone with the same problems. . . . I find this depressing." Another woman hates "going into dark places, bumping into people and having them wonder what's the matter with me." Several men surveyed relate the problem of asking a woman out for a date, and hoping that she is able and willing to drive.

Personal adjustment
Most of those surveyed report having been embarrassed by their RP. Falling down and bumping into objects are the most common reasons given. The respondents indicate that most other people do not understand their type of impairment, and often regard those with it as clumsy or inattentive. Some respondents try to ignore the disorder and do things as they always have.

Most of the respondents have someone with whom they can talk about the condition. However, while a very large majority state that a close friend knows of their disorder, a smaller number say they actually can talk to their close friend about it. Further, only half of those receiving counseling at the time surveyed feel that they can talk with their counselor about

their disorder. One-fifth of the respondents report that they have no one with whom they can talk about their RP (see Table 2).

Going blind is obviously the greatest concern the respondents have. Corollary to this is their fear of losing independence and not being self-supporting after vision declines. Because the rate of visual deterioration is so uncertain, many express a fear of the future. Understandably, their hope is that their condition will not worsen. Another major concern is passing the condition on to children. Other fears reported include a limited social life, feelings of inadequacy, embarrassment, and being "abnormal."

Of those who express hope that their vision remains stable, some plan to continue with the job they have based on this hope. This seems to imply that many young adults may not have fully realized the irreversibility and progression of the disorder and its implications. As Vernon (1983) explains, only after the person is fully aware of the reality, can "constructive and effective coping with permanent disability begin." Some young adults with RP may benefit from counseling that deals with this crucial principle.

Counseling services needed
Only thirty-nine percent of those surveyed have ever received any type of counseling related to their eye disorder (see Table 2). However, a large majority of respondents indicate that young people with RP have a need for special counseling to help them accept and adjust to their condition (see Table 2).

To ensure appropriate and comprehensive counseling, the counselor should be knowledgeable about the nature and progression of RP, so that a client need not spend valuable time teaching his or her counselor about its implications. The professional should be especially attuned to the social and recreational barriers faced by the young man or woman with RP. Also, opportunities for peer counseling and interaction should be made more available.

Steps Taken by the RP Foundation Fighting Blindness
Some positive steps have been taken toward addressing the problems of young adults with RP. Several years ago, the RP Foundation Fighting Blindness established the Young Adult Program for young people with RP and allied retinal disorders to offer them the opportunity to meet others with RP, share experiences, and learn more about their disorders. The Young Adult Program has been successful in promoting

peer interaction through its nationwide newsletter column, telephone network system and letter exchange program. In addition, the Foundation maintains an ongoing information and referral program. Besides research and medical questions, the information and referral coordinator responds to inquiries on such topics as genetics, education, employment, low vision aids, community services, legal issues and government programs. Referrals are frequently made to appropriate organizations, agencies and local Foundation affiliiates.

References
Boughman, J.A., Conneally, P.M., & Nance, W.E. (1980). Population genetic studies of retinitis pigmentosa. *American Journal of Human Genetics, 32,* 23-235.

Fishman, G., Vasquez, V., Fishman, M., & Berger, D. (1979). Visual loss and foveal lesions in Usher's syndrome. *British Journal of Ophthalmology, 7,* 484-488.

Karp, A. (1985). Hearing loss associated with retinitis pigmentosa. *Journal of Visual Impairment & Blindness. 79,* 404-405.

Schein, A. (1976). Counseling issues in RP. *American Archives of Rehabilitation Therapy, 23*(1), 9-14.

Schein, J.D., & Delk, M.T., Jr. (1974). *The deaf population of the United States.* Silver Spring, Md.: National Association of the Deaf.

Vernon, M. (1983). *Parental and physician reaction to retinitis pigmentosa in a child.* Pamphlet published by National Retinitis Pigmentosa Foundation.

Vernon, M., Boughman, A., & Annala, L. (1982). Considerations in diagnosing Usher's syndrome: RP and hearing loss. *Journal of Visual Impairment & Blindness, 70,* 258-261.

U.S. Bureau of the Census (March, 1982). *1980 census of population: Detailed population characteristics.* Part 1, Washington, D.C.

U.S. Bureau of the Census (1982). *Statistical abstract of the United States: 1982-1983.* (103rd edition). Washington, D.C.

U.S. Department of Health and Human Services (June, 1980). *Epilepsy.* (N.I.H. Publication No. 80-1612). Washington, D.C.: U.S. Government Printing Office.

U.S. Department of Health and Human Services (February, 1981). *Prevalence of selected impairments, United States 1977.* (DHHS Publication No. [PHS] 81-1562). Washington, D.C., U.S. Government Printing Office.

Louise Nemshick is a graduate of Western Maryland College; McCay Vernon, Ph.D., is professor of psychology at Western Maryland College; and Fran Ludman, M.L.A., is director of human services for the R.P. Foundation Fighting Blindness. Inquiries should be addressed to the authors at Western Maryland College, Westminster, MD 21157.

The Usher's Syndrome Adolescent: Programming Implications for School Administrators, Teachers, and Residential Advisors

Wanda M. Hicks and Doin E. Hicks

OVERVIEW

Usher's Syndrome, first described in 1858, is a condition of congenital deafness accompanied by progressive loss of vision through retinitis pigmentosa. In childhood, the syndrome is characterized by poor adaptation to darkness (night blindness), progressing to limited peripheral vision that usually becomes increasingly evident by the teenage years. During the middle-aged or later years, there is degeneration of central vision. It is difficult, however, to generalize about the disease since the rate of visual deterioration varies considerably from individual to individual, and there is a wide range of concomitant handicaps.

The incidence data on Usher's Syndrome are somewhat sketchy and thus open to conjecture. Available estimates indicate the disease occurs in approximately 3 per 100,000 in the general population (Kloepfer, Laguaite, & McLaurin, 1966). This may seem like a small number, placing the disease almost in the rare category. But when applied to the deaf population, and particularly to those persons who are congenitally deaf, the data are much more meaningful and significant.

Regarding those persons who were born deaf, the literature has variously reported the incidence of Usher's Syndrome at 4% (Nance, 1971, 1973) and 3-6% (Vernon, 1973). Bergsma

Wanda Hicks is a specialist with the Office of Special Services, Division of Pre-College Programs at Gallaudet College in Washington, D.C. Doin Hicks is the Vice President for Research, Division of Research at Gallaudet College.

(1973) reported, however, that the incidence of Usher's Syndrome among the deaf population may be substantially higher than previous estimates since the symptoms of retinitis pigmentosa may not be present or detected until well after the student has started school. Nevertheless, Vernon (1969) estimates that 16,000 persons in the United States suffer from Usher's Syndrome. Recent estimates from the Office of Special Education, Department of Education, support Vernon's estimate by indicating there are 3,000 to 5,000 severely vision and hearing-impaired school-aged individuals in the United States.

Although this is a relatively small segment of the total school-aged handicapped population (estimated at 7,000,000), it is a group that requires and deserves extensive assistance in order to achieve its potential. Vernon (1974) puts the situation in perspective by stating, "It is almost unbelievable that a condition which causes 3% to 6% of deaf children to become blind is still relatively ignored by professionals working with deaf adults and children." To dramatize further the significance of Usher's Syndrome, Vernon (1969) reported that half of all deaf-blindness was due to this disease.

USHER'S SYNDROME: SYMPTOMATOLOGY AND STAGES

When inquiring about the condition of Usher's Syndrome, educators usually ask questions relating to symptoms of the condition, its stages, and, most importantly, programmatic considerations. Doin Hicks (1978) has provided a comprehensive outline and discussion of the characteristics of the condition that should be taken into consideration for programmatic planning. He summarizes the five stages as: (a) *Stage 1* — "Awareness Stage" (chronological ages of 6-12); (b) *Stage 2* — "General Counseling Stage" (chronological ages of 13-20); (c) *Stage 3* — "General Planning and Community Resource Identification Stage" (early adult years); (d) *Stage 4* — "Specific Planning and Adjustment Counseling Stage" (middle adult years; and (e) *Stage 5* — "Adjustment Stage" (late adult years or sooner).

In the same article, Hicks points out that careful, comprehensive, and well-coordinated programming should be undertaken from the point of initial diagnosis through the late adult years. He recommends professionals be forthright and candid with the person having the condition.

Even in the first stage, the initial symptoms of the disease should be described to the individual and he or she should be alerted to compensatory measures that should be taken to cope with the night vision problems. Even at this early age, the family should be provided with supportive counseling. Genetic counseling should be included in such a program.

As the loss of night vision becomes compounded with loss of peripheral vision during the early adolescent years, career counseling should be implemented. Additional genetic counseling is important for the family and the individual, along with specific counseling regarding the nature of the disease, phases of the disease, and variations in the rate of disease progression.

PROGRAMMING CONSIDERATIONS

Schools and programs serving individuals with Usher's Syndrome must tailor a special academic program to meet these students' present and future needs. Such programmatic planning must carefully take into consideration the symptomatic progression of the disease from the initial loss of night vision to the loss of peripheral vision and later the loss of central vision. Depending upon the age of a deaf-visually-impaired person and the severity of visual disability, a comprehensive program could well include such things as (a) vision health care, (b) orientation and mobility training, (c) prevocational training, (d) typing, (e) orientation to Braille, (f) physical conditioning, (g) counseling, and (h) regular evalua-

tions. As a result of such individualized activities, the visually-impaired student should learn the skills necessary to begin to function adequately with limited sight. In addition, he or she can achieve a realistic concept of present abilities and limitations, as well as how those abilities can serve the individual in the near and distant future.

The Usher's Syndrome student should be provided with an appropriate education to understand intellectually his or her handicap, as well as appropriate counseling services to help the student emotionally accept the handicap. The educational program, particularly in the late teenage years, should assist the person in establishing appropriate vocational goals.[1] Such students need to develop a comprehensive understanding of community, state, and national resources providing followup services.

Wanda Hicks (1978) has noted the increased interest of community and state organizations in providing services to deaf-blind postsecondary persons. Services include recreational and leisure activities provided by smaller organizations such as community clubs, religious groups, private service organizations, and park services. Vocational and health-oriented services, as well as habilitation and treatment programs, are generally provided by the larger state and federal service agencies. Hicks (1978) also summarizes some of the changes taking place in educational programming for deaf-blind adults. She points out that these changes are met with a number of problems and concerns:

A few programs established for the deaf and the blind are opening their continuing education classes to deaf-blind. Many problems are being encountered, however. For example, special support services such as one-to-one interpreting or special materials must usually be provided by the individual himself or by other service agencies. Further, the small number enrolled in these classes indicates a need for analyzing the results of this mainstreaming approach and consideration of the alternative approach of developing continuing education classes specifically designed and organized to meet the needs of the deaf-blind. (p. 396)

Local, state, and federal service agencies generally have not assumed direct responsibility

---

[1] *It is important that students have the widest possible choice within "appropriate" areas. For example, a career goal requiring moderate visual acuity may be acceptable so long as the student is fully aware that a career change will be necessary as vision changes.*

for providing services to deaf-blind persons until after they have completed their ongoing educational programs. Traditionally, these agencies have worked not only independently from one another, but also separate from school systems. A rather new concept that has been proposed (Hicks & Pfau, 1979) is cooperative and systematic planning of life-long services for Usher's Syndrome individuals. This planning is conceptualized as involving representatives from educational programs and all local, state, and federal agencies that serve such individuals. Such cooperation is intended to help avoid the service gaps that commonly exist in the habilitative/rehabilitative programs of individuals who are handicapped.

In order that a continuum of life-long services exists, vocational rehabilitation agencies must be called in by school programs to assist in planning Individualized Education Programs (IEP's) whenever the Usher's Syndrome person approaches his or her 16th birthday, or as soon as vocational rehabilitation agencies are permitted by state regulation to begin providing client service.

As suggested by Hicks and Pfau (1979), the educational program should have a case manager who works with the vocational rehabilitation case manager. The educational case manager would assume a leadership position in program planning until the student is released from the educational programs. At that time, the vocational rehabilitation case manager would assume primary responsibility for coordinating and/or providing the needed services. Again, the key is joint and systematic planning from diagnosis of the condition to the late adult years.

IMPLICATIONS FOR SCHOOL ADMINISTRATORS

The administrator of a school must assume overall responsibility for the education and welfare of all students in the school program. This is an awesome responsibility when considering the implications of providing an appropriate education to a range of multiply handicapped students. Schools for the deaf have always had students with additional handicaps in their programs. Because of the small number of such students, however, little systematic planning and coordination generally occurred. Often, a staff or faculty member

would take an interest in a particular multi-handicapped student, or be assigned such a responsibility, to help the student get through the program.

In recent years, the situation has changed dramatically in schools and programs for the deaf. The number of children from the 1964-65 rubella epidemic having at least one secondary handicap (in addition to deafness) ranges as high as 40%. This change in demographic characteristics of the student body, along with some recent federal and state legislation, means this substantial number of students can no longer be ignored. Future populations of deaf students—after the rubella group has completed postsecondary education—also will have a high incidence of multiple handicaps. This is because the disease or condition that caused deafness frequently causes other problems. In addition, a higher incidence of drug and alcohol abuse and venereal disease exists among expectant mothers. All of these situations contribute to a higher probability of single or multiply handicapping conditions.

The good administrator not only reviews and analyzes the past, but assesses the present situation and systematically plans for the future. Usher's Syndrome students comprise a significant percentage of the total multihandicapped student population in a program for the deaf. These students must be integrated, to the extent possible, within the school's total academic, residential, psychosocial, and recreational programming. In order for this to occur, in-school and out-of-school support units must be organized and developed, the physical facilities must be altered, and special programming must be implemented using management/planning teams. Comprehensive and systematic planning involves at least three major steps:

1. Analyze the demographic characteristics, including the present and future abilities and deficiencies, of individual students within the program;
2. Develop and analyze the demographic profile of the total school population that identifies common and unique characteristics of groups of students; and
3. Develop a comprehensive, coordinated, and systematic program that allows each child to progress at his/her maximum rate in all intellectual, social, emotional, and motoric areas.

The administrator has the ultimate responsibility to Usher's Syndrome students of providing and/or arranging for appropriate academic and support services—medical, family, instructional, psychosocial, career/vocational, and community/environment. Recruitment and employment of specially trained and experienced staff and faculty who understand the unique needs of this multihandicapped child may be necessary. It may be necessary also to conduct a variety of in-service workshops and institutes to provide orientation and training needed by faculty and staff. Below are six major areas in which administrative program planning is essential.

A. *Medical Considerations*
1. What are the results of audiological testing (e.g., severity of hearing loss, age of onset, slope of audiometric curve, amount of functional hearing)?
2. What are the results of the visual screening test and, if the visual screening test was failed, what are the results of the in-depth comprehensive follow-up visual testing?
3. What additional health-related problems or handicaps does the student have?
   a. Does the student report them to the nurse?
   b. Does he or she cry easily?
   c. Does the student have a number of health-related complaints, and is there a consistency in such complaints?

B. *Family Profile Considerations*
1. What is the socioeconomic status of the family?
2. How many were in the household (e.g., number of siblings, one or two parents, grandparents)?
3. What are the family expectations for this student, and how much support will the family give to the school?
4. What is the disease-related history of the family?
   a. Are there other deaf members in the family?
   b. If there are other deaf members in the family, have any of them been diagnosed as having Usher's Syndrome?
   c. Does the family have immunization records?

5. Does the family live on a farm, in the inner city, or in the suburbs?
6. Does the family eat nutritionally-balanced meals?
7. What is the family's attitude toward this student?
8. Does the family need counseling or training in community skills?
9. Does the family provide a better residence environment than a dormitory situation would?
10. Does the family provide an environment which is culturally rich or is that environment one which is culturally deprived?

C. *Academic Considerations*
1. Can academic tests standardized on deaf students be administered to the Usher's Syndrome students in a satisfactory manner?
2. If standardized tests cannot be used, how can the school best determine the student's academic deficiencies and strengths?
3. If the student has visual problems, have the tests taken into consideration such factors as optimal lighting, large print, appropriate administrative instruction, and do they give the individual time to respond?
4. If the student is taking medication, how does this influence his or her academic performance?
5. What special accommodations are needed in the classroom (e.g., optimal class size, large print, lighting, content, programming sequence, peer attitude, teacher awareness)?
6. What special academic-support services are needed to support class activities?
7. What considerations are given to the student's preferred learning style, deficiencies, and competencies?

D. *Psychosocial Considerations*
1. Does the Usher's Syndrome student understand the nature of his or her condition?
2. Is the student able to cope with the present symptoms of his or her condition and with the disease's anticipated progression?
3. Is the student able to cope with peer reactions?

4. Is the student able to sustain emotional balance without special counseling via a trained psychologist?

E. *Career/Vocational Considerations*
   1. What are some realistic career options for an individual with Usher's Syndrome?
   2. What career prerequisites (e.g., academic, social, communication, training, competencies, experience) are essential for career entry?
   3. What are the postsecondary educational interests and capabilities of the individual?
   4. What are the career/vocational interests and capabilities of the individual?

F. *Community Resource Considerations*
   1. What resources are available to a student with Usher's Syndrome within his or her home community?
   2. What state and federal resources are available to this student?
   3. Has liaison been established between the school and community/state/federal resources on behalf of the student?
   4. For the residential school student, what degree of independence is realistic for his or her return to a home community?
   5. What are the perceptions of members of the individual's community, including representatives from business and industry, toward multiply handicapped individuals?

After reviewing the preceding questions, one can see that the school administrator has a wide range of responsibilities in providing leadership and coordination for educational programming on behalf of the Usher's Syndrome student. The good administrator is concerned with not only diagnosis and planning but also educational assessment, program implementation, and coordination with service-providing institutions. Though these functions are necessary for all deaf students in the school program, they are particularly crucial for students with Usher's Syndrome.

IMPLICATIONS FOR TEACHERS AND SERVICE SUPPORT PERSONNEL

Though the chief administrative officer has overall responsibility for program planning and coordination, the classroom teacher and service support personnel are responsible for day-to-day program implementation. For the Usher's Syndrome student, the general goal of the school might be stated as follows: "To provide an appropriate academic environment and support services, as well as appropriate methodology and media/materials, which allows and encourages the Usher's Syndrome student to participate fully and to make the maximum progress of which he or she is capable in school program areas—academic, residential, psychosocial, recreational, physical, extracurricular, and others."

In order for the student with Usher's Syndrome to have a culturally rich home environment—with prerequisite learning experiences that foster progress in school—the school needs to develop and implement a parent orientation and education program. This is, assuming that the condition of Usher's Syndrome has been diagnosed prior to school entry. It is well known that many Usher's Syndrome youngsters are not accurately diagnosed until after they are well into their elementary school years. Every attempt should be made to diagnose the condition at the earliest possible date.

Teachers and service support personnel should complete inservice training related to the condition of Usher's Syndrome in order to plan and implement the most appropriate educational program possible. After a complete student assessment is made, the teachers and support personnel will be able to develop realistic goals for the student. In addition to general goals, it is important that realistic, specific, and measurable educational objectives be formulated, along with procedures for evaluating the degree to which they have been attained. It is realistic, then, to plan and implement programming strategies.

Placement Considerations

A number of factors must be considered in making a determination of the student's optimal placement in a secondary program. Some of the more important factors include the following:
   1. Academic achievement level;
   2. Intellectual ability;
   3. Vocational interests, competencies, and experiences;
   4. Psychosocial maturity;
   5. Characteristics of the family, including expectations for the student;

6. Community resources;
7. Degree of orientation and mobility training;
8. Severity of hearing loss and visual problems;
9. Number, type, and severity of additional handicapping conditions (in addition to hearing and vision impairment);
10. Receptive and expressive communication ability in the oral/aural, reading/writing, manual communication, and Braille modalities;
11. Health history, present health condition, and health prognosis;
12. Apparent rate of visual deterioration.

Physical Considerations for Classroom Environment

In preparing for and instructing the Usher's Syndrome student, the teacher should bear in mind a number of considerations. One of these is that a significant reduction in peripheral vision generally exists, sometimes accompanied by some loss of central vision. Consequently, it is recommended that the students be seated in a tight configuration. Other students and the teacher should not be more than 10 feet from the Usher's Syndrome student, with the optimal distance being 6 feet.

Regarding seating arrangements, a number of options are adequate. Horseshoe seating (with the Usher's Syndrome students at either end) and a circle arrangement (providing the diameter is not greater than 10 feet) are both excellent. The rectangular configuration and the shallow curve arrangement are fair to good, providing that Usher's Syndrome students are seated on the end chairs. One suggestion is to allow the Usher's Syndrome student to choose the seating location that allows for best vision and communication. Other important considerations are as follows:

1. *Lighting* — The lighting, either fluorescent or incandescent, should be adequate and of adjustable intensity; individual desk lamps should be provided when possible; if natural light is present, glare should be eliminated if possible.
2. *Teacher Area* — The teacher should try to stay in the same general area while lecturing or giving group instructions; clutter should be avoided and a continuous background should exist if possible.
3. *Windows* — Windows should be only in the rear of the classroom unless nonglare windows exist (then windows on sides of classroom may be appropriate).
4. *Chalkboards* — The chalkboard should always be kept clean for maximum contrast; letters should be in upper and lower case (avoiding use of all capital letters), and 3-4' high for easy reading.
5. *Color* — Colors in background teaching areas should be somewhat neutral (soft), nonglare and textured if possible; other areas of the classroom may be cheerful and bright; dark browns and dark reds should be avoided on floors and carpets (since these colors make other objects hard to see for the Usher's Syndrome students) in preference for softer colors.
6. *Furniture Arrangement* — Furniture should be arranged in a way that allows for considerable freedom of movement in open spaces; it should also be stable and free from sharp edges; if any changes are made in furniture arrangement, these should be discussed with the students; also, all doors and drawers (classroom, cabinet, etc.) should be kept closed.

Other Classroom Considerations

All instructional materials should include print that is above average in size, from a minimum of 12 points to a maximum of 18 points. If the student's vision is very poor, type size up to 36 points may be used. However, it must be remembered that larger print, above a certain size (approximately 18 points), is more difficult to read.

All print should have the maximum contrast possible; thus, dense ink should be used. Black on white nonglare paper is best. For teacher-prepared materials, the IBM "bookcase" typing element is very good. The illustrations and pictures should be clear with definite and broad lines, and an uncluttered background.

Visual materials, and a visual communication modality, should be continued as long as the Usher's Syndrome student has functional vision. The sense of touch, however, should also be taught and developed in a systematic and thorough manner. Texture should be used whenever possible, and the teacher should keep in mind that the tactile and olfactory senses will become the primary sensory modalities for the

Usher's Syndrome individual as central vision becomes seriously impaired and nonfunctional. Thus, these senses must be developed to their fullest extent.

There may be some adjustments necessary in order for efficient communication to occur. For example, if a student's central acuity is less than 20/80, speechreading will be reduced by approximately 80%. Because of night blindness, communication methods that rely on the visual modality are almost impossible in dark or semi-dark conditions. For those students who still have good central acuity but a greatly restricted visual field, it may be necessary to substantially modify normal sign language procedures.

Keeping in mind the three major components of sign language—point of location, movement, and configuration—it may be necessary to reduce the magnitude of the movements, increase the duration of each sign, and make each signed configuration clearer and more concise.

As the field of vision becomes more restricted and as central vision deteriorates, other communication methods will have to be considered (e.g., guided-wrist method, touch method—alphabet in palm of hand, block print on body, Braille, manipulative alphabet).

In summary, the classroom teacher must take into consideration not only where the Usher's Syndrome student is functioning at the present time, but where he or she will be functioning in the immediate and distant future. The teacher must take maximum advantage of all the student's assets and capabilities and must also prepare him or her for the most probable eventuality. For the teacher to function in this desirable manner, it is necessary to have a thorough understanding of the limitations and capabilities of each student and also of the nature of the Usher's Syndrome condition.

Service support personnel also must have a thorough understanding of the condition of Usher's Syndrome. These personnel include those working in such areas as (a) health (e.g., nurse, general physician, otologist, ophthalmologist), (b) counseling (e.g., counselor, psychologist, psychiatrist), (c) media and materials support (e.g., librarian, curriculum designer, educational technology specialist), (d) testing (e.g., audiologist, diagnostician, optometrist), and (e) other service providers (e.g., speech therapist/speech pathologist, reading special-

ist, art/music specialist, physical education personnel, dormitory personnel, supervising teacher, principal). These service providers must not only be able to communicate effectively with Usher's Syndrome students, but must have a thorough understanding of the functioning status of each student, realistic goals and expectations, and prognoses for them.

IMPLICATIONS FOR RESIDENTIAL ADVISORS OR HOME/ COMMUNITY CONTACTS

Residential advisors (also termed "house parents," "cottage parents," or "RA's") and others who work with students in out-of-class programs must also understand the symptoms and progression of Usher's Syndrome and how it affects students, the family, and peer interactions. The residential advisors must understand the normal adaptive behaviors of Usher's Syndrome students, and must know how to plan activities that do not put the students at a disadvantage. They must also know how to make the residential environment a comfortable place where such students can live, interact, and mature.

Although this role of the residential advisor is emphasized in the following, it should be stressed that the family and/or others in the community must assume responsibility for such observation, support, and intervention, as appropriate.

The residential advisor may have to plan activities for Usher's Syndrome students that are more flexible than for other students. Such students should be "free to be me." Though there should be definite regulations and guidelines, any constraints should take into consideration the present and future sensory deprivation of such students. They should be provided with a variety of activities. Some additional tutoring may be necessary in order to assist them in completing homework activities. Also, some general counseling may be required to assist these students to work out their more than average social and psychological problems. Residential advisors should be apprised of the following common behaviors of the Usher's Syndrome students:

1. They may appear quiet in a large group;
2. They frequently exhibit shy-type behaviors, particularly in group situations;
3. They may edge themselves to one side

when placed in a group;

4. They frequently bump into objects in the room such as tables and chairs;
5. They are bothered particularly by bright lights and complain that glaring lights hurt their eyes;
6. They frequently fail to understand or miss group instruction that is given by residential advisors or classroom teachers;
7. They are frequently last in completing group activities;
8. They exhibit symptoms of anxiousness in new areas;
9. They are frequently last to enter a room and may bump into other students and objects;
10. They may appear unconcerned and may fail to fully participate in group activities;
11. They frequently must rely on a friend for information;
12. They have repetitive behavior (they seem to do the same things in the same ways or continue to order the same things);
13. They may frequently have accidents at mealtime with objects placed at their sides;
14. They express a desire to enter a room that will be darkened (such as a movie theatre) very early;
15. They have a tendency to avoid conversations in darkened areas;
16. They may choose to stay home alone rather than be faced with the embarrassment of not being able to see in dark or poorly lit places;
17. They may appear awkward when exiting from the inside to the outside of a building (where they are faced with bright lights);
18. They may avoid participating in outdoor sports when the sun is very bright;
19. They may request sunglasses whenever they are asked to participate in activities in the bright sunlight;
20. Without sunglasses, they are nearly always seen shading their eyes or squinting when in the sunlight;
21. They avoid walking or running fast in unfamiliar areas, particularly when there is bright sunlight or when they are in darkened areas;
22. They frequently hesitate at the top or bottom of stairs (in an attempt to orient themselves);

23. When walking down the street, they frequently stumble over curbs or slight elevations/depressions in walking surface;
24. They may hesitate when first meeting someone, or appear to ignore them;
25. They have difficulty reading in dimly lit areas (such as menus in restaurants);
26. When walking along a road at night, they may appear to stagger or lose their balance after an oncoming car has passed (as a result of bright lights);
27. They may avoid social activities when such activities take place in dimly lit areas;
28. They may appear to ignore you if you are standing at their side;
29. They prefer to sit at the side of a large group;
30. They prefer conversation at distances of 4 to 6 feet;
31. They may appear to be constantly visually scanning a group.

The above behaviors, though possibly appearing somewhat bizarre to the untrained observer, are logical when considering the students' reduced peripheral vision, inability to adapt to substantial changes in illumination, night blindness, and impaired central vision. The residential advisors must become informed, and they must build an awareness among all students not affected by Usher's Syndrome. A considerable amount of student and family guidance and counseling is also important.

The residential advisors may wish to lead group discussions (informal counseling and guidance sessions) in such areas as (a) understanding the functioning and limitation of their eyes, (b) understanding the progressive nature of Usher's Syndrome, (c) sharing problems and events that have occurred associated with the condition, (d) sharing concerns about their future (e.g., visual prognosis, career/vocational expectations, marriage and the family, everyday living, recreation), and (e) resources that might be available to the students (e.g., resource personnel, agencies and programs, aids and devices, financial resources, places where additional education and training may be obtained).

The residential advisors should assume responsibility for advocacy on behalf of these students. The advisors should help the students seek out and use available resources, and they should encourage the students to be more independent and self-reliant.

The residential advisors should arrange adequate and appropriate lighting for the Usher's Syndrome students. In conversation areas, the lighting should be at least 79 candle power. In hallways, baths, laundry rooms, and activity rooms, the lighting should also be evenly lit with approximately 79 candle power. Outside lighting should provide even illumination, avoiding very bright or dark spots. Student rooms should be decorated in soft, lighter colors. Colors or materials that cause glare should be avoided. To the extent possible, the windows should face in a direction of least glare from the sun. If this arrangement is impossible, an opaque heavy shade should be installed. Students should have desk/study lamps that contain both fluorescent and incandescent bulbs. If possible student rooms should have lighting that is controlled by a rheostat which allows the student to set the lighting at optimal conditions for his/her unique visual functioning.

Residential advisors should also be aware that small group activities are preferable to large group activities. If a large group activity is necessary, it is important to provide an interpreter or mini-groups within the larger group. Some other specific suggestions are listed below:

1. Flashlights should be provided for night travel, or the "Sighted Guide" method may be appropriate if the person is seriously visually impaired and if the activity is in an unfamiliar area;
2. Specially lighted conversational areas should be provided during parties, dances, and other activities (that are traditionally dimly lit);
3. Arrangements should be made so that students may arrive early to a movie to allow the students to be seated before the lights go out;
4. Students should be allowed to remain in their seats a few minutes after the movie is over;
5. Students should be permitted to choose the best location to sit or stand for any activity;
6. Sunglasses should be provided for outside activities during the day, particularly if there is bright sunlight;
7. If possible, students should be provided with a position during outdoor activities and games that allows their backs to be to the sun;

8. Students should be alerted to any change in the level of a surface when walking, particularly when facing the sun;
9. A comprehensive program of peer awareness should be implemented;
10. Skilled and understanding counselors should be available at all times; and
11. Candid and objective answers should be given to the students who have questions about different aspects of Usher's Syndrome.

Residential advisors play a very important role in the lives of the Usher's Syndrome residential student. In order to provide the kind of program that is optimal for the student, residential advisors must have an indepth understanding of the progressive characteristics and symptoms of Usher's Syndrome. They must attempt to analyze and understand the behaviors of the students and modify the environment where necessary to reduce psychological and physical risks.

Counseling and guidance activities are an important responsibility of the residential advisor for students with Usher's Syndrome. A thorough understanding of the condition will allow the advisor to provide information that will reduce stress and anxiety and thus make the dormitory a more interesting, rewarding, and enjoyable place in which to live.

CONCLUSION

Described herein are a number of considerations for school staff members, family, and others who work closely with the young persons with Usher's Syndrome. Specific roles and responsibilities will vary as a function of particular school and community organizational structures. Accordingly, the reader is encouraged to consider the suggestions provided as a generic approach to service delivery, even though responsibilities are categorized. Conspicuously missing is a specific explanation of the role of school counselor or other psychologically oriented clinicians. Obviously the area of social/personal/genetic, as well as career development, counseling would well be and should be largely vested within the school counselor role. Unfortunately, many schools for the deaf and other programs serving hearing- and vision-impaired students do not have comprehensive counseling services. A complete explication of the potential counselor role is, therefore, appropriate for another descriptive article. The overriding consideration here is that the young person with Usher's Syndrome has every opportunity to achieve optimum development. It has been said that the silent minority of deaf persons is "among the most misunderstood sons of man." How then can one describe the implications of the added problem of limited vision? It is this monumental problem which we seek to place in perspective.

REFERENCES

Bergsma, D. R. Opthalmologic aspects of Usher's Syndrome. In *Symposium on Usher's Syndrome,* Washington, D.C.: Gallaudet College, April 19, 1973.

Hicks, W. M. Continuing education for deaf blind youth and adults. *American Annals of the Deaf,* 1978, 123, 395–399.

Hicks, W. M., & Pfau, G. S. Deaf-visually impaired persons: Incidence and services. *American Annals of the Deaf,* 1979, 124, 76–92.

Hicks, D. E. Usher's Syndrome: Programmatic considerations. *American Annals of the Deaf,* 1978, 123, 365–371.

Kloepfer, H. W., Laguaite, J. K., & McLaurin, J. W. The hereditary syndrome of congenital deafness and retinitis pigmentosa. *Laryngoscope,* 1966, 86.

Nance, W. E. The principles and practice of genetic counseling. *Annals of Otology, Rhinology, and Laryngology,* 1971, p. 80.

Nance, W. E. Genetic aspects of Usher's syndrome. *Proceedings of Usher's Syndrome Conference.* Washington, D.C.: Gallaudet College, April 1973.

Vernon, M. Usher's Syndrome—Deafness and progressive blindness. *Journal of Chronic Diseases,* 1969, 22, 133–151.

Vernon, M. Overview of Usher's Syndrome: Congenital deafness and progressive loss of vision. In *Symposium on Usher's Syndrome,* Washington, D.C.: Gallaudet College, April 19, 1973.

Vernon, M. Overview of Usher's Syndrome: Congenital deafness and progressive loss of vision. *Volta Review,* Feb. 1974.

Services for Children and Youths who are Deaf-Blind: An Overview

A.M. Zambone; K.M. Huebner

Abstract: The uniqueness and complexity of needs and characteristics of the population of children who are deaf-blind make it extremely difficult to determine who they are. Consequently, identifying and meeting their needs through appropriate intervention models and strategies is also difficult. This paper provides an overview of what is currently known about the population of children who are deaf-blind, a description of the service delivery and resource systems currently in place, and a discussion of current and future issues relevant to providing intervention.

Determining prevalence is critical to meeting the needs of children and youths who are deaf-blind. An inaccurate count can result in inadequate funding, because federal resource distribution is determined by a formula that is based on the number of persons being served. Misclassification and misidentification result in inappropriate or incomplete intervention and are significant barriers to monitoring the quality of educational programs being provided (Baldwin & Bullis, 1988). A comprehensive effort to determine the prevalence of children and youths who are deaf-blind was conducted by Teaching Research in 1985. They received a grant from the Office of Special Education Programs (SEP) to compile national census information on persons between birth and 21 years of age who are deaf-blind. Their findings revealed the following (Baldwin, 1986; Baldwin & Bullis, 1988):

• In 1985, 4,227 Americans between birth and 21 years of age were reported as having deaf-blindness. That number increased to 5,477 in the 1987 count.

• The mean number of persons aged 21 and under who should have been identified as deaf-blind was 8,186—a discrepancy of nearly 3,000 persons. This number was determined by reviewing the significant discrepancies between the reports of the U.S. state departments of special education (SEA) and the state and regional coordinators for services to students who

are deaf-blind, by empirically estimating prevalence by normal distribution of the population, and by utilizing nine sample states as a "criterion group" to establish a baseline.

• A conservative estimate of two standard deviations below the mean results in a total of 5,442 deaf-blind persons aged 21 and under. Thus, the 1987 count represents, at best, a low-end range estimate.

Prevalence

There are numerous speculations about the reasons for the inaccuracies of prevalence data on deaf-blindness. The most obvious reason is the heterogeneous nature of the deaf-blind population. As Wolf, Delk, and Schein (1982) and Ward (1987) reported, there is significant variance in sensory abilities, additional impairments, levels of intelligence, communication abilities, and other attributes in the deaf-blind population. Chelimsky (1983) estimated that 66 percent of the children served by deaf-blindness centers have additional disabilities. Also, Wolf et al. (1982) indicated that the degree of sensory impairments is very difficult to measure in a large percentage of the deaf-blind population because of additional disabilities and other barriers to communication that limit response to typical evaluation procedures.

Identification is further complicated by significant discrepancies in definitions adopted by the various SEAs, SEP (based on educational law guidelines), and by the Helen Keller National Center, which uses the definition found in Section 313 of the Rehabilitation Act (Ward, 1987). Since 1971, there has been a voluntary

The authors would like to thank Jeri F. Traub, Ph.D., coordinator of international education and training, Hilton/Perkins Program, for her assistance in the preparation of this article.

national registry of children and youth who are deaf-blind. In 1980, SEP began to coordinate their data collection and analysis activities with the registry. Because it is a voluntary registry, however, several states do not participate, and others report only incomplete data (Ward, 1987).

Etiology

It has been difficult to determine etiology as prevalence for deaf-blindness. Wolf et al. (1982) examined rubella data collected since the epidemic of 1963 to 1965. Rubella continues to be a significant etiology for deaf-blindness, and its prevalence varies across geographic regions from year to year. There are many other causes of deaf-blindness, including genetic anomalies; congenital disabilities and malformations; toxicity due to drug ingestion during pregnancy; irradiation; infectious diseases, such as encephalitis and meningitis; and child abuse, trauma, or accident (Dantona, 1977; Chelimsky, 1983; Ward, 1987).

Despite the difficulty in counting and describing the population of children who are deaf-blind, there have been extensive efforts to ensure the availability of services specific to their unique needs through targeted funding initiatives from the U.S. federal government. These initiatives have significantly shaped the response to intervention needs since the rubella epidemic of the early 1960s resulted in a marked increase in the incidence of deaf-blindness.

Funding sources and program models

Specific legislation to ensure that the educational needs of children and youths who are deaf-blind would be met began to evolve in 1965 with the passage of P.L. 89-313. This law amended Title I of the Elementary and Secondary Education Act (ESEA) to establish grants to state agencies responsible for providing a free education in state-operated or -supported programs to children who are disabled, many of whom were labeled severely disabled or deaf- blind. ESEA was again amended in 1967 with the passage of P.L. 90-247, establishing Part C of Title VI in response to the increased incidence, due to the rubella epidemic, of deaf-blindness in children.

The legislation appropriated funds and described guidelines for establishing regional centers to provide educational services to children who are deaf-blind (U.S. Department of Education, 1983). These services included diagnosis and periodic medical evaluations, special education programs and therapy, consultation with and technical assistance from staff and caregivers, coordination of delivery of services among agencies, development of new services to fulfill unmet needs, professional and paraprofessional training, dissemination of information, and research.

Part C of Title VI of ESEA was again amended in 1970 and incorporated into the Education of the Handicapped Act (EHA), P.L. 91-230. These amendments authorized the continuation of direct services to children who are deaf-blind. Part 212c of P.L. 93-380, passed in 1975, assured continuity of funding under the title of "Deaf-Blind Centers and Services Program." That program name was again changed in 1983 by Section 622 of the Education of the Handicapped Act Amendments, P.L. 98-199, to "Services for Deaf-Blind Children and Youth."

Section 622 of the Education for the Handicapped Act, as amended by P.L. 98-199, refined the focus of the program. This new legislation placed increased emphasis on making funds available to projects to provide special education and related services to those children and youths who are deaf-blind to whom the states are not obligated to provide services under Part B of P.L. 94-142 (such as children whose ages are beyond the state-mandated range for services). Section 622 provided support to states to either make available a free, appropriate education under Part B of P.L. 94-142 or to provide services under some other authority, such as P.L. 98-313. Additionally, Section 622 supported technical assistance to SEAs to increase their effectiveness in delivering appropriate services to students eligible for services under Part B.

As this article went to press, the Department of Education, Office of Special Education and Rehabilitation Services, was beginning the process of reviewing responses to requests for proposals for continuing with these projects. It is anticipated (phone conversation with Charles Freeman, project officer, OSERS, June, 1992) that there will be between 40 to 50 single and multi-state centers in operation for the next three years.

The funding redistribution has also reflected the changes in the priorities for services to children and youths who are deaf-blind from no differentiation of eligibility among this population under Part C and Part 212c to special education and related services under Section 622 only for those children not covered under the state-mandated age ranges of P.L. 94-142 (Dantona, 1977). The services, as defined in the first of the three priorities of Section 622, include vocational and transitional services; diagnosis and educational evaluation; programs of adjustment, education and orientation; and consultation, counseling, and training for parents, other caregivers, and families.

Under the second priority, Section 622 supports technical assistance to states to increase their effectiveness in serving children eligible for special education under Part B. Technical assistance can be provided to all agencies serving children and youths who are deaf-blind through preservice or in-service training for professionals and paraprofessionals; replication of successful and innovative approaches in the provision of education or related services; encouragement of parental involvement; consultation and counseling services to professionals, paraprofessionals, parents, and others who are significant in the lives of children and youths who are deaf-blind.

The third priority allows any remaining funds to be used to provide services for children for whom the state is obligated to provide a free appropriate public education under P.L. 94-142. While this priority is still maintained in the law, regulation and SEP policy have prohibited the use of funds for this group of children for the past several years.

General and specialized services

Several studies were conducted in 1981 under the U.S. federal funding initiatives to evaluate the services provided to children and youths who are deaf-blind and to examine the ability to meet their needs through existing services, particularly during the transition to postschool environments. These studies yielded conflicting data on the need for separate funding initiatives specifically for students who are deaf-blind, and on the states' ability to provide services without reliance on Section 622 funds, particularly related services and extended day and year services (Lewis, 1981; Scott, Campeau, Wheeler, & Ferrara, 1982; Wolf, Delk, & Schein, 1982; Hanley, Clark, & Hanley, 1982). Additional points of conflict were raised in relation to the issue of separate intervention needs for this population as compared to the overall population of learners with severe disabilities.

A review of the 1981 studies and subsequent policy analysis efforts coordinated by SEP were conducted by Ward (1987), who concluded that the states have not yet reached a consensus "on whether Section 622 funds should be targeted for only indirect services or whether Section 622 funds should be phased out in the next two to three years" (p. 32).

Changing priorities
In addition to the policy and procedural conflicts under Section 622 and the dearth of definitive data about population prevalence and characteristics, services to children and youths who are deaf-blind have been challenged by changing priorities and values in service delivery under P.L. 94-142 and its amendments of 1986, P.L. 99-457. Specifically, with the priority for funds available through these mandates going to those children with the most severe disabilities, the mandate for service provision in the least restrictive environment being interpreted as full integration, the trend toward noncategorical delivery of services, and the lack of requirements under P.L. 99-457 to identify and categorize children according to their disabling conditions; conflict has arisen in several areas. These areas include the nature of services to be provided based on assumed needs, the agencies most appropriate to provide services and thus receive funding and technical assistance, and the competencies required of the personnel providing those services. These conflicts have resulted in the following:
• Dissension between providers of services to children with severe disabilities other than sensory impairments and providers of services to individuals with hearing and-or visual impairments. This dissension has created significant breakdowns in collaboration between the two areas of potentially applicable expertise and conflicting efforts to influence both the political arenas and the direct service arenas providing support to services for children who are deaf-blind (Zambone, 1989).
• The formation of the National Coalition on Deaf-Blindness, a coalition of professionals, parents, and organizations concerned with children with single and dual sensory impairments for the purpose of advocacy on behalf of separate funding and other forms of program support at the federal, state, and local levels (Collins, 1989).

• Frequently incomplete or inadequate service delivery to children who are deaf-blind and their caregivers in both programs for children with severe disabilities other than deafness or blindness and for children who are deaf-blind with additional disabilities (Orlansky, 1989).
• Significant confusion on the part of caregivers and direct service providers about optimal service delivery settings and services and additional resources needed (McDonald, 1989).
• Professional and consumer isolation within the larger context of special education (Orlansky, 1989).
• Inadequate knowledge and skills necessary to identify and meet the needs of children and youths who are deaf-blind and disagreement over effective service delivery models, best practices, and optimal service settings (Orlansky, Barrett, Collins, & Zambone, 1989).

Educational settings
Currently, children who are deaf-blind are served in a variety of settings, ranging from residential schools for children who are blind or deaf to integrated classrooms for nondisabled children, with support from teachers trained in visual or hearing impairments or severe disabilities. Within this range, a large number of children are served in categorical day and residential programs for students with severe disabilities. There is, however, a risk of inadequate service provision in all settings because of lack of teachers who represent a range of expertise across the disability areas, lack of related and support services specific to sensory impairments, and lack of resources and skills to address either those disabilities accompanying the deaf-blindness or the deaf- blindness itself.

Issues and responses in service delivery

Transition services
In addition to the difficulty of delivering a comprehensive, appropriate educational program to children who are deaf-blind, there is a crisis in effecting transition to appropriate postschool placements and services. Because the initial population of persons who are deaf-blind as a result of the rubella epidemic is too old to be eligible for school services, service providers are increasingly concerned with ensuring the continuity of support and training beyond the age of 21. Although vocational rehabilitation must first serve those individuals with severe disabilities, because these services are provided as an

entitlement rather than as an educational mandate, a breakdown in the continuity of school to postschool support has occurred. Conversely, since 1988 there has been a significant increase—to 117 agencies—in supported employment services to persons who are deaf-blind (Barrett, 1989).

There is also a severe shortage of personnel specifically trained to meet the educational needs of students who are deaf-blind. Parent support models specific to deaf-blindness are limited in scope and number, and there is ongoing disagreement among professionals, parents, and consumers about optimal service models and programs.

New initiatives
Efforts to address the problems just discussed are multifaceted. They include the following:
• The National Coalition on Deaf-Blindness and other advocacy and consumer groups are continuing their efforts to preserve access to categorical funds for the maintenance and continued development of services specific to children and youths who are deaf-blind. The strong commitment to specialized services for this population is based on a belief that they have needs that are specific and unique as a result of the deaf-blindness. There are other groups that believe that the needs of children who are deaf-blind should be addressed within the context of services for the population of children with various combinations of severe multiple impairments, because 1) there are limited dollars to be distributed between these two need-intensive groups of children, 2) the needs of both populations are similar and thus there are few programmatic discrepancies in providing services to both groups, and 3) providers of general services are committed to full integration and those serving the population of persons who are deaf-blind do not share that commitment. Each group believes the other is inadequately prepared fully to meet the needs of children who are deaf-blind. The groups' differences are further exacerbated by the dearth of empirical data documenting the needs of this population, and the limited prevalence of the population, rendering it difficult to make available a full range of services across numerous distant and discrepant settings. Although these differences of philosophy and approach have not been resolved, there is renewed attention to reserving some U.S. federal resources specifically for children who are deaf-blind.

- Extensive efforts, such as the inclusion of topics in deaf-blindness in the TASH, AER, CEC, and other programs to provide opportunities to identify critical issues, and for different professional, consumer, and parent group representatives to begin exploring ways to work together on behalf of children and youths who are deaf-blind.

- Increasing numbers of parent groups specifically for those caregivers whose children have deaf-blindness are emerging. The Hilton/Perkins National Program is involved in supporting and expanding this very important network. Consequently, new groups are being formed around the country. A large number of parent members are also individual members of the National Association for Parents of the Visually Impaired (NAPVI).

- The U.S. Congress has continued its support of the Helen Keller National Center for Deaf-Blind, the only dedicated national program in deaf-blindness that includes a direct service component. The center is authorized, through a cooperative agreement with the Rehabilitation Services Administration and Department of Education, under the 1967 Amendment to the Vocational Rehabilitation Act.

- The distribution of discretionary funds for personnel preparation programs addressing the needs of low-prevalence populations, including those who are deaf-blind. Currently, there are few graduate degree programs with emphasis specifically on deaf-blindness. There are several summer institutes, but these do not lead to certification in or a degree in deaf-blindness.

Grants

Funding has been made available through the U.S. Department of Education, Office of Special Education Programs, for distribution to projects that will identify best practices and needs, articulate the values that must underlie service delivery, and translate those values into practice. Recent grants have been awarded to the following:

- Teaching Research, Western Oregon State College, for refining counting procedures, developing a mechanism for identifying best practices and optimal settings, and applying the results of this identification to the evaluation of existing programs and services.

- TRACES (Teaching Research Assistance to Children and Youth Experiencing Sensory Impairments), for its national effort assisting state and multi-state deaf-blindness centers in identifying training needs

and developing technical assistance plans; developing a consultant pool of experts to plan and deliver technical assistance; selecting quality project reports, research findings and other materials pertaining to services to children who are deaf-blind; developing materials addressing topical issues; and providing planning and managerial support for annual meetings of directors of projects serving children and youths who are deaf-blind.

- The American Foundation for the Blind's Deaf-Blind Project: A National Consortium Effort, which is a four-year project funded to identify, collect, evaluate, develop, and disseminate in-service training and self-study materials for personnel working with children who are deaf-blind. The project emphasizes communication and mobility.

- The Deaf-Blind Clearinghouse, a recently funded collaborative effort led by Teaching Research and including the American Foundation for the Blind, Helen Keller National Center, and the Hilton/Perkins National Program.

Conclusion

Essentially, the needs of children and youths who are deaf-blind are addressed as a part of the larger mission of the organizations serving people who are deaf, blind, or severely disabled. Efforts to meet the children's needs more effectively, although commonly acknowledged as important, frequently result in conflicts and fragmented services because of discrepant values, priorities, traditions, and professional assumptions. These conflicts have increased because of competition for funds, resulting in increased commitment to serving the unique needs of those coming from a sensory-disability priority. The resolution of the conflicts, however, depends on cooperation among all groups concerned with the deaf-blind population, and, more importantly, a significant increase in accurate data reporting of their prevalence and characteristics, knowledge about effective practice, and the priorities of caregivers and consumers.

References

Baldwin, V., & Bullis, M. (1988). Prevalence data on students with deaf-blindness. In A. Covert, & T. Carr, (Eds.), *Value-based services for young adults with deaf-blindness*. New York: Helen Keller National Center for Deaf-Blind Youths and Adults, Technical Assistance Center, and The Association for Persons with Severe Handicaps Technical Assistance Project.

Barrett, S. (1989). *Vocational and community services*. Paper presented at the Josephine L. Taylor Leadership Institute, Atlanta, GA.

Chelimsky, E. (1983). Deaf-blind children and the centers serving them. 98th Congress, 1st session, *Hearings before the Subcommittee on Select Education*. Washington, D.C.: U.S. General Accounting Office.

Collins, M. (1989). *Educational Services*. Paper presented at the 1989 Josephine L. Taylor Leadership Institute, Atlanta, GA.

Dantona, R. (1977). A history of centers and services for deaf-blind children. In E.L. Lowell & C.C. Rouin (Eds.), *State of the art: Perspectives on serving deaf-blind children* (pp. 18-22). Sacramento, CA: California State Department of Education.

Hanley, M.J., Clark, D., & Hanley, D.E. (1982). *The deaf-blind: Perceptions from the '70s—Directions for the 80's: Recommendations and policies, priorities and actions for serving the deaf-blind*. Unpublished manuscript, Denver, CO: Mountain Plains Regional Center.

Lewis, L.M. (Preparer). (1981). *Selected issues in service delivery to deaf-blind children* (Project FORUM). Washington, D.C.: National Association of State Directors of Special Education.

Orlansky, M., Barrett, S., Collins, M., & Zambone, A. (1989). *Services to persons with multiple impairments and deaf-blindness*. Panel presentation at the Josephine L. Taylor Leadership Institute, Atlanta, GA.

Scott, A.C., Campeau, P.L., Wheeler, J.D., & Ferrara, S. (1982). *Evaluability assessment of the deaf-blind centers and services programs*. (Contract No. 300-80-0825), Palo Alto, CA: American Institutes for Research.

Ward, M. (1987). *An analysis of the issues associated with the new data collection process for deaf-blind children and youth under section 622 of the Education of the Handicapped Act as amended by P.L. 98-199*. Unpublished dissertation.

Wolf, E.G., Delk, M.T., & Schein, J.D. (1982). *Needs assessment of services to deaf-blind individuals* (Contract No. 300-81-0426). Silver Spring, MD: REDEX, Inc.

Zambone, A. (1989). *Summary and reaction*. Paper presented at the Josephine L. Taylor Leadership Institute, Atlanta, GA.

Alana M. Zambone, Ph.D., coordinator of international outreach services, Asia/Pacific and Latin American regions, Hilton/Perkins International Program, 175 North Beacon Street, Watertown, MA 02172; Kathleen M. Huebner, Ph.D., director, National Program Associates and AFB Deaf-Blind Project, American Foundation for the Blind, 15 West 16th Street, New York, NY 10011.

Perspectives of Parents Whose Children Have Dual Sensory Impairments

Michael F. Giangreco, Chigee J. Cloninger, Patricia H. Mueller, Susan Yuan, and
Susan Ashworth
University of Vermont

Although educators and other professionals acknowledge the importance of involving parents in their childrens' education, few researchers have investigated parental perceptions of educational and related services. This qualitative study identified four major themes during interviews with 28 families whose children have dual sensory impairments. These concerns clustered around parental perceptions of a "good life" for their children, as well as their experiences with fear, frustration, and change. Implications from the analysis may assist teachers, related service professionals, and administrators working with families to understand more fully parental perspectives.

DESCRIPTORS: dual sensory impairment, families, parent-professional relations, parents, qualitative research, quality of life, rural services, special education

Professional educators readily acknowledge the importance of family involvement in the education of children with special needs (Benson & Turnbull, 1986; Carney, 1987; Lipsky, 1989; Turnbull & Turnbull, 1990). Far too often, however, educators pass judgment on the quality of that involvement with little or no knowledge of family circumstances. Educators may concern themselves with issues such as lack of skill generalization from school to home, but seldom inquire into the demands, expectations, or priorities of the family (Featherstone, 1980). Systems change is promoted to accommodate evolving exemplary practices with all the best intentions for students, yet parents are not asked what impact these changes may have on their lives, nor how they define "quality of life" for themselves and their children (Hill, Rotegard, & Bruininks, 1984; Schalock, 1990).

Recognizing the importance of understanding family perspectives within the educational arena, this study explored the experiences and opinions of families of children with limited vision and hearing (dual sensory impairments), many of whom had other significant cognitive, orthopedic, and medically related disabilities (Vadasy & Fewell, 1986). To date, relatively little educational research has been conducted regarding children and youth with dual sensory impairments (DSI), or more specifically, their parents' perceptions of educational and related services (Baldwin & Bullis, 1988).

Due to the low incidence and multiple nature of their disabilities, students with dual sensory impairments pose unique challenges to the educational system in terms of (a) curriculum, (b) instruction, (c) receiving education within general education schools/classrooms, (d) planning for meaningful transitions, and (e) post-school opportunities (Covert & Carr, 1988; Ellis, 1986; Goetz, Guess, & Stremel-Campbell, 1987; Helmstetter, Murphy-Herd, Roberts, & Guess, 1984). The impact of the limitations of our collective knowledge of this group of students has resulted in the development of curricula that do not match family-focused outcomes, unduly restrictive educational placements, and the development of educational programs that limit options and do not promote a higher quality of life after graduation (Bullis & Otos, 1988; Covert & Carr, 1988; Meyer & Eichinger, 1987). Clearly, significant gaps exist in the research regarding appropriate service delivery practices for students with dual sensory impairments. The impact of these practices on the family unit is yet to be understood fully.

Frequently, parents, brothers, and sisters are the only persons providing continuity throughout the student's entire school career (Benson & Turnbull, 1986; Powell & Ogle, 1985). Thus, it becomes crucial for the family to participate in the design and implementation of a child's educational program (Turnbull & Turnbull, 1990). Given the number and variety of professionals involved in the education of students with dual sensory impairments and the complexity of student needs, families of these children may face intense pressures. Understanding these pressures may shed light on similar areas of concern for a much broader spectrum of families whose children have special needs as well as for the professionals who serve them. Therefore, the purpose

Partial support for the preparation of this manuscript was provided by the United States Office of Education, Office of Special Education and Rehabilitative Services, Demonstration Projects for Deaf-Blind Children and Youth (#H086H80017) awarded to the Center for Developmental Disabilities at the University of Vermont. The content of this article reflects the ideas and positions of the authors and do not necessarily reflect the ideas or positions of the U.S. Department of Education; therefore, no official endorsement should be inferred.

of this research was not only to listen intently and record as faithfully as possible what these families said, but to capture their meaning. This information can affect how teachers, related service professionals, and administrators who work with families whose children have dual sensory and multiple impairments will operate in the future. As the services mandated by P. L. 99–457 are implemented, professionals will be expected to use a family-centered approach to identify and respond to the strengths and concerns of families in meeting the needs of their children. (Bailey, Winton, Rouse & Turnbull, 1990; McGonigel & Garland, 1988). This study is an effort to move in that direction.

Methods

The nature of the questions posed by this study prompted the selection of semistructured interviews as the method of research. The descriptive and inductive approach inherent in qualitative methods determined the study design. The primary objective was to understand better parental perspectives regarding the impact of educational and related services on the lives of children with dual sensory impairments. The research design was based on the conceptual underpinnings of established qualitative methods and techniques (Bogdan & Biklen, 1982; Patton, 1980; Taylor & Bogdan, 1984).

Study Participants

From December 1988 through June 1989, 35 students were listed on the *Vermont Report of Students with Dual Sensory Impairments (DSI)* (analogous to the Federal Deaf-Blind Registry). The Vermont Department of Education defines a student with dual sensory impairments as one who ". . . is visually impaired and who is hearing impaired in accordance with Vermont regulations, and cannot be accommodated in special education programs solely for the child with hearing impairments or the child with visual impairments, without adaptations designed for these dual sensory impairments". Students are also included in the State Report if they are considered to be at risk for dual sensory impairments. A student is at risk for dual sensory impairments ". . . when there are inconsistent or inconclusive responses during clinical hearing and/ or vision evaluations, and/or inconsistent responses to auditory and/or visual stimuli in the environment, or the student has a chronic or degenerative health impairment that may potentially result in dual sensory impairments" (Vermont Department of Education, 1987). These definitions do not imply that special education programs are necessarily provided in segregated special education settings. Rather, special education programs and services for students with severe disabilities, including those with dual sensory impairments, are provided in the least restrictive environment. Increasingly, this includes general education classrooms

(*Daniel R. R. v. State Board of Education*, 1989; Lipsky & Gartner, 1989; Stainback, Stainback, & Forest, 1989; Williams et al., 1986).

Parents of 28 students from the State DSI Report agreed to participate in this study. The remaining seven families declined participation or could not be contacted. All families interviewed were Caucasian. Twenty of the children lived with both of their biological parents; one lived with his biological mother, and two lived with their grandparents. Of the remaining five children, three lived in two-parent adoptive families. Two children lived in single-parent families, one with a foster mother and another with an adoptive mother. Family size ranged from three to eight with the average being 4.7. Consistent with Vermont's rural nature, 17 of the families lived in towns with populations under 1,000. Five families lived in communities with populations ranging from 1,000 to 5,000, and five resided in communities of 5,000 to 15,000. Only one family lived in a small city of approximately 38,000.

As indicated in Table 1, twenty-six mothers, three fathers, and two grandmothers (who were guardians) were interviewed. Students ranged in age from 3 to 20 years with the majority ($n = 20$) being under 10 years of age. Seventeen of the students were females; 11 were males. Thirteen students received their education in special classes, eight in general education classes, six in home-based programs, and one in a residential school.

As a group, these youngsters had significant cognitive and physical impairments. The labels of mild, moderate, severe, or profound retardation used in Table 1 are an indication of their level of functioning and are not meant to offer a measure of ability. In nearly all cases, it was difficult to differentiate which disability or combination led to the student's level of functioning.

Data Collection Method

The research team met to discuss the purposes of the research, the study design, and a list of potential questions for data collection. The appropriateness of the questions from the parental perspective was addressed by the member of the research team who was a parent of a child with severe disabilities. The team agreed upon a set of questions to ensure that each interviewer inquired about the same issues (see Table 2). The research team agreed that questions were not to be presented to families in standardized ways, or necessarily in the same order. Rather, each team member would individualize his or her question-asking style to match the individual interviews and would follow various paths of questioning based on parental responses.

Parents were contacted by telephone and asked if they were willing to be interviewed. Those who agreed to participate were given the option of being interviewed face-to-face or by phone. Twenty-three parents were interviewed face-to-face; 19 of these interviews were conducted in parents' homes, and the remainder in

Table 1
Summary of Information Regarding Families, 1988–1989

	Student Initials (Pseudonym)	Sex	Student Age	Person(s) interviewed	Number of interviews	Interviewer	Educational Placement	Student Characteristics (DSI = Dual Sensory Impairment)
1	JT	M	3	Mother	1	PM	Early education (Special education)	DSI, Severe retardation, Severe orthopedic disability
2	SK	M	3	Mother and Father	1	SA	Early education (Integrated)	DSI, Severe retardation
3	AR	F	3	Mother	2	SY MG[a]	Early education (Home-based)	DSI, hydrocephalus, Health impaired
4	KK	F	4	Mother	1	PM	Early education (Home-based)	DSI, Moderate retardation, Marshall-Smith Syndrome
5	JB	M	4	Mother	1	PM	Early education (Special education)	DSI, Moderate retardation, Sturge-Weber Syndrome
6	JL	M	4	Mother	1	MG	Early education (Special education)	DSI, Severe retardation
7	ED	F	4	Mother	1	PM	Early education (Home-based)	DSI, Within normal range of intelligence
8	CF	F	5	Mother	1	SY	Early education (Home-based)	DSI, Profound retardation, Severe orthopedic disability
9	JY	F	5	Grandmother	2	CC MG[a]	Early education (Integrated)	DSI, Severe retardation Severe orthopedic disability
10	JA	M	6	Grandmother	2	SA MG[a]	Kindergarten (Regular)	DSI, Severe retardation Severe orthopedic disability
11	KH	F	7	Mother	1	MG	Special Class	DSI, Profound retardation, Severe orthopedic disability
12	BV	M	7	Mother	1	SY	Grade 1 (Regular)	DSI, Down Syndrome
13	AT	F	7	Mother	1	CC	Grade 2 (Regular)	DSI, Profound retardation, Severe orthopedic disability
14	AE	M	7	Mother	1	PM	Grade 2 (Regular)	DSI, Severe retardation, Severe orthopedic disability
15	SW	M	7	Mother and Father	2	MG MG[a]	Grade 2 (Regular)	DSI, Profound retardation Severe orthopedic disability
16	CT	M	7	Mother	2	MG MG[a]	Special Class	DSI, Profound retardation, Severe orthopedic disability
17	SB	M	8	Mother	1	MG	Residential School	DSI, Mild retardation, Attention deficit disorder
18	JH	F	8	Mother	1	MG	Special Class	DSI, Profound retardation, Severe orthopedic disability
19	RH	F	9	Mother and Father	1	SY	Home-based	DSI, Profound retardation, Severe orthopedic disability, Medically fragile
20	LM	F	9	Mother	1	PM	Grade 3 (Regular)	DSI, Severe retardation Severe orthopedic disability
21	DG	M	11	Mother	1	MG	Special Class	DSI, Mild retardation
22	LG	F	11	Mother	1	MG	Special Class	DSI, Profound retardation, Severe orthopedic disability
23	HP	F	13	Mother	1	SY	Special Class	DSI, Severe retardation, General motor delays
24	BJ	F	13	Mother	1	MG	Special Class	DSI, Profound retardation, Severe orthopedic disability
25	ED	F	15	Mother	1	MG	Special Class	DSI, Profound retardation, Severe orthopedic disability
26	PJ	F	15	Mother	1	SA	Special Class	DSI, Profound retardation, Severe orthopedic disability
27	DJ	F	17	Mother	2	MG MG[a]	Special Class	DSI, Profound retardation, Severe orthopedic disability
28	MF	F	20	Mother	1	SA	Home-based	DSI, Profound retardation, Severe orthopedic disability

[a] Member check.

Table 2
Issues Addressed in the Interview Questions

1. Can you tell me about your child's educational history? When did s/he start school? What kinds of classes was s/he in and what other kinds of services did s/he receive? How have services been provided (e.g., directly, consultation)?
2. How much involvement does your child have with nonhandicapped students during school and after school hours? How do you feel about this involvement? Have you always felt the same way about this involvement or have your opinions changed over time?
3. What is it about your child's current educational placement that you like the best and think is most important? What, if anything, about your child's current educational placement would you change to make it better?
4. What do you think are the most important things your child should learn while in school and why are these things important? What do you hope will be the outcome of your child's education?
5. What do you think would happen to your child if s/he was placed in an educational situation that was very different from what it is currently (e.g., if she is now in a self-contained special class what would happen if she was placed in a regular class)?
6. How far in advance do you think about planning for your child's life? Next week? Next year? Adulthood? How do you feel about long-range planning?
7. When your child completes his/her eligibility for public school services, what would a high quality life consist of? What kinds of settings would you like to see for your child and what kinds of activities?
8. How have nonhandicapped children and parents of nonhandicapped children responded to the presence of your child in the public school (building or classroom)?
9. Can you recall any experiences that you or your child had related to school that were extremely negative?
10. Do you feel that you are considered as a full member of the educational team? Do you have an equal voice in decision-making (e.g., selection of IEP goals)? Has this always been the case?
11. How do you feel regarding the involvement and coordination of the specialists (e.g., vision specialists, PT, OT) who work with your child?
12. Can you recall one or two experiences that you or your child had related to school that were extremely positive?
13. Is there any other information about your child's school experiences that you feel are important in helping professionals better consider the needs of families?

other, mutually agreed upon locations (e.g., restaurant, office). Five parents were interviewed by telephone. The interviews ranged in length from approximately 1 to 2 hr. The five members of the research team were assigned families based primarily on geographic convenience.

Each interview began with a review of the purposes of the research and assurances of confidentiality. The parents were then asked the questions listed in Table 2. Data were recorded during these discussions by writing as many direct quotes as possible and taking notes on the substance of the parent response to each question. At times this resulted in short periods, typically less than a minute, of nonspeaking time between questions. Interviewers attempted to augment direct quotes and capture the essence of the parent response by following a pattern of asking, listening, writing, and asking follow-up questions to verify a shared understanding of the parent's remarks. Abbreviated notetaking was used during the interview to maintain the flow of conversation. The same day of the session, the interviewer expanded on these abbreviated notes. The fieldnotes included descriptive information on the setting, parents' comments and responses to questions, and interviewer comments. Fieldnotes were organized by pairing the questions asked with the parental responses. Any written information that was not data directly from parents, such as interviewer comments or perspectives, was labeled as such and listed under the specific parent response that prompted the interviewer's comment. General interviewer comments were also labeled and included at the end of the fieldnotes. All fieldnotes were

organized in a similar format and typed for review by other members of the research team.

Data Analysis Procedures

Following the initial 28 interviews, fieldnotes were analyzed using a qualitative coding procedure (Bogdan & Biklen, 1982). The narrative data were coded and subsequently organized by similarity of theme into categories. Coding consisted of reviewing the text to identify repeated words, phrases, and ideas. Initially, coding resulted in the identification of over 50 categories of data. The data were repeatedly reorganized in an attempt to understand the meaning of parental responses and to make the categories more manageable in size and content. The second major recategorization consolidated the data into 20 categories.

Benefits of group data analysis were apparent as the process went forward. The first round of coding resulted in categorization that was far different from the categories ultimately presented in this article. Initial categories such as "educational placement," "integration," "service delivery," and "curriculum" were educationally driven and did not represent the parental perspective adequately. Recategorization with research team members led to new and different categories that more accurately reflected the ways parents thought about the issues. This interpretation was further studied by team members to determine whether the analysis matched their understanding of the data, based on their personal field experiences. Supporting data were identified in the fieldnotes and a search was conducted for any data that were contrary to the tentative categorizations.

Member Checks

Once the research team reached agreement on coding categories and the subsequent analysis, member checks (Ferguson, Ferguson, & Jones, 1988; Lincoln & Guba, 1985) were conducted with 6 of the 28 families to reduce the possibility that the professional perspectives of the research team might overshadow parental views. These follow-up interviews were crucial for achieving the intended purpose of the research, because internal reliability among research team members is of limited value if the team's analysis does not reflect accurately the meaning of those being interviewed. To minimize bias, therefore, member checks are necessary for establishing agreement on the interpretation of the data between researchers and those being interviewed.

Three families whose children attended special classes and three whose children attended regular classes were selected for member check interviews. Parents who expressed divergent opinions and perspectives during the initial interviews were purposely chosen. During these follow-up telephone calls, which lasted approximately 45 min to 1 hr, participants were presented with the team's analysis and asked to indicate (a) whether the team's analysis matched their own experiences, (b) whether the team's analysis adequately represented a parental rather than professional viewpoint, and (c) whether the data "made sense." Additionally, they were asked to offer opinions that might assist the research team in understanding more fully the parental perspective. The six parents who participated in the member checks indicated strong agreement with the analysis. In a number of cases, parents responded to a finding with sudden laughter, because the team's analysis had "hit a nerve." This laughter was always followed by a confirming statement and often by a story supporting or illustrating the point.

Results

Parents interviewed during this study identified four major areas that dominated their thinking about their child's school experience. These four areas include parental perceptions of a "good life" for their child, as well as their experiences with fear, frustration, and change. The results section culminates with a summary of what parents said they wanted from school professionals.

Quality Indicators: "I want my child to have a good life"

The aspirations of parents whose sons and daughters have dual sensory impairments parallel what might be expected from any parent. When asked what would constitute a quality life for their child, parents identified five major characteristics. The need for a safe, comfortable, stable home was paramount. Parents wanted their children to live in a home and clearly sought to avoid congregate care facilities, such as nursing homes, large group homes, or institutions. It was also vital to establish and maintain a social network of "people who care." Parents wanted their children to be productive with their time by engaging in work that is valued by society as well as meaningful, interesting, image-enhancing, and preferred by the individual. Although work was considered important by some parents, those who viewed employment as an unlikely option for their children focused their attention on some of its nonmonetary benefits. "He needs duties, activities, not necessarily to make money, but to make him feel important, something he's good at, to be useful." Based on these attitudes, parents identified a variety of potentially acceptable post-school options, such as competitive or supported employment, volunteering, continued education or training, and leisure activities. Parents also wanted their children to have ongoing access to multiple environments and activities so that their life would be full and interesting. "I can't picture her being home-based; it's not enough." They consistently indicated that having a variety of opportunities, experiences, and settings was a major part of what distinguished an enjoyable life from a boring existence. Lastly, given the medically complicated problems of many children with dual sensory impairments, parents hoped their children could pursue these quality of life indicators in a state of health and comfort. After indicating that her child's "first year of (his) life was filled with excruciating pain," one mother explained that all other indicators of a good life hinge on relative health and comfort.

The development of social networks was identified as a major unmet need. "My first goal is that he'll have a circle of friends, some peer support; it's just as important as skills." Almost all of the respondent families indicated that the interactions of their children were limited to family members or friends of family members. These children had few friends or even acquaintances of their own. Regardless of the status of the child's social network, the most positive and negative school-related experiences of these families pertained to interactions with nonhandicapped people. Parents stated that some people who made up the social network at school questioned the child's worth and treated the child as though he/she were unwanted. "Sometimes when she is in therapy, I feel they treat her more as an object than a child." Another parent recalled, "Other people have always written him off. His preschool teacher told us that he wasn't worth wasting time on in terms of equipment and teaching when her time could be better spent with other kids who could learn better." Conversely, parents reported their most positive experiences had been when their children were included, welcomed, and treated with dignity and worth. Parents described a variety of positive, neutral, and negative interactions between their children and nonhandicapped people. Parents reported that people who interacted with their children in negative or neutral ways tended to be those with limited or superficial interactions, whereas individuals who "take the time to get to know people with disabilities are more positive."

Parents whose children had access to interactions with nonhandicapped peers in school reported that over the years, different nonhandicapped children demonstrated "genuine concern and interest" as well as "exceptional insights into the needs and feelings" of the children with dual sensory impairments. As one mother reported, "This year it was Lance. He would comfort him when he cried; he invited him to his house; he pushed him on the swings and helped him on the slide." Although parents were unable to explain why these particular children seemed to gravitate toward their children, they did share a common belief of perceived benefits from these interactions. Although parents indicated that their children with dual sensory impairments may or may not have gained anything positive from these interactions, they were confident that the nonhandicapped child "got a lot out of it."

As already stated, the aspirations of parents whose children have dual sensory impairments, as well as possible other numerous severe handicaps, closely parallel the hopes of any parent. Home, health, meaningful personal relationships, valued activity, and varied experiences form a hopeful vision for them. In the best circumstances, parents whose children have dual sensory impairments may face formidable obstacles to realizing their vision. In the worst circumstances, the human service systems in place to assist families (e.g., schools) may, by their organizational design, block the paths to the desired outcomes. The next three sections describe school-based family experiences that illustrate potential obstacles from the parent perspective.

Fear: "Everybody's afraid"

Fear of the future led many parents to indicate they were "uncomfortable" and "avoided" long-range planning for their children because "it's too big an unknown." Parents explained that thinking of the future was too painful and that avoiding it, as an act of commission or omission, was a coping mechanism to reduce stress and unnecessary worry about events over which parents perceived they had little or no control. Having a child with a reduced life expectancy contributed to the avoidance of long-range planning. "I don't think about the future; I don't know if she'll be alive." "It's so hard to visualize the future, especially when I don't see older people (alive) with such severe handicaps."

An additional contributing factor in avoiding long-range planning was parental beliefs about their children's futures. Those parents who had a positive vision of their child's future progress seemed willing, in some cases even anxious, to engage in long-range planning. Those with a pessimistic view of their children's future

tended to avoid long-range planning. "My expectations are very limited; I never had high hopes." These pessimistic feelings were exacerbated when parents perceived a never-ending responsibility for child rearing. "With most children at some point it's up to the children, but not with a handicapped child; it's a lifetime project." In avoiding long-range planning, most parents preferred to take a short-range, "wait and see," "leave it open" approach. As one mother said, "If I think too far ahead I get depressed, so I've learned to take it 1 day at a time."

Although parents acknowledged that some of their own behavior was affected by fear, they believed fear also affected the behavior of professionals. For example, parents indicated that itinerant vision and hearing specialists were involved minimally with their children, although these children with dual sensory impairments presumably need such services. The more severe and multiple the handicaps (e.g., physical disability, mental retardation, behavioral disorders), the less likely the vision or hearing support staff were involved. Parents said they believed vision and hearing specialists could be of assistance in supporting the education of their children, but perceived professionals as "afraid to admit when they didn't know something." Parents believed professionals dealt with their own fears of not being experts by either "not working with the child" or "pretending to know the answers when they don't."

Often parents are described as "overprotective," but parents attached that descriptor to professionals, who, they believed, acted out of fear and not knowing what to do. "School is overly worried about little things; he fell over in circle one day; that's no reason to call." "They're afraid of his seizures even though they are under control." "They always want to send him home as sick when it doesn't warrant coming home; they just don't know how to handle him." Some parents indicated they thought the school district was afraid the child would die, and they didn't want it happening in school. As one parent said, "If something is going to happen, it will happen. I won't blame the school." Another parent echoed this sentiment by saying, "We know the risks; we're not going to sue them. I'd rather have my child die in a regular class at 5 years old than at 20 in an institution."

Frustration: "Dealing with schools can be tough"

For parents, one major frustration with school programs serving students with dual sensory impairments is the sheer number of professionals. "I can remember at one time I just wanted them to leave me alone; it seemed so overwhelming." As one mother quipped, "most kids collect stamps; he collects professionals." Despite the fact that many parents perceived the well-meaning parade of professionals as "hectic," "confusing," and an "invasion of privacy," they cushioned their discontent by saying they had "no objections to lots of people, as long as it helps."

A few parents reported that the multitude of professionals did help, but as one parent stated, being in the process felt like, ". . . a ping-pong ball because everyone has a different idea about what's right for your child, and we do too." "They don't see him as a whole person, just different disability segments. Everyone likes to segment him. None of the specialists know what to do when a child has more than one disability. It's frustrating." Many parents said such experiences prompted them to view specialists as people who did not have expertise beyond a narrow band of knowledge.

Statements by parents indicated deficiencies in coordination and communication among team members. "They [professionals] ask the same questions; they need to talk to each other." Those families who had a designated case manager or liaison with the school felt more satisfied. "No matter how many people work with Janie, there is only one contact person." Case managers can help "take the hassle off me." This was especially important to families when the staff changed frequently due to moving, pregnancy, illness, transfers, and so forth.

Parents said they viewed themselves as the coordinators of services because they knew the child best and had both the historical perspective and a vested interest in a future vision for the child. Although parents strongly expressed their desire to have input in their child's educational program, many indicated that "the school staff doesn't feel I'm part of the team." "They share information with me," but "they question whether I know what I am saying." Some parents said it was acceptable to be merely informed "as long as the teachers do a good job." More often than not, parents indicated that being informed rather than included resulted in irrelevant educational planning or decisions that did not match the needs of the child or the family. Parents said they sometimes had to be aggressive and that such an approach was unpopular but necessary. "That was a big problem (being excluded by the team); I raised hell and now it's better." Those families who were frustrated by the behaviors of professionals and who decided not to be aggressive often withdrew from the educational process. They reasoned, "I can speak up, but there is nobody to listen"; therefore, "it doesn't matter what I say because they [professionals] are going to do what they want anyway."

Change: "Sometimes change is harder on us than it is on them"

As students with all types of severe and multiple disabilities are increasingly included in regular schools and classes, parents may be confronted with potential changes in their child's educational placement. Parents whose children received special education in self-contained (special) classes were asked how they thought a change in placement to a general education class would affect their child. They responded with a consistent list of negative outcomes. Parents said if their child were integrated he/she would regress, be neglected or overlooked, be exposed to undesirable behaviors, not receive enough appropriate stimulation, miss his/her classmates, lack needed learning opportunities, and that the change would be disruptive. Interestingly, when parents whose children received special education services in general education classes were asked how they thought a change in placement to a more segregated class would affect their child, they responded with the exact same list of negative effects. When parents were presented with this apparently contradictory finding during member check interviews, they explained that the issue was not so much integration as it was change. "People are comfortable where they are as long as everything is going OK." Parents indicated they didn't want to risk making a change when they perceived the current situation as acceptable.

Regardless of the extent to which the child's placement was segregated or integrated, a parent's level of satisfaction with his/her son's or daughter's educational placement was strongly attributed to teachers and staff who demonstrated a genuine concern for the child by working hard to make the school experience positive and meaningful. Parents whose children received special education services in general education classes identified several major benefits: (a) the opportunity to absorb as much as possible, given the child's unknown learning potential, (b) building ongoing social networks, and (c) developing a positive self-image. Parents whose children received special education in self-contained classes identified major benefits as stability, a protective environment, and individualized attention. Given the perceived security of a placement where the child was "happy and welcomed," few parents liked the idea that educators had "changed the rules of the game midstream" from segregated to integrated. Upon reflection, several parents came to the conclusion that they would probably have been more favorably disposed toward educational integration if it initially had been clearly the direction of the school. They indicated that any change to a more integrated setting would most likely be harder on tnem than on their child; "even good change can be difficult."

Advice from Parents

Parents were clear and consistent in their advice to professionals. First and foremost, parents wanted professionals to listen to them and trust they know the child best. Secondly, parents wanted professionals to treat their family as individual and unique, treat kids with respect and dignity, and "treat them like kids no matter how little you think they understand."

Parents wanted an educational program with stability that avoided shifting the student to different locations convenient for the school system but disruptive to the child and family. "Based on where you live, most parents know where their child will go to elementary, middle, and high school, but not us; our kid gets moved around to different schools all over the place every year just because he's handicapped." One parent put things in perspective when she said, "Everything about Sam is unstable and uncertain; anything that we find to maintain stability helps us cope."

Parents longed for professionals who would be honest with them and be secure enough to "admit when they don't know something." Lastly, parents wanted to be included in decisions about changes (e.g., integration) that would have a direct impact on their family. To be heard, trusted, treated as individuals, attain some basic level of stability, to expect honesty, and inclusion in important decisions that affect families, were the requests from these parents. They have challenged the professional school community to practice what they preach.

Discussion and Implications

Although the results of this study highlight a number of perspectives shared by parents whose children have dual sensory impairments, the heterogeneity of people who have dual sensory impairments and their life circumstances indicate that caution should be observed when interpreting these data or making generalizations. The following limitations should be considered. Interviews of self-reported perceptions can be strengthened by comparing the findings with participant observations and analysis of pertinent documents. Also, only three fathers were interviewed and all three of those conversations included the children's mothers. Even though the common link among the 28 families in this study was the children's diagnosis of dual sensory impairment, the vast majority were also identified as having significant cognitive and orthopedic disabilities. The multiplicity and severity of the disabilities, not exclusively the vision and hearing impairments, may have affected parental responses. The majority of these families resided in rural areas and included two parents. It is unknown whether responses would be different from single-parent families or those who live in urban areas. Because the majority of parents interviewed had preteenage children, it is also not known whether responses would change significantly as families faced the challenges associated with the transition to adulthood during the teenage years.

Future research may clarify whether the responses of parents whose children have severe and multiple disabilities parallel those of other parents whose children are less significantly handicapped or nonhandicapped, thus identifying whether the phenomenon of parenthood varies in kind or merely degree. Additional research may determine whether responsiveness to the issues identified in this study affects the level of parental stress or facilitates achieving the quality of life that the parents sought for their children.

Focusing on Quality of Life Indicators

The parameters that parents identified as indicators of a quality life (e.g., home, health, meaningful personal relationships, valued activity, and varied experiences) can be a focal point for services to children. Putting these indicators into practice should include establishing a clear link between what we want for a child and what we do.

Although educators typically place a high emphasis on skill attainment, the parents generally placed minimal emphasis on skill development for their child. If the skills targeted for instruction were both matched to a family-centered vision for the child and clearly linked to one or more quality of life indicators, parents might find the educational planning process more relevant. For example, during IEP preplanning, many educators meet with parents to identify their priorities for the child. Skill inventories are frequently used in which items are organized into categories such as *socialization*, *communication*, *self-care*, *motor*, and *cognition*. Some educators and parents can see clearly the link between these skills and quality of life indicators; others may not. For those who may not, or those for whom the link is unclear, reorganizing and describing skills to show their relationship to quality of life indicators would be helpful. Instead of sections labeled *communication* and *socialization*, these skills might be categorized as those that *facilitate the development of meaningful relationships or social networks* or *provide enhanced access to varied environments and activities*. Even though many skills will overlap more than one quality of life indicator, purposely linking skills to quality of life indicators can establish and maintain a shared focus among team members (Giangreco, Cloninger & Iverson, 1990).

Because parents focused attention on the development of meaningful personal relationships for their children, it is interesting to note that current service delivery models tend to place children with dual sensory impairments in residential schools, special schools, and special classes (Bullis & Otos, 1988; Vadasy & Fewell, 1986). Such placement dramatically reduces the possibility that relationships will develop between children with severe disabilities and their nonhandicapped peers, who may have genuine concern and interest in them as well as exceptional insights into their needs and feelings. If one makes the assumption that such nonhandicapped individuals exist, and the evidence reported by parents suggests that they do, then opportunities for such interactions must occur if social networks are to be established. G. Kishi (personal communication) suggested that these types of relationships could be supported by fully integrated educational placements and the inclusion of people with severe disabilities in a wide variety of typical environments and activities. Such situations provide opportunities for interactions with many people, some of whom may gravitate toward people with disabilities.

Acknowledging Fear

If parents are correct in their perceptions, both family and professional actions are controlled, in part, by fear of the unknown future, the limitations of their own knowledge, and lack of control over certain events. Parents' comments in the present study were consistent with the perspectives shared by Turnbull, Summers and Brotherson (1986, p. 57), who wrote, "A major coping strategy for many families of retarded children is passive appraisal, which involves maintaining a strong present rather than future orientation, and taking one day at a time." Featherstone (1980, p. 29) expressed a similar view when she stated, "Professionals who have not themselves fought free of crippling fears sometimes misunderstand parents' efforts to safeguard the quality of their daily life. This issue can feed into the tension between parents and professionals. Teachers often complain that parents are too present-centered."

In order to cope, parents may suppress their fear, whereas professionals may mask their fear to maintain an illusion of expertise. In both cases, each party engages in behaviors that threaten to expose the fears of the other. Parents ask professionals questions for which they have inadequate answers, and professionals ask parents to engage in the potentially discomforting task of long-range planning. Potential solutions to this dilemma are far more easily proposed than accomplished. For professionals to acknowledge their fears and expose them freely will require a level of security not frequently found in public schools and will likely require a shift in professional socialization from perceived expertise to collaboration. Professionals should be increasingly aware that factors such as severity of disability, multiplicity of disability, age, life expectancy, and parental beliefs about their child's future have an impact on the family's willingness to engage in long-range planning (Vadasy & Fewell, 1986). Given these and other factors, time projections for future planning for students with disabilities must be individualized. Rather than the frequent application of environmental analysis of planning for post-school options, the future may be defined differently by each family (e.g., next year, 5 years from now, post-school). By asking parents how far into the future they wish to plan, rather than telling them to plan for post-school, educators can demonstrate their recognition that each family is individual and unique.

Dealing with the Sources of Frustration

For bureaucratic or benevolent reasons, educational service systems assign professional staff to students based on disability labels. If a child is labeled visually impaired, a teacher for students with visual impairments is assigned. If a child has physical disabilities, a motor specialist such as an occupational or physical therapist is assigned. In the case of children with dual sensory impairments and accompanying multiple disabilities, this compartmentalized, more-is-better approach often perpetuates three major frustrations of parents: (a) too many professionals, (b) segmentation of the child based on disability labels, and (c) fragmented service coordination.

The assignment of so many professionals, each with a different speciality, often ignores the reality that the disciplines traditionally associated with students who have dual sensory impairments (i.e., special education, vision support, orientation and mobility, hearing support, audiology, speech language pathology, occupational therapy, physical therapy) have some degree of overlap in roles and functions. When team members explore potential overlaps and adopt an only-as-special-as-necessary approach to service provision, students can still access needed services while minimizing the unnecessary involvement of too many professionals (Giangreco, 1990a; Giangreco & Eichinger, 1990).

Recent evidence indicates that professionals from many disciplines typically generate an individual focus for service delivery based on what is valued by their discipline (Giangreco, Edelman & Dennis, in press). This is problematic because the ideas of group members do not converge on a shared set of goals. Rather, their potential impact is dissipated as each professional pursues a separate set of goals. The absence of a shared focus is further emphasized because teachers, parents, and specialists often disagree about who should maintain the authority for making service delivery decisions (Giangreco, 1990b). Emerging models that are "discipline-free" may address identified parental frustrations by exploring the interdependencies among disciplines, establishing individualized communication mechanisms, and offering opportunities for families to engage fully in educational service development (Benson & Turnbull, 1986; Giangreco, 1990b; Giangreco, Cloninger & Iverson, 1990; Iverson & Cloninger, 1990; Vandercook, York & Forest, 1989; Williams, Fox & Fox, 1989).

Accepting and Participating in Change

In the relatively short time since the parent interviews were completed, eight students who previously received their education in special classes or through home-based instruction (see Table 1) have been transitioned to regular class placements with special education support. This highlights the fact that change in educational placement continues to be an issue facing families. Parents often indicate having concerns about change—not only how it will affect their children, but how it might affect them (Hanline & Halvorsen, 1989). It is not surprising that parents feel left out when school systems go about the business of enacting significant educational reforms without adequately involving them. Although extensive elaboration about the theory and practice of educational change (Bolman & Deal, 1984; Fullan, 1982), and specifically regarding school integration change (Giangreco, 1989; Lipsky & Gartner, 1989), is beyond the scope of this discussion, it is suggested that school personnel must work actively to include all relevant constituencies, including families, in changes that will affect them.

If signals are received from the school organization that change (e.g., integration) is about to take place, parents as well as professionals may benefit from opportunities to develop an anticipatory mind set, begin considering how the potential change might affect them, and to engage in reciprocal consultation with others involved in the change (Bolman & Deal, 1984). This opportunity to weigh personal costs can have a positive impact on subsequent outcomes (Cuban, 1984). Crucial considerations affecting adoption and retention of school change include both opportunities for major constituency groups to participate in planning and a realistic time frame that allows for psychological preparedness (Fullan, 1982; Sarason, 1974).

Listening to Families

Underlying everything that parents said during interviews was their concern that too often professionals do not listen to families or take into account how the children's needs are interdependent with those of other family members. The desires of parents to be trusted as authorities on their children, to be treated honestly and individually by professionals, and to expect a basic level of stability in services challenge the educational community to become increasingly reflective (Schon, 1983). In part, this reflective evaluation may highlight that what we do affects not only the children in our classrooms, but the families with whom they live. The results of this study remind us that despite platitudes about parent involvement, many parents remain dissatisfied with their level of involvement and their role in the educational process. As the 1990s begin, the success of educational programs may be determined, in part, by our ability and willingness truly to include parents as partners in education.

References

Bailey, D. B., Winton, P. J., Rouse, L., & Turnbull, A. (1990). Family goals in infant intervention: Analysis and issues. *Journal of Early Intervention, 14*(1), 15–26.

Baldwin, V., & Bullis, M. (1988). Prevalence data on students with deaf-blindness. In A. M. Covert & T. S. Carr (Eds.), *Value-based services for young adults with deaf-blindness* (pp. 33–40). Sands Point, NY: Helen Keller National Center for Deaf-Blind Youth and Adults Technical Assistance Center, in cooperation with The Association for Persons with Severe Handicaps Technical Assistance Project.

Benson, H., & Turnbull, A. (1986). Approaching families from an individualized perspective. In R. Horner, L. H. Meyer,

& H. D. B. Fredericks (Eds.), *Education of learners with severe handicaps: Exemplary service strategies* (pp. 127–157). Baltimore: Paul H. Brookes.

Bogdan, R. C., & Biklen, S. K. (1982). *Qualitative research for education: An introduction to theory and methods.* Boston: Allyn and Bacon.

Bolman, L. G., & Deal, T. E. (1984). *Modern approaches to understanding and managing organizations.* San Francisco, CA: Jossey-Bass.

Bullis, M., & Otos, M. (1988). Characteristics of programs for children with deaf-blindness: Results of a national study. *The Journal of the Association for Persons with Severe Handicaps, 13,* 110–115.

Carney, I. H. (1987). Working with families. In F. P. Orelove & D. Sobsey (Eds.), *Educating children with multiple disabilities: A transdisciplinary approach* (pp. 315–338). Baltimore: Paul H. Brookes.

Covert, A. M., & Carr, T. S. (1988) *Value-based services for young adults with deaf-blindness.* Sands Point, NY: Helen Keller National Center for Deaf-Blind Youth and Adults Technical Assistance Center, in cooperation with The Association for Persons with Severe Handicaps Technical Assistance Project.

Cuban, L. (1984). *How teachers taught: Constancy and change in American classrooms, 1890–1980.* New York: Longman.

Daniel R. R. v. State Board of Education, F. 2d (5th Cir., June 12, 1989).

Ellis, D. (1986). *Sensory impairments in mentally handicapped people.* San Diego: College-Hill.

Featherstone, H. (1980). *A difference in the family: Living with a disabled child.* New York: Penguin Books.

Ferguson, P. M., Ferguson, D. L., & Jones, D. (1988). Generations of hope: Parental perspectives on the transitions of their children with severe retardation from school to adult life. *The Journal of the Association for Persons with Severe Handicaps, 13,* 177–187.

Fullan, M. (1982). *The meaning of educational change.* New York: Teachers College Press, Columbia University.

Giangreco, M. F. (1989). Facilitating integration of students with severe disabilities: Implications of "Planned Change" for teacher preparation programs. *Teacher Education and Special Education, 12*(3), 139–147.

Giangreco, M. F. (1990a). Effects of a consensus-building process on team decision-making: Preliminary data. Burlington: University of Vermont, Center for Developmental Disabilities. Manuscript submitted for publication.

Giangreco, M. F. (1990b). Making related service decisions for students with severe handicaps: Roles, criteria, and authority. *The Journal of the Association for Persons with Severe Handicaps, 15,* 22–31.

Giangreco, M. F., Cloninger, C., Iverson, V. (1990). *Cayuga-Onondaga assessment for children with handicaps (C.O.A.C.H.) Version 6.0.* Stillwater: Oklahoma State University, National Clearing House of Rehabilitation Training Materials.

Giangreco, M. F., Edelman, S., Dennis, R. (in press). Common professional practices that interfere with the integrated delivery of related services. *Remedial and Special Education.*

Giangreco, M. F., & Eichinger, J. (1990). Related services and the transdisciplinary approach: A parent/professional training module. In M. Anketell, E. J. Bailey, J. Houghton, A. O'Dea, B. Utley, & D. Wickham (Eds.), *A series of training modules for educating children and youth with dual sensory and multiple impairments.* Monmouth, OR: Teaching Research Publications.

Goetz, L., Guess, D., & Stremel-Campbell, K. (1987). *Innovative program design for individuals with dual sensory impairments.* Baltimore: Paul H. Brookes.

Hanline, M., & Halvorsen, A. (1989). Parent perceptions of

the integration transition process: Overcoming artificial barriers. *Exceptional Children, 55,* 487–493.

Helmstetter, E., Murphy-Herd, N., Roberts, S., & Guess, D. (1984). *Individualized curriculum sequence and extended classroom models for learners who are deaf and blind.* Lawrence: University of Kansas, Curriculum Development Project for Secondary Age Severely Handicapped Deaf-blind Students.

Hill, B. K., Rotegard, L. L., & Bruininks, R. H. (1984). The quality of life of mentally retarded people in residential care. *Social Work, 29*(3), 275–281.

Iverson, V. S., & Cloninger, C. (1990, in preparation). *Vermont integration planning process (VIPP).* Burlington: University of Vermont, Center for Developmental Disabilities.

Lincoln, Y., & Guba, E. (1985). *Naturalistic inquiry.* Beverly Hills, CA: Sage.

Lipsky, D. K. (1989). The roles of parents. In D. K. Lipsky & A. Gartner (Eds.), *Beyond separate education: Quality education for all* (pp. 159–179). Baltimore: Paul H. Brookes.

Lipsky, D. K., & Gartner, A. (1989). Building the future. In D. K. Lipsky & A. Gartner (Eds.), *Beyond separate education: Quality education for all* (pp. 255–290). Baltimore: Paul H. Brookes.

McGonigel, M. J., & Garland, C. W. (1988). The individual family service plan and the early intervention team: Team and family issues and recommended practices. *Infants and Young Children: An Interdisciplinary Journal of Special Care Practices, 1*(1), 10–21.

Meyer, L. H., & Eichinger, J. (1987). Program evaluation in support of program development: Needs, strategies, and future directions. In L. Goetz, D. Guess, & K. Stremel-Campbell (Eds.), *Innovative program design for individuals with dual sensory impairments* (pp. 313–353). Baltimore: Paul H. Brookes.

Patton, M. Q. (1980). *Qualitative evaluation methods.* Beverly Hills, CA: Sage.

Powell, T. H., & Ogle, P. A. (1985). *Brothers and sisters: A special part of exceptional families.* Baltimore: Paul H. Brookes.

Sarason, S. (1974). *The culture of the school and the problem of change.* Boston: Allyn & Bacon.

Schalock, R. L. (1990). *Quality of life: Perspectives and issues.*

Washington, DC: American Association on Mental Retardation.

Schon, D. A. (1983). *The reflective practitioner: How professionals think in action.* New York: Basic Books.

Stainback, S., Stainback, W., & Forest, M. (1989) *Educating all students in the mainstream of regular education.* Baltimore: Paul H. Brookes.

Taylor, S. J., & Bogdan, R. (1984). *Introduction to qualitative research methods. 2nd edition.* New York: John Wiley and Sons.

Turnbull, A. P., Summers, J. A., & Brotherson, M. J. (1986). Family life cycle: Theoretical and empirical implications and future directions for families with mentally retarded members. In J. J. Gallagher & P. M. Vietze (Eds.), *Families of handicapped persons: Research, programs, and policy issues* (pp. 45–65). Baltimore: Paul H. Brookes.

Turnbull, A. P., & Turnbull, H. R. (1990). *Families, professionals, and exceptionality: A special partnership (second edition).* Columbus, OH: Merrill Publishing.

Vadasy, P. F., & Fewell, R. R. (1986). Mothers of deaf-blind children. In R. R. Fewell & P. F. Vadasy (Eds.), *Families of handicapped children: Needs and supports across the life span* (pp. 121–148). Austin, TX: Pro-Ed.

Vandercook, T., York, J., & Forest, M. (1989). The McGill Action Planning System (MAPS): A strategy for building the vision. *The Journal of the Association for Persons with Severe Handicaps, 14,* 205–215.

Vermont Department of Education (1987). *Guidelines for identification of students with dual sensory (vision and hearing) impairments in the state of Vermont.* Montpelier: Vermont Department of Education. Author.

Williams, W., Fox, W., Christie, L., Thousand, J., Conn-Powers, M., Carmichael, L., Vogelsburg, R. T., & Hull, M. (1986). Community integration in Vermont. *The Journal of the Association for Persons with Severe Handicaps, 11,* 294–299.

Williams, W., Fox, T., & Fox, W. (1989). *Integrating the instruction of students with intensive educational needs into regular education classrooms: Individual program design procedures manuals.* Burlington: University of Vermont, Center for Developmental Disabilities.

Functional Vision Screening for Severely Handicapped Children

BETH LANGLEY, M.A.
REBECCA F. DUBOSE, PH.D.
Ms. Langley is educational diagnostician and Dr. DuBose is associate professor, Faculty of Special Education, Model Vision Project, George Peabody College for Teachers, Nashville, Tennessee.

Abstract: *Ophthalmologists traditionally have been unable to provide teachers and parents with useful information about a severely handicapped child's functional vision. Literature concerning the assessment of vision in handicapped children is reviewed and a guide is proposed for use by teachers in evaluating the severely handicapped child's functional vision.*

Severely handicapped children with some form of visual impairment are often placed in educational settings accompanied by inadequate reports giving some indication of visual classification and an unintelligible description of the specific impairment. References are repeatedly made to the difficulties involved in assessing the child's visual problems and to the hesitancy with which the ophthalmologist makes his judgment. In centers where a multidisciplinary team evaluates the child, vision experts tend to rely on the functional visual information provided by the classroom teacher or the educational diagnostician. A more practical assessment of visual functioning in severely handicapped children will therefore become available if those agents most familiar with the child's everyday use of vision actually participate in the assessment.

This paper describes some of the difficulties found in testing the visual acuity of severely handicapped children, surveys formal and informal measures used in testing visual acuity or functional vision, suggests guidelines for teachers to use in observing visual behaviors, and proposes a functional vision checklist that may be used by teachers or paraprofessionals to gain insight into how a child is using his residual vision.

FORMAL ASSESSMENT OF VISUAL ACUITY The problems inherent in determining visual acuity of multiply handicapped children have been stated by Allen (1957), Wolfe and Harvey (1959), Hoyt (1963), Sloan and Savitz (1963), Ffooks (1965), Borg and Sundmark (1967), Faye (1968), Lippman (1969), Macht (1971), and Sheridan (1973). Under the conditions imposed by the instruments used for testing visual acuity, low functioning children are easily distracted, lose interest in the test, fear the testing situation, fail to understand the tests, and give unreliable and inconsistent responses. Special educators and ophthalmologists have tried to find visual acuity tests that are effective with severely handicapped children, since visual impairment is frequently found with other handicapping conditions. Blackhurst and Radke (1968) found that moderately retarded children had four times as many visual impairments as the normal school population; Vernon (1969) reported that approximately 25 percent of deaf children had some form of visual impairment, and Wolf and Anderson (1973) provided evidence of visual limitations in 50 percent of cerebral palsied children.

What is Visual Acuity?

Wolfe and Harvey (1959) defined visual acuity as the ability to distinguish small spatial separations, or intervals, between portions of the visual field. Since it depends upon the ability of the eye to resolve a given visual angle, acuity is greater the closer together are two points that can be distinguished. Wolfe and Harvey distinguished sensory from visual acuity as an individual's reaction to low-keyed sensory data of mild duration and extent. Lippman (1969) suggested that sensory impressions developmentally advance from discriminative and perceptual stages to a conceptual stage.

Sheridan (1970) segmented acuity into two separate processes which are particularly relevant to multiply handicapped children: *seeing* and *looking*. Described as a physiological process dependent upon intact visual mechanisms, *seeing* is "the reception of mobile and static patterns of light, shade, and hue by the eye and transmission of this information to the central nervous system" (Sheridan, 1973). Primarily a psychological process, *looking* combines perceptual and conceptual operations to attend to visual stimuli with purposeful interpretation of their meaning.

As the child's awareness of his world increases so does his ability to distinguish visually and to respond to more abstract forms of stimuli through gradual refinement of his acuity to its mature state. Sheridan (1973) believes that by 12 months a child has a visual acuity comparable to adult vision, although it is not efficiently developed. A child of kindergarten age should be able to attend to an object for at least 20 seconds, pursue a moving target in all directions with a minimum of head movement, and localize different visual stimuli within the environment (Banus, 1971).

The majority of multiply handicapped children with significant visual deficiencies retain some functional vision and do see. However, their limited experiential and cognitive repertoires—essential to the integration of sensation into meaningful stimuli—prevent them from looking.

FORMAL TESTS AND PROCEDURES The formal tests that offer the most promising information about the extent of visual functioning of multiply handicapped children are Sheridan's Stycar Vision Tests and Koehler's New York Flashcard Vision Test (Faye, 1968). These tests were developed specifically for use with handicapped children and to assess near as well as distant vision.

Lippman (1969) found the Stycar to be the most reliable test in screening visual acuity of preschool children. Although Sheridan devised a distant screening chart consisting of only nine capital block letters chosen on the basis of simple vertical and horizontal lines (L H T), the circle (O), the cross (X), the part-square (U), the triangle (A), and the part-triangle (V), her Miniature Toys Test and Rolling Balls Test (subtests in the Stycar battery) are in fact more useful for evaluating vision in multiply handicapped children.

The Miniature Toys Test was developed for use with severely handicapped children who were unable either to match letters or name and match colored pictures of common objects placed individually on cards. After experimenting with numerous toys, Sheridan found the most effective ones to be a car, plane, doll, chair, knife, fork, and spoon, all 2″ high; a larger knife and spoon 3¼″ high; and a doll 5″ high. She found that children as young as 21 months successfully matched the objects and that their interest in the task lasted for its duration.

Designed paticularly for use with children from six to 30 months, the Rolling Balls Test consists of a series of graded balls projected a distance of 20 feet. The child is required to retrieve them one by one after they have been rolled horizontally across his line of vision.

The New York Flashcard Vision Test was developed out of a need for assessing the visual acuity of multiply handicapped children, visually handicapped preschool children, and the nonreader of any age (Faye, 1968). Only three symbols (heart, house, and umbrella) make up the test. They are presented one at a time on 12 reversible 4″ x 5″ flashcards. Snellen acuity notation is printed on every card, three symbols for each acuity level from "200" characters to "10." As long as they are consistent, children may verbally or manually label symbols anything they like or, if unable to express themselves, can point to large matching symbols. Average children of 27 months consistently attended and responded appropriately to the three symbols, and Faye successfully screened trainable mentally retarded children with the cards. The test is administered to the conventional method of acuity testing, except that the test distance is ten

feet or less and notations can be converted to the 20-foot reading.

Unsuitable Tests

Other formal measures of visual acuity have required skills not in the repertoire of multiply handicapped children. Sloan and Savitz (1963) identified two major forms of visual acuity tests, those based on indicating directions and those requiring identification of pictures.

In reviewing tests based on indicating directions, Sheridan (1973) felt that the Snellen E, the Sjorgen-Hand Test, and Landolt's Broken Rings included three major factors that significantly influenced the low functioning child's ability to perform adequately on them. Because multiply handicapped, as well as preschool children, have difficulty in coping with diagonals, they responded only to figures pointing up, down, left, or right. Directionality also complicates the assessment of multiply handicapped children as they confuse left and right and, although they may perceive laterality, they experience confusion in duplicating the position of the symbols. Because the patterns presented are constant, no opportunity is available to observe the child's ability to discriminate differences in configuration (Sheridan, 1973 and Ffooks, 1965).

Picture identification tests have been most frequently employed in testing handicapped populations though numerous adapted procedures have been necessary. Osterberg (1965) specified three requirements to bear in mind in the selection and development of pictorial visual acuity charts: 1) optometric principles must be adhered to as closely as possible; 2) objects must belong to the child's world of ideas; and 3) presentations of pictures must be adapted to the child's demands for recognition of pictures greatly variant from adults' needs. Other authors (Allen, 1957; Wolfe & Harvey, 1959; Hoyt, 1963; Faye, 1968; and Sheridan, 1973) have stressed the importance of using pictures of objects within the child's experiential repertoire. General criticisms of picture charts were that the pictures inaccurately projected angles at a nodal point corresponding to the highly accepted Snellen E symbol and required personal experience and ability to recall labels. More specific concerns have been expressed by Sloan and Savitz (1963), Borg and Sundmark (1967), and Ffooks (1965). Sloan and Savitz (1963) and Ffooks (1965) stated that picture tests were too dependent on psychological interpretations of figures before they could be understood and recognized by children.

INFORMAL TESTING OF VISUAL ACUITY Adaptations of formal tests have included deleting items; projecting them onto large screens; manipulating three dimensional response materials; converting response forms into puzzles; altering the type of figure, outline, silhouette, background, or color of the target and response figure; and applying operant technology (Courtney & Heath, 1971 and Macht, 1971). Although numerous tests have been developed and adapted with handicapped children in mind, none have proved satisfactory for use with this population unless administered through some form of operant procedure.

Employing an operant approach, Courtney and Heath (1971) trained and evaluated color vision in 39 trainable and 71 educable mentally retarded children using the AO HRR Color Vision Tester to determine the percentage of color blindness among the population of mentally retarded individuals. They found the AO HRR effective, as it offered four training and six testing plates graded for both type and severity of color blindness. The test proved to be highly motivating, required no verbal responses, no ability to read conventional numbers, and no need for the coordination essential for tracing paths. Training the children to take the color form of the test was accomplished through a black and white adaptation of the colored symbols O, X, and Δ. Identical forms were painted on slabs hinged to a box which dispensed M & M's whenever a correct response was given. Most children required about five minutes of training, but the authors succeeded in testing one 12-year-old Mongoloid child with an IQ of 35 after 40 minutes of training. No difference was found in the prevalence of color blindness among mentally retarded individuals and that of normal individuals reported in the literature.

Macht (1971) applied operant technology to obtain a subjective measure of visual acuity in five mentally retarded children between five and seven years of age. He included in his subject population two adults of normal intellectual and visual functioning to verify his results. Through the use of a specially constructed wheel displaying two stimulus Snellen Illiterate E's, one at the top and the other at the bottom of the wheel, and a table containing a response mechanism, Macht not only devised a way to evoke responses to the Snellen Illiterate E Chart, but also included an elaborate training system. The children were placed at the table 20 feet from the wheel and were trained to respond by pushing the response lever to the upright E, as opposed to the E which inverted as the wheel turned. Subjects were reinforced with M & M's and small candies for appropriate responses. The initial training E was larger than the 20/200, but for the actual testing the 20/200, 20/100, 20/70, 20/50, 20/40, 20/30, and 20/20 E's were utilized. Obtaining significant successful results that correlated with the adults' responses, Macht attributed children's previous failures to respond to the Snellen E and other visual acuity tests to procedural inadequacies rather than to the presence or absence of some quality in the child himself.

Macht and Courtney, with their promising results, offered the field of visual assessment valuable implications for successful application of tests that had previously proved ineffective with multiply handicapped children. Teachers cognizant of how children functionally use their vision can give ophthalmologists information that is helpful in determining visual capacities. Assessing functional vision in the severely handicapped child is a first step in planning educational programs relevant to his needs.

Informal Teacher-Oriented Visual Screening

Informal teacher-oriented visual screening procedures can effectively obtain important, practical information regarding what a child sees and how well he sees it. Although informal, the evaluation should be carried out systematically. Establishing a working rapport with the child, the setting, and stimulus materials is of primary importance. With a particularly young child, it may be necessary to hold and rock or sing to him for several minutes to quiet him. Sharing a manipulative toy often helps the evaluator to gain the confidence of an older child. The setting should be small, uncluttered, and quiet. Working with the child on the floor, where the evaluator has easy access to both the child and materials, facilitates administration of stimulus materials, puts the child and evaluator on the same level, and prevents attempts to leave a table, slip from a chair, or push materials from the table. Multiply handicapped children are more responsive to highly motivating materials, although in this assessment they must be limited in sound components to insure that the child is attending visually rather than aurally.

Suggested materials for eliciting visual behaviors outlined in the checklist are brightly colored soft rubber squeak toys with the squeaker removed (this toy can be squeezed to produce action but the sound is eliminated), a penlight or small flashlight, fluorescent rubber toys containing lights, and mechanical toys having flints producing sparks when operated. Especially motivating for severely handicapped children are rattles encasing moving parts; large and small spinning tops and easily rolled cars; fluorescently colored inch cubed blocks; small candies or cereals such as M & M's, Fruit Loops, cake decorating items; and roly poly action toys. Other suggested materials are a small box, paper and brightly colored magic markers; plastic pegs and board; brightly colored, textured books with thick pages; large beads; stacking cones; a primary puzzle with approximately three pieces; multicolored counting bears; shape sorting chips or parquetry blocks; simple pictures in duplicate glued to small index cards; or commercially produced pictures and duplicates of different colored toys for matching.

The first stage of the visual assessment should be to observe the child for immediately obvious visual abnormalities and behaviors indicating deficient vision. Primary questions to be answered should focus on the presence or absence of basic visual responses, and the types of visual stimuli (light, movement, color) to which the child attends. Observing not only the manner and direction in which the child reacts to visual stimuli, but also the distance and size of objects eliciting the most consistent response, provides insight into the positioning of specific materials useful in obtaining maximum visual attention. Equally important is the assessment of the child's ability to integrate visual stimuli with cognitive and motor processing skills to perform discrimination, association, figure-ground, and eye-hand coordination activities. Simple techniques for use in assessing five aspects of visual function are given below. Figures I through V suggest check lists a teacher may use for recording information about a multiply handicapped child's performance.

Techniques for Functional Vision Screening

I. Presence and Nature of the Visual Response

a. Direct a penlight into the child's eyes from 12″ away and observe whether the pupils constrict, then dilate when the light is removed. Be sure to observe his eyes before shining the light as blind children often exhibit hippus, a continual constricting and dilating of the pupil.

b. Assessing a tendency of the eyes to deviate can be done by flashing a beam from a penlight into the child's eyes from 30″ away. If the light is reflected simultaneously in the middle of each pupil, no deviation is present. If the reflection is centered on one pupil but off-center in the other, some form of muscle imbalance is indicated.

c. Place the child on his back and kneel behind his head. Pass your hand across his eyes, pause and repeat. A blinking reflex indicates some light perception and possibly some object perception.

I. Presence and Nature of the Visual Response

a. Pupillary reaction: ___present ___absent ___R ___L
b. Muscle imbalance: ___present ___absent ___R ___L
c. Blink reflex: ___present ___absent ___R ___L
d. Visual field loss: ___present ___absent ___R ___L
e. Peripheral field loss: ___present ___absent ___R ___L
f. Visual field preference: ___present ___absent ___R ___L
g. Eye preference: ___present ___absent ___R ___L

II. Reaction to Visual Stimuli

a. Inappropriate visual behaviors: ___present ___absent
b. Tracking ability: ___present ___absent
  ___light ___objects: ___vertical ___circular
  ___horizontal ___oblique
c. Reaches for toys: ___present ___absent
  ___in front of him ___to his right ___to his left
  ___above eye level ___below eye level
d. Shifts attention: ___present ___absent
  ___both sides ___one side ___R ___L
e. Scanning ability: ___present ___absent

III. Distance and Size of Objects and Pictures

a. Locates dropped toy: ___present ___absent ___distance
  ___peg or candy ___inch cubed blocks ___shape chips
b. Small toy observed: ___present ___absent ___distance
c. Large toy observed: ___present ___absent ___distance
d. Objects matched: ___present ___absent ___distance
  ___large toys ___distance
  ___small toys ___distance

IV. Integration of Visual and Cognitive Processing

a. Visual pursuit: ___present ___absent
b. Causality: ___present ___absent
c. Object permanence: ___present ___absent
d. Object concept: ___present ___absent
e. Means-ends: ___present ___absent

V. Integration of Visual and Motor Processing

a. Approach:
  1. pegs: ___visual ___tactual Reach: ___O ___U
  2. stacking cone: ___visual ___tactual Reach: ___O ___U
  3. puzzles: ___visual ___tactual Reach: ___O ___U
  4. pounding bench: ___visual ___tactual Reach: ___O ___U
  5. beads: ___visual ___tactual Reach: ___O ___U
b. Matching:
  1. colored blocks:
    ___matches ___does not match ___near distance ___far distance
  2. shapes:
    ___matches ___does not match ___near distance ___far distance
  3. pictures:
    ___matches ___does not match ___near distance ___far distance

---

d. Assess the child's perception of light using a penlight. From 12″ or closer flash the light and note whether he attends to it. The light should be flashed slightly above, below, to the left, and right of the child's face to determine the range of visual field. Note whether he fails to attend to the light in any plane.

e. Sitting behind the child, bring the light slowly into his right, then his left visual field. Note at which point he turns to look at the light. He should notice it when it is directly in line with the lateral portion of the eye.

f. Present the child with play objects of equal interest simultaneously in the right and left visual fields and gesture for him to touch them, switch their positions and repeat. Observe whether the child attends to a toy in only one position rather than both.

g. While holding a motivating toy 12″ to 18″ in front of the child's eyes, alternately cover each eye. Observe whether he resists having one or both eyes covered or if he remains indifferent to the covering. Children having limited or no vision in an eye will not mind having that eye covered but will strongly resist covering of the functional eye.

II. Reaction to Visual Stimuli

---

a. Observe the child for any inappropriate visual behaviors such as light flicking with fingers or objects or eye poking.

b. Evaluate the child's ability to localize, track, and scan by holding puppets, small squeeze toys, or penlights within the child's range of vision. Move them slowly from left to right, up and down, and in oblique angles. Note whether he locates an object efficiently and attends for at least 20 seconds.

c. Place toys at all levels and in all directions and watch to see if he turns and reaches for them. These items should be interspersed throughout the evaluation to maintain interest in looking.

d. Note whether the child is able to shift his attention by holding two toys of equal interest approximately one foot apart in front of the child. Shake one, pause, then shake the other. Observe whether he shifts his gaze to the other toy.

e. Observe his ability to scan by placing three objects in front of him and watch to see if he shifts his attention from one toy to the next in line.

III. Distance and Size of Objects and Pictures

---

a. While interacting with the child, scatter small pegs or candies ¼″ in diameter, inch cubed blocks, counting bears, or shape chips around the child and encourage him to find them. Note the distance at which he most consistently attends to the various sized objects.

b. Project large (6″ to 8″ in diameter) and small (2″ to 3″ in diameter) toys to the left, right, and forward from the child and observe how far they travel before he looks away or ceases in his efforts to retrieve them.

c. Using a set of toys that duplicate, except for color, those used in B, have the child match his objects with yours as you display them singly. Begin at 10 feet for large and 5 feet for small objects. Obtain the maximum distance at which the child sees the objects without straining by moving backwards or forwards in 2-foot intervals until he consistently matches four or five objects.

IV. Integration of Visual and Cognitive Processing

a. Tap or pour blocks and pellets from containers in front of the child. Note whether he looks at them as they tumble before him.

b. Scribble large circular motions with magic marker on white paper in front of the child. Note whether he watches or attempts to take the marker.

c. Give the child M & M's to hold, help him place them in a small box and shake them around. Take the box from the child and quickly remove the candies. Watch to see if he looks for the candies when you return the box.

d. Give him a large colorful book to look at. Note whether he bends to look at the pictures or pats them.

e. Give the child a toy which has continuous action and attracts his attention. As he watches, push the toy out of his sight and note if he looks for the toy. Replace it before him without the motion and observe whether he attempts to reactivate it.

V. Integration of Visual and Motor Processing

a. On activities involving the pegs, stacking cone, puzzles, pounding bench, and beads, watch to see if he directly inserts or applies pieces, overreaches (O), or underreaches (U). Does he look for the recess and the hole or does he only tactually approach them?

b. When shown one colored block, shape, or 2″ picture at a time, can he match it, given only two choices? Watch to see which colors, shapes, and pictures he matches and if he attends to color or configuration. Observe the distance from the materials at which he works, then have him match them at a far distance. Note the farthest distance at which he correctly matches each.

Summary

Traditional tests of visual functioning and acuity have lacked the impetus essential for assessing children with multiple impairments. Although operant measures have been successful in eliciting behaviors required to respond to these tests, Sheridan and Koehler have offered the most promising formal tests for this population. Until the use of the New York Flashcard Vision Test and the Stycar Vision Test is more widespread, the task of visual assessment remains primarily with the teacher. Obtaining even a gross indication of the child's functional visual field—a preferred eye, distance at which he most efficiently works with various sized objects, and the level of complexity of the visual stimuli that the child successfully interprets—provides the teacher with basic information needed to design an educational program relevant to the child's visual and developmental needs. ■

References

Allen, H. F. Testing of visual acuity in preschool children: Norms, variables, and a new picture test. *Pediatrics*, 1957, **19**, 1093-1100.

Banus, B. S. *The developmental therapist.* Thorofare, N.J.: Charles B. Slack, Inc., 1971.

Blackhurst, R. & Radke, E. Vision screening procedures used with mentally retarded children—A second report. *Sight Saving Review*, 1968, **38**, 84-88.

Borg, G. & Sundmark, U. A comparative study of visual acuity test for children. *Acta Ophthalmologica*, 1967, **45**, 105-113.

Courtney, G. R. & Heath, G. G. Color vision deficiency in the mentally retarded: Prevalence and a method of evaluation. *American Journal of Mental Deficiency*, 1971, **76**, 48-52.

Faye, E. E. A new visual acuity test for partially-sighted non-readers. *Journal of Pediatric Ophthalmology*, 1968, **5**, 210-212.

Ffooks, O. Vision test for children: Use of symbols. *British Journal of Ophthalmology*, 1965, **49**, 312-314.

Gorman, J. J., Cogan, D. G. & Gellis, S. S. An apparatus for grading the visual acuity of infants on the basis of optokinetic nystagmus. *Pediatrics*, 1957, **19**, 1088-1092.

Hoyt, W. F. Neuro-ophthalmologic examination of infants and children. *International Ophthalmology Clinics*, 1963, **3**, 757-775.

Lippman, O. Vision of young children. *Archives of Ophthalmology*, 1969, **81**, 763-767.

Macht, J. Operant measurement of subjective visual acuity in non-verbal children. *Journal of Applied Behavior Analysis*, 1971, **4**, 23-26.

Osterberg, G. A Danish pictorial sight-test chart. *American Journal of Ophthalmology*, 1965, **59**, 1120-1123.

Sheridan, M. D. *Manual for the Stycar Vision Tests.* Windsor, Ontario: NFER Publishing Company, Ltd., 1973.

Sloan, A. E. & Savitz, R. A. Vision screening. *International Opthalmology Clinics*, 1963, **3**, 815-831.

Vernon, M. Multiply handicapped deaf children: Medical, educational, and psychological considerations. Washington, D.C.: *Council for Exceptional Children Monograph*, 1969.

Wolf, J. M. & Anderson, R. M. *The multiply handicapped child.* Springfield, Ill.: Charles C Thomas, 1973.

Wolfe, W. & Harvey, J. The evaluation and development of techniques for testing the visual and auditory acuity of TMR children. *Eric document 002 802.* Austin, Tx.: College of Education, Texas University, 1959.

 **IN BRIEF**

Developmental Scales versus Observational Measures for Deaf-Blind Children

MARTIN H. DIEBOLD
W. SCOTT CURTIS
REBECCA F. DuBOSE

Comprehensive evaluation is a critical first step in developing appropriate individualized educational plans for exceptional children. Historically, approaches to evaluation have included the use of standardized tests and developmental scales as well as systematic observation of daily behavior. However, there has been a lack of research aimed at determining whether measures of performance obtained through the administration of standardized tests and developmental scales are related to measures of performance obtained through systematic observation (Herbert, 1970).

The purpose of this study, therefore, is to determine:

1. The maximum relationship between two sets of measures: (a) standarized tests and developmental scales and (b) systematic behavior observation ratings.
2. Whether significant relationships between individual measures of both sets could be demonstrated.
3. Whether any systematic observation measures could efficiently predict any measures of performance obtained through the administration of standardized tests and developmental scales.

Method

Instruments

The Cattell Infant Intelligence Scale (Cattell, 1947/1960) or the Stanford-Binet Intelligence Scale (Terman & Merrill, 1973) was used to obtain a score (i.e., mental age) for intellectual development. The Stanford-Binet was used in lieu of the Cattell in instances where a subject's intellectual functioning exceeded the ceiling on the Cattell. Social age was obtained through administration of the Maxfield-Buchholz Scale of Social Maturity for Use with Preschool Blind Children (Maxfield & Buchholz, 1957). Gross motor age and fine motor age were obtained through administration of the Peabody Developmental Motor Scales (Folio & DuBose, 1974). Either the Receptive-Expressive Emergent Language (REEL) scale (Bzoch & League, 1970) or the Preschool Language Scale (Zimmerman, Steiner, & Evatt, 1969) was used to obtain a receptive language age and expressive language age for each subject. The Preschool Language Scale was used in lieu of the REEL in instances where a subject's language functioning exceeded the ceiling on the REEL.

The Telediagnostic Protocol (TDP) (Curtis

& Donlon, 1972) was the systematic observation instrument used to obtain seven measures of behavioral functioning: receptive communication, referent communication, expressive communication, adjustment, affective learning, sensory motor learning, and intellectual learning. The TDP employs behavior observation and rating of videotapes of a child in eight structured and unstructured everyday situations. The purpose of the TDP is to provide an idiographic description of a deaf-blind child's daily behavior using a trait rating system (e.g., curiosity, attentiveness, flexibility). Normally, the TDP provides a nonquantitative description of behavioral functioning. However, for the purpose of this study a scoring system was applied to obtained ratings (Diebold, 1975).

Subjects

Subjects were 24 ambulatory deaf-blind children between the ages of 6 years, 2 months, and 13 years, 11 months. Mean chronological age for the group was 9 years, 10 months. All subjects were candidates for admission to any of seven educational programs for deaf-blind children in seven eastern states.

Procedure

All developmental scales were administered to each subject by an experienced evaluator from the deaf-blind program at the Kennedy Child Study Center, Peabody College. In addition, experienced evaluators from the Deaf-Blind Project at the University of Georgia videotaped each subject. The 24 stimulus tapes were then presented to three psychoeducational consultants who served as judges. Judges independently viewed and rated each subject's behavior for the eight situations in a manner consistent with that described by Curtis and Donlon (1972). A scoring system was applied to obtained ratings so that a mean judge rating score was obtained for each subject in each of the seven areas of behavioral functioning.

Results

Table 1 displays various descriptive statistics for each of the systematic behavior observation and the standardized test and developmental scale variables, respectively. Data

associated with the observation variables demonstrated variability, reflecting differences between the variables with respect to maximum possible scores versus obtained scores. The range of group means for the observation variables was 31.96 to 175.77. Overall performance of the group, expressed in percentage of maximum possible score, was 55%.

Compared with the descriptive data of the observational variables, the developmental scale variables demonstrated much less variability with respect to differences between the means. The range of group means for the developmental scale variables was 17.75 months to 38.44 months. Using mean group chronological age as a frame of reference (i.e., 118 months), the developmental scale variables depicted the subject group as functioning within 24% of their mean group chronological age. In summary, the developmental scale variables tended to depict the group's performance as low with little variability. In contrast, the observation variables depicted the group's performance as comparatively high and variable.

A computerized canonical correlation analysis program (Barr & Goodnight, 1972) was used to determine the maximum relationship between the two sets of measures. The analysis produced six canonical correlation coefficients. One coefficient (0.93) was significant beyond the .05 level (p = .0008).

A correlation matrix was also obtained through a product moment correlation analysis (Barr & Goodnight, 1972). The results of this analysis indicate that: (a) interrelationships among the observation variables were lower than the interrelationships for the developmental scale variables; (b) one developmental scale variable, social age, consistently demonstrated higher relationships between the other developmental scale variables; (c) relationships within the two sets were higher than relationships between the two sets; (d) three observation variables— adjustment, affective learning, and intellectual development—correlated the highest with the developmental scale variables; (e) all three observation variables concerned with communication demonstrated moderate relationships but low common variances with the developmental scale variables; (f) one observation variable, sensory motor learning, demonstrated low, nonsignificant relationships

TABLE 1
Descriptive Statistics
for Each of the
Observation and Developmental Scale Variables

Observation variables	Possible score	Mean score	SD	Mean expressed as percentage	Range of group performance expressed as percentage
Receptive communication	160	77.68	10.70	49%	37% - 60%
Referent communication	80	40.96	6.23	51%	40% - 63%
Expressive communication	80	31.96	5.45	40%	27% - 54%
Adjustment	240	175.77	33.45	73%	48% - 91%
Affective learning	264	151.86	38.83	58%	33% - 78%
Sensory motor learning	120	95.54	10.02	80%	60% - 88%
Intellectual learning	192	53.06	21.61	28%	12% - 52%

Developmental scale variables	Mean chronological age in months	Mean developmental age in months	SD	Mean developmental age expressed as percentage of mean chronological age	Range of developmental age expressed as percentage
Receptive language age	118	21.87	21.50	19%	0% - 63%
Expressive language age	118	17.75	17.10	15%	2% - 63%
Social age	118	38.44	17.86	33%	13% - 56%
Gross motor age	118	33.46	21.32	28%	14% - 55%
Fine motor age	118	33.62	22.88	28%	7% - 65%
Mental age	118	25.78	16.70	22%	5% - 60%

with all the developmental scale variables; and (g) both the developmental scale variables concerned with communication demonstrated moderate correlations but low common variances with all the observation variables including the three observation variables concerned with communication.

Multiple correlation analysis employing a stepwise regression analysis (Barr & Goodnight, 1972) was used to determine whether any observation variables predicted group performance on each of the developmental scale variables. The results demonstrated that at least one observation variable was a significant predictor of each developmental scale variable. Multiple R's ranged from 0.80 to 0.90. Table 2 displays the observation variables that effectively predicted each developmental scale variable.

Conclusions

The purpose of this study was to determine whether the performance of a group of deaf-blind children on developmental scales was significantly related to measures of their performance obtained through systematic behavior observation.

Results indicate that, as a set, observation measures significantly correlate with the set of developmental scale measures. Furthermore, at least one observation measure served as a significant predictor of group performance for each developmental scale measure. However, the magnitude of correlation and low common variance associated with each relationship between individual measures of both sets indicates that they are not linear relationships. This suggests that information obtained from one evaluation approach is not completely redundant when combined with the information obtained through the use of the other approach. Therefore, the frequent recommendation that both evaluation approaches be used in accomplishing comprehensive evaluation of exceptional children would appear to be supported.

TABLE 2
Independent Variable Predictors
of Dependent Variables

Dependent (developmental scale) variables	Predictor (observation) variables
Receptive language development	Sensory motor learning
	Intellectual learning
Expressive language development	Sensory motor learning*
	Adjustment
	Referent communication
Social development	Adjustment*
	Sensory motor learning
	Expressive communication
Gross motor development	Intellectual learning*
	Sensory motor learning
Fine motor development	Intellectual learning*
	Sensory motor learning
	Adjustment
Intellectual development	Intellectual learning*

* Arranged in order of greatest contribution to the prediction; $p < .05$.

References

Barr, A. J., & Goodnight, J. H. *A user's guide to a statistical analysis system.* Raleigh NC: Department of Statistics, North Carolina State University, 1972.

Bzoch, K. R., & League, R. *Receptive-expressive emergent language scale.* Gainesville FL: The Tree of Life Press, 1970.

Cattell, P. *The measurement of intelligence of infants and young children.* New York: Psychological Corporation, 1960. (Originally published, 1947.)

Curtis, W. S., & Donlon, E. T. *The development and evaluation of a videotape protocol for the examination of multihandicapped deaf-blind children* (Final Report). Syracuse NY: Syracuse University, 1972.

Diebold, M. H. *A comparison of two approaches to the assessment of deaf-blind children.* Unpublished doctoral dissertation, University of Georgia, 1975.

Folio, R., & DuBose, R. F. *Peabody developmental motor scales* (Experimental Edition). Nashville TN: Institute on Mental Retardation and Intellectual Development, George Peabody College for Teachers, 1974.

Herbert, J. *Direct observation as a research technique. Psychology in the Schools,* 1970, 7(2), 127-138.

Maxfield, K. & Buchholz, S. *A social maturity scale for blind preschool children.* New York: American Foundation for the Blind, 1957.

Terman, L. M., & Merrill, M. A. *Stanford-Binet intelligence scale: Manual.* Boston: Houghton Mifflin, 1973.

Zimmerman, I. L., Steiner, V. G., & Evatt, R. L. *Preschool language manual.* Columbus OH: Charles E. Merrill, 1969.

MARTIN H. DIEBOLD *is Coordinator, Special Education Programs, Auburn University, Auburn, Alabama;* W. SCOTT CURTIS *is Professor, Speech Pathology and Audiology, University of Georgia, Athens; and* REBECCA F. DuBOSE *is Professor and Chairman, Special Education, George Peabody College, Nashville, Tennessee. This study was completed while the senior author was a graduate student at the University of Georgia. Funds in support of this study came from a US Office of Education Trainee Fellowship and from a grant from the US Department of Health, Education, and Welfare, Office of Education, Bureau of Education for the Handicapped (Grant No. OEG-0-72-5460).*

Early Intervention for Infants with Deaf-Blindness

MARTHA G. MICHAEL
PETER V. PAUL
Ohio State University

ABSTRACT: Few individuals labeled deaf-blind are, in fact, totally deaf and totally blind. Many of these individuals have residual sight and hearing, but may not receive adequate early training in using these senses effectively. Effective early sensory training with infants entails the use of consistent reinforcement methods in natural social contexts. Preservice and inservice teachers must become knowledgeable in high-quality programming components in which the goal is to increase the abilities of students with dual sensory impairments—in both mobility and communication—and to help them become independent, responsible adults.

☐ In recent years, educators and researchers have directed their attention to early childhood and early intervention programs for infants with severe disabilities (Bickman & Weatherford, 1986; Ramey, Trohanis, & Hostler, 1982). Specifically, this focus has resulted in an increase of interest in services and programs for infants with dual sensory impairments (Freeman, 1985; McInnes & Treffry, 1982). In relation to early intervention and deaf-blindness, however, there is a need for improvement in university-level preservice training programs, development of better identification and educational placement procedures, and the establishment of research-based intervention programming.

In this article, we briefly discuss the effects that definitions of deaf-blindness may have on educational placements and services for infants with dual sensory impairments and on the training of preservice university students interested in becoming professionals in this area. Several intervention theories and their effects on current special education practices are also presented. In essence, we argue that the establishment of appropriate early intervention programs entails methods that address the use of residual sight and hearing, as well as the development of other senses. Thus, much of our focus in programming is on assessment and training in the use of vision and audition.

EFFECTS OF DEFINITION ON PROGRAMS AND TRAINING

Problems in the development of effective intervention programming and the training of professionals have resulted from the range of interpretations for the federal government's educational definition of deaf-blindness (Baldwin, V., 1986; Bullis & Bull, 1986). In general, the federal definition does not suggest the multiplicity of services and the types of professional training needed to support these individuals with such diverse characteristics.

Many students with dual sensory impairments are categorized as multihandicapped (D'Zamko & Hampton, 1985). Their sensory impairments are not recognized as primary disabilities. Thus, these students may be placed in programs that lack sufficient supportive and consistent services to meet their needs effectively (Fredericks & Baldwin, 1987). For example, most teachers of students with severe or multiple disabilities may not be familiar with vision and auditory assessments; residual visual-training and auditory-training methods; coactive, cooperative, and reactive learning techniques (Van Dijk, 1965; 1968); and alternative modes of communication (e.g., communication boards, American Sign Language). In general, these teachers may have little or no knowledge of programming for students with dual sensory impairments.

Even some universities may not be equipped to provide preservice students with necessary skills to deal with the multiplicity of programming needs for teaching children with deaf-blindness (Baldwin, V., 1986; Bullis & Bull, 1986; Covert & Fredericks, 1987). For example, some preservice training programs for certification in multihandicaps or severe handicaps do not address functional visual or auditory training and assessment. In many states that offer certification for multihandicaps, the requirements are so generic they do not specify the skills necessary for dealing effectively with individuals who are deaf with additional handicapping conditions (Curtis & Tweedie, 1985; D'Zamko & Hampton, 1985).

FUNCTIONAL INTERPRETATION OF DEAF-BLINDNESS

The number of persons with deaf-blindness has not increased substantially since 1974; however, interpretations of the definition of the population have changed drastically. The need for quality services and qualified personnel, both in education and in adult services, has been recognized (Barrett, 1987). Commendably, recent adult service delivery definitions have included more functional interpretations of the term *deaf-blind* (Konar & Rice, 1982). For example, individuals categorized as having deaf-blindness can represent any of the following: (a) those with moderate-to-profound auditory and visual impairments, with or without other educationally disabling conditions, who need services to increase independence; (b) those with central-processing problems that result in cortical blindness or central auditory dysfunction; and (c) those with progressive sensory impairments such as Usher's syndrome. The formulation of more recent functional interpretations, such as category *a*, have allowed some states to include children with functional impairments and other children whose primary disability is mental retardation (K. Arnold, personal communication, December 1987).

Regardless of the categories of dual sensory impairments, approximately 94% of these children have either residual hearing or residual sight (Fredericks & Baldwin, 1987; Ouellette, 1984). Thus, intervention programming and university-level preservice training should consider auditory and visual assessment and training, as well as other sensory training techniques (e.g., tactile, olfactory, and kinesthetic) and innovative communication strategies (Barraga & Morris, 1982;

Goetz, Utley, Gee, Baldwin, & Sailor, 1981; Siegal-Causey & Downing, 1987). These areas should also be considered in developing early intervention theories and programs for infants with deaf-blindness.

INTERVENTION THEORIES

Several theories have provided the philosophical underpinnings of current intervention practices. Biological-developmental theorists have described psychological growth in holistic, interactionist terms (Lewin, 1951; Piaget, 1952; Vygotsky, 1962). These theorists argued that, from birth, organisms use, assimilate, and construct conceptions. Cognitive growth results from communicative interactions.

On the other hand, radical behaviorists assert that the mind is a machine that is formulated by stimulus input from birth and that reflects the accumulation of this learning by the output of behavior (Skinner, 1953). Behavior is explained by a causal mechanism that does not depend on the functional value of the behavior. Determinism is one of the basic tenets of behaviorism (Baldwin, A., 1980).

Special education programs seem to be influenced by educational ideologies such as environmental transmission, which parallels behaviorism, and a combination of romanticism and progressivism. Romanticism emphasizes the value of childhood, the discovery of an inner self, and interaction with others. Progressivism, which parallels the developmental theory of Piaget, also emphasizes interaction with others, as well as interaction with the environment. It is based on the Hegelian belief that development is a progression through stages and that knowledge is an active change in patterns of thought influenced by problem-solving situations (Baldwin, A., 1980). In other words, organisms are proactive in constructing their own developmental progress from birth throughout life.

It seems that intervention programs for high-risk infants, including those with dual sensory impairments, lack a firm theoretical base. The development of these programs may be the result of the accumulation of nontheoretical research data (Walker & Crawley, 1983). Most curricula for infants with disabilities, however, tend to adhere to the tenets of a biological-developmental or cognitive-developmental approach (Bailey, Jens, & Johnson, 1983). That is, developmental milestones are emphasized, and skills must be developed in a specific hierarchical order regardless of the ages of children with disabilities. The developmental order of skills corresponds to what has been observed in younger children without disabilities (Bailey et al., 1983).

On the other hand, some programs use curricula that emphasize functional (i.e., ecological or environmental learning) approaches in which instructional practices rely on task-analysis of functional and chronological age-appropriate activities, analysis of discrepancies between needed skills and previously acquired skills, and the use of operant-conditioning methods. Bailey et al. (1983) analyzed 15 curricula for infants with disabilities and found that only 3 curricula employed a functional approach. In general, the functional approach was used in conjunction with principles from 1 of the developmental approaches.

Only 1 of these 15 curricula for infants has been field tested. In addition, very few data are available on the effectiveness of the various theoretical approaches. It has been argued that principles from several theories can be combined in curriculum and instruction of early intervention programs (Bailey et al., 1983). We think that a creative approach, using aspects of both the environmental-learning theories and the cognitive-developmental theories, is appropriate for infants, especially infants with dual sensory impairments. Specifically we recommend the incorporation of systematic training in the area of auditory and visual development in natural settings and using age-appropriate materials. It has also been documented that the use of instructional operant-conditioning methods in these natural, meaningful settings can increase residual sense function and generalization of acquired skills (Barraga & Morris, 1982; Goetz & Gee, 1987; Lundervold, Lewin, & Irwin, 1987).

EARLY INTERVENTION

Early intervention is the establishment of educational and support services for children, age 3 and younger, with or at risk for disabilities, and their families. The importance of early intervention for children with handicapping conditions has been widely documented (Bronfenbrenner, 1975; Hayden, 1979; McInnes & Treffrey, 1982; Peterson, 1983). In the case of infants with two or more handicapping conditions, such as deaf-blindness, the need for early intervention is greater. The senses of vision and audition are dynamically and

neurologically linked, and both senses should be addressed on a consistent, systematic basis to prevent problems in cognitive, linguistic, and social-emotional development.

Identification

The methods for identifying infants are case finding, registries, and screening. To provide appropriate and crucial intervention services to infants and families, it is vital that the identification process be improved. States should be encouraged to establish registries that include (a) functional tracking (i.e., description of a child's placement and intervention methods), (b) directional services (i.e., services that direct families to available programs), and (c) listing of programming options for children with dual sensory impairments and their families. Firm connections should be established with the appropriate personnel within the medical community such as obstetricians, neonatologists, and pediatricians to facilitate the identification process. This should enable agencies to assist families in finding appropriate services for their children (Michael, Arnold, & Niswander, 1988; Watson, Barrett, & Brown, 1984).

Early Intervention for Infants with Deaf-Blindness

Early intervention programming may need to be eclectic, using techniques that emphasize, at least, the development of motor and functional communication skills, and particularly, the distance senses (vision and audition) (Fredericks & Baldwin, 1987; Goetz & Gee, 1987). Classroom teachers need to know how to interpret the results of both clinical and functional assessments and improve the sensory functional abilities of infants (Curtis & Tweedie, 1985; D'Zamko & Hampton, 1985). Adequate assessment, followed by a comprehensive intervention program, should lead to improvement in an infant's use of residual senses for communication and mobility skills (Freeman, 1985; McInnes & Treffrey, 1982).

Relatively few data are available concerning the enhancement of residual vision and hearing functions, using sequential, simultaneous, or contingent methods, in infants with deaf-blindness. Some methods focus on the functional use of one sense or the other; however, they have been designed to aid classroom teachers of older children (Goetz & Gee, 1987; Goetz et al., 1981;

Smith & Cote, 1982). In addition, these methods have not specifically focused on the development of residual senses in relation to communication, mobility or self-image in infants. Given the available information, we present some effective visual and auditory tests and examples of training for infants with dual sensory impairments. These examples can be incorporated into programming by classroom or home-bound teachers. A transdisciplinary team, which includes eye (e.g., optometrists) and ear (e.g., audiologists) specialists, should help interpret formal test results and provide directions in determining appropriate adaptations for each child's specific needs.

DEVELOPMENT OF RESIDUAL VISION

Visual Assessment

Visual assessment and subsequent intervention are critical for infants with dual sensory impairments for two main reasons: efficient vision use is important for learning, and visual function can improve (Goetz & Gee, 1987; Lundervold et al., 1987). Developing a formal vision-training program may require great effort from members of the transdisciplinary team. For example, the team must conduct a battery of both clinical and functional tests over a period of time to determine visual effectiveness and subsequent curricular planning and instructional intervention. Cress (1989) suggested that assessments be followed by ongoing observation and recording of children's visual behaviors during activities in natural, meaningful environments. To plan accurately for intervention, teachers of children with dual sensory impairments need to have the ability to interpret clinical findings, perform functional assessments, and record ongoing data of the child's performance.

A child who does not respond to conventional testing may be a candidate for several physiological tests that focus on visual acuity. These formal tests should be administered by qualified clinical or medical personnel. The tests include the Visually Evoked Response (VER), also known as Visually Evoked Potential (VEP), and the Electroretinogram (ERG). The VER has been used extensively to determine the visual acuity of infants (Baraldi, Ferrari, Fonda, & Penne, 1981) and children with neurological handicaps (Mohn & Van Hol-Van Duin, 1983). The ERG yields useful information about the functioning level of the retina.

Functional tests assess the visual behavior of the individual rather than just the physiological condition of the eyes. That is, these tests assess the ability to track objects, use visual fields, develop eye-hand coordination, and perform other functions that reflect visual development. The tests are portable and can be administered by trained personnel, such as teachers.

Functional vision assessments have been developed both for individuals with visual impairments only and for those with multiple handicaps. Some assessments developed for clients with multiple handicaps include *Functional Vision Inventory for the Multiple and Severely Handicapped* (Langley, 1980) and the *Visual Assessment Manual* (Sailor, Utley, Goetz, Gee, & Baldwin, 1982). Since neither of the two assessments have reported reliability or validity data, no comparisons on their applicability and effectiveness can be made (Cress, 1985).

The Opkinetic Nystaqmx (OKN) provides information on the acuity threshold of the infant through the use of spinning cards to determine fixation ability. The Forced Preferential Looking Test (FPL), based on Fantz's work (1963) with infants, is another test that seems promising for infants up to 6 months old and for difficult-to-test children such as those with dual sensory impairments. The Operant Preferential Looking Test (OPL), which pairs a discerned reinforcing consequence with the behavior of fixation, is specifically geared toward infants over the age of 6 months (Teller, 1979), but has produced promising results for individuals with multiple disabilities (Duchman & Selenow, 1983; Mohn & Van Hol-Van Duin, 1983). The Teller Acuity Card Technique, normed on 0-to-3-year-old children without disabilities, has been shown to be effective for children who are developmentally delayed or at risk for this condition (Cress, 1989; Mohn & Van Hol-Van Duin, 1983; Teller, McDonald, Preston, Sebris, & Dobson, 1986). In addition, this procedure is useful for mass screening of infants.

In sum, to obtain accurate data on the visual functioning level of infants with dual sensory impairments, one must use a variety of clinical and functional tests over a certain period of time. It may be necessary to provide visual training to young children to improve their ability to be assessed (Cress, Johnson, Spellman, Sizemore, & Shores, 1982). For example, some children can be trained to fixate visually through operant conditioning. The infant's need for low-vision aides (e.g., eyeglasses) should be determined as early as possible. Methods for adapting the classroom and home environments, positioning the child, and enhancing optimal vision use should result from the assessments and be part of the programming (Courtwright, Mihok, & Jose, 1975; Jose, 1983). One must complete an assessment battery before developing a training program.

Visual Training

In our view, a vision training program should follow a functional, hierarchical sequence, using activities similar to those outlined, for example, in the manual *Look at Me* (Smith & Cote, 1982) or in the article "Functional Vision Programming" (Goetz & Gee, 1987). For each visual skill listed here, a separate instructional strategy package should be implemented for each infant when appropriate. Implementation begins in natural, meaningful contexts (e.g., going to the store, mealtimes) after decisions are made on the targeted visual skills to be learned to enhance participation.

1. Awareness of light (orient to presence of stimulus).
2. Attention to light (fixation either bifoveal or monofoveal).
3. Localization of light source in various areas of the visual field (awareness and attention).
4. Light tracking.
5. Awareness of presence or absence of light.
6. Visual tracking of objects or persons.
7. Attention to presence or absence of light.
8. Localization of objects (scanning).
9. Use of peripheral vision.

These components can be systematically taught via prompting methods (e.g., see Sailor et al., 1982), and continuous loop strategies (Goetz & Gee, 1987). The target visual behavior must be performed consistently before proceeding to the next behavior. Contingent reinforcement is used, as well as a pairing of the visual objective to a functional skill that requires the use of the target visual skill. For example, a functional skill for infants, such as grasping a bottle, is paired with the visual objective of fixation. Older or more skilled infants may be expected to locate visually an article of clothing such as their shoe or to discriminate between two desired objects and choose one. Event recording techniques can be used to measure the targeted visual behavior during the observation periods.

In general, infants with dual sensory impairments progress very slowly. Parents should be shown, through modeling, procedures and strategies for achieving objectives step by step. They should be encouraged to incorporate the activities into their normal day-to-day routines with their infants at home. An example of one level of this training is presented as follows.

Level 1: Awareness of light (orient to presence of stimulus).

Rationale: In training very young children to be aware of light, there may be a need to orient them to the presence of a stimulus, and then pair the preferred stimulus with the stimulus of light. When children become aware of various stimuli in their environment, this is the first step in their reaction to the outside world.

Objective: The purpose is to build awareness of a sensory stimulus by orienting behaviors toward the stimulus. The reactions of children should be monitored.

Target Behaviors:
1. Head turn.
2. Gaze shift.
3. Brief fixation.
4. Ability to respond consistently to light stimulus.

Activity: Child will perform target behavior selected when blinds in the home are opened in the morning.

DEVELOPMENT OF RESIDUAL HEARING

Auditory Assessment

As in vision assessment, a variety of clinical and functional hearing tests should be administered to infants with dual sensory impairments over a period of time before establishing an intervention program. Hearing should be assessed to (a) determine the extent and degree of impairment; (b) evaluate the effects of medical treatment or the use of prosthetic devices, such as hearing aids; and (c) provide individual, appropriate educational programming (e.g., Erber, 1982; Sanders, 1982). As discussed previously, early intervention, particularly amplification and auditory training, is important because of the pervasive effects of hearing impairment on the child's cognitive, linguistic, and socioemotional development.

In the assessment of middle ear function, the three major objective measures that involve physiological responses to auditory stimuli and require no instructed behavior responses are static compliance, tympanometry, and acoustic reflex evaluation (Orchik & MacKimmie, 1984). These tests have been useful with some special-needs populations, such as children with behavioral disturbances, language delays, and mental retardation. For children under 1 year of age, standard immittance audiometry is not feasible; however, a technique known as acoustic otoscopy or acoustic reflectometry can be used for these difficult-to-test children (Teele & Teele, 1984). Another useful and efficient test is the Sensitivity Prediction Acoustic Reflex (SPAR) method (Niswander, 1988).

Behavioral hearing assessments require overt behavioral responses to auditory stimuli. Traditional methods are inappropriate for children with dual sensory impairments (Niswander, 1987). Many of these children do not have the necessary cooperative and receptive language skills to participate. It seems that effective testing programs involve the pairing of visual/tactile and auditory stimuli, and then fading these stimuli so that the level of auditory response can be determined.

For infants without the use of efficient vision, there seem to be no best testing procedures available that are supported by research. The Auditory Brainstem Response (ABR) and Behavior Observation Audiometric (BOA) methods are recommended for hard-to-test individuals; however, they are not always accurate in determining auditory function (Hecox, Gerber, & Mendel, 1983; Niswander, 1987; Spradlin, 1985). For example, in BOA procedures, the child is placed in a soundproof test booth. The audiologist presents stimuli and observes changes in the child's behavior such as eye blinks, startle reactions, and cessation or increase in activity.

Other behavioral audiometric procedures that have been adapted for use with hard-to-test children include the use of classical and operant conditioning to train responses. For example, visual stimuli may be used to reinforce correct localization responses (Goetz, Gee, & Sailor, 1985). This classical conditioning testing is named the Visual Reinforcement Audiometry (VRA). Adaptations for individuals who are visually impaired may include the use of vibrotactile reinforcement (Spradlin, 1985). An example of operant conditioning testing is Tangible Reinforcement Oper-

ant Conditioning Audiometry (TROCA). This highly structured test originally was developed for assessing children with mental retardation (Lloyd, Spradlin, & Reid, 1968). Typically, candy or little toys are dispensed if a child depresses a button on a box after hearing a sound. If a visual reinforcer is used, this test is labeled Visual Reinforcement Operant Conditioning Audiometry (VROCA).

In most cases, children with dual sensory impairments need to be trained to make reliable responses to auditory stimuli. TROCA and other alternative procedures can be used to train children before formal audiological evaluations are made. Because of children's varying abilities, no one procedure is appropriate for all children. As stated aptly by Cress (1989):

> A knowledge of the specific child's response capabilities and reinforcer preferences is crucial in selecting one of the training procedures described above. Even more crucial, perhaps, is a commitment by service providers to devote the time necessary to accomplish this training. (pp. 16-17)

Cress also has argued that training children to respond to auditory stimuli rarely occurs in instructional practices with young children with dual sensory impairments.

In addition to interpreting the results of formal audiological measures, classroom teachers should be able to conduct informal assessments of their students' hearing. In general, informal tests involve presenting various auditory stimuli to students and recording reliable changes in behaviors. These tests are important because formal test results do not provide information about how well students use their residual hearing; that is, the functional use of hearing in the classroom (Erber, 1982; Sanders, 1982). In essence, the findings of formal and informal tests can be used to establish instructional programs that help students to improve skills, such as localizing and discriminating sounds, and to train students for subsequent formal audiological assessments.

Several factors should be considered in evaluating students' responses to sounds (e.g., Sailor et al., 1982). These include (a) students' characteristics, such as age and capabilities; (b) the use of a natural, meaningful setting (e.g., in the home); (c) the nature of the auditory test stimuli; and (d) the range of response modes, particularly in students with severe disabilities. We recommend that several test stimuli be selected from each of three general categories: speech (e.g., child's name, name of favorite toy, babbling), environmental sounds (e.g., water pouring, door slam), and noise makers (drum, telephone, toys) (Erber, 1982; Sailor et al., 1982; Sanders, 1982). Test stimuli should use sounds with a wide range of frequencies to increase the possibility of obtaining responses. To obtain reliable results, the selected sounds should be placed on a tape for testing purposes. Depending on age and ability, students can be required to detect sounds (presence or absence), discriminate between them (same or different), identify them (pointing to labels or pictures), or comprehend them (e.g., reacting or responding to requests, commands, questions) (e.g., see Erber, 1982).

Auditory Training

There are a number of approaches for the development of audition, ranging from unisensory (i.e., audition only) to multisensory (e.g., vision, audition, and taction) (Calvert, 1986; Ling, 1984). Some approaches include a strong speech component. Because of varying characteristics and abilities of students, there is no auditory training program that will work for all children with dual sensory impairments. Some fundamentals are the involvement of parents or caregivers (especially for language development); the use of natural, meaningful environments; the use of age-appropriate activities; and adherence to a developmental sequence.

Whether the normal development sequences of auditory behavior also apply to people with severe disabilities is an open question (e.g., Sailor et al., 1982). Although the developmental sequence may not be observed precisely for every student, it should provide a general framework for understanding auditory functioning and for establishing an intervention program. For example, from birth to age 3 months, the infant's responses to sound are largely reflexive and may include a startle response, widening or blinking of the eyes, or a sudden change in activity. Typically, infants respond to gross sounds (e.g., door slamming); however, they will also respond to speech. The use of familiar sounds, such as speech, might be effective in eliciting early attending responses (e.g., see Northern & Downs, 1984). Auditory feedback emerges around the 4th month. Subsequently, the child's babbling becomes more like speech and he or she begins to monitor productions of sounds. At 9 months of age, the child can accurately identify the location of sound sources at all angles from the ear (Northern & Downs, 1984). The association of particular sounds and their sources to meaning occurs during the last 3 months of the 1st year of life. Early intervention programming for children with severe disabilities should contain the major aspects of the normal acquisition process, that is, detection, awareness, attention, discrimination, feedback, self-monitoring, identification, and associating sounds with meaning (see discussions in Erber, 1982; Ling, 1984; Mischook & Cole, 1986).

The auditory process is inseparable from speech and language development (e.g., Ling & Ling, 1978; Pollack, 1985). For example, in associating sounds with meaning, the child begins to realize which acoustic cues are significant. Several factors contribute to a child's capacity to learn auditorily, for example, early identification of hearing loss; early and consistent use of amplification systems, such as group and individual hearing aids; the extent, severity, and etiology of the hearing loss; the quantity and quality of auditory stimulation; an intact capacity to learn; and interrelations among parents and specialists (Ling, 1984). Although several auditory training and learning programs exist (e.g., Erber, 1982; Sanders, 1982), it may be beneficial if a program follows a functional sequence that correlates to what has been observed in infants without disabilities, deviating only in the time of achievement of the various targeted behaviors. Boothroyd (1982) has outlined seven target behaviors that should be components of a successful program:

1. Attend to sounds.
2. Attend to differences among sounds (discrimination).
3. Recognize objects and events from the sounds they make.
4. Be alerted to sounds.
5. Use hearing for the perception of space (pertinent for a child with severe visual loss).
6. Use hearing for the perception of speech.
7. Use hearing to control the production of speech.

Boothroyd's sequence of behaviors can serve as a conceptual framework for the training components of an auditory-training program. An example of one level is as follows:

Level 1: Develop an awareness of sounds (attend without meaning).

Rationale: The initial cognitive level to be achieved is a basic awareness of the presence and dimensions of sound without any necessary recognition of this auditory stimulus.

Objective: To provide very young children with a knowledge of the presence of sound.

Some suggested target behaviors include the following (Michael et al., 1988, pp. 13-14):

1. Eye-widening (eyebrow movement).
2. Eye-blinking.
3. Startle.
4. Stirring or arousal from sleep.
5. Cessation of movement.
6. Slight head turn toward the sound.
7. Any combination of the above behaviors.

Activity: Child will perform target behavior when the radio is turned on in the crib.

INTEGRATED SENSORY APPROACH

Among researchers on deafness, there is no clear consensus that an integrated multisensory approach (i.e., involving both senses simultaneously) is better than a unisensory approach that focuses on only one sense (i.e., audition), especially for language development (Ling, 1984). There is agreement, however, that an integrated sensory approach should be used and should offer opportunities for children to formulate ideas about the environment. That an integrated approach is important, especially for children with dual sensory impairments, is supported by researchers in the field of perception who are concerned with the notion of cross-modal transfer (McKenzie & Day, 1987).

As with other approaches, there is no one best integrated sensory approach that will work for all children with dual sensory impairments. The following example is adapted from a qualitative report involving an 8-month-old child considered cortically blind who eventually saw himself in the mirror after a period of several months (J. Miller, personal communication, April 1989).

Target behavior: To assist the child in learning to fixate on his or her own face in the mirror.

Preliminary target behaviors: Awareness of light, fixation on light, attention to light.

Items needed: Large plastic mirror, penlight, and optical aids.

Training:

1. Position infant so that he or she is facing mirror, shine light on mirror, and tap behind the mirror where the light is shining. Look for changes in infant's behavior, such as cessation or increase of movement and increased vocalization.
2. Turn off light and stop tapping. Look for changes in behavior.
3. Repeat until response of looking at mirror is paired with light.
4. Slowly fade light back in line with infant's face, but keep tapping at previous location of light on mirror.
5. Fade out tapping.
6. Fade out light.

CONCLUSION

Programming for infants and children with dual sensory impairments should be designed to fulfill the needs of these individuals regardless of how they are categorized or where they are placed. Children with dual sensory impairments should receive specialized services, such as alternative modes of communication, functional sensory training, and orientation and mobility. We have emphasized effective programming, rather than programs, to highlight the necessity of fulfilling specialized needs. Infants and children with dual sensory impairments are found in a variety of program settings. Thus, it is crucial that supplemental information and instruction be available to the direct care providers, including family members, for the further development of the abilities of the children.

RECOMMENDATIONS

1. There is a need for adequate programming in sense utilization for young children with dual sensory impairments.
2. The development of appropriate preservice training is important, not only in the management of auditory and visual impairments, but also in methods of instruction to increase ability.
3. More research is needed to determine the best methods for helping children acquire functional sensory skills to become more independent.
4. Parents or caregivers and other members of the family should be involved as early as pos-

sible in creating communicative environments that stress the use of residual senses.

REFERENCES

Bailey, D., Jens, K., & Johnson, N. (1983). Curricula for handicapped infants. In S. Garwood & R. Fewell, *Educating handicapped infants: Issues in development and intervention* (pp. 387-415). Rockville, MD: Aspen.

Baldwin, A. (1980). *Theories of child development.* New York: Wiley.

Baldwin, V. (1986). *Prevalence of students with deaf-blindness* (Final Project Report). Washington, DC: Office of Special Education and Rehabilitation, Special Education Programs, U.S. Department of Education.

Baraldi, P., Ferrari, B., Fonda, S., & Penne, A. (1981). Vision in the neonate (full term and premature): Preliminary result of the application of some testing methods. *Documenta Opthalmologica, 51,* 101-112.

Barraga, N., & Morris, J. (1982). *Program to develop efficiency in visual functioning.* Louisville, KY: American Printing House for the Blind.

Barrett, S. (1987). Trends and issues in developing community living programs for young adults who are deaf-blind and profoundly handicapped: In response to Lyle T. Romar. In A. Covert & B. Fredericks (Eds.), *Transition for persons with deaf-blindness and other profound handicaps* (pp. 39-50). Monmouth, OR: Teaching Research Publication.

Bickman, L., & Weatherford, D. (1986). *Evaluating early intervention programs for severely handicapped children and their families.* Austin, TX: PRO-ED.

Boothroyd, A. (1982). *Hearing impairments in young children.* Englewood Cliffs, NJ: Prentice-Hall.

Bronfenbrenner, U. (1975). *Is early intervention effective? A report on longitudinal evaluation of preschool programs.* (DHEW Publication No. [OHD] 74-25, Vol. 2). Washington, DC: U.S. Government Printing Office.

Bullis, M., & Bull, B. (1986). *Review of research on adolescents and adults with deaf-blindness.* Washington, DC: The Catholic University, National Rehabilitation Center.

Calvert, D. (1986). Speech in perspective. In D. Luterman (Ed.), *Deafness in perspective* (pp. 167-191). San Diego, CA: College-Hill.

Courtwright, G., Mihok, T., & Jose, R. (1975). Reading stands: A nonoptical aid. *Optometric Weekly, 66,* 449-451.

Covert, A., & Fredericks, H. (1987). Introduction. In A. Covert and H. Fredericks (Eds.), *Transition for persons with deaf-blindness and other profound handicaps: State-of-the-art* (pp. 1-3). Monmouth, OR: Teaching Research Publication.

Cress, P. (1985). Visual assessment. In M. Bullis (Ed.), *Communication development in young children with deaf-blindness: Literature Review I* (pp. 31-59). Monmouth, OR: Teaching Research Publication.

Cress, P. (1989). *Sensory assessment manual.* Lawrence: University of Kansas, Bureau of Child Research, Parsons Research Center.

Cress, P., Johnson, J., Spellman, C., Sizemore, A., & Shores, R. (1982). The development of a visual acuity test for persons with severe handicaps. *Journal of Special Education Technology, 5,* 11-19.

Curtis, W., & Tweedie, D. (1985). Content and process in curriculum planning. In E. Cherow, N. Matkin, & R. Trybus (Eds.), *Hearing-impaired children and youth with developmental disabilities* (pp. 246-270). Washington, DC: Gallaudet College Press.

Duchman, R., & Selenow, A. (1983). Use of forced preferential looking for measurement of visual activity in a population of neurologically impaired children. *American Journal of Optometry and Physiological Optics, 60,* 817-821.

D'Zamko, M., & Hampton, I. (1985). Personnel preparation for multihandicapped hearing-impaired students: A review of the literature. *American Annals of the Deaf, 32,* 9-11.

Erber, N. (1982). *Auditory training.* Washington, DC: Alexander Graham Bell Association for the Deaf.

Fantz, R. (1963). Pattern vision in newborn infants. *Science, 140,* 296-297.

Fredericks, H., & Baldwin, V. (1987). Individuals with sensory impairments: Who are they? In L. Goetz, D. Guess, & K. Stremel-Campbell (Eds.), *Innovative program design for individuals with dual sensory impairments* (pp. 3-15). Baltimore, MD: Brookes.

Freeman, P. (1985). *The deaf-blind baby: A program of care.* London, England: William Heinemann Medical Books.

Goetz, L., & Gee, K. (1987). Functional vision programming: A model for teaching visual behaviors in natural contexts.. In L. Goetz, D. Guess, & K. Stremel-Campbell (Eds.), *Innovative program design for individuals with dual-sensory impairments* (pp. 76-97). Baltimore, MD: Brookes.

Goetz, L., Gee, K., & Sailor, W. (1985). Using a behavior chain interruption strategy to teach communication skills to students with severe disabilities. *The Journal of the Association for Persons with Severe Handicaps, 10,* 21-30.

Goetz, L., Utley, B., Gee, K., Baldwin, M., & Sailor, W. (1981). *Auditory assessment and program manual for severely handicapped deaf-blind students.* (San Francisco State University, Bay Area Severely Handicapped Deaf-Blind Project. U.S. Department of Education 300780038). Washington, DC: U.S. Government Printing Office.

Hayden, A. (1979). Handicapped children, birth to 3. *Exceptional Children, 45,* 510-516.

Hecox, K., Gerber, S., & Mendel, M. (1983). Development of auditory brainstem responses. In S. Gerber & G. Mencher (Eds.), *The development of auditory behavior* (pp. 77-90). New York: Grune & Stratton.

Jose, R. (1983). *Understanding low vision.* New York: American Foundation for the Blind.

Konar, V., & Rice, D. (1982). *Strategies for serving deaf-blind clients.* Hot Springs: Arkansas Research and Training in Vocational Rehabilitation.

Langley, M. (1980). *Functional vision inventory for the multiple and severely handicapped.* Chicago: Stoelting.

Lewin, K. (1951). *Field theory in social science.* New York: Harper & Row.

Ling, D. (Ed.). (1984). *Early intervention for hearing impaired children: Oral options.* San Diego, CA: College-Hill.

Ling, D., & Ling, A. (1978). *Aural habilitation: The foundations of verbal learning in hearing-impaired children.* Washington, DC: Alexander Graham Bell Association for the Deaf.

Lloyd, L., Spradlin, J., & Reid, M. (1968). An operant audiometric procedure for difficult-to-test patients. *Journal of Speech and Hearing Disorders, 33,* 236-245.

Lundervold, D., Lewin, L., & Irwin, L. (1987). Rehabilitation of visual impairments: A critical review. *Critical Psychology Review, 7,* 169-185.

McInnes, J., & Treffrey, J. (1982). *Deaf-blind infants and children: A developmental guide.* Buffalo, NY: University of Toronto Press.

McKenzie, B., & Day, R. (Eds.). (1987). *Perceptual development in early infancy: Problems and issues.* Hillsdale, NJ: Lawrence Erlbaum.

Michael, M., Arnold, K., & Niswander, P. (1988). *A study of the differential effects of providing functional vision and auditory training to very young children who are deaf-blind.* Ohio State University, Great Lakes Area Regional Center for Deaf-Blind Education. Grant proposal submitted to Office of Special Education and Rehabilitation Services (OSERS).

Mischook, M., & Cole, E. (1986). Auditory learning and teaching of hearing-impaired infants. *Volta Review, 88,* 5, 67-81. [Special Issue].

Mohn, G., & Van Hol-Van Duin, J. (1983). Behavioral and electrophysiological measure of visual functions in children with neurological disorders. *Behavioral Brain Research, 10,* 177-187.

Niswander, P. (1987). Audiometric assessment and management. In L. Goetz, D. Guess, & K. Stremel-Campbell (Eds.), *Innovative program design for individuals with dual sensory impairments* (pp. 99-127). Baltimore, MD: Brookes.

Niswander, P. (1988). *Audiological assessment of the difficult-to-test child.* Unpublished manuscript, Ohio State University, Nisonger Center.

Northern, J., & Downs, M. (1984). *Hearing in children* (3rd ed.). Baltimore, MD: Williams & Wilkins.

Orchik, D., & MacKimmie, K. (1984). Immittance audiometry. In J. Jerger (Ed.), *Pediatric audiometry* (pp. 45-70). San Diego, CA: College-Hill.

Ouellette, S. (1984). Deaf-blind population estimates. In D. Watson, S. Barrett, & R. Brown (Eds.), *A model service delivery system for deaf-blind persons* (pp. 7-10). Little Rock: University of Arkansas.

Peterson, N. (1983). Early intervention with the handicapped. In E. Meyer (Ed.), *Exceptional children* (pp. 94-143). Denver, CO: Love Publishing.

Piaget, J. (1952). *The origins of intelligence in children.* New York: Norton.

Pollack, D. (1985). *Educational audiology for the limited-hearing infant and preschooler* (2nd ed.). Springfield, IL: Charles C Thomas.

Ramey, C., Trohanis, P., & Hostler, S. (1982). An introduction. In C. Ramey & P. Trohanis (Eds.), *Finding and educating high-risk and handicapped infants* (pp. 1-18). Baltimore, MD: University Park Press.

Sailor, W., Utley, B., Goetz, L., Gee, K., & Baldwin, M., (1982). *Vision assessment and program manual for severely handicapped and/or deaf-blind students.* (San Francisco State University, Bay Area Severely Handicapped Deaf-blind Project. U.S. Department of Education 300780038). Washington, DC: U.S Government Printing Office.

Sanders, D. (1982). *Aural rehabilitation: A management model* (2nd ed.). Englewood Cliffs, NJ: Prentice-Hall.

Siegal-Causey, E., & Downing, J. (1987). Nonsymbolic communication development: Theoretical concepts and educational strategies. In L. Goetz, D. Guess, & K. Stremel-Campbell (Eds.), *Innovative program design for individuals with dual-sensory impairments* (pp. 15-48). Baltimore, MD: Brookes.

Skinner, B. F. (1953). *Science and human behavior.* New York: Free Press.

Smith, A., & Cote, K. (1982). *Look at me.* Philadelphia: The Pennsylvania College of Optometry.

Spradlin, J. (1985). Auditory evaluation. In M. Bullis (Ed.), *Communication development in young children with deaf-blindness: Literature review I* (pp. 49-61). Monmouth, OR: Teaching Research Publications.

Teele, D., & Teele, J. (1984). Detection of middle ear effusion by acoustic reflectometry. *Pediatrics, 104,* 832-838.

Teller, D. (1979). The forced-choice preferential looking procedure: A psychophysical technique for use with human infants. *Infants Behavior Development, 2,* 135.

Teller, D., McDonald, M., Preston, K., Sebris, S., & Dobson, V. (1986). Assessment of visual acuity in infants and children: The acuity card procedure. *Developmental Medicine and Child Neurology, 28,* 779-789.

Van Dijk, J. (1965). The first steps of the deaf/blind child toward language. *Proceedings of the conference on the deaf/blind, Refsnes, Denmark* (pp. 47-50). Boston, MA: Perkins School for the Blind.

Van Dijk, J. (1968). *Movement and communication with rubella children..* Paper presented at the annual meeting of the National Association for Deaf-Blind and Rubella Children, St. Michielsgestel, Netherlands.

Vygotsky, L. (1962). *Thought and language.* Cambridge, MA: Massachusetts Institute of Technology Press.

Walker, J., & Crawley, S. (1983). Conceptual and methodological issues in studying the handicapped infant. In S. Garwood & R. Fewell, *Educating handicapped infants* (pp. 158-209). Rockville, MD: Aspen.

Watson, D., Barrett, S., & Brown, R. (Eds.), (1984). *A model service delivery system for deaf-blind persons.* Little Rock, AR: Research & Training Center on Deafness.

ABOUT THE AUTHORS

MARTHA G. MICHAEL is a Program Manager at the Center for Special Needs Populations, College of Education; and PETER V. PAUL is an Associate Professor in the Department of Educational Services and Research at The Ohio State University, Columbus.

Exceptional Children, Vol. 57, No. 3, pp. 200-210.
©1990 The Council for Exceptional Children.

Instructional Strategies for Learners with Dual Sensory Impairments in Integrated Settings

June Downing
University of Arizona

Joanne Eichinger
California State University at San Bernardino

This article presents information on instructional strategies and the effective use of personnel needed for educating students with dual sensory impairments in integrated learning environments. To counter the practice of educating students in separate environments according to their most apparent weaknesses and limitations, the authors contend that learners with dual sensory impairments can benefit from shared learning environments (cross-categorical) and from daily interactions with nondisabled peers. Specific examples and practical intervention strategies to accommodate for the sensory losses are provided.

DESCRIPTORS: adaptations, curricula, dual sensory impairment, educational placement, instructional strategies, integration, least restrictive environment, placement, sensory impairment, service delivery

Learners with dual sensory impairments (deaf-blindness) traditionally have been educated in segregated and specialized environments. These learners, however, possess many of the same characteristics as other learners with severe disabilities who have been successfully integrated into regular schools and classes (Ford & Davern, 1989).

Instead of developing completely unique programs for students with dual sensory impairments, it would be beneficial to examine programs targeting other severe disabilities to determine appropriateness. Qualities of "most promising educational practices" for students with severe disabilities have been well documented (Fox et al., 1986; Meyer, Eichinger, & Park-Lee, 1987) and hold considerable promise for students who are severely handicapped by their sensory deficits.

While considerable documentation exists to support

both heterogeneous groupings of children with differing abilities (Baumgart & Van Walleghem, 1986; Usilton & Filler, 1988) and integration with nondisabled peers (Brinker, 1985; Voeltz, 1980, 1982; Ziegler & Hambleton, 1976), little information exists that addresses specific variations in instructional strategies needed to reach these goals.

The authors of this paper recognize the unique learning needs of learners labeled deaf-blind, yet feel that certain modifications and adaptations can effectively accommodate such learners without segregation. The purpose of this article is to provide curricular, instructional, and administrative strategies that can be employed to serve students with dual sensory impairments. Specifically, it will describe ways in which special educators, even those with no training or experience with students having sensory deficits, can plan for and effectively instruct these students. Suggestions for intervention that allow maximal integration with other students with disabilities and nondisabled students will be provided. Administrative decisions and support needed to achieve quality educational programming will be discussed.

Characteristics of the Target Population

Individuals labeled deaf-blind may experience diverse combinations of hearing and visual impairments with normal or gifted intelligence or they may have additional mental, physical, and behavioral disabilities. For the purpose of this paper, learners labeled deaf-blind or having dual sensory impairments will be considered to have moderate to severe visual and hearing impairments as well as moderate to profound mental retardation and possibly other concomitant disorders.

Although 93.8% of all individuals labeled deaf-blind typically have some functional vision and/or hearing (Fredericks & Baldwin, 1987), the disability is such that it hinders the development of communication and social interaction skills, especially when there is an accompanying mental disability. Because these individuals do not receive clear and consistent information from either

The authors wish to extend their appreciation to Fred Orelove, Michael Giangreco and Nancy Johnson-Dorn for their helpful feedback.

sensory modality, a tendency exists to turn inward to obtain the desired level of stimulation. The individual therefore may appear passive, nonresponsive, and/or noncompliant. Students with dual sensory impairments may not respond to or initiate appropriate interactions with others and often exhibit behavior that is considered socially inappropriate (e.g., hand flapping, finger flicking, head rocking) to satisfy basic needs (Smithdas, 1981; Van Dijk, 1985). When students with dual sensory impairments are placed in the same classroom for instruction, opportunities for peer interaction and group instruction are greatly minimized.

Administrative and Personnel Issues

The authors contend that it is effective and efficient to teach students with dual sensory impairments in neighborhood schools. Administrative decisions can be made that facilitate the inclusion of students with dual sensory impairments in regular school settings. Primarily, this involves the use of personnel specially trained in sensory impairments, a transdisciplinary approach to related services, and the heterogeneous grouping of students with disabilities.

Vision and Hearing Specialists

Placing students with dual sensory impairments in classrooms for students with other types of disabilities or in regular classrooms means that teachers with training in mental retardation, physical handicaps, behavior disorders, or general education may be responsible for students who do not fit traditional expectations. Teachers certified in other disability areas or in regular education may feel quite inadequate in addressing the needs of students who do not communicate using speech and who cannot rely on visual or auditory input to receive information. Students with dual sensory impairments, especially those who do not have functional vision or hearing, may not learn effectively through visual or auditory means. Because most educators rely on imitation and visual and auditory cues for instructional purposes, the inability to use visual or auditory input can be perceived as problematic. Also, most teachers of students with severe handicaps and regular education teachers often do not receive training in the effects of sensory losses on learning; thus, this information must be obtained from vision and hearing specialists. These specialists can be employees of a particular school district, or special education cooperatives, or can be brought in as consultants from state schools, university training programs, or private consulting agencies.

Specialists trained in sensory deficits can provide information on necessary adaptations (both materials and teaching style), distance and field in which to present stimuli, availability and benefits of optical and auditory aids, and specific training techniques to improve residual sensory skills. Vision specialists can provide information and training on orientation and mo-

bility skills (e.g., sighted guide, trailing techniques, limited cane techniques, and community travel). Specialists in the area of hearing impairments can address the particular communication difficulties that a hearing impairment produces. These specialists alert the teacher and other service providers to the effects that sensory losses have on the developing child and what adaptive (and sometimes unusual) behaviors may result.

Children with dual sensory impairments often have functional vision and/or hearing and may not physically appear to have a sensory deficit. Too often, teachers assume that their students can see and hear, when actually they receive minimal sensory information. Vision and hearing specialists can help the teacher gain an appreciation for the effects of sensory deprivation and acquire a greater sensitivity toward their student's sensory difficulties. Ongoing services for staff and students as well as inservice training should reflect the unique needs of individual students labeled deaf-blind and the real or perceived inability of direct service providers to meet those needs. Inservice presentations to regular education and special education staff could include such topics as developing alternative forms of communication, adapting materials, using tactile teaching, creating social opportunities, teaching use of vision and/or hearing within functional activities, and teaching orientation and mobility skills. Inservice topics appropriate for nonhandicapped peers could include communicating to a peer who is deaf-blind, playing with someone who is deaf-blind, understanding what it is like to be deaf-blind, and learning by touch. Districts can utilize existing needs assessment instruments to determine inservice training needs for this population, such as the one developed in 1985 by Norman, Brookfield-Norman, and Meyer (see Meyer & Eichinger, 1987 for a copy of this assessment).

Transdisciplinary Model for Related Services

To provide cohesive, functional programs for students with dual sensory impairments, administrators will need to develop and support a transdisciplinary model for providing services (Orelove & Sobsey, 1987; York, 1984). The transdisciplinary model of service delivery incorporates the expertise of all educational team members into one holistic program for a particular student. Individual team members do not assess the student by isolated tests related only to a given specialty area (e.g., speech and language, fine motor, visual functioning). Nor do individual team members provide direct instruction in isolated specialty rooms at arbitrarily assigned times of the day (e.g., vision training on Thursdays from 10:00 to 10:30 a.m.). Instead, identified specialists work collaboratively with the entire educational team to help identify problem areas related to their given area of expertise as they arise during meaningful activities throughout the day. Intervention targeting basic skills such as vision and hearing is not provided in isolation but is incorporated into functional activities for the student that occur in the classroom, school environment, and community (Downing & Bailey, 1990). For example, a child with some residual vision would not practice tracking a light in a black box under the supervision of a vision specialist for 10 minutes twice a week. Rather, the vision specialist would demonstrate to the teaching staff ways in which the student should use her residual vision in functional everyday activities (e.g., tracking her spoon when eating, scanning an augmentative communication board to indicate a desired message).

Instead of transporting similarly disabled students to a certified teacher's classroom, the transdisciplinary model requires that the teacher travel to the students to ensure that the special education needs of each student are being met. The specialist can analyze the activities that cause difficulties for a given student with a visual or hearing loss and provide direct instruction, develop adaptive aids, and/or train the staff so that further instruction will incorporate the specialist's suggestions. The specialist must work cooperatively with direct service providers to assist in the development, implementation, and ongoing evaluation of the student's programmatic needs.

Heterogeneous Groupings of all Students

Several authors have questioned the value of homogeneous groupings of students having severe disabilities (Brown, Nietupski & Hamre-Nietupski, 1976; Certo & Kohl, 1984; Ford et al., 1986). Homogeneous grouping becomes particularly problematic when applied to students with dual sensory impairments, since this type of grouping drastically reduces student interaction.

Students who require tactile input for learning and social interactions need more direct one-to-one instruction just to receive the necessary information. Therefore, grouping students who all require considerable one-to-one instruction makes even small group learning difficult, adding to the time individual students are forced to wait. If, however, the student with dual sensory impairment is with two or three other students who can make use of auditory and visual information, more interactions are possible, and the teacher can provide the necessary tactile instruction while maintaining the attention of the group through visual and auditory means.

Heterogeneous groupings allow certain students with severe disabilities to assist other students who may have more difficulty in a given activity. Pairing students with diverse skills also eases instruction that occurs in community settings (Baumgart & Van Walleghem, 1986). For example, classrooms with students who all require assistance in mobility (either use of a sighted guide or wheelchair transportation) will make travel to and from instruction in the community quite difficult. Classrooms having some students who can walk, respond appropriately to visual and auditory cues, and carry objects will require less assistance. These students can assist their peers who do not have these skills. Grouping students by chronological age and balancing student strengths and limitations to avoid grouping by ability level will greatly facilitate teacher effectiveness by reducing the intensity of intervention required by each student.

Administrators can ensure not only that students with differing needs and abilities are heterogeneously grouped to complement learning strengths with limitations but also that students with severe disabilities, such as deaf-blindness, have daily learning opportunities with their nonhandicapped peers. Administrators can encourage and support their teachers in specifically planned integration activities. Support of such programs is critical because physical integration within a typical public school is a necessary but not sufficient condition (Meyer & Kishi, 1985; Stainback & Stainback, 1985). Efforts must be made to ensure frequent and structured contact between students with dual sensory impairments and their nondisabled peers to promote social interactions, language skill development, and friendships (Sasso & Rude, 1988; Stainback & Stainback, 1987; Strully & Strully, 1985).

Instructional and Curricular Strategies

With the support of the entire educational team, the teacher will need to make certain adjustments in intervention strategies to accommodate the needs of the learner with dual sensory impairments. However, these adjustments need not be so unique that they are an undue hardship for the special educator or that they do not benefit students with other disabilities. Some of these instructional and curricular strategies include enhancing visual and auditory stimuli, emphasizing tactile techniques of teaching, recognizing the nonvisual and nonauditory aspects of functional activities, targeting visual and auditory skills within meaningful contexts, keeping group size small, fostering cooperative learning in heterogeneous groups, and employing the principle of partial participation.

Enhancing Visual and Auditory Stimuli

Most students with the deaf-blind label have sufficient vision or hearing, or both, to make use of information presented through these sensory modes (Fredericks & Baldwin, 1987; Van Dijk, 1985). These students require enhanced visual and auditory information and need to have their attention drawn to these stimuli. Therefore, teaching techniques used effectively with students having other disabilities can also prove effective with students having dual sensory impairments. These students benefit from the same systematic procedures of instruction: modeling, visual cueing, physical prompting, giving feedback, and reinforcing desired behaviors (Snell & Zirpoli, 1987). The only adaptations needed may be modification of the materials and their presentation to make use of remaining visual and auditory skills. For example, pictures can be enlarged, outlines made darker and bolder, and contrast improved by using black on yellow vs. black on white. Contrast also can be improved by ensuring that the object of interest draws visual attention and stands distinctly apart from the background (e.g., a picture of a chocolate milkshake on a solid pale blue backing). To avoid glare, clear plastic coating (lamination) can be replaced by yellow acetate sheets. Pictures for student schedules or communication devices can be held in upright nonglare plastic photograph holders. Seating arrangements and lighting can be adapted to allow sufficient illumination while decreasing glare. Pictures can be paired with objects to clarify intent or paired with sign and speech that is slightly slower and louder to facilitate communication. Visual stimuli should always be presented within the student's field of vision, and the size, clarity, and depth should accommodate the student's visual limitations. Both visual and auditory information may need to be presented to the student at a very proximal distance, which may mean moving either the student or the stimuli. These suggestions for adapting the learning environment can be used effectively with all students who have severe disabilities, including those with no sensory impairments. However, rearranging the environment to facilitate learning should not detract from an overall pleasant and attractive classroom. Learning environments in the school should be clean, organized, accessible, and decorated in a manner that reflects the chronological age of the students (Rikhye, Gothelf, & Appell, 1989).

Tactile Teaching Techniques

For those students who do not make use of auditory or visual stimuli, information must be obtained through another mode. When auditory and visual senses are impaired, the clearest information is provided by the sense of touch. Tactile input is not meant to replace either visual or auditory information but is added to these two sense modalities to increase the amount of information available. Instead of relying solely on visual or auditory cues (pictures, speech), the teacher must eliminate the distance between child and stimuli and must target tactile information.

Itard (1862) pronounced touch the only true sense, referring to its lack of illusory qualities. Yet teachers must be aware of the sometimes limited information that the sense of touch provides. The individual receives only partial information at any one time and must synthesize that information into an understandable whole. The larger the object, the more difficult the synthesis (at the other end of the continuum, extremely small objects are equally difficult to understand through tactile stimuli). The teacher needs to be aware that, due to this incomplete view of the world, the individual will need considerably more access to the same tactile information before an adequate level of understanding is reached.

The most efficient tactile cues are physical cues present in the natural environment, rather than those artificially produced. Using natural cues will facilitate transfer of learning from the training environment to other environments where the skill will be used (Ford & Mirenda, 1984; Horner, Bellamy, & Colvin, 1984). For example, feeling the toilet paper dispenser could serve as a natural cue to prompt the student to get off the toilet seat, versus a direct instructional prompt to stand up. Teaching in natural environments (where the skill is needed) and in natural sequences and contexts minimizes the need for the student to transfer skills and provides a sound rationale for instruction. For example, Sam (age 7) works on the fine motor skill of opening jars during snack time when he opens the peanut butter jar and spreads its contents on a piece of bread. The peanut butter jar and the time of day serve as natural cues for Sam to anticipate expected behavior. Because individuals with dual sensory impairments have less sensory input and therefore fewer natural cues to aid in the transfer of skills or to understand the purpose of the activity, teaching in natural environments and emphasizing natural cues to prompt desired behavior are critical. Using real objects and practicing skills in real activities will provide students with a clearer understanding of their world as well as the expectations of others.

When natural cues are insufficient to evoke the desired response, teachers must prompt the student physically. A student with limited vision and hearing learning a new skill or activity may need considerable physical prompting to clarify expectations. Once a student has engaged in an activity and has some awareness of the required skill sequence, additional prompting can follow a continuum from minimal to maximal assistance (Holowach, 1987; Snell & Zirpoli, 1987). The level of assistance will depend on the needs of the individual student and is contingent on a sufficient wait period to allow the student time to respond independently. The tendency of direct service providers to intervene with full physical manipulation without first using less intrusive and more indirect cues may lead to a dependency and learned helplessness that may be difficult to diminish at a later date.

During times when the teacher is trying to evoke communication skills from the student, physical prompting becomes awkward and interferes with the typology of a normal conversation. The teacher is not only the conversational partner but also the prompter. To avoid this confusion, it may be best to concentrate on peer-to-peer interactions by facilitating both conversants, or by making use of a teaching assistant, volunteer, speech and language pathologist, or peer to provide the needed physical prompting. This type of prompting, a modified form of shadowing (Foxx, 1981), maintains the speaker-listener interaction while providing the necessary physical assistance needed to shape the desired communicative responses and initiations. The student is directed to respond to whomever initiated the interaction (or to initiate the interaction himself) by minimal physical prompting from behind. For example, at snack time the teaching assistant could shadow the student with dual sensory impairments and physically assist him in touching his peer on the arm to get his attention, making an approximation of the sign "want" and pointing to a cookie. After the peer responds with "Here's a cookie" and provides the plate of cookies, the teaching assistance could again shadow tactilely the student from behind and provide the physical cue for the student to reach out and accept the desired items.

The disadvantage of the shadowing technique is the need for additional teaching support. The advantages include the ability to prompt spontaneous communication and fade the prompting while maintaining the typology of a normal conversation. Such a technique is recommended for students with other disabilities who do not initiate interactions or respond as desired and who wait until acted upon by an adult.

Determining Whether Activities Require Vision or Hearing

Many activities do not require vision and hearing, and many do not require one or the other for full participation. Vision or hearing may make these activities more enjoyable or easier to perform, but often they are not necessary. The following are examples of such activities: skiing, skating, swimming, going on amusement rides, giving/getting a message, cooking, doing macrame, creating with pottery/clay, assembling items, playing with dolls/trucks, riding horses, using exercise equipment, cleaning, hiking, and boating. Some activities are dependent on one or both primary senses, and, consequently, should be avoided by the individual who does not make use of visual or auditory information. Such activities include: watching movies or television, listening to music, playing video games, looking at picture books or magazines, coloring or painting, and working on a computer. Before restricting an individual's participation in a given activity, it would be advisable to consider that individual's sensory impairment (residual hearing and vision needing correction, needed amplification), individual preference, and ability to partially participate (Baumgart et al., 1982).

Targeting Visual and Auditory Skills Within Meaningful Contexts

Teaching a student to use visual and auditory skills is most effective when incorporated into a meaningful activity. Having a child look at bright lights or flashing lights or listening to sounds has little practical value to any individual. There are, however, many times throughout each day when the use of both visual and auditory skills assist the child in performing certain activities. For example, the student who leaves the toilet unflushed can be encouraged to listen for the noise accompanying the act as a check on one's own behavior. Similarly, the student who leaves water running can be encouraged to use both vision and hearing to correct the error. Any time the student must respond to meaningful sounds (fire alarm, the start or cessation of music at a dance, having one's name called), auditory skills are being developed. There are even more frequent opportunities to use vision skills (checking hair/makeup in a mirror, reaching for an object, using a pictorial communication device, looking at television or books, etc.). Developing instruction that targets vision and/or hearing skills out of the normal and natural context of an activity will not enhance the student's ability to use those skills when they are more needed for real world activities (Lunderwold, Lewin, & Irwin, 1987).

Teaching in Small Groups

Most teachers of students with homogeneous severe disabilities find large group instruction ineffective. These students typically do not demonstrate sufficient attending skills to accommodate large instructional groupings (six to eight students). Small group instruction (two to four pupils) or one-to-one instruction are more typical scenarios in the average classroom (Reid & Favell, 1984). Some professionals in the area of deaf-blindness advocate a one-to-one instructional model for students with dual sensory impairments (McInnes & Treffry, 1982). This recommendation stems from the belief that these individuals are unable to benefit from instruction without direct and continuous teacher intervention. However, continual one-to-one instruction separates the individual with dual sensory impairments from peer-to-peer interactions and may teach the individual to respond only in situations where direct one-to-one intervention with an adult is available, making the child overly dependent. Such a one-to-one ratio is often not practical in classrooms or work environments (Reid & Favell, 1984). It therefore may be more beneficial to teach interaction in small groups (two to four pupils) as well as providing one-to-one instruction. Furthermore, evidence exists to support the claim that small group instruction is just as effective as one-to-one instruction (Bourland, Jablonski, & Lockhart, 1988). Large group instruction may also prove beneficial in some instances when a student labeled deaf-blind is receiving instruction with a group of nonhandicapped children.

In general, the class size should be small enough for quality instruction to occur. When several students with severe disabilities are placed in one class, the amount and quality of instructional time is affected negatively. If school districts are committed to providing quality education to all students, factors such as class size, class location, and teaching support (in terms of staff, materials, and transportation) must be addressed to meet educational needs.

Cooperative Learning Strategies

For students receiving instruction in a special education class in a regular public school, structured peer integration programs can be developed. Special education teachers can establish programs in which individual students are paired with nondisabled age peers for social activities such as games, cooking activities, school jobs, or art or music activities. Frequently in peer integration programs, students are paired with one another over a period of time in order for relationships to develop (Voeltz, 1980, 1982). The selection of activities should consider the degree of sensory impairment. For example, students with total sensory losses would benefit more from a cooking activity that includes olfactory and tactile stimuli than from a video game that requires some auditory or visual skills.

Cooperative learning (see Johnson & Johnson, 1989) is one strategy that has been used successfully to increase social interactions between nondisabled students and students with severe disabilities (Eichinger, 1990; Putnam, Rynders, Johnson, & Johnson, 1989). For example, two students can be given one set of ingredients and utensils to make pizza along with a picture or tactile recipe designating who is to do each step of the task. In the cooperative model, students would be told to work together to make the pizza and help each other whenever necessary. This type of structure incorporates the "sink or swim together" philosophy of cooperative learning as well as the jigsaw method of sharing materials (Johnson & Johnson, 1987).

Within these structured activities, students can acquire the important social skill of turn taking. Students labeled deaf-blind, students with other disabilities, and typical students all need to modify their behaviors to accommodate interactions. Greater emphasis will need to be placed on nonsymbolic and tactile types of interactions and less emphasis on verbal and highly symbolic modes. Peers can be a particular asset when teaching the individual labeled deaf-blind the importance of taking turns in all play and social interactions. For students to make use of tactile signs, nondisabled peers will need to learn how to communicate in this manner. Another method to facilitate communicative interactions among peers is to develop and teach the use of an augmentative communication device. The speech and language therapist with the assistance of the teacher and vision specialist can devise a simple and portable system of objects, parts of objects, and/or pictures with the printed word (Calculator, 1988; Rowland & Schweigert, 1989) that would allow a student who is deaf-blind to communicate more readily with nonhandicapped friends. Teaching these interactive skills helps nondisa-

bled peers become aware of the many ways to communicate other than speech. This awareness can form the basis for recognizing and accepting differences.

As a by-product of cooperative learning situations and interactions among students of widely differing abilities, nonhandicapped peers can become a valuable resource for developing some of the adaptive aids required by students labeled deaf-blind. Typical students can help identify problem areas that prevent students labeled deaf-blind from actively participating in school activities (socially or physically). As part of a class assignment, students can create the adaptations or aids needed to resolve the identified problem. This valuable use of a natural resource in a school system not only benefits the student with a disability but also encourages the creativity and problem solving skills of typical students.

Partial Participation

The principle of partial participation states that students with severe disabilities who may not be totally independent in a given activity can be given the opportunity to learn those steps that they are capable of performing, thus partially participating in a wide range of school-based and nonschool environments and activities (Baumgart et al., 1982). This construct has tremendous utility when instructing learners with dual sensory impairments. For example, Steve, age 9, has a total hearing loss, moderate vision impairment, and spastic quadriplegia. For the past 3 months, he has been involved with 10-year-old Leon in a structured peer integration program. Three times a week Leon comes to Steve's room while his other fifth grade classmates have recess. One of the activities the boys enjoy together is playing a video game. Since Steve is unable to activate the joystick in the typical manner, he uses an adaptive pressure pad switch. Although he has no hearing, he responds to the visible stimuli of the airplanes hitting the targets. Either the teacher or Leon sets up the game, and Steve partially participates by taking his turn when Leon gives him a touch prompt on the forearm.

Summary

Students with dual sensory impairments have severe handicaps that require special consideration to ensure effective programming. The inability of some students to use visual and auditory information efficiently requires the teacher and other direct service providers to adapt materials and teaching strategies. Daily decisions are made with regard to accentuating visual and auditory information or adapting the activity to bypass the need for that type of sensory input. These adaptations target the individual with dual sensory impairments but also can be effective strategies for students with other severe disabilities.

In this article a case was made for the inclusion of students with dual sensory impairments in classrooms for students having other disabilities, as well as in regular education classrooms. Heterogeneous grouping can be viewed in a positive light for all students with disabilities if it provides them with the opportunity to interact with and learn from students with different abilities and limitations. Furthermore, it is imperative that learners with dual sensory impairments be educated in integrated settings to have sustained contact and instruction with nondisabled peers. Nonhandicapped students are needed to model appropriate behavior, provide opportunities for social interaction, and respond consistently to limited interactive behavior. Friendships need to be developed at an early age to provide needed support from nonhandicapped peers in the future.

Classroom teachers of students without sensory impairments usually are not experienced with learners having dual deficits and may be unfamiliar with strategies that compensate for sensory losses. However, if these teachers can be encouraged to seek assistance from specialists as needed, and to recognize the importance of adapting to the sensory loss, meeting the needs of students with dual sensory impairments can be achieved without jeopardizing the instruction of other students. Instead of requiring students to meet the expectations of a particular classroom, teachers must individualize instruction to accommodate different abilities and needs. The challenge of teaching should be in adapting to individual needs, not in subordinating individual differences to the strengths of the teacher.

References

Baumgart, D., Brown, L., Pumpian, I., Nisbet, J., Ford, A., Sweet, M., Messina, R., & Schroeder, J. (1982). Principle of partial participation and individualized adaptations in educational programs for severely handicapped students. *Journal of The Association for the Severely Handicapped, 7*(2), 17–27.

Baumgart, D., & Van Walleghem, J. (1986). Staffing strategies for implementing community-based instruction. *Journal for The Association of Persons with Severe Handicaps, 11*, 92–101.

Bourland, G., Jablonski, E., & Lockhart, D. (1988). Multiple-behavior comparison of group and individual instruction of persons with mental retardation. *Mental Retardation, 26*(1), 39–46.

Brinker, R. P. (1985). Interactions between severely mentally retarded students and other students in integrated and segregated public school settings. *American Journal of Mental Deficiency, 89*, 587–594.

Brown, L., Nietupski, J., & Hamre-Nietupski, S. (1976). The criterion of ultimate functioning and public school services for severely handicapped students. In M. A. Thomas (Ed.), *Hey, don't forget about me! Education's investment in the severely and profoundly handicapped* (pp. 2–15). Reston, VA: The Council for Exceptional Children.

Calculator, S. (1988). Promoting the acquisition and generalization of conversational skills by individuals with severe disabilities. *Augmentative & Alternative Communication, 4*(2), 94–103.

Certo, N., & Kohl, F. L. (1984). A strategy for developing interpersonal interaction instructional content for severely handicapped students. In N. Certo, N. Haring, & R. York (Eds.), *Public school integration of severely handicapped students: Rational issues and progressive alternatives* (pp. 221–244). Baltimore: Paul H. Brookes.

Downing, J., & Bailey, B. (1990). Developing vision use within functional daily activities for students with visual and multiple disabilities. *RE:view. 21*, 209–220.

Eichinger, J. (1990). Effects of goal structure on social interaction between elementary level nondisabled students and students with severe disabilities. *Exceptional Children, 56*, 408–417.

Ford, A., & Davern, L. (1989). Moving forward with school integration: Strategies for involving students with severe handicaps in the life of the school. In R. Gaylord-Ross (Ed.), *Integration strategies for students with handicaps* (pp. 11–31). Baltimore: Paul H. Brookes.

Ford, A., Dempsey, P., Black, J., Davern, L., Schnorr, R., & Meyer, L. (Eds.) (1986). *The Syracuse community-referenced curriculum guide for students with moderate and severe handicaps.* Syracuse, NY: Syracuse City School District.

Ford, A., & Mirenda, P. (1984). Community instruction: A natural cues and corrections decision model. *Journal of The Association for Persons with Severe Handicaps, 9*, 79–87.

Fox, W., Thousand, J., Williams, W., Fox, T., Towne, P., Reid, R., Conn-Powers, C., & Calcagni, L. (1986). *Best educational practices '86: Educating learners with severe handicaps.* Burlington: University of Vermont, Center for Developmental Disabilities.

Foxx, R. M. (1981). *Effective behavioral programming: Graduated guidance and backward chaining.* Champaign, IL: Research Press.

Fredericks, H. D., & Baldwin, V. (1987). Individuals with sensory impairments: Who are they? How are they educated? In L. Goetz, D. Guess, & K. Stremel-Campbell (Eds.), *Innovative program design for individuals with dual sensory impairments.* (pp 3–14). Baltimore: Paul H. Brookes.

Holowach, K. (1987). *Teaching that works: The individualized critical skills model.* Oakland, CA: Special Education Resource Network (SERN).

Horner, R. H., Bellamy, G. T., & Colvin, G. T. (1984). Responding in the presence of nontrained stimuli: Implications of generalization error patterns. *Journal of The Association for Persons with Severe Handicaps, 9*, 287–295.

Itard, J. M. G. (1862). *The wild boy of Aveyron.* New York: Appleton-Century-Crofts.

Johnson, D. W., & Johnson, R. T. (1987). *Learning together and alone: Cooperative, competitive, and individualistic learning* (2nd ed.). Englewood Cliffs, NJ: Prentice Hall.

Johnson, D. W., & Johnson, R. T. (1989). Cooperative learning and mainstreaming. In R. Gaylord-Ross (Ed.), *Integration strategies for students with handicaps* (pp. 233–248). Baltimore: Paul H. Brookes.

Lunderwold, D., Lewin, L., & Irwin, L. (1987). Rehabilitation of visual impairments: A critical review. *Clinical Psychology, 7*, 169–185.

McInnes, J. M., & Treffry, J. A. (1982). *Deaf-blind infants and children: A developmental guide.* Toronto: University of Toronto Press.

Meyer, L., & Eichinger, J. (1987). Program evaluation in support of program development: Needs, strategies and future directions. In L. Goetz, D. Guess, & K. Stremel-Campbell, (Eds.), *Innovative program design for individuals with dual sensory impairments* (pp. 313–353). Baltimore: Paul H. Brookes.

Meyer, L., Eichinger, J., & Park-Lee, S. (1987). A validation of program indicators in educational services for students with severe disabilities. *Journal of The Association for Persons with Severe Handicaps, 12*, 251–263.

Meyer, L. M., & Kishi, G. S. (1985). School integration

strategies. In C. Lakin, & J. R. Bruininks (Eds.), *Strategies for achieving community integration of developmentally disabled citizens* (pp. 231–252). Baltimore: Paul H. Brookes.

Orelove, F., & Sobsey, D. (1987). *Educating children with multiple disabilities: A transdisciplinary approach.* Baltimore: Paul H. Brookes.

Putnam, J. W., Rynders, J. E., Johnson, R. T., & Johnson, D. W. (1989). Collaborative skill instruction for promoting positive interactions between mentally handicapped and nonhandicapped children. *Exceptional Children, 55*(6), 550–557.

Reid, D., & Favell, J. (1984). Group instruction with persons who have severe disabilities: A critical review. *Journal of The Association for Persons with Severe Handicaps, 9,* 167–177.

Rikhye, C., Gothelf, C., & Appell, M. (1989). A classroom environment checklist for students with dual sensory impairments. *Teaching Exceptional Children, 22*(1), 44–47.

Rowland, C., & Schweigert, P. (1989). Tangible symbols: Symbolic communication for individuals with multisensory impairments. *Augmentative & Alternative Communication.* 226–234.

Sasso, G., & Rude, H. (1988). The social effects of integration on nonhandicapped children. *Education and Training in Mental Retardation, 23*(1), 18–23.

Smithdas, R. (1981). Psychological aspects of deaf-blindness. In S. Walsh & R. Holzberg (Eds.), *Understanding and educating the deaf-blind/severely and profoundly handicapped* (pp. 38–42). Springfield, IL: Charles C. Thomas.

Snell, M., & Zirpoli, T. (1987). Intervention strategies. In M. Snell (Ed.), *Systematic instruction of persons with severe handicaps* (3rd ed.) (pp. 110–149). Columbus, OH: Charles E. Merrill.

Stainback, S., & Stainback, W. (1985). *Integrating students with severe handicaps into regular schools.* Reston, VA: Council for Exceptional Children.

Stainback, W., & Stainback, S. (1987). Facilitating friendships. *Education and Training in Mental Retardation, 22*(1), 18–25.

Strully, J., & Strully, C. (1985). Friendship and our children. *Journal of The Association for Persons with Severe Handicaps, 10,* 224–227.

Usilton, R., & Filler, J. (1988). *Training module: Heterogeneous groupings.* San Francisco: California Research Institute, San Francisco State University.

Van Dijk, J. (1985). An educational curriculum for deaf-blind multi-handicapped persons. In D. Ellis (Ed.), *Sensory impairments in mentally handicapped people* (pp. 374–382). San Diego, CA: College-Hill Press.

Voeltz, L. (1980). Children's attitudes toward handicapped peers. *American Journal of Mental Deficiency, 84*(5), 455–464.

Voeltz, L. (1982). Effects of structured interactions with severely handicapped peers on children's attitudes. *American Journal on Mental Deficiency, 86,* 180–190.

York, J. (1984). *A transdisciplinary model of service delivery for educational teams who serve students with severe and multiple handicaps: Implications for developmental therapists.* Unpublished manuscript. University of Wisconsin-Madison.

Ziegler, S., & Hambleton, D. (1976). Integration of young TMR children into regular elementary school. *Exceptional Children, 42*(8), 459–461.

Strategies for Educating Learners with Severe Disabilities Within Their Local Home Schools and Communities

Jacqueline S. Thousand and Richard A. Villa

In a number of schools in North America, we now can walk into elementary and secondary classrooms and observe students who could be labeled severely or multiply handicapped receiving their education together with similar-aged classmates who have no identified special education needs (Biklen, 1988; Blackman & Peterson, 1989; Brown et al., 1989; Forest, 1988; Nevin, Thousand, Paolucci-Whitcomb, & Villa, 1990; Porter, 1988; Schattman, 1988; Villa & Thousand, 1988; York & Vandercook, 1989). Inclusionary educational practices for learners with intensive educational needs have evolved over the last decade in Vermont. A number of administrative, organizational, instructional, and teacher preparation strategies support the education of intensively challenged or challenging learners in general education environments, and we call for national policy changes to support inclusive schooling for all students.

WHO ARE LEARNERS WITH SEVERE HANDICAPS?

Whether a student is considered as having severe handicaps often depends upon the idiosyncratic definition adopted by the state and community in which the student resides. A U.S. federal definition identifies students with severe handicaps as those who:

> 1) may possess severe language and/or perceptual-cognitive deprivations, and evidence abnormal behaviors such as: i) failure to respond to pronounced social stimuli, ii) self-mutilation, iii) self-stimulation, iv) manifestation of intense and prolonged temper tantrums, and v) the absence of rudimentary forms of verbal control, and 2) may also have extremely fragile physiological conditions. (20 U.S.C. 1401(7); Former 45 CFR 121.1)

Brown et al. (1983, p. 77) offered an alternative definition of "severely handicapped" students as school-aged students who function intellectually within the lowest 1% of their particular age groups. This 1% includes learners who may have labels such as physically handicapped; multiply handicapped; dual sensory impaired (i.e., deaf-blind); autistic or psychotic; trainably mentally retarded; or moderately, severely, or profoundly retarded.

Jacqueline Thousand is an assistant professor at the Center for Developmental Disabilities of the University of Vermont, Burlington. Richard Villa is Director of Instructional Services and Staff Development for the Winooski (Vermont) School District.

At the local school level, formal definitions such as the two just presented have little functional meaning or use. What is considered a "severe handicap" varies from one school to the next and is contingent upon each school community's beliefs about and experience with students whose educational needs go beyond the school's standard curriculum or instructional practices. For example, a school community with little experience accommodating for individual students may think of a new student with Down syndrome as "severely handicapped." A second school, with extensive experience educating students who have a broad range of needs, may view much more challenged student as "just another student" with unique needs that must be met. Given this phenomenon of "relativity," terms such as *students with intensive educational needs, students who present intensive challenges to school personnel,* and *challenged* or *challenging students* are used here to represent students with "severe handicapping" characteristics described in the previous paragraph, as well as other students who, for whatever reason, are perceived by school personnel as "most challenging" to the current school culture or ecosystem.

WHO BELONGS IN GENERAL EDUCATION CLASSROOMS?

Currently there is an emerging recognition of the benefits of educating students with intensive educational needs in their local communities and schools (Brown et al., 1989; Sailor, 1989). There is, however, disagreement within the field as to whether students with intensive educational needs belong in general education classrooms; "the major placement issue of the day is whether students with severe intellectual disabilities should be based in regular or special education classrooms in home schools" (Brown et al., p. 12).

Writing for school principals, Burrello and Tourgee (1990) sorted out "students with severe disabilities" as the subpopulation of students with handicaps for whom "maintaining a self-contained setting in a centrally located place in the building with socialization opportunities was the most realistic program" (p. 3). Jenkins, Pious, and Jewell (1990) determined that, although the regular education initiative (Will, 1986) should apply to most students with handicaps, students with intensive educational needs should be excluded, because their needs extend beyond the normal developmental curriculum that the classroom teacher is responsible for delivering and adapting for individual learners.

Others have devoted entire texts to describing strategies for including *all* students, regardless of perceived exceptionalities, within general education and community environments (Lipsky & Gartner, 1989; S. Stainback, & W. Stainback, in press; S. Stainback, W. Stainback & Forest, 1989; W. Stainback & S. Stainback, 1990a). Williams, Villa, Thousand, and Fox (1990) go so far as to suggest that the special versus regular class placement issue really is a non-issue for a number of reasons. The successful placement and education of students with intensive educational challenges in regular classes has been occurring for a number of years in schools throughout North America (Thousand et al., 1986). Furthermore, Public Law 94-142, the Education for All Handicapped Children Act, clearly specifies that placement of any student must be based upon the student's identified needs, not the student's handicapping condition or categorical label.

To even raise the question of whether regular class placement is appropriate for a category of learners (i.e., students with intensive educational needs) "assumes that placement can be made based upon handicapping condition without documentation of an individual student's needs and examination of whether the needs could be met in a regular class-based placement" (Williams et al., 1990, p. 333). Finally, learning and social benefits for students with and without identified handicaps have been documented (S. Stainback & W. Stainback, 1990a; Thousand & Villa, 1989), as have benefits for teachers, when educators collaborate to invent individualized, responsive educational programs (Nevin et al., 1990; Thousand et al., 1986; Thousand & Villa, 1990; Villa & Thousand, in press).

The special/regular class placement question may be a non-issue. Yet, the norm within most North American schools is still for intensively challenged students to be educated in schools or classrooms other than those of their neighbors' children. Why? First, systems change takes time. Second, people thinking about change are more likely to "take the plunge" if they have models to observe, visit, and imitate. These are now available, and teachers, parents, students, and school board members can now share their stories about how to create schools in which students with intensive needs are welcome and successful.

A CASE STUDY IN VERMONT

Background and a Demonstration of Success

Vermont is a small, sparsely populated state, notorious for its strong small-town community spirit and interest in local community control in decision making. It is one of the few places where the populace of each small town turns out for a day-long annual town meeting to debate and decide upon issues large and small. Vermont is also a state with a long history of educating students who have mild handicaps in their local school general education classroom, with resource room and consulting teacher support to the classroom teacher (Christie, McKenzie, & Burdett, 1972; Idol, Paolucci-Whitcomb, & Nevin, 1986; Knight, Meyers, Paolucci-Whitcomb, Hasazi, & Nevin, 1981, McKenzie, 1972; McKenzie et al., 1970).

In the latter half of the 1970s, special classes for students with intensive education needs were established in public schools. Up to this time most of these children were not in public school and had not been offered educational services at home or in the institution in which they resided. To provide training and technical assistance to special class teachers in the new role of educating these "most challenging" students, an interdisciplinary support team—the I-Team—was jointly created with state and federal funding by the Vermont Department of Education and the University of Vermont (McKenzie, Hill, Sousie, York, & Baker, 1977). As members of this team traveled throughout Vermont, providing training and technical assistance, they noticed that some schools chose not to send their intensively challenged students to the newly formed special classes but instead chose to educate them along with their agemates in their local schools. This observation led to development of a pilot project demonstrating the successful transition of two students with intensive needs back to their home schools from a regional special class program.

The Homecoming Model Project

Encouraged by these results, funding was sought and secured from the federal Office of Special Education Programs to expand the effort with 26 schools in four school districts (Williams et al., 1986). The project's objectives were to develop, field-test, and evaluate a "model to bring 'home' students [with intensive challenges] from regional special education programs and prevent other students from ever being placed in them" (Thousand et al., 1986, p. 6). The project, known as *Homecoming*, achieved its objectives by its end, in the fall of 1986.

A total of 77 students, ranging in age from 5 to 17 years, benefited from the *Homecoming* model. Of these students, 58 have been transitioned from regional special educational programs to regular classrooms in their local schools. An additional 19 students who were at risk of being placed in self-contained special classes or out-of-district programs continue to be maintained within regular education environments of their local schools. (Thousand et al., 1986 p. 6)

Of the original 58 students who transitioned to their home schools in the mid-1980s, all avoided re-referral to out-of-school placements. And, four years following the project's end, hundreds of additional Vermont students with various handicapping conditions have been returned from former regional and special class programs to dozens more local schools (O'Connor, 1990).

What has all this change taught us? What are the critical elements for a school district to successfully transition and maintain challenging students in local educational settings? An important outcome of the Homecoming project was the identification of conditions considered essential for intensively challenged students to be transitioned to and maintained within home school classrooms. Six critical ingredients, described in detail in *The Homecoming Model* (Thousand et al., 1986), are briefly presented in Table 1.

Best Educational Practices for Educating Intensively Challenged Students

Along with the introduction of an increasing number of students with intensive educational needs into general education settings of Vermont schools was a pressing need to provide instructional staff with guidelines for delivering special education and related services to optimize student participation in integrated school and community settings. With Vermont Department of Education leadership and University of Vermont support, guidelines representing current *best educational practices* were generated, resulting in a document of 55 quality indicators in the nine best practice areas described in Table 2. These statements of best practice were validated by general and special education educators, administrators, and parents (Williams, Fox, Thousand, & Fox, 1990) and adopted by the Vermont Department of Education as guidelines for local education agencies. In 1987 they were made widely available for use by school personnel, parents, school board members, and community members.

Best Practices for Meeting the Needs of All Students

As educational personnel became more experienced and skilled in integrating intensively challenged students into the routine and culture of their local schools, additional exemplary educational practices (e.g., team teaching, cooperative group learning models, peer tutoring programs, peer support networks) and "critical ingredients" (e.g., expansion of the curriculum to include social skills development and community service, a new instructional role of employment special-

TABLE 1
Critical Elements for Transitioning and Educating Students in Their Home School

Elements	Indicators
1. Administrative commitment	The superintendent of schools, the special education administrator, and the building principals demonstrate, through their actions, support for the concept of educating all students within regular education environments in local schools. District administrators initiate review of current policies and procedures to determine barriers to age-appropriate regular class placement of all learners and make needed modification.
2. Instructional staff commitment	Despite varying levels of commitment, instructional staff are expected to demonstrate behaviors that support implementation of a model to serve all students in regular education environments. A variety of strategies are employed to develop staff commitment.
3. A means for accessing expertise	A collaborative relationship is established for expertise to be shared through the development of local planning teams, which include members of the school and greater community.
4. A process allowing for cooperation	Staff members receive training in collaborative teaming processes and skills so that members of local planning teams may effectively share expertise and accomplish team objectives.
5. A process for developing transition and maintenance plans	A structured (15-step) planning process designed for the transition and maintenance of students within regular education environments is used by local planning teams.
6. Access to consultative support	Members of local planning teams have access to professional(s) who have background and experience in developing integrated educational programs for intensively challenging students. The professional(s) provide consultation, training, and technical assistance.

ist to expand vocational education to include job development and training) emerged, which benefited many students. With the practice of more and more generic inclusionary educational strategies, the original best practices clearly were too "special education" in nature and in the language (see Table 2). They communicated an inappropriate and unwanted message that educational practices effective for students with intensive educational needs were very different from the practices effective for the rest of the school population.

This led to revision of the best practice categories and

TABLE 2
Best Practices Areas

1. *Age-appropriate placement in local public schools*
   The placement of choice for all students (with and without handicaps) should be within chronologically age-appropriate regular classrooms in the students' local public schools.

2. *Integrated delivery of services*
   IEP's and instructional programs should indicate the integration of instruction on education and related service goals into everyday school, home, and community activities. Related service providers should offer consultation and assistance to special and regular educators, parents, and others in developing, implementing, and integrating instruction on related service goals.

3. *Social integration*
   Students with handicaps should have access to the same environments as nonhandicapped peers of similar chronological age. Primary goals of social integration should be to increase the number of integrated community and school environments and to improve the quality of interactions in those environments.

4. *Transition planning*
   Transition planning should occur well in advance of major moves (e.g., early education, special education to elementary school, elementary to high school, high school to adult services). Transition objectives should be included in IEPs and reflect the input of significant parties affected by the transition.

5. *Community-based training*
   Students should have the opportunity to acquire and demonstrate specific skills within appropriate community settings. Conditions and criteria of IEP goals and objectives should include performance in natural environments.

6. *Curricular expectations*
   Curricula or curriculum guidelines should progress from no skills to adult functioning in all areas of integrated community life, with a system for longitudinal monitoring of student progress.

7. *Systematic data-based instruction*
   There should be written schedules of daily activities, clearly defined objectives, reliably implemented instructional programs, and systematic data collection and analysis. Instructional decisions should be based upon documentation of student's progress.

8. *Home-school partnership*
   Parents should have ongoing opportunities to participate in the development of their child's IEP and the delivery of educational and related services. There should be a clearly delineated system for regularly communicating with parents and providing parents with information. Parental concerns should be reflected in IEP goals and objectives.

9. *Systematic program evaluation*
   Educational and related services should be evaluated on a regular basis. Evaluations should actively involve the entire program staff and provide administrators and staff with information regarding the achievement of program goals; student progress; discrepancies requiring remediation; directions for future program change; and program impact upon students, their families, and the community.

indicators to reflect exemplary practices from both general and special education. As the items in Table 3 illustrate, the new best practice document is intended for use with *all* school-aged students (Fox & Williams, 1990). The categorical labels and the language used to define the items in Table 3 versus the original best practice items reveal a shift toward the conceptualization of best educational practices as supporting a single system of education responsive to all children versus a dual system of general and special education (W. Stainback & S. Stainback, 1984; Wang, Reynolds, & Walberg, 1988).

State-Level Support for Inclusionary Educational Practices

The shift of educational services for more challenging students from regionalized self-contained special classes to local schools, coupled with a dramatic rise in special education costs and the national interest in restructuring schools, created a need to examine the state's system for funding special education and to establish state board of education and department of education policies to support services in local school generated education classrooms. The "old" funding formula for special education services was founded upon the notion of "placement" rather than "services needed." It provided fiscal incentives for serving children in more restrictive environments; the more restrictive the placement (e.g., residential, special class), the greater the state's share of funding for that placement.

A 3-year collaborative and consensus-building effort among the Vermont State Board of Education, the Vermont State Department of Education, key state legislators, and the Vermont Education Coalition (representing the Vermont Headmasters Association, the Vermont Superintendents Association, the Vermont-National Educational Association, the Vermont Parent Teacher Organization, and the Vermont Coalition for Disability Rights) resulted in new educational goals, new legislation, and a new funding mechanism. The new education goals articulate the need to restructure schools to support very high performance for all students. They forward the vision that "there is no special education as we used to know it. Children are different from one another in lots of ways, and the schools [must] accommodate everyone with an inventive array of special services" (Vermont Department of Education, 1990, p. 2).

Legislation in 1988 defined the state's share of special education costs at 50% and created a mechanism to fund educational services for students regardless of the place in which they were delivered. A 1990 modification of this legislation declared the following.

School Climate and Structure

Indicator #1
The school's philosophy statement and objectives should be developed by administrators, staff, students, parents, and community members and should reflect the school's commitment to meeting the individual needs of all students in age-appropriate integrated school and community settings.

Indicator #7
The school's instructional support system (e.g., classroom-based model for delivering support services, teacher assistance team, individual student planning teams, special education prereferral process, volunteer system) should be developed by administrators, staff, students, parents, and community members and should be available to all students and staff.

Collaborative Planning

Indicator #9
The school should provide time during school hours for instructional support teams (e.g., individual student planning teams, teacher assistance teams, teaching teams) to meet and for individual team members to monitor services, and to provide timely consultation, support, and technical assistance to families and staff.

Social Responsibility

Indicator #13
The school should provide opportunities for students to develop a sense of responsibility and self-reliance through age-appropriate activities such as peer tutoring/mentoring, student government, participation in decision making about important school issues, and school and community jobs.

Curriculum Planning

Indicator #18
The school's curricula should be developed by administrators, staff, students, parents, and community members, and should identify age-appropriate content (e.g., reading, math, history, social/emotional, arts, health) and process-oriented (problem-solving and collaboration skills, study skills) goals and objectives that set a high standard of excellence and address the needs of all students.

Indicator #24
The system for monitoring the progress of students with intensive needs in basic skill and/or social areas should include: (a) indications of level of independence on identified skills/activities; (b) indications of environments in which those skills/activities have been demonstrated; (c) an annual summary; and (d) post-school follow-ups of employment, self-esteem, and socialization for purposes of program improvement.

Delivery of Instructional Support Services

Indicator #25
Instructional support services and staff (e.g., Chapter I, special education, speech and language, guidance, peer tutoring) should be incorporated into ongoing school and community activities.

Individualized Instruction

Indicator #30
The school should provide opportunities for all staff to become proficient in using a variety of instructional methods (e.g., cooperative learning, whole language, peer tutoring, drill and practice, incidental teaching, computer-assisted instruction), matching methods to individual student needs, and incorporating methods into ongoing activities.

Indicator #32
A variety of instructors (e.g., teachers, teacher assistants, same-age peer tutors, cross-age peer tutors, peer mentors, volunteers) should be available to students and matched to individual student needs.

Transition Planning

Indicator #41
There should be procedures for facilitating the smooth transition of all students from one educational setting to another, and from school to post-school life.

Family-School Collaboration

Indicator #44
The school should provide families with frequent opportunities to visit the school and to regularly communicate with school staff on topics important to both the family and the school.

Planning for Continued Best Practice Improvement

Indicator #49
A plan for improving best practice-based services within the school should be developed every three to five years by a school planning team consisting of administrators, staff, students, parents, and community members.

Note: Indicators were selected from a total of 58 indicators included in a July 3, 1990 draft of *Selected Best Practices From Regular and Special Education* (Fox & Williams, 1990).

> It is the policy of the state that each local school district design and implement, in consultation with parents, a comprehensive system of education services that will result, to the maximum extent possible, in all students succeeding in the regular classroom. (Vermont Act 230, 1990, p.1)

This legislation also dedicates 1% of the total state special education budget to training teachers and administrators in strategies for providing in-class supports to students and requires each public school to establish a prereferral system—an "instructional support team"—to problem solve regarding any child who might need additional classroom support.

Change at the "micro" level (i.e., demonstrations of educating intensively challenged students in general education classrooms) and change at the "macro" level (e.g., promulgation of a funding formula and training dollars to support inclusive schooling) are always inextricably intertwined, continually interacting to alter the beliefs and practices of the time. Collaboration and advocacy on the part of parents, educators, and policy makers can result, and have resulted, in dramatic changes in the educational scene, as the Vermont history illustrates.

WHAT SCHOOL LEADERSHIP CAN DO

The formal leadership personnel of a school district are the ones charged with publicly representing the district's vision or mission and coordinating the actions of school personnel and students to be consistent with this vision. The educational leadership, then, is in the position of shaping the organizational structure of the schools within the district and the beliefs of the school community. These structures and beliefs can work to support or to inhibit a school's capacity to support the education of intensively challenged students in general education settings. The recommendations offered in this section are derived from research findings, model demonstration outcomes, and surveys of teachers and general and special education administrators in Vermont who are concerned with educating *all* students in heterogeneous local school and community environments (Villa & Thousand, 1990).

Promoting an Inclusive Vision

Administrators involved in including intensively challenged students in their local schools stress the importance of clarifying for themselves, school staff, and the community a vision based upon at least the following assumptions: (a) all children are capable of learning; (b) all children deserve the opportunity to receive educational services with similar-aged peers in heterogeneous local school classrooms; and (c) the school district is charged with meeting the unique educational and psychological needs of all of its community's children. To articulate such an inclusive vision is necessary but not sufficient for school staff to adopt the desired school mission. Efforts have to be taken to foster understanding and consensus regarding the vision.

One strategy for building consensus is through education of the school staff. Smith (in press) has noted that how teachers interact with students depends, at least in part, upon the conceptual framework and the language they use to think and talk about students. Therefore, the district leadership must (a) develop and deliver a comprehensive inservice training agenda exposing the school community to information regarding the theoretical, ethical, and data-based rationale for inclusionary education, and (b) offer them opportunities to acquire a common knowledge base, language, and set of technical skills for communicating about and implementing exemplary educational practices.

A second powerful strategy for securing support for an inclusive vision is to involve representatives of school and community stakeholder groups in formulating the school district's mission and objectives for supporting students with intensive educational needs in regular education. People who participate as decisionmakers more likely develop a sense of ownership for their decisions and act to promote agreed-upon outcomes than if decisions are imposed upon them (Thousand et al., 1986; Thousand, Nevin, & Fox, 1987; Thousand, Villa, Paolucci-Whitcomb, & Nevin, in press).

Schools that are successful in realizing a vision (e.g., the education of all intensively challenged students in integrated environments) are ones that attend to the development of a spirit of enthusiasm and devotion to the common goal by creating rewards and incentives and publicly recognizing staff and students who model or actively promote the district mission of inclusion. In structuring rewards, administrators are advised to reward *groups* as well as individuals, as this highlights the district's valuing of collaborative team efforts. Staff and students should be asked what *they* consider rewarding. Any person holding any job (e.g., bus driver, secretary, cafeteria worker, community volunteer) within the school district can forward or thwart the inclusionary mission.

All members of the school community, then, need to be viewed as candidates for acknowledgement. Short notes of praise, posting of "thank you" notes from visitors, retreats for collaborative planning efforts, opportunities for conference attendance or presentations are just a few examples of recognition methods that administrators have successfully structured.

Strategies for building understanding and consensus will always be unique to the history, characteristics, and values of each school community. Although system-wide support for an educational mission is the ideal, not *all* members of the school community will or need to believe in that vision in order for the formal leadership to take actions to increase the district's capacity to provide quality support to intensively challenged students and quality instructional services to all students in heterogeneous learning environments.

Expanding the Curriculum

Those who have worked in both the historically separate general and special education systems know that the curriculum and effective instructional strategies employed in the two systems are fundamentally the same. Students eligible for special services are simply at a different place in the curricular sequence than their agemates. For students with intensive educational needs, the curriculum, with its focus upon work, social life, and recreation skills and use of the community as a learning environment, may seem to be notably different. A closer look, however reveals that the general education curriculum clearly addresses vocational instruction, social skills (e.g., cocurricular activities and clubs, speaking and listening competencies), life skills (e.g., technology education, family living), and recreation needs (e.g., physical education, music, art). Furthermore, general education has always employed the community as an instructional setting (e.g., field trips, vocational placements, behind-the-wheel driving).

District leadership has to lead the school community in discovering the sameness of the curriculum for learners with and without intensive challenges and to work with them to reorganize content, instructional staff, and instructional settings so that a generic set of services may be made available to any student. The content of all courses has to be examined closely. Duplicate content should be eliminated (e.g., a special education basic skills class in math addresses much of the same content as the general education consumer math class), and responsibility for teaching common content has to be distributed across the instructional staff members who formerly worked exclusively in general or special education.

New curricular domains, such as social competence and responsibility, may have to be developed; and new job roles (e.g., integration or support facilitator, school-based employment specialist) may have to be developed to deliver the expanded curriculum in integrated school and community settings (W. Stainback & S. Stainback, 1990b). Community training sites should be examined for potential use by a broader range of students. An IBM plant may offer an intensively challenged student an assembly line job experience, an advanced computer science student programming experience,

and the opportunity to acquire the social behaviors expected in a workplace.

Developing Partnerships for Change

More often than not, no one school district possesses all of the diverse human and material resources it may need to successfully initiate a change process (i.e., attempting the inclusion of intensively challenged and challenging students in a school system for the first time). The development of professional partnership relationships with State Department of Education personnel, faculty of institutions of higher education, consultants, and other school districts with similar interest in creating more responsive schools in a recommended administrative practice for gaining access to much needed human and fiscal resources.

State Department of Education personnel may be able to provide fiscal incentives or regulatory relief so that innovative model demonstration projects may be initiated. They also may provide valuable support in the public relations area—articulating in publications, circulars, and public presentations the need for school restructuring and the value of creating schools that welcome and exemplify excellence for all children.

People with specific expertise not yet available within the district (e.g., nonverbal communication specialists, experts in approaches for establishing constructive and positive school conduct, teachers with experience adapting curriculum for intensively challenged students, experts in cooperative group learning models) may be hired to provide needed technical assistance and training. Staff, students, parents, and administrators from school districts with experience in educating students with intensive educational needs in general education can provide training and should be tapped as trainers regarding the "how to's" of inclusion. They also are likely to have valuable insights to help forward the change process, insights based upon their own real life experiences with being in the middle of change.

School districts attempting to accommodate students with intensive challenges are advised to collaborate with institutions of higher education for the mutual benefit of both organizations. Together the two organizations might design and solicit state or federal support for model demonstration projects in the school district, arrange for valuable internship opportunities for graduate students in integrated educational settings, conduct research to document the impact (e.g., student achievement, social development, post-graduation employment, teacher competence and morale) of inclusive educational practices and local placement of all students, co-design and deliver a district's inservice training program, or co-develop and deliver preservice teacher preparation course content for new or emerging roles (e.g., integration or support facilitator) necessary for supporting a more diverse group of students, their teachers, and their families.

Finally, school districts that share a common vision of inclusive education should form partnerships with one another and exchange personnel (e.g., reciprocal inservice presenters) and resources, jointly problem solve the barriers to change, form a coalition to advocate for changes in teacher preparation programs and state-level policy or funding, and celebrate the positive outcomes of structuring heterogeneous learning opportunities for children.

Restructuring to Create a Climate of Equality and Equity

We cannot ask students to do what we, as adults and educators, are not willing to do ourselves. More specifically, we cannot expect children to support and respect one another in heterogeneous educational groupings if we are not willing to also create heterogeneous collaborative planning and teaching teams, actively involve families in decision making regarding their children's educational programs, and empower students to join in as instructors, advocates for themselves and others, and decision makers regarding schoolwide issues.

Redefining the Role of the Teacher and the Expert As Members of a Collaborative Team

Schools attempting to educate a diverse group of students have taken various steps to merge the instructional resources of general and special education to meet the needs of a heterogeneous student body. Some schools have dropped professional labels and distributed job functions across a number of school personnel (Villa & Thousand, 1988). The Winooski (Vermont) School District has created a single job description for all professional educators (classroom teachers, consulting teachers, speech and language pathologists, guidance personnel), which emphasizes collaboration and shared responsibility for educating all of the community's children.

Some schools have formed long-term team teaching arrangements among faculty (e.g., Bauwens, Hourcade, & Friend, 1989). Thousand and Villa (1990) describe the *teaching team*—"an organizational and instructional arrangement of two or more members of the school and greater community who distribute among themselves planning, instructional, and evaluation responsibilities for the same students on a regular basis for an extended period of time" (p. 152). By looking to the entire adult and student community as potential team members, teaching teams result in better instruct-

or/learner ratios and ongoing exchange of knowledge and skill among team members—outcomes that benefit more students than just those requiring intensive support.

Personnel in schools that have been most successful in responding to the needs of intensively challenging students consistently identify as the cornerstone to their success a strong *collaborative team*, which engages in problem-solving and decision-making processes referred to as "collaborative teaming" (Thousand et al., 1986). Any adult or student interested in supporting the education of an intensively challenged student is a potential member of the student's team. In collaborative planning and teaching teams, members agree to coordinate their work to achieve common, publicly agreed-upon goals. Collaborative processes employed by the team are based upon the principles of cooperative group learning (Johnson & Johnson, 1987a), which prescribe five elements for effective team functioning (Thousand & Villa, 1990):

1. Face-to-face team interaction on a frequent basis.
2. An "all for one, one for all" feeling of positive interdependence.
3. A focus on the development of small-group interpersonal skills in trust building, communication, leadership, creative problem solving, decision making, and conflict management.
4. Regular assessment of the team's functioning and goal setting for improving relationships and task achievement.
5. Methods for holding one another accountable for personal responsibilities and commitments.

Instructional support teams, or teaching assistance teams, have long been available to teachers as a support in problem solving regarding students who present educational or behavioral challenges (Chalfant, Pysh, & Moultrie, 1979). The power of these teams and the individual student support teams that employ collaborative teaming processes lies in their capacity to merge the unique skills of talented adults and students, enfranchise team members through the participatory decision-making process, and distribute leadership authority beyond the administration to the broader school community (Thousand & Villa, 1990).

True collaborative teams also promote a climate of equality and equity in a number of ways. Effective collaborative teams have no single leader; leadership roles are distributed and rotated among all members. Specialists or experts have no extra authority; they are "just another member" of the team. Everyone in the group engages in collaborative consultation, alternately playing the consultant/expert and the consultee/recipient role and modeling learning as well as teaching (Thousand et al., in press).

Family-Focused Education Goal Setting

Families of children with identified handicaps are guaranteed, through PL 94-142, certain rights of participation in the development of their children's education program. Family members of a child with intensive educational needs sometimes find themselves in a struggle with school personnel over what they and their child view as "the good life" and the role of the school in this life, and what professional educators and support personnel (e.g., physical therapist, occupational therapist, speech and language therapist) have been trained to believe are necessary educational goals and experiences for the child (Giangreco, Cloninger, Mueller, Yuan, & Ashworth, in press).

The *C.O.A.C.H.* (Giangreco, Cloninger, & Iverson, 1990) assessment and planning instrument for learners with intensive educational needs has been designed expressly for the purpose of assisting family members and the educators of their child to jointly develop educational objectives and integrated school and community experiences considered relevant to the family. The tool is based upon six assumptions regarding families of children with intensive needs:

1. Families know aspects of their children better than anyone.
2. Families have the greatest vested interest in their children's learning.
3. Families likely are the only adults involved in their child's entire schooling.
4. Families have unique access to information about their children in the home and community.
5. Families can positively influence the quality of community services.
6. Families must live with the outcomes of educational decisions every day of the year.

C.O.A.C.H. is unique in that it puts the family in the position of driving the educational goal-setting process and requires family members and professionals to behave as equal members of a collaborative team. The respect for family members' knowledge and wishes structured into the assessment process is illustrated by Part 1 of the instrument. Included in this section are questions regarding five "quality of life indicators" identified by parents of children with multiple handicaps as parameters of a "good life" (Giangreco, Cloninger, & Iverson, 1990, p. 19). The family's answer to these questions are meant to offer team members a mutual understanding of the child's current status and issues important to the family.

Empowering Students to be Instructors, Advocates, and Decision Makers

The term *collaboration* usually conjures up the image of adults, usually *professional* educators, working together. Schools attempting to educate a diverse student population have expanded the list of potential collaborators to include students and other adults (e.g., parents, support personnel, instructional assistants, community volunteers). Villa and Thousand (1990) offer a rationale for placing students in the collaborative role.

First, given the diverse educational and psychological needs of an increasingly heterogeneous student population, school personnel have to take advantage of any and all available human resources. Students provide a rich pool of expertise, refreshing creativity, and enthusiasm at no cost to the school district.

Second, futurists suggest "a new collaborative role for teachers and students in which students accept an active senior partnership role in the learning enterprise" (Benjamin, 1989, p. 9). Educational reform recommendations also call for more active student participation in their learning and more opportunities for students to develop and use higher-level thinking skills (Boyer, 1983; Costa, 1985; Glasser, 1986; Hunter, 1982). This means involving students in planning, instruction, problem solving, and evaluation activities.

Third, futurists advise schools to offer opportunities for students to practice being contributing and caring members of society and to develop empathy for others (Benjamin, 1989; Falvey, Coots, & Bishop, 1990). By encouraging students to advocate for the educational interests and needs of a fellow student (e.g., a student with intensive educational needs), schools create opportunities such as these.

Fourth, given the current information explosion and the increasingly complex nature of a diverse global society, which will require people to pool their knowledge and skills through collaborative efforts, collaborative skills emerge as a core curriculum area for today's schools.

School personnel, then, have a responsibility to model collaboration by sharing their decision-making power with students, in a climate of mutual respect. Among the collaborative arrangements or strategies recommended for schools attempting to create a heterogeneous learning community that includes students with intensive educational challenges are:

- Students as instructors in partner learning, cooperative group learning and adult-student teaching team arrangements.
- Students as members of collaborative planning teams,

determining accommodations for classmates with intensive challenges.

- Students functioning as an advocate for a peer in transition or individualized education plan (IEP) planning meetings.
- Students supporting a challenged classmate in a "peer buddy" system or a Circle of Friends (Forest & Lusthaus, 1989).
- Students as coaches for their teachers, offering feedback regarding the effectiveness and consistency of their instructional and discipline procedures.
- Students as members of curriculum, inservice, and other school governance committees (e.g., school board).

We contend that collaborative arrangements such as these promote the desired outcomes of a quality integrated schooling experience for intensively challenged students, active participation and problem solving on the part of the student body, equity and parity among students and adults, and a spirit of community within the school (Villa & Thousand, in press).

ADAPTING CURRICULUM AND INSTRUCTION: SELECTED STRATEGIES

Recently reviews have proliferated regarding methods for "individualizing" curriculum and providing "individualized" instruction (e.g., Glatthorn, 1987; Nevin et al., 1990; Villa & Thousand, 1988; Slavin, 1987; W. Stainback & S. Stainback, 1989; Wang, 1989). Several strategies considered appropriate and effective for responding to the individual needs of intensively challenged or challenging students are discussed in this section.

Data-Based Strategies
For Adapting Curriculum and Instruction

In Glatthorn's (1987) summary of research on methods for adapting curriculum and instruction to respond to individual student differences, three specific sets of approaches were offered as having the strong support of quality research: mastery learning, computer-assisted instruction, and cooperative group learning.

Mastery Learning Models

Common to all of these mastery learning or outcome-based instructional models are the following teacher behaviors (Block & Anderson, 1975; Brookover et al., 1982; Vicker, 1988):

1. Frequent, brief diagnostic assessment of each student.

2. Individualization of learning objectives with clear pre-set mastery criteria.
3. Frequent specific provision of feedback regarding student performance.
4. Adjustment or supplementation of instruction or practice time, for students who do not meet their mastery criteria.

An underlying assumption of mastery learning models is that all children can learn, given time and the appropriate resources. This assumption, combined with the extensive effectiveness data that make mastery learning models so compelling for use in classrooms, includes intensively challenging students.

Computer-Assisted Instruction (CAI)

As Glatthorn (1987) notes, CAI is particularly useful in three areas of instruction:

1. *Tutorial*, in which new information is presented.
2. *Drill and practice*, in which old information is reviewed for the purpose of remediation or accelerating rate or level of mastery.
3. *Simulations*, in which concept learning or more complex problem solving is the focus.

For students who are physically challenged, nonverbal, or verbally unintelligible to the general public, computers frequently are used as an alternative or augmentive mode of communication as well as a learning tool.

Cooperative Group Learning

As with effective collaborative teams, cooperative learning models (Johnson & Johnson, 1987b; Slavin, 1983) share five common elements:

1. Face-to-face interaction among a heterogeneous group of students.
2. Positive interdependence (structured through common goals or products, joint rewards, division of labor and roles, division of materials or information).
3. Teaching a small-group interpersonal skills.
4. Regular assessment and goal setting regarding the appropriate use of small-group and interpersonal skills.
5. Individual accountability for achieving individualized academic and social objectives.

In Vermont, more than 20 integration facilitators (teachers with the job function of arranging supports for students with intensive educational needs) regularly work with classroom teachers to structure heterogeneous cooperative group lessons that meaningfully include intensively challenged students. How are lessons adapted to integrate a low-achieving student or a student identified as handicapped? Johnson and Johnson (1987b) describe several proven strategies, but sample lessons designed by classroom teachers with the assistance of an integration facilitator best illustrate how adaptations can be made (Villa & Thousand, in press).

Example #1: A cooperative group lesson adapted for a young student with multiple handicaps. When this lesson occurred, John was 8 years old. He had recently transitioned from a special class for students with multiple handicaps to a combined first/second grade classroom in his local school. John occasionally vocalized loudly but did not yet use vocal behavior to communicate. One of the IEP goals for John was to develop his use of various switches as a first step in developing an augmentative communication system. Other IEP goals were for John to remain with a group throughout an activity, to keep his hands off others' materials, and to refrain from making loud vocalizations in a group.

In this lesson students were assigned to groups of five each. All group members, John included, were expected to sit in a circle, stay with their group, and use an "indoor" voice level. These social and behavioral expectations, by the way, directly addressed two of John's IEP goals.

Groups first were assigned the task of listening to a "talking book" story tape and following along with the illustrations from the story book. Each group had a copy of the story tape, a tape recorder, and the illustrated book. Each child in a group was assigned a specific job or role to perform during the lesson. One job was to turn the pages of the story book to correspond with the tape recording; another was to operate the tape recorder. John was assigned the role of tape recorder operator. His tape recorder was adapted so that he could activate it by pushing on a panel switch.

Being assigned the role of tape recorder operator gave John a valuable and needed role in his group, and it also addressed two of his IEP goals. First, it allowed for assessing the switch's potential for use in a meaningful real-life situation. Second, it inhibited John's grabbing behavior; during the lesson at least one of his hands was engaged in a behavior (pushing the switch to turn on the tape recorder) incompatible with grabbing. Tape recorders also are a popular-leisure time device for children and adults, so are appropriate for John to learn to use.

After listening to the story, groups generated and agreed upon answers to questions concerning the story. They then met as a large group and shared their responses. John's objectives for this part of the lesson continued to be behavioral in nature—to stay with the group and to refrain from making loud noises or grabbing other's materials.

Example #2: A cooperative group lesson adapted for an adolescent with multiple handicaps. Bob, a young man with multiple handicaps, attended his local junior high school. At the time of the biology lesson presented here, Bob was 13 years old and in seventh-grade classes. For this lesson students were arranged in groups of three or four students to dissect a frog for the purpose of identifying body parts. Bob was assigned to a group of four. Whereas other groups used lab tables to do their dissection work, Bob's group used, as their work space, the lap tray attached to his wheelchair.

Bob's objectives for this lesson were different from those of his classmates. He was engaged in a structured communication program (a two-choice discrimination task between real objects randomly placed on either side of his lap tray), which was simple to deliver and which his peers could, and did, easily implement along with their dissection activities at points throughout the class period.

Another of Bob's objectives was to increase the frequency of his vocalizations. Bob's teammates were instructed to regularly use his name as they worked, which they frequently did. The classroom teacher and her collaborating integration facilitator had instructed Bob's fellow group members regarding the two programs. During the activity no adult was directly involved in guiding the peers' interactions with Bob, although a teacher assistant sat near Bob's group, collecting data for the structured programs.

Partner Learning and Peer Tutoring Systems

Another powerful approach for adapting instruction is partner learning or peer tutoring. As Gartner and Lipsky (1990, p. 84), noted, "evidence of the instructional, social, and cost effectiveness of tutoring is mounting." The many benefits for the tutor and the tutee have been summarized in research reviews and a meta-analysis of research (Cohen, Kulik, & Kulik, 1982; Madden & Slavin, 1987; Pierce, Stahlbrand, & Armstrong, 1984). The documented benefits to students receiving instruction (learning gains, the development of positive social interaction skills with another student, and heightened self-esteem) are typical areas of concern for educators and families of intensively challenged students. As with other instructional and peer support strategies that utilize *peer power* (Villa & Thousand, 1988), "peer-tutoring partnerships are a cost-effective way for teachers to increase the amount of individualized instructional attention available to their students (Armstrong, Stahlbrand, Conlon, & Pierson, 1979)" (Villa & Thousand, 1988, p.146). Good and Brophy (1987) suggest that peers trained as tutors may be more effective than adults. They use more age-appropriate and meaningful vocabulary and examples; as recent learners of material being taught, they are familiar with the tutee's potential frustrations and problems; and they tend to be more direct than adults.

Same-age and cross-age partner learning systems can be established within a single classroom (Maheady, Sacca, & Harper, 1988), across more than one classroom, or across an entire school. Clearly, formalized school-wide peer tutoring systems cannot and do not arise overnight. The readers are referred to Villa and Thousand (in press) for an example of how a school-wide partner learning system can evolve over a 2- to 3-year period. The following two individual student examples from Villa and Thousand (in press) illustrate the power of partner learning for behaviorally challenging students.

Example #1: Andrew as a second-grade tutor. Serving as a tutor may have a powerfully positive impact on students identified as seriously emotionally disturbed (SED). Consider, for example, Andrew. During his sixth-grade year, Andrew served as a cross-age tutor the last 45 minutes of each school day in a second grade classroom. This privilege was contingent upon daily demonstration of appropriate behavior as outlined in his behavioral contract. Although this young man still presented intensive behavioral challenges to his own teachers and agemates, the second-grade teacher considered him a model of appropriate behavior and a valued instructional asset. His second-grade tutoring time was one or two times during the day when an instructional assistant was *not* assigned to be available in case of disruptions. Andrew demonstrated the importance of his tutoring role the week before the Christmas holiday vacation, when he chose to forego his own class party to present individual gifts to the entire second-grade class and its teacher.

Example #2: Rebecca's role as a tutor. The tutoring role was intended to help Rebecca, a fourth grader identified as SED, to identify and moderate her own antisocial behavior. Following each tutoring session with second-grade students, she was asked to analyze her effectiveness in teaching and managing the students' behavior. Her tutees' be-haviors that interfered with teaching and management were highlighted, and analogies were drawn to her own behaviors and their effects upon learning. Strategies then were discussed for effectively moderating her own social behaviors.

Creative Problem Solving by Peers

A number of Vermont teachers who have students with dual sensory impairments (i.e., deaf-blind) use an elegantly simple method for determining meaningful curricular and instructional modifications for intensively challenged stu-

dents as regular class members (Giangreco, 1990). As a routine part of the introduction of a lesson, these teachers ask, "How can we make sure (student's name) is included in this lesson?" or "How can we make (student's name) a meaningful part of this activity?" Teachers report that students are highly creative problem solvers and that they generate a great many realistic modification strategies from which to select.

In a more formal application of creative problem solving, students are taught a five-step problem-solving method (Parnes, 1981, 1988). In a Vermont second-grade classroom, students were guided through the five-step process in order to address the general issue of inclusion for their classmate with dual sensory impairments and multiple disabilities. During the initial 10-minute brainstorming stage of the 45-minute activity, the class generated more than 70 ideas for integrating the classmate into the daily routines of the school. When the ideas were assessed for feasibility in the next step of the process, most ideas were found to be usable. More important, the collaborating integration facilitator reported that in the weeks that followed, initiations directed by peers and staff toward the target student increased in both type and frequency.

Curriculum-Based Assessment

"Curriculum-based assessment" (CBA) refers to a set of criterion-referenced assessment methods for identifying a student's instructional needs by examining the student's ongoing performance within the selected curriculum the school uses with the student. Unlike norm-referenced assessment, CBA is not concerned with comparing students with one another but instead with examining a student's performance in comparison with a preset criterion or standard. CBA gives teachers information about what to teach, closely linking assessment with instruction. Of course, to use CBA, teachers have to identify and select or create a curriculum sequence that is both appropriate and specific enough to give teachers information for designing instructional programs. For in-depth descriptions of CBA methodologies, readers are referred to Deno and Mirkin (1977); Howell and Morehead (1987); Idol, Nevin, and Paolucci-Whitcomb (1986); Shapiro (1987); and Shriner, Ysseldyke, and Christenson (1989).

User-Friendly Measurement Systems

Meyer and Janney (1989) have pointed out that the measurement systems we use in general education settings with intensively challenging students must be "user-friendly"

(p. 265)—capable of documenting desired outcomes and assisting teams to make decisions about instruction while at the same time being unintrusive. A user-friendly measurement system is one "which does not interrupt the flow of instruction or intervention in the classroom, requires minimal time to complete, and allows professionals and paraprofessionals to share both their objective and subjective observations" (p. 265). Meyer and Janney describe a variety of measurement systems that meet these criteria and that teachers in general education settings are more likely to use and find meaningful than trial-by-trial data collection practices, which once were viewed as "good" research methodology or best practice in handicapped-only classrooms.

A Decision-Making Process

Tools are now available to assist teams to creatively design an integrated daily schedule for students with intensive challenges (Giangreco, Cloninger, & Iverson, 1990; Iverson & Cloninger, 1990). One of these is known as the IEP-General Education Matrix. Figure 1 presents a sample completed matrix for a third grader. Notice that the student's team has listed, across the top of the matrix, normally scheduled general class activities, including major transition times (e.g., arrival, departure). (For older students these activities would be replaced with class offerings from the school's master schedule.) Along the left column the team has listed abbreviations for the student's IEP goals, general curriculum areas in which the student has learning outcomes, and any management needs (e.g., regular repositioning, personal care needs such as toileting, administration of medication, hearing aid battery checks).

The matrix offers a visual representation of when and where IEP and other learning goals *might possibly* be met. It is intended to assist a student's planning team in choosing when and where learning goals will be addressed in general education activities.

Options for the Delivery of Support Services

The matrix also may help the team to identify the types of curriculum modifications and instructional supports the student may need for educational objectives to be adequately addressed. Special services and supports may be delivered in general education settings in four broad ways, identified in Table 4 (Giangreco, Cloninger, & Iverson, 1990; Giangreco & Meyer, 1988). When initially exploring potential possibilities for inclusion, the team is advised to consider and decide which of these four options for delivering support is best suited or most likely to occur for each of the activities

included in the matrix. As illustrated in Figure 1, codes may be entered on the matrix to represent the most likely adaptation option for each activity. When coding the matrix, however, these notations do not designate how the student actually is included in classroom activities when the daily schedule is finalized. At this point, the matrix is simply meant to offer a visual representation of how learning and management needs *might* be addressed in general education environments. It also is used to highlight when IEP objectives or management needs do not easily mesh with general education activities.

Problems in Meshing Learning Objectives And General Education Activities

At times it appears that no, or very few, general education opportunities are available to address a learning objective. This meshing challenge shows up on the matrix as an entire row or column of blank spaces. When an entire row is blank, the team must question whether the learning objective for that row is appropriate—whether it is both *functional* (likely to lead to more independent adult functioning or an enhanced social support network) and of *high priority*.

If the answer is "yes" to both of these criteria questions, the team should engage in creative problem solving to avoid the loss of an integration opportunity. Iverson and Cloninger (1990) offer specific strategies and examples for meeting various "match-up" challenges. Peers may be enlisted to help problem solve or to serve as peer tutors or buddies. If other students need alternative instruction, small groups can be arranged within a classroom. In cases where the objective is considered either nonfunctional or of low priority, the team may wish to review the IEP and assess whether the objective should be rewritten so that it is more functional, "put on hold," or dropped altogether.

Sometimes the IEP-General Education Matrix may reveal one or more general educational activities or classes during which few, if any, learning objectives or management needs seem to fit. These blocks of the school day may be used to focus upon objectives that have to be addressed outside of the classroom (e.g., community-based instruction, job experiences, toileting). Consideration should be given, however, to *including* the student in activities or classes that do not specifically address learning objectives, particularly when they offer incidental learning opportunities in areas that have not yet been targeted as objectives or opportunities for social interaction and friendship building.

Designing an Integrated Daily Schedule

The culmination of the matrixing process is in designing a daily schedule for the student. In the elementary grades,

TABLE 4
Student Participation Options in
General Education Classroom Activities

Same:
Students who pose intensive challenges can participate in regular class activities by doing what all the other students are doing. Suppose a class is scheduled for Music and students are practicing songs for the annual holiday concert. All the students, including the student with special educational needs, pursue the *same* objectives within the same activities.

Multi-Level:
Multi-level curriculum/instruction occurs when students are all involved in a lesson within the same curriculum area but are pursuing different objectives at multiple levels based on their individual needs (Campbell, Campbell, Collicott, Perner, & Stone, 1988). For example, all the students may be in a reading lesson. The student with special needs is learning to identify (read) representations on a communication board (e.g., photos, line drawings, symbols) while others are learning to read orally with appropriate pauses to match punctuation. Multi-Level Curriculum/Instruction merely suggests an extension to include students with a wider range of abilities than is typically pursued within regular education. For example, in a math lesson one student is applying computational skills to a word problem and another is learning to count with correspondence. Both students are pursuing math learning outcomes but at different levels within the same activity or lesson.

Curriculum Overlapping:
Curriculum overlapping occurs when a group of students is involved in the same lesson, but pursuing goals/objectives from different curricular areas (Giangreco & Meyer, 1988, p. 257; Giangreco & Putnam, 1991). Suppose students are in science lab learning about properties of electricity. A student with special needs may be involved in these activities for the primary purpose of pursuing objectives from other curriculum areas (e.g., communication, socialization) such as following directions, accepting assistance from others, or engaging in a school job with a nonhandicapped peer. When curriculum overlapping takes place, the regular class activity is primarily a vehicle used to attain other goals. This approach opens many opportunities for students to participate in classes previously considered "inappropriate." These settings are selected because they offer opportunities to address identified needs.

Alternative:
Occasionally students may need to pursue *alternative* activities if the regular class does not offer reasonable opportunities to address relevant learning outcomes through multi-level curriculum/instruction or curriculum overlapping. For example, during a time when general education students are taking a half-hour paper-and-pencil test, it may be appropriate to work on community-based activities such as pedestrian skills, because activities such as this may not be addressed adequately within the regular class schedule. Similarly, certain management needs are appropriately met in private (e.g., catheterization or postural drainage may be carried out in the health office). Caution should be exercised when selecting alternative activities, because most student needs can be met in regular class situations given creative planning, a commitment to inclusion, and collaboration among professionals and families.

Source: From M. Giangreco, C. Cloninger, and V. Iverson (1990) C.O.A.C.H.—Cayuga-Onondaga Assessment for Children with Handicaps (6th ed.) (pp. 38–39) (Stillwater: Oklahoma State University). Copyright 1990 by National Clearinghouse of Rehabilitative Training Materials. Adapted by permission.

where classroom routines remain relatively stable, teams have found the information represented on the matrix to be particularly helpful in identifying when additional peer or adult support is needed and when adaptations in materials, instructional strategies, or curriculum are needed. In the middle and secondary grades, where students move from class to class and have individual schedules, the matrix has been used to select classes.

Even though a student with intensive needs will have scheduled "regular education" experiences, the schedule must remain flexible so that the student's team may arrange for alternative instruction (e.g., individual instruction, vocational education) when particular units or topics fail to match the student's needs. Even at the high school level, meshing challenges have been overcome and have resulted in intensively challenged students receiving *more* services in integrated versus separate activities (Giangreco, Cloninger, & Iverson, 1990).

EDUCATIONAL ROLES FOR DELIVERING THE CURRICULUM

As already mentioned, one of the responsibilities of school district leadership is to guide the school community through a process of curriculum examination in order to discover the "sameness" of general and special education curricula, merge duplicate content taught in separate programs (e.g., general versus special versus compensatory education) and distribute instruction of this content across instructional staff of formerly separate programs, and develop new curricular domains (e.g., social skills and responsibility). An associated responsibility of school leadership is to examine the need for new job roles or job functions so that the expanded curriculum may be delivered in integrated school and community settings. The *school-based employment specialist* and the *integration* or *support facilitator* are two specific job roles that have emerged in the last several years to enable an expanded curriculum to be delivered to a broader range of students in heterogeneous school and community settings.

School-Based Employment Specialists

Recent follow-up studies indicate high dropout and low employment rates for students with handicaps who have exited school (Hasazi & Clark, 1988; Hasazi, Gordon, & Roe, 1985; Mithaug, Horiuchi, & Fanning, 1985). In their examination of young adults labeled moderately, severely, and profoundly retarded, Wehman, Kregel, and Seyfarth (1985) found only 12% employed either part-time or full-time. In addition, their wages were extremely low. These data clearly attest to the need for additional vocational options to enhance

Regular Class Schedule

<table>
<thead>
<tr><th>Name: Tommy Smith
Grade: 3</th><th></th><th>Arrival</th><th>Current Events</th><th>Reading</th><th>Math</th><th>Lang. Arts</th><th>LUNCH</th><th>Recess</th><th>Science</th><th>Social Studies</th><th>P.E.</th><th>Art</th><th>Music</th></tr>
</thead>
<tbody>
<tr><td rowspan="8">IEP GOALS</td><td>Summons Others</td><td>ML</td><td></td><td></td><td></td><td>ML</td><td>CO</td><td>CO</td><td></td><td></td><td>CO</td><td>CO</td><td></td></tr>
<tr><td>Makes Choices</td><td></td><td>ML</td><td>CO</td><td>CO</td><td>ML</td><td>CO</td><td>CO</td><td>CO</td><td>CO</td><td>CO</td><td>CO</td><td>CO</td></tr>
<tr><td>Initiates Interactions</td><td>S</td><td></td><td></td><td></td><td>CO</td><td>ML</td><td>CO</td><td>CO</td><td>CO</td><td>CO</td><td>CO</td><td>CO</td></tr>
<tr><td>Imitates Skills</td><td>ML</td><td>CO</td><td>CO</td><td>CO</td><td>CO</td><td></td><td>CO</td><td>CO</td><td>CO</td><td>CO</td><td>CO</td><td>CO</td></tr>
<tr><td>Leisure with Others</td><td>ML</td><td></td><td></td><td>CO</td><td></td><td>ML</td><td></td><td></td><td></td><td></td><td></td><td></td></tr>
<tr><td></td><td></td><td></td><td></td><td></td><td></td><td></td><td></td><td></td><td></td><td></td><td></td><td></td></tr>
<tr><td></td><td></td><td></td><td></td><td></td><td></td><td></td><td></td><td></td><td></td><td></td><td></td><td></td></tr>
<tr><td></td><td></td><td></td><td></td><td></td><td></td><td></td><td></td><td></td><td></td><td></td><td></td><td></td></tr>
<tr><td rowspan="9">GENERAL CURRICULUM</td><td>Physical Education</td><td></td><td></td><td></td><td></td><td></td><td></td><td></td><td></td><td></td><td>ML</td><td></td><td></td></tr>
<tr><td>Music</td><td></td><td></td><td></td><td></td><td></td><td></td><td></td><td></td><td></td><td></td><td></td><td>S</td></tr>
<tr><td>Art</td><td></td><td></td><td></td><td></td><td></td><td></td><td></td><td></td><td></td><td></td><td>S</td><td></td></tr>
<tr><td>Socialization</td><td>ML</td><td>CO</td><td>CO</td><td>CO</td><td>CO</td><td>ML</td><td>ML</td><td>CO</td><td>CO</td><td>CO</td><td>CO</td><td>CO</td></tr>
<tr><td>Communication</td><td>ML</td><td>ML</td><td>CO</td><td>CO</td><td>ML</td><td>S/CO</td><td>ML</td><td>CO</td><td>CO</td><td>CO</td><td>CO</td><td>CO</td></tr>
<tr><td>Personal Management</td><td>ML</td><td></td><td></td><td>ALT</td><td>ALT</td><td>ALT/ML</td><td></td><td>ALT</td><td>ALT</td><td></td><td></td><td></td></tr>
<tr><td>Recreation/Leisure</td><td>ML</td><td></td><td></td><td></td><td>CO</td><td></td><td>ML</td><td></td><td></td><td></td><td></td><td></td></tr>
<tr><td>School</td><td></td><td>ML</td><td>CO</td><td>CO</td><td>CO</td><td></td><td></td><td></td><td></td><td></td><td></td><td></td></tr>
<tr><td>Vocational (class jobs)</td><td>CO</td><td>CO</td><td>CO</td><td>CO</td><td>CO</td><td>CO</td><td>CO</td><td>CO</td><td>CO</td><td>CO</td><td>CO</td><td>CO</td></tr>
<tr><td rowspan="4">MGMT NEEDS</td><td>Teach Others Commun.</td><td>CO</td><td>CO</td><td></td><td></td><td>CO</td><td></td><td>CO</td><td></td><td>CO</td><td></td><td></td><td></td></tr>
<tr><td>Provide Personal Care</td><td>ML</td><td></td><td></td><td>ALT</td><td>ALT</td><td>ML</td><td>ML</td><td>ALT</td><td>ALT</td><td></td><td></td><td></td></tr>
<tr><td>Positioning</td><td>ML</td><td>CO→</td><td></td><td>→</td><td></td><td>→</td><td></td><td>→</td><td></td><td>→</td><td></td><td>→</td></tr>
<tr><td>Access Modifications
+ (use of)</td><td></td><td>CO</td><td></td><td></td><td></td><td></td><td></td><td>CO</td><td></td><td>CO</td><td></td><td></td></tr>
</tbody>
</table>

S=Same   ML=Multi-Level   CO=Curriculum Overlapping   A=Alternative

From M. Giangreco, C. Cloninger, and V. Iverson, 1990, *C.O.A.C.H.—Cayuga-Onodaga Assessment for children with Handicaps* (6th ed.) (p. 41) (Stillwater: Oklahoma State University, National Clearinghouse of Rehabilitative Training Materials. Copyright 1990 by National Clearinghouse of Rehabilitative Training Materials. Reprinted by permission.

FIGURE 1
Sample IEP—General Education Matrix

challenged students' employability.

The school-based employment specialist (SBES) is a secondary educator who works with a school district's guidance and vocational education department and community employers to expand the work experience and job skill training options so that students with intensive challenges and other students have needed work experiences before graduation. Cobb, Hasazi, Collins, and Salembier (1988) have provided a detailed description of the job functions of the SBES and have outlined the graduate-level program at the University of Vermont that prepares educators to serve as an SBES.

Integration/Support Facilitators

The integration facilitator or support facilitator is a second educational role that now is in place in a number of North American schools striving to educate intensively challenged students in local general education environments. An integration/support facilitator (ISF) may work at the elementary and/or secondary level in one or more school buildings or school districts. Job functions of the ISF include (W. Stainback & S. Stainback, 1990b):

• Fostering professional peer collaboration by team

teaching and organizing and serving on teacher and student support teams.

- Locating material, equipment, and specialized technical human resources.
- Adapting curriculum and instructional methods.
- Organizing students into peer tutoring, peer buddy, and other peer support systems.
- Facilitating home-school partnership and communication.
- Lobbying for necessary support (e.g., an instructional assistant for a classroom, state or federal grant support).
- Facilitating community "ownership" for integration activities and removal of traditional special education labels assigned to students, classrooms, teachers and programs.

Since 1986 the University of Vermont has offered a graduate training concentration that "retools" educators to serve as ISFs in inclusionary public schools (Thousand & Fox, 1989). Students in the program work four days a week in the school districts in which they are or will be functioning as an ISF. On the fifth day they attend courses on the university campus. Central to their training are competencies in collaborative teaming and consultation (Thousand et al., 1986; Nevin et al., 1990; Thousand et al., in press) as well as the other competency areas described in Table 5. As of this writing more than one third of Vermont's school districts employ at least one trained ISF in one or more of their schools.

Pitfalls to Avoid

S. Stainback and W. Stainback (1990b) have identified several potential pitfalls of creating an integration/support facilitator role within a school. These same potential pitfalls apply equally to the employment specialist role and any other educational role that emerges in response to the needs of a subgroup of the total school population.

One potential pitfall is that the ISF may be expected to work exclusively with intensively challenged students. This expectation is in conflict with the intended focus of the ISF role, which is to "serve as a resource to the teacher, family, principal, and the class as a whole in building support networks" (p. 34). Restricting the range of students with whom the ISF may work has many potential negative consequences. For one, it denies other students and staff access to valuable expertise. In addition, exclusive association of the ISF with certain students may set those students apart from their peers and interfere with their forming natural peer support networks and friendships.

A second pitfall has to do with the ISF being perceived as the new "expert" in the system. Contrary to the desired role of the ISF as a model and coach in effective collaborative teaming and joint decisionmaking, many educators in the new ISF role find themselves being looked to as the expert responsible for solving the problems regarding certain students. Educators new to the role of ISF must be careful to demonstrate, through their behaviors, their belief in collaborative processes; they must model and expect others to demonstrate equity and parity (equal responsibility and power) in decisionmaking.

The Winooski (Vermont) School District dealt with this potential pitfall by initially training all support personnel (consulting teachers, speech and language pathologists, resource teachers) in core ISF competencies. Training in these same competency areas then was made available to all teachers, instructional assistants, and administrators. This training not only ensured that all support personnel and many other staff had enhanced skills for collaborating in heterogeneous classrooms; it also prevented perceptions that one person or one group of people were the "super special educators."

Finally, the ISF must be vigilant in *not* "oversupporting" a student. For a challenged student to increase independence and have access to natural peer support, adults (teaching assistants, the ISF, other support personnel) sometimes must step back a bit and observe what the student and the natural school ecosystem can do on its own to facilitate learning and relationship building.

The Role of Instructional Assistants And Common Concerns

As noted by Lindeman and Beegle (1988), employment of instructional assistants or paraprofessionals has increased dramatically since enactment of PL 94–142 in 1975. For many students with intensive educational challenges, particularly physically challenged students who will need personal attendants throughout their lives, the instructional assistant (IA) plays a vital support role. As a member of the classroom teaching team, the IA can provide a broad range of supports. These include assisting the teacher with clerical work, record keeping, and developing and preparing materials. IAs may provide students with physical assistance; and they may instruct, thereby bettering the adult/student ratio in the classroom and enhancing possibilities for individualized instruction. Studies suggest that IAs do spend most (60% to 70%) of their day instructing students, often in one-to-one arrangement (Harrington & Mitchelson, 1987; Mintzes, 1985; Vasa, Steckelberg, & Ronning, 1983).

While recognizing the tremendous potential of the IA as a support option for students with intensive educational needs, we must point out five commonly expressed concerns re-

TABLE 5
Competency Clusters for Integration/Support Facilitators

1.0 *Training others.* Trainees will demonstrate their ability to train others (members of collaborative teams, general and special educators, teacher assistants, students with and without handicaps, parents and other family members, other school and community members) to implement effective instructional programs for learners who pose intensive challenges, demonstrate collaborative teaming skills, and articulate an understanding of best educational practices.

2.0 *Technical assistance.* Trainees will demonstrate their ability to provide technical assistance to general and special educators, administrators, and community agency personnel to implement best educational practices and improve the education of learners who are challenged within their local schools and communities.

3.0 *Best educational practices.* Trainees will identify, provide a rationale for, and be able to clearly articulate the benefits of "best educational practices" for all learners that address the issues of school climate and structure, collaborative planning, social responsibility, curriculum planning, delivery of instructional support services, individualized instruction, transition planning, family-school collaboration, and planning for continued best practice improvement.

4.0 *Consultation, communication, and small-group skills.* Trainees will demonstrate knowledge of and the ability to implement techniques for building trust, effectively communicating, giving and receiving positive and negative feedback, and exhibiting appropriate leadership and conflict resolution styles with building-based support team members and other individuals concerned with the education of challenging learners.

5.0 *Collaborative teaming and cooperative group learning.* Trainees will collaborate with building-based support teams of parents, general and special educators, students, and administrators to plan, implement, and evaluate strategies for edu-

cating all learners within their local public schools. Trainees will develop and implement cooperative learning lessons that accommodate learners with intensive challenges and their typical peers.

6.0 *Supervision and peer coaching.* Trainees will provide direct feedback to teacher assistants, volunteers, peer tutors, peer buddies, and general and special educators, regarding the effectiveness of their instruction with learners who have intensive challenges, through clinical supervision and peer coaching conferences.

7.0 *Strategies from general education and theory of instruction for adapting curriculum and instruction to promote the inclusion of learners with intensive challenges.* Trainees will identify and be able to clearly articulate characteristics of "effective schools" and strategies in general education for adapting curriculum and instruction promoting the inclusion of learners with challenges in general education learning environments. These strategies include peer tutoring, cooperative group learning, outcomes-based instruction, computer-assisted instruction, multi-aged groupings, and theory of instruction regarding cognitive learning.

8.0 *Organizational skills (self and others).* Trainees will demonstrate the ability to manage their time and plan, schedule, and document their professional activities so they may evaluate their efficiency and effectiveness in achieving their goals and objectives.

9.0 *Establishment, implementation, and evaluation of a service delivery model for serving all learners in local school general education settings.* Trainees will establish, implement, and evaluate their role as a specialist who supports local school general education placement for students with moderate and severe challenges within their respective school districts and assigned schools.

---

garding the role of IAs in facilitating the inclusion of intensively challenged students:

1. The classroom teacher may not accept "ownership" for a student who comes with an IA, delegating responsibility for the child's instruction primarily to the IA.
2. The IA may become overprotective, overinvolved, or "attached at the hip" to the student.
3. The physical presence of the IA may impede interactions with peers.
4. IAs often are not included as members of student planning teams, even though the decisions of these teams usually have a great impact upon what the IA does on a day-to-day basis (most often expressed as a concern by IAs themselves). In addition, although IAs often are the least trained member of the team, they frequently are asked to engage in the most complex work (adapt-

ing, designing and implementing instruction) without adequate supervision or evaluation.
5. An administrative concern is the cost associated with hiring a full-time IA for each intensively challenged student or every student with a particularly "frightening" label.

Clearly, all of these concerns are valid. Administrators and teachers in Vermont schools, who are experienced with educating intensively challenged students in regular education, have wrestled with all of these issues and offer some strong advice:

1. Spend adequate time discussing and clarifying with the school community that the purpose of support is to enable a student to gain independence and form natural relationships with peers.

2. Clearly delineate the IA's job as a support to the teacher and the classroom as well as the challenged student.

3. Use collaborative teaming processes in planning, delivering, and evaluating instruction, and expect IAs to join the team as equally valued and vocal members.

4. Do not presume that all or certain intensively challenged students require full-time or part-time IA support. Instead, establish procedures for documenting the need for an IA. The documentation should require a description of the other types of accommodations and support already attempted.

5. Develop and regularly reexamine a plan for fading out the direct instructional and personal support the IA provides to the student. Many other adults and students can provide the same support, and an IA can in many ways share the responsibility with the challenged student's classmates for enhancing the quality of education.

PERSONNEL PREPARATION

Recommended Changes
For Teacher Preparation Programs

School personnel are graduates of our colleges and universities. It is there that they learn there are at least two types of human beings and if you choose to work with one of them you render yourself *legally* and conceptually incompetent to work with the others. (Sarason, 1982, p. 258)

Sarason goes on to say that public schools are simply mirror images of today's colleges and universities. Sarason's words provide a powerful illustration of how the current division of teacher preparation programs into separate, distinct, and categorical special education programs (e.g., severe handicaps, learning disabilities, emotional disturbance, English as a second language) and general education concentrations hampers the ability of professionally prepared educators to either visualize or structure heterogeneous learning experiences that include students who, because of their *disabilities* or their exceptional *capabilities* and talents, are considered a challenge to educate. Graduates of personnel preparation programs have few models of adults collaborating across their disciplines or areas of expertise. Is it any wonder that general and special education have evolved as separate systems (Wang et al., 1988) or that Sarason and colleagues long ago called teaching the "lonely profession" (Sarason, Levine, Godenberg, Cherlin, & Bennet, 1966, p. 74)?

S. Stainback and W. Stainback (1989) have offered a rationale and steps for facilitating merger of personnel preparation programs. They recommend that general and special education faculty sit down and analyze their curricula and

identify agreed-upon knowledge and skills concerning philosophies and processes of instruction and learning that they considered critical. A core set of courses, such as that recommended in Table 6, then could be developed and required of all education majors. In addition to this core, each student would take courses in one or more areas in which they wish to develop special competence (e.g., reading, behavior management, history, alternative communication systems, employment, individualized and adaptive learning strategies).

Integration/support facilitators simply would be school personnel with expertise in competency areas such as collaborative teaming and consultation, curriculum and instructional modification, and partner and cooperative learning structures. By restructuring professional preparation programs in this manner, graduates no longer would get the message that they have to perpetuate a dual system of education. Instead they would have the cognitive set and the preparation to instruct a diverse student body in their respective selected specialty areas.

TABLE 6
Common Professional Core of Courses
For All Educators

Courses	Credit Hours
1. Historical/Philosophical Foundations of Education	3
2. Child and Adolescent Development	3
3. Human Relations and Sensitivity to Human Differences	3
4. Classroom Organization, Management, and Motivational Strategies	3
5. Curriculum Design and Adaptations	3
6. Educational Measurement and Curricular-Based Assessment	3
7. Adapting Instruction to Individual Differences	3
8. Utilization of Audiovisual/Media/Computer Technology	3
9. Home, School, and Community Relations	3
10. Issues and Trends in Education	3
Total	30

Source: From S. Stainback & W. Stainback, 1989, "Facilitating Merger Through Personnel Preparation" in *Educating All Students in the Mainstream of Regular Education*, S. Stainback, W. Stainback, & M. Forest (Eds.), (Baltimore, Paul H. Brookes Publishing Company). Reprinted by permission.

A Recommended School District
Inservice Training Agenda

Staff of schools committed to educating all of their students in the mainstream of regular education need to acquire a common conceptual framework, language, and set of technical skills in order to communicate about and implement practices which research and theory suggest will enable them to better respond to a diverse student body. If personnel employed within the school have not received this training through their teacher preparation program, it becomes the job of those responsible for planning inservice for the local education agency to facilitate the formulation and ratification of a comprehensive inservice training agenda. This agenda may need to extend across several years to ensure that instructional personnel have the opportunity to progress from acquisition to mastery. (Villa, 1989, p. 173)

This statement acknowledges what many teachers have reported (Lyon, Vaassen, & Toomey, 1989), that neither their professional preparation nor their relatively isolated teaching experiences have adequately prepared them to meet the needs of a heterogeneous student population, including students who present intensive challenges. Fortunately, as Villa (1989) points out, schools do not have to wait for higher education to "get its act together" (p. 175) to empower staff to collaborate in the education of all children. He prescribes a four-tiered long-range inservice training agenda for school districts (see Table 7), which targets the entire community as the audience for the first tier of training. Training format options and incentives for encouraging participation also are suggested.

Higher Education, State Department of Education And School District Collaboration

In Vermont, collaboration between the State Department of Education and the state higher education institutions has been a critical factor in forwarding inclusionary education practices since the 1960s. In 1968, for example, this unique partnership created the *consulting teacher* special education professional preparation program (Christie et al., 1972; McKenzie et al., 1970), which enabled students with mild handicaps to receive special education support within regular classrooms. This mutually beneficial collaboration, envied throughout the United States, quickly expanded to include local school personnel as trainers of other adults. Classroom teachers and their consulting teacher partners provided practicum experiences for "consulting teachers-in-training" and coursework for local personnel to develop curriculum-based assessments, increase their behavior management and instructional adaptation skills, and keep abreast of current educational innovations.

In 1987, the Vermont Department of Education, integration/support facilitators from Vermont school districts, and University of Vermont faculty embarked upon yet another collaborative effort to jointly plan and deliver intensive week-long Summer Leadership Institutes to provide local school teams with critical knowledge and skills to educate students with intensive needs in regular education.

For a school team to attend the institute, two criteria must be met. First, the team must be *heterogeneous*, with representation from as many constituency groups as possible (e.g., the administration, general and special educators, parents, students, teaching assistants, guidance personnel, health personnel, speech and language pathologists). Second, the team must select at least one target student who is transitioning to the local school or for whom the team wishes to develop a more integrated daily schedule.

Training focuses upon four of the 10 competency core clusters in the integration/support facilitator training program (see Table 6), best educational practices (refer to Table 2 and 3); consultation, communication, and small-group skills; collaborative teaming; and strategies for adapting curriculum and instruction to promote the inclusion of learners with intensive challenges. The instructional format alternates between team work sessions and formal presentations by parents, administrators, teachers, related service personnel (e.g., occupational therapists, physical therapists, speech and language pathologists), instructional assistants, and students with and without handicaps. Each team has an assigned "facilitator" (a university faculty member, State Education Department technical assistant, or a trained integration/support facilitator) who is available to answer technical questions, guide team work, and observe and process with group members their effectiveness in collaborating and managing conflict. By the week's end, each team has developed a 16-step "action plan" for delivering support to their target student and enhancing collaboration among the adults and students of their school.

The primary objective of the institute is to create a sense of group cohesion and a common conceptual framework and language among team members so they are able to support one another in transferring their newly acquired knowledge and skills to colleagues in their "home school" in the fall. As of this writing, nine Summer Leadership Institutes have been attended by over 500 Vermont educators, parents, and community members from the majority of the state's 60 superintendencies. Teams from several U.S. states and Canadian provinces also have attended and replicated the institute in their own communities. In Vermont, local school teams, regional groups of integration/support facilitators, and the state I-Team (which supports students with multiple handicaps) have replicated the summer training or extended the training as a one- or two-semester course offering within local school districts.

SUMMARY

Skrtic (1987; 1988) has described schooling in North

TABLE 7
A Recommended Public School Inservice Training Agenda

Tier I   *Generic content relevant for all members of the school and greater community*

- General education research regarding the characteristics of "effective schools" (Brookover et al., 1982) and current exemplary "best educational practices" from general and special education (Williams & Fox, 1990).
- Models for adult collaboration and teaming and the development of small-group social skills Johnson & Johnson (1987a, 1987b); Thousand et al. (1986); Thousand et al. (in press).

Tier II   *Selected content to respond to self-identified training needs of parents and community members; for example:*

- Legal rights and safeguards
- IEPs
- Behavior management
- Community-based training
- Transition between school environments
- Transition to adult services
- Post high-school follow-up

Tier III   *Training in assessment, behavior management, and instructional strategies for instructional personnel*

- Outcome-based instructional models (Block & Anderson, 1975; Guskey, 1985; Hunter, 1982), assessment models (Blankenship, 1985; Brown et al., 1989; Giangreco, Cloninger, & Iverson, 1990; Deno, 1985; Idol, Paolucci-Whitcomb, & Nevin, 1985; 1986; Ysseldyke & Christenson, 1987), and curriculum adaptation approaches (Campbell et al., 1988; Giangreco & Meyer, 1988) that enable teachers to discuss learner characteristics and make decisions about their own instructional behavior.
- Cooperative group learning models (Johnson, Johnson, Holubec, & Roy, 1984; Slavin, 1984).
- Computer-assisted instruction (Heerman, 1988).
- Classroom and school-wide behavior management and discipline approaches (Becker, 1986; Glasser, 1986; Curwin & Mendler, 1988).
- Methods for teaching and reinforcing students' use of positive social skills (Hazel, Schumaker, Sherman, & Sheldon-Wildgen, 1981).
- The use of student peers as tutors in partner learning, buddies in nonacademic situations, and members of individual student IEP planning teams (Good & Brophy, 1987; Pierce, Stahlbrand, & Armstrong, 1984; Villa & Thousand, 1988).

Tier IV   *Training in peer coaching and clinical supervision for supervisory personnel*

- (Cummings, 1985; Joyce & Showers, 1980; 1988).

Source: From Richard A. Villa, 1989, "Model Public School Inservice Programs: Do they exist?" *Teacher Education & Special Education, 12,* 173–176. Copyright 1989 by Special Press, San Antonio, TX. Adapted by permission.

America as a professional bureaucracy and argues that this paradigm diminishes teachers' ability to individualize for a great many students, including students with intensive educational needs. Skrtic explains:

> The biggest problem is that schools are organized as professional bureaucracies . . . a contradiction in terms: Professionalization is intended to permit personalization; bureaucratization is intended to assure standardization. To blame the inability to individualize instruction totally on the capacity or will of professionals is misguided in that it blames the teacher for the inadequacies and contradictions of the organizational structure. This is the same kind of distortion of reality we make when we blame particular students for not learning from the existing standardized programs of the school organization. These students are the ones we call "handicapped," which is what I mean when I say that school organizations create "handicapped students." In both cases our tendency is to blame the victims—teachers who fail to individualize and students who fail to learn—for the inadequacies of the system. (Thousand, 1990, p. 31)

To enhance the capacity of schools to individualize for students, a "paradigm shift" is recommended: Educators should consider organizing into ad hoc teams (Patterson, Purkey, & Parker, 1986) or an *adhocracy* (Skrtic, 1987) so that educators may "mutually adjust their collective skills and knowledge to invent unique, personalized programs for each student" (Thousand, 1990, p. 32). In this new paradigm, the teacher is an inventor who has an implicit understanding that educational programs will have to be:

> . . . continuously invented and reinvented by teachers in actual practice with students who have unique and changing needs. . . . The value of the adhocracy is that it is configured for diversity whereas the professional bureaucracy is configured for homogeneity, and so must remove diversity from the system through means like special education and other pull-out programs. (Thousand, 1990, p. 32)

What is suggested here is the need for organizational restructuring of schools. This restructuring already has begun. Ad hoc collaborative problem-solving and teaching teams composed of adults and students currently are emerging across North America in inclusion-oriented schools (see Nevin et al., 1990; Thousand & Villa, 1989; 1990; Villa & Thousand, in press). These schools are right in the *middle* of a paradigm shift toward an "ideal" school structure of multiple ad hoc groups, which form and dissolve as needed to address the instructional and organizational barriers to the invention of personalized learning opportunities. Thousand et al. (in press) offer a detailed description of this ideal school for the 21st century and a scenario of how a school in the middle of a paradigm shift might transfer to the adhocratic structure.

We encourage an end to discussions of *where* students labeled severely or multiply handicapped can or should be educated. Instead, we propose that the discussion go another way, that it focus upon how to document, further refine, and disseminate the instructional, organizational, and technological innovations that allow neighborhood schools to respond to the diverse educational and psychological needs of any learner (Williams, Villa, Thousand, & Fox, 1990). Furthermore, teachers and administrators of each school building need to discuss how they will reorganize so that educators, students, and community members may form planning and teaching teams empowered to invent the future in the adhocratic fashion Skrtic prescribes.

"Student diversity is only a problem because of the kind of school organization we have" (Holmes Group, 1990). But that organization can and is now changing. We, therefore, propose a united advocacy effort to promulgate national policy prohibiting segregated education for any youngster entering school in the 21st century. This gives us this entire last decade of the 20th century to further research and refine strategies for inclusion and personalized instruction, not only for students with intensive educational needs, but for all students.

REFERENCES

Armstrong, S. B., Stahlbrand, K., Conlon, M. F., & Pierson, P. M. (1979, April). *The cost effectiveness of peer and cross-age tutoring.* Paper presented at international convention of Council for Exceptional Children. (ERIC Document Reproduction Service No. ED 171 058)

Bauwens, J., Hourcade, J. J., & Friend, M. (1989). Cooperative teaching: A model for general and special education integration. *Remedial & Special Education, 10*(2), 17–22.

Becker, W. (1986). *Applied psychology for teachers: A behavioral cognitive approach.* Chicago: Science Research Associates.

Benjamin, S. (1989). An ideascape for education: What futurists recommend. *Educational Leadership, 47*(1), 8–14.

Biklen, D. (Producer). (1988). *Regular lives* [Videotape]. Washington, DC: State of the Art.

Blackman, H., & Peterson, D. (Eds.). (1989). *Totally integrated neighborhood schools.* LaGrange, IL: Department of Special Education.

Blankenship, C. (1985). Using curriculum-based assessment data to make instructional decisions. *Exception Children, 54,* 233–238.

Block, J., & Anderson, L. (1975). *Mastery learning in classroom instruction.* New York: Macmillan.

Boyer, E. L. (1983). *High School.* New York: Harper & Row.

Brookover, W., Beamer, L., Efthim, H., Hathaway, D., Lezzotte, L., Miller, S., Passalacqua, J., & Tornatzky, L. (1982). *Creating effective schools: An inservice program for enhancing school learning climate and achievement.* Holmes Beach, FL: Learning Publications.

Brown, L., Long, E., Udvari-Solner, A., Schwarz, P., Van-Deventer, P., Ahlgren, S., Johnson, F., Gruenewald, L., & Jorgensen, J. (1989). Should students with severe intellectual disabilities be based in regular or in special education classrooms in home schools? *Journal of The Association for Persons with Severe Handicaps, 14,* 8–12.

Brown, L., Nisbet, J., Ford, A., Sweet, M., Shiraga, B., York, J., & Loomis, R. (1983). The critical need for nonschool instruction in educational programs for severely handicapped students. *The Journal of The Association for the Severely Handicapped. 8*(3), 71–77.

Burrello, L., & Tourgee, B. (Eds.). (1990, June). *Principal letters: Practices for inclusion.* Bloomington: Indiana University, National Academy/CASE.

Campbell, S., Campbell, S., Collicott, J., Perner, D., & Stone, J. (1988). Individualizing instruction. *Education New Brunswick - Journal of Education,* pp. 17-20.

Chalfant, J., Pysh, M., & Moultrie, R. (1979). Teacher assistance teams: A model for within building problem solving. *Learning Disability Quarterly, 2,* 85–96.

Christie, L., McKenzie, H., & Burdett, C. (1972). The consulting teacher approach to special education: Inservice training for my classroom teachers. *Focus on Exceptional Children. 4*(5), 1–10.

Cobb, B., Hasazi, S., Collins, M., & Salembier, G. (1988). Preparing school-based employment specialists. *Teacher Education & Special Education, 11,* 64–71.

Cohen, P. A., Kulik, J. A., & Kulik, C. C. (1982). Educational outcomes of tutoring. *American Educational Research Journal, 19,* 237–248.

Costa, A. (1985). Developing minds: *A research book for teaching thinking.* Alexandria, VA: Association for Supervision & Curriculum Development.

Cummings, C. (1985). *Peering in on peers.* Edmonds, WA: Snohomish Publishing Co.

Curwin, R., & Mendler, A. (1988). *Discipline with dignity.* Alexandria, VA: Association for Supervision & Curriculum Development.

Deno, S. L. (1985). Curriculum-based measurement: The emerging alternative. *Exceptional Children, 52,* 219–232.

Deno, S. L., & Mirkin, P. K. (1977). *Data-based program modification: A manual.* Reston, VA: Council for Exceptional Children.

Falvey, M., Coots, J., & Bishop, K. (1990). Developing a caring community to support volunteer programs. In W. Stainback & S. Stainback (Eds.), *Support networks for inclusive schooling: Interdependent integrated education.* Baltimore: Paul H. Brookes Publishing Co.

Forest, M. (1988). Full inclusion is possible. *IMPACT, 1,* 3–4.

Forest, M., & Lusthaus, E. (1989). Promoting educational equality for all students: Circles and maps. In S. Stainback, W. Stainback, & M. Forest (Eds.), *Educating all students in the mainstream of regular education* (pp. 43–57). Baltimore: Paul H. Brookes Publishing Co.

Fox, T., & Williams, W. (1990, October). *Quarterly progress report. State-wide systems change: Vermont model for statewide delivery of quality comprehensive special education and related services to severely handicapped children.* Burlington: University of Vermont, Center for Developmental Disabilities.

Gartner, A., & Lipsky, D. (1990). Students as instructional agents. In W. Stainback & S. Stainback (Eds.), *Support networks for inclusive schooling: Interdependent integrated education* (pp. 81–93). Baltimore: Paul H. Brookes Publishing Co.

Giangreco, M. F. (1990, June). Including students with disabilities in regular classes through creative problem-solving. *I-Team News.* (Available from Center for Development Disabilities, University of Vermont, Burlington, VT)

Giangreco, M. F., & Cloninger, C. J., Facilitating inclusion through problem-solving methods. *TASH Newsletter, 16*(5), 10.

Giangreco, M. F., Cloninger, C. J., & Iverson, V. S. (1990). *C.O.A.C.H.—Caguga-Onondaga assessment for children with handicaps* (6th ed.) Stillwater: Oklahoma State University, National Clearing House of Rehabilitative Training Materials.

Giangreco, M. F., Cloninger, C. J., Mueller, P., Yuan, S., & Ashworth, S. (in press). A quest to be heard: Perspectives of parents whose children are dual sensory impaired. *The Journal of The Association for Persons with Severe Handicaps.*

Giangreco, M. F., & Meyer, L. H. (1988). Expanding service delivery options in regular schools and classes for students with disabilities. In J. L. Graden, J. E. Zins, & M. J. Curtis (Eds.), *Alternative educational delivery systems: Enhancing instructional options for all students* (pp. 241–267). Washington, DC: National Association of School Psychologists.

Giangreco, M. F., & Putnam, J. (1991). Supporting the education of students with severe disabilities in regular education environments. In L. H. Meyer, C. Peck,

& L. Brown (Eds.), *Critical issues in the lives of persons with severe disabilities* (pp. 245-270). Baltimore: Paul H. Brookes Publishing Co.

Glasser, W. (1986). *Control theory in the classroom.* New York: Harper and Row.

Glatthorn, A. (1987). How do you adapt the curriculum to respond to individual differences? In A. Glatthorn, *Curriculum renewal* (pp. 99–109). Alexandria, VA: Association for Supervision & Curriculum Development.

Good, T. L., & Brophy, J. E. (1987). *Looking into classrooms* (4th ed.). New York: Harper and Row.

Guskey, T. (1985). *Implementing mastery learning.* Belmont, CA: Wads-worth Publishing Co.

Harrington, R. G., & Mitchelson, D. (1987, Winter). Special education paraprofessionals: How effective are they? *New Directions,* 3–4.

Hasazi, S. B., & Clark, G. M. (1988). Vocational preparation for high school students labeled mentally retarded: Employment as a graduation goal. *Mental Retardation, 26,* 343–349.

Hasazi, S., Gordon, L., & Roe, C. (1985). Factors associated with the employment status of handicapped youth exiting high school from 1979 to 1983. *Exceptional Children, 51,* 455–469.

Hazel, J., Schumaker, J., Sherman, J., & Sheldon-Wildgen, J. (1981). *Asset: A social skills program for adolescents.* Champaign, IL: Research Press.

Heerman, B. (1988). *Teaching and learning with computers.* San Francisco: Jossey-Bass Publishers.

Holmes Group, The. (1990). *Tomorrow's schools: Principles for the design of professional development schools.* East Lansing, MI: Author.

Howell, K. W., & Morehead, M. K. (1987). *Curriculum-based evaluation for special and remedial education.* Columbus, OH: Charles E. Merrill.

Hunter, M. (1982). *Mastery teaching.* El Segundo, CA: TIP Publications.

Idol, L., Nevin, A., & Paolucci-Whitcomb, P. (1986). *Models of curriculum-based assessment.* Rockville, MD: Aspen Publishers.

Idol, L., Paolucci-Whitcomb, P., & Nevin, A. (1986). *Collaborative consultation.* Austin, TX: Pro-Ed.

Iverson, V. S., & Cloninger, C. J. (1990). *Vermont integration planning process—V.I.P.P.,* Burlington: University of Vermont, Center for Developmental Disabilities.

Jenkins, J., Pious, C., & Jewell, M. (1990). Special education and the regular education initiative: Basic assumptions. *Exceptional Children, 56,* 479–491.

Johnson, D. W., & Johnson, R. T. (1987a). *Learning together and alone: Cooperation, competition, and individualization* (2d ed.). Englewood Cliffs, NJ: Prentice-Hall.

Johnson, D. W., & Johnson, R. T. (1987b). *A meta-analysis of cooperative, competitive and individualistic goal structures.* Hillsdale, NJ: Lawrence Erlbaum.

Johnson, D. W., Johnson, R. T., Holubec, E., & Roy, P. (1984). *Circles of learning.* Arlington, VA: Association for Supervision & Curriculum Development.

Joyce, B., & Showers, B. (1980). Improving inservice training: The messages of research. *Educational Leadership, 37,* 379–385.

Joyce, B., & Showers, B. (1988). *Student achievement through staff development.* New York: Longman Publishing Co.

Knight, M. F., Meyers, H. W., Paolucci-Whitcomb, P., Hasazi, S. E., & Nevin, A. (1981). A four year evaluation of consulting teacher services. *Behavior Disorders, 6,* (2), 92–100.

Lindeman, D., & Beegle, G. (1988) Preservice teacher training and use of the classroom paraprofessional—A national survey. *Teacher Education & Special Education, 11,* 183–186.

Lipsky, D. K., & Gartner, A. (1989). *Beyond separate education—Quality education for all.* Baltimore: Paul H. Brookes Publishing Co.

Lyon, G. R., Vaassen, M., & Toomey, F. (1989). Teachers' perceptions of their undergraduate and graduate preparation *Teacher Education & Special Education, 12,* 164–169.

Madden, N. A., & Slavin, R. E. (1987). *Effective pull-out programs for students at risk.* Baltimore: Johns Hopkins University, Center for Research on Elementary and Middle Schools.

Maheady, L., Sacca, M. K., & Harper, G. F. (1988). Classwide peer tutoring with mildly handicapped high school students. *Exceptional Children, 55,* 52–59.

McKenzie, H. S. (1972). Special education and consulting teachers. In F. Clark, D. Evans, & L. Hammerlynk (Eds.), *Implementing behavioral programs for schools* (pp. 103–125). Champaign, IL: Research Press.

McKenzie, H., Egner, A., Knight, M., Perelman, P., Schneider, B., & Garvin, J. (1970). Training consulting teachers to assist elementary teachers in the management and education of handicapped children. *Exceptional Children, 37,* 137–143.

McKenzie, H., Hill, M., Sousie, S., York, R., & Baker, K. (1977). Special education training to facilitate rural, community-based programs for the severely handicapped. In E. Sontag (Ed.), *Educational programming for the severely and profoundly handicapped* (pp. 96–108). Reston, VA: Division on Mental Retardation, Council for Exceptional Children.

Meyer, L., & Janney, R. (1989). User-friendly measures of meaningful outcomes: Evaluating behaviors interventions. *The Journal of The Association for Persons with Severe Handicaps, 14,* 263–270.

Mintzes, S. S. (1985). Education's stepchildren: The role of paraprofessionals in special education. *New Directions, 6,* pp. 1–2.

Mithaug, D. E., Horiuchi, C. N., & Fanning, P. N. (1985). A report of the Colorado statewide follow-up survey of special education students. *Exceptional Children, 51,* 397–404.

Nevin, A., Thousand, J., Paolucci-Whitcomb, P., & Villa, R. (1990). Collaborative consultation: Empowering public school personnel to provide heterogeneous schooling for all. *Journal of Educational & Psychological Consultation, 1*(1), 41–67.

O'Connor, K. (1990, June 29). Special kids joining peers in the classroom. *Rutland Herald, 34*(156), 1,4.

Parnes, S. J. (1981). *The magic of your mind.* Buffalo, NY: Creative Education Foundation, Inc. in association with Bearly Limited.

Parnes, S. J. (1988). *Visioning: State-of-the-art processes for encouraging innovative excellence.* East Aurora, NY: D. O. K. Publishers.

Patterson, J., Purkey, S., & Parker, J. (1986). *Productive school systems for a nonrational world.* Alexandria, VA: Association for Supervision & Curriculum Development.

Pierce, M. M., Stahlbrand, K., & Armstrong, S. B. (1984). *Increasing student productivity through peer tutoring programs.* Austin, TX: Pro-Ed.

Porter, G. (Producer). (1988). *A chance to belong* [Videotape]. Downsview, Ontario: Canadian Association for Community Living.

Sailor, W. (1989). The education, social vocation integration of students with the most severe disabilities. In D. Lipsky & Gartner (Eds.), *Beyond separate education: Quality education for all* (pp. 53–75). Baltimore: Paul H. Brookes Publishing Co.

Sarason, S. (1982). *The culture of the school and the problem of change.* Boston: Allyn and Bacon.

Sarason, S., Levine, M., Godenberg, I. I., Cherlin, D., & Bennet, E. (1966). *Psychology in community settings: Clinical, educational, vocational and social aspects.* New York: John Wiley & Sons.

Schattman, R. (1988). Integrated education and organizational change. *IMPACT, 1,* 8–9.

Shapiro, E. S. (1987). *Behavioral assessment in school psychology.* Hillsdale, NJ: Lawrence Erlbaum Associates.

Shriner, J., Ysseldyke, J., & Christenson, S. (1989). Assessment procedures for use in heterogeneous classrooms. In S. Stainback, W. Stainback, & M. Forest (Eds.), *Educating all students in the mainstream of regular education* (pp. 159–181). Baltimore: Paul H. Brookes Publishing Co.

Skrtic, T. (1987). The national inquiry into the future of education for students with special needs. *Counterpoint, 4*(7), 6.

Skrtic, T. (1988). The crisis in special education knowledge. In E. Meyen & T. Skrtic (Eds.), *Exceptional children and youth: An introduction* (3d ed.) (pp. 415–448). Denver: Love.

Slavin, R. E. (1983). *Cooperative learning.* New York: Longman.

Slavin, R. E. (1984). Review of cooperative learning research. *Review of Educational Research, 50,* 315–342.

Slavin, R. E. (1987). Ability grouping and student achievement in elementary school: A best-evidence synthesis. *Review of Educational Research, 57,* 293–336.

Smith, C. (in press). What's in a word? *Teacher Education and Special Education.*

Stainback, S., & Stainback, W. (1989). Facilitating merger through personnel preparation. In S. Stainback, W. Stainback, & M. Forest (Eds.), *Educating all students in the mainstream of regular education* (pp. 139–150). Baltimore: Paul H. Brookes Publishing Co.

Stainback, S., & Stainback, W. (1990a). Inclusive schooling. In W. Stainback & S. Stainback (Eds.), *Support networks for inclusive schooling: interdependent integrated education* (pp. 3–24). Baltimore: Paul H. Brookes Publishing Co.

Stainback, S., & Stainback, W. (1990b). Inclusive schooling. In W. Stainback & S. Stainback (Eds.), *Support networks for inclusive schooling: Interdependent integrated education* (pp. 25–36). Baltimore: Paul H. Brookes Publishing Co.

Stainback, S., & Stainback, W. (in press). *Teaching in the inclusive classroom: Curriculum design, adaptation, and delivery.* Baltimore: Paul H. Brookes Publishing Co.

Stainback, S., Stainback, W., & Forest, M. (1989). *Educating all students in the mainstream of regular education.* Baltimore: Paul H. Brookes Publishing Co.

Stainback, W., & Stainback, S. (1984). A rationale for the merger of special and regular education. *Exceptional Children, 51*, 102–111.

Stainback, W., & Stainback, S. (1989). Practical organizational strategies. In S. Stainback, W. Stainback, & M. Forest (Eds.), *Educating all students in the mainstream of regular education.* Baltimore: Paul H. Brookes Publishing Co.

Stainback, W., & Stainback, S. (1990a). *Support networks for inclusive schooling: Interdependent integrated education.* Baltimore: Paul H. Brookes Publishing Co.

Stainback, W., & Stainback, S. (1990b). The support facilitator at work. In W. Stainback & S. Stainback (Eds.), *Support networks for inclusive schooling: Interdependent integrated education* (pp. 37–48). Baltimore: Paul H. Brookes Publishing Co.

Thousand, J. (1990). Organizational perspectives on teacher education and renewal: A conversation with Tom Skrtic. *Teacher Education & Special Education, 13*, 30–35.

Thousand, J., Fox, T., Reid, R., Godek, J., Williams, W., & Fox, W. (1986). *The homecoming model: Educating students who present intensive educational challenges within regular education environments* (Monograph No. 7–1). Burlington: University of Vermont, Center for Developmental Disabilities.

Thousand, J., & Fox, W. (1989). *Certificate of advanced study program: Preparing post-masters level specialists to support local school placement for students with moderate and severe handicaps within rural Vermont.* (Available from Jacqueline Thousand, Center for Developmental Disabilities, 499C Waterman Bldg. University of Vermont, Burlington, VT 05452)

Thousand, J., Nevin, A., & Fox, W. (1987). Inservice training to support the education of learners with severe handicaps in their local public schools. *Teacher Education & Special Education, 10*(1), 4–13.

Thousand, J., & Villa, R. (1989). Enhancing success in heterogeneous schools. In S. Stainback, W. Stainback, & M. Forest (Eds.), *Educating all students in the mainstream* (pp. 89–103). Baltimore: Paul H. Brookes Publishing Co.

Thousand, J., & Villa, R. (1990). Sharing expertise and responsibilities through teaching teams. In W. Stainback & S. Stainback (Eds.), *Support networks for inclusive schooling: Integrated and interdependent education* (pp. 151–166). Baltimore: Paul H. Brookes Publishing Co.

Thousand, J., Villa, R., Paolucci-Whitcomb, P., & Nevin, A. (in press). A rationale for collaborative consultation. In S. Stainback & W. Stainback (Eds.), *Divergent perspectives in special education.* Boston: Allyn and Bacon.

Vasa, S. F., Steckelberg, A. L., & Ronning, L. U. (1983). *Guide for effective utilization of paraprofessionals in special education.* Lincoln: University of Nebraska-Lincoln, Department of Education.

Vermont Department of Education (1990). *Vermont Education Goals.* Vermont Department of Education, 120 State Street, Montpelier, VT 05602.

Vermont Act 230 (1990). Vermont Department of Education, 120 State Street, Montpelier, VT 05602.

Vicker, T. R. (1988). Learning from an outcomes-driven school district. *Educational Leadership. 45*(5), 52–55.

Villa, R. (1989). Model public school inservice programs: Do they exist? *Teacher Education & Special Education, 12*, 173–176.

Villa, R. & Thousand, J. (1988). Enhancing success in heterogeneous classrooms and schools: The powers of partnership. *Teacher Education & Special Education, 11*, 144–154.

Villa, R., & Thousand, J. (1990). Administrative supports to promote inclusive schooling. In W. Stainback & S. Stainback (Eds.), *Support networks for inclusive schooling: Integrated interdependent education* (pp. 201–218). Baltimore: Paul H. Brookes Publishing Co.

Villa, R., & Thousand, J. (in press). Student collaboration: The essential curriculum for the 21st century. In S. Stainback & W. Stainback (Eds.) *Adapting the regular class curriculum: Enhancing student success in inclusive classrooms.* Boston: Allyn and Bacon.

Wang, M. (1989). Accommodating student diversity through adaptive instruction. In S. Stainback, W. Stainback, & M. Forest (Eds.), *Educating all students in the mainstream of regular education* (pp. 183–197). Baltimore: Paul H. Brookes Publishing Co.

Wang, M. C., Reynolds, M. C., & Walberg, H. J. (1988). Integrating children of the second system. *Phi Delta Kappan, 70*, 248–251.

Wehman, P., Kregel, J., & Seyfarth, J. (1985). Transition from school to work for individuals with severe handicaps: A follow-up study. *Journal of the Association for Persons with Severe Disabilities, 10*, 132–139.

Will, M. (1986). *Educating students with learning problems, a shared responsibility: A report to the Secretary.* Washington, DC: U.S. Department of Education. Office of Special Education and Rehabilitative Services.

Williams, W., Fox, T., Thousand, J., & Fox, W. (1990). Levels of acceptance and implementation of best practices in the education of students with severe handicaps. *Education & Treatment in Mental Retardation, 25*, 120–131.

Williams, W., Fox, W., Christie, L., Thousand, J., Conn-Powers, M., Carmichael, L. Vogelsberg, T., & Hull, M. (1986). Community integration in Vermont: Evolution and revolution. *Journal of the Association for the Severely Handicapped, 11*, 294–299.

Williams, W., Villa, R., Thousand, J., & Fox, W. (1990). Is regular class placement really the issue? A response to Brown, Long, Udvari-Solner, Schwartz, Van Denventer, Ahlgren, Johnson, Grunewald, & Jorgensen. *Journal of the Association for Persons with Severe Handicaps, 14*, 333–334.

York, J., & Vandercook, T. (1989). *Strategies for achieving an integrated education for middle school aged learners with severe disabilities.* Minneapolis: Institution on Community Integration.

Ysseldyke, J. E., & Christenson, S. L. (1987). *The instructional environment scale.* Austin: Pro-Ed.

A Classroom Environment Checklist for Students

with Dual Sensory Impairments

Catherine H. Rikhye
Carole R. Gothelf
Madeline W. Appell

■A primary goal of programs for students who have dual sensory impairments is to help them get in touch and keep in touch with their environment (Gothelf, Rikhye, & Silberman, 1988). These students receive limited and fragmented sensory information from the environment. They live from moment to moment in a world where events may appear to occur in a random and unpredictable manner. They characteristically display withdrawal and self-stimulatory behaviors, and they rarely initiate social interactions or activities (McInnes & Treffry, 1981).

In order to help them anticipate events and develop a sense of spatial and temporal organization, teachers must provide a classroom environment that is stable and structured, highlighting relevant information and making it enticing. They must establish clear routines, boundaries that define areas throughout the classroom, and a sensory environment that facilitates self-dependence (Gothelf, Rikhye, & Silberman, 1988).

An increasing number of students with dual sensory and multiple impairments are now being served by their local school systems. Many administrators, special education teachers, and related services personnel are providing instruction and support to these students for the first time. The checklist described here is intended to provide these professionals with the information they need to adapt the classroom environment to the needs of their students and develop age-

appropriate functional programs for them.

Classroom Environment Checklist

The teacher completes a comprehensive evaluation of the classroom environment using the 20 questions that follow (hereafter referred to as the checklist).

Background

A first draft of the checklist was developed from a review of literature focusing on classroom design (Duncan, Gish, Mulholland, & Townsend, 1977; Falvey, 1986; Gothelf, Rikhye, & Silberman, 1988; Meyer & Eichinger, 1987; Milner, 1981; Woods, 1985). The instrument was field tested by project staff, classroom teachers, and administrative personnel in a public school serving students from 7 to 18 years of age who had dual sensory impairments as well as cognitive and physical disabilities. It was revised to reflect suggestions made by the field testers concerning readability, clarity, facility of administration, and relevance of individual questions to program design. Follow-up pilot testing was carried out at a second public school. The checklist provides a means whereby school personnel can evaluate the quality of environmental design and incorporate information about it into instructional programs and procedures. Its use can help staff identify critical environmental features that

promote student anticipation of events, communication, independent mobility, and self-initiation of activities.

Checklist Content

There are 20 items in the checklist, each with a simple yes/no response format. The items reflect a variety of considerations including ambience, safety, equipment specifications, and environmental characteristics that facilitate self-dependence. The brief discussions of the items that follow can serve as a manual for the checklist administration.

✔ *Would you want your relative to spend the day in this classroom?* The ultimate measure of any program's desirability is whether or not it is good enough for the observer's own family; if it is not, then the program is not suitable for anyone. This question both begins and ends the checklist in order to discern any differences between a first impression and a more informed investigation.

✔ *Is the classroom cheerful and pleasant?* This second item incorporates factors such as overall cleanliness, odor, the condition and colors of the walls, floor and equipment, lighting, and orderliness. If the answer is negative, the observer must note and analyze the specific elements that prompted the negative response.

✔ *Are the equipment, decor, furniture, and wall displays age-appropriate?*

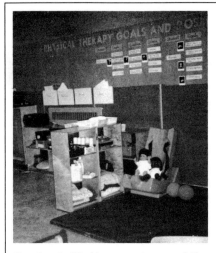

Question 1: Would you want your relative to spend the day in this classroom?

Question 2: Is the classroom cheerful and pleasant?

Question 10: Is each student's equipment in good working order?

Would the classroom decor and equipment be suitable for the nonhandicapped peers of these students?

✔ *Is the environment safe?* The observer must determine what safety features are necessary in view of the age of the students in the classroom. The element of safety must be balanced with the need for appropriate risk. There are some safety features that should be present regardless of students' age (e.g., covered and anchored electric wires, clearly posted evacuation routes and procedures, elimination of sharp edges and broken furniture, availability of locked cabinet areas for cleaning supplies).

✔ *Are work areas organized, neat, labeled, and accessible?* The observer must evaluate the overall level of classroom order. Labels can include written or braille words, pictures, raised line drawings, thermoform representations, or tangible symbols (Rowland & Stremel-Campbell, 1987).

✔ *Is the classroom organized to allow for privacy during change of clothing, diapering, and toileting?* These activities should be carried out in privacy. If there is no space for a changing area in the bathroom, an area of the classroom should be screened off from public view.

✔ *Is there an appropriate level of sensory stimulation in the classroom?* Are there too many visually stimulating objects hanging from the ceiling or on the walls? Is the environment

visually bland and undifferentiated? Is music being played when it is not part of an activity? Is the noise level too high?

✔ *Is the furniture the correct size for each student?* Are students able to maintain good posture and body alignment when seated? Can they reach materials that should be independently obtained from shelves, cubbies, and closets? Are students' feet firmly planted on the floor when they are seated on the toilet? Are tables the proper height for table work? Can the environment be adapted by using footstools and adjustable chairs?

✔ *Does each student have and use appropriate adaptive equipment or corrective aids?* Students who have dual sensory impairments as well as cognitive and physical disabilities are often denied opportunities to participate in activities due to their inability to complete all the necessary skills in a task sequence. Individualized adaptations can be developed that allow them to participate. These might include built-up utensils, cut-out cups, switches, Velcro fasteners, tactually and/or color-coded dials and gauges, or nonslip placemats. Is special equipment (e.g., wedges and bolsters) in evidence? Are students wearing prescribed braces, splints, hearing aids, and eyeglasses?

✔ *Is each student's equipment in good working order?* Equipment should be checked on a daily basis. Even properly maintained equipment breaks down; therefore, the teacher

must have both alternate plans and spare parts available.

✔ *Are lighting levels sufficient, and are light sources individualized and adjustable?* Lighting can make a significant difference in promoting optimal use of residual vision. Glare and reflections can be eliminated through the use of matte surfaces. Individual student needs should determine the intensity of the lighting selected and the best placement of that light. Some people with low vision are extremely light sensitive, while others benefit from high levels of illumination.

✔ *Does the classroom have adequate sound-dampening and -enhancing features?* Sound-dampening wall, ceiling, and/or floor treatments such as sound-absorbent room dividers, acoustic tiles, and carpeting should be evident. Sound is focused when space is divided; therefore, teachers should create surfaces and spaces that absorb sound and reduce excessive reverberation of noise.

✔ *Does the organization of the room promote orientation and independent mobility?* Clearly demarcated pathways and landmarks promote orientation and self-dependent mobility. Specific objects that can serve as cues (e.g., room dividers, furniture, tactual or visual runners along walls, or varied floor surfaces) should be added to the environment. Significant places should be distinguished by special cues.

Question 15: Are each student's belongings tactually or visually identified?

Question 17: Are individual students' IEP objectives, conditions, and criteria posted?

References

Duncan, J., Gish, C., Mulholland, M. E., & Townsend, A. (1977). *Environmental modifications for the visually impaired: A handbook.* New York: American Foundation for the Blind.

Falvey, M. A. (1986). *Community-based curriculum: Instructional strategies for students with severe impairments.* Baltimore: Paul H. Brookes.

Gothelf, C. R., Rikhye, C. H., & Silberman, R. K. (1988). *Working with students who have dual sensory impairments and cognitive disabilities: A handbook for special education teachers and related services personnel.* Albany: New York State Education Department, Office for Education of Children with Handicapping Conditions, Title VI-C.

McInnes, J. M., & Treffry, J. A. (1981). *Deaf-blind infants and children: A developmental guide.* Toronto: University of Toronto.

Meyer, L. H., & Eichinger, J. (1987). Program evaluation in suport of program development: Needs, strategies, and future directions. In L. Goetz, D. Guess, and K. Stremel-Campbell, (Eds.), *Innovative program design for individuals with dual sensory impairments* (pp. 313–353). Baltimore: Paul H. Brookes.

Milner, M. (1981). *Breaking through the deafness barrier: Environmental accommodations for hearing impaired people.* Washington, DC: Physical Plant Department, Gallaudet College.

Rowland, C., & Stremel-Campbell, K. (1988). Share and share alike: Conventional gestures to emergent language for learners with sensory impairments. In L. Goetz, D. Guess, & K. Stremel-Campbell, (Eds.), *Innovative program design for individuals with dual sensory impairments* (pp. 49–76). Baltimore: Paul H. Brookes.

Woods, D. E. (Ed.). (1985). *The more we do together: Adapting the environment for children with disabilities.* (Monograph M-31). New York: World Rehabilitation International.

✔ *Does the organization of the room promote anticipation of scheduled events?* Distinct, identifiable work areas such as vision and auditory training areas, a leisure area, an area for individual work, and an activities of daily living area will promote students' recognition of where they are and what activities occur in that space.

✔ *Are each student's belongings tactually or visually identified?* To facilitate independent identification of each student's materials, equipment, and personal belongings, a consistent and meaningful symbol should be attached to all such items.

✔ *Is the class schedule posted?* The purpose of posting a schedule that includes all the related services students are receiving is so that anyone can readily reference where individual students are and which activities should be occurring. Fixed schedules not only indicate where students and instructional staff are located but also assist students in developing anticipation and communication skills.

✔ *Are individual students' IEP goals, objectives, conditions, and criteria posted?* This reinforces the objectives, conditions, and criteria of student programs for all personnel working in the classroom. The actual IEP should not be posted, because the document is confidential.

✔ *Is the means of recording student progress in view?* Monitoring progress provides guidelines for continuing or altering instructional interventions. Therefore, the data sheets used to record student performance should be in view and readily obtainable. This can be accomplished with clipboards or manila envelopes holding individual student data sheets, or with data sheets posted on boards near work areas.

✔ *Are photographs and descriptions of prescribed positions for students who have physical impairments posted?* This helps clarify handling and positioning techniques.

✔ *Would you want your relative to spend the day in this classroom?* Now that the observer has scrutinized the classroom, the observer is asked to re-evaluate the response to the first question.

Conclusion

The checklist should be used on a monthly basis to monitor progress and pinpoint ongoing and changing needs. As students learn and develop, the teacher should modify the classroom environment to meet changing needs. Use of the checklist can help teachers identify incongruities between environmental arrangements and students' assets and needs. It can also motivate school staff to consider alternative environmental elements. Finally, the checklist offers a useful model for classroom design for all programs serving students with disabilities.

Catherine Rikhye (CEC Chapter #45) is Project Coordinator, St. Luke's/Roosevelt Hospital Center, Developmental Disabilities Center, New York, New York. **Carole R. Gothelf** (CEC Chapter #45) is Director of Educational Services, The Jewish Guild for the Blind, New York, New York. **Madeline W. Appell** (CEC Chapter #45) is Director of the Developmental Disabilities Center, St. Luke's/Roosevelt Hospital Center, New York, New York. *The checklist described here was developed by staff of the Field-Based, Multisite Training Program for Teaching and Related Services Personnel of School-Age Deaf-Blind Children and Youth. The project was supported by a grant from Office of Special Education and Rehabilitation Services (Grant Number G008730425) Inservice Training for Severely Handicapped Including Deaf-Blind Children and Youth, 84-086R. The information presented herein does not necessarily reflect the policy of the Office of Special Education and Rehabilitation Services and no official endorsement should be inferred.*

Clarifying the Role of Classroom Interpreters

By P. Lynn Hayes

P. Lynn Hayes is an assistant professor in the Hearing and Speech Department of Kansas University Medical Center.

"Tutor algebra? Me? The last time I looked at a math book was in 1976."

"I've been interpreting for four hours with one 10-minute break. My arms are ready to fall off. And it's dark in here. How can the students possibly see me?"

"I have no idea whether he did his report last night. Why do people ask me these questions?"

"*Hamlet!* Have you ever tried to interpret Shakespeare? 'A slave that is not twentieth part of the tithe...'"

"Interpret football practice? I just don't think so..."

Most educational interpreters face a bewildering array of challenges in the course of a typical day. Using the term "interpreter" broadly--to mean interpreters and transliterators working in educational settings, this demanding and rewarding job is the fastest growing category in the field of sign interpretation.

The far-reaching impact of PL 94-142 and subsequent laws, which encouraged the enrollment of deaf and hard of hearing students in mainstream schools, has also led to declining enrollments in residential programs and specialized day schools. An article in the 1991 Directory Issue of **The American Annals of the Deaf** indicated that 77 percent of students who are deaf currently attend public day schools and classes.

As the numbers of deaf students mainstreamed in regular classes continues to rise, so does the need for qualified educational interpreters. And with interpreters increasingly visible in school settings, there is a growing need to clarify their roles and responsibilities.

Recently, I had opportunity to interview 35 working educational interpreters in an attempt to pinpoint their most persistent problems and to seek workable solutions. This article is based on the results of those interviews, as well as on my own experience as an educational interpreter. Many of the suggestions for solving interpreting problems are based on in-service training courses provided for interpreters and transliterators in Kansas, and on additional interviews with educational interpreters in Pittsburgh, PA.

The educational interpreters who volunteered to be interviewed were very candid about their most common problems. Most expressed continuing concern about:

o Defining their professional role and responsibilities--in and beyond the classroom.

o The bewildering variety of sign systems used in school settings.

o Their relationships with the students they serve: the development of student IEPs and the issue of confidentiality.

o Communication among interpreters and other educational personnel.

o Opportunities for professional growth, and supervision and evaluation of their work.

Pardon Me...
What Is It That You Do?

Educational interpreters reported overwhelmingly that few of the educators they work with understand their role--in the classroom or beyond. They proposed that school districts write clear-cut job descriptions, designating exactly what is expected of educational interpreters. Faculty and staff members who work with interpreters should have copies of those job descriptions for their own reference.

The interpreters also suggested that mainstream teachers of students who are deaf and hard of hearing should be offered extensive in-service training at the beginning of every school year. Workshops should describe effective teaching strategies for deaf and hard of

hearing students, and focus on the role and responsibilities of the classroom interpreter. A well-planned training program could clarify a variety of matters:

o Optimal standards for student seating, classroom lighting, and effective teaching materials.

o The appropriate pace for instruction and discussions.

o The differences between manual and oral communication.

o The issue of student/interpreter confidentiality.

o The interpreter's need for regular breaks and early notification of changes in routine (movies, guest speakers, field trips, etc.).

Teacher training could also include discussions of effective ways of integrating interpreters into the educational team. Students--both hearing and deaf--should also be made aware of the interpreter's role in and out of class. Two of the interviewees, frustrated with students' lack of pertinent information, developed an "Introduction to Deafness" workshop for incoming freshmen in a high school with a large deaf student population.

Me? A Substitute Teacher?

Fewer than 20 percent of the interpreters interviewed had teaching certificates, and most were uncomfortable in that role. They reported, however, that they were often asked to solve discipline problems, administer tests, and tutor students in various subject areas.

Many interpreters reported similar problems: substitute teachers often rely on their help with teaching and discipline, and regular teachers expect them to manage the class when they are absent.

An interpreter should attempt to fill such requests only when the job description includes those duties.

It was suggested that copies of the interpreter's job description be made available to substitutes as well as to regular teachers. School administrators should also clarify some of those issues when substitute teachers report for work.

What Language Is That?

It would seem obvious that everyone working with deaf students in a specific setting should use a consistent sign system and vocabulary. But educational interpreters often find little consistency in classroom communication. It is not unusual to observe one teacher using conceptual Signed English and another using literal Signed English with the same student. If possible, teachers and interpreters should meet weekly or biweekly to discuss vocabulary and figurative expressions.

Interpreters should also become familiar with the procedures used to develop and record signs for technical vocabulary. In specialized disciplines that lack established sign vocabulary, fingerspelling often seems to be the only option. Some interpreters prefer, however, to "invent" the signs they need to convey specific information.

For example, one interviewee was assigned to interpret for an anthropology class. Frustrated with the lack of established sign vocabulary, she and her co-workers developed a working vocabulary of special signs to use in anthropology classes throughout the school district. They created a journal with drawings and descriptions of each sign, including hand shape, movement, orientation, and location. Students were told that the new signs had been developed specifically for their anthropology classes, but were not for use outside the school setting.

The signing community discourages the tendency to invent new signs, so it should only be done as a last resort. Resources are available to help interpreters find existing technical vocabulary. The Technical Sign Project (TSP), housed at National Technical Institute for the Deaf (NTID) collects, evaluates, records, and publishes newly accepted signs for general use.

How to Relate to My Students?

Many of the interpreters interviewed expressed concern about their responsibilities toward the students for whom they interpret. One issue was the development of the IEP. Because of their ongoing interactions with students throughout the day, interpreters often feel qualified to offer valuable information to IEP teams, but they are rarely consulted. Many tended to feel they are overlooked because teachers and school administrators do not consider them professional educators. Others, when invited to attend IEP meetings, were unsure about the process or their role in it.

Most interpreters agreed that they should be included in the development of IEP's for students they work with. They suggested that teachers meet with the interpreter before the meeting, to explain the development of the IEP and how the interpreter might contribute.

Another important issue was the need for interpreters to develop a relationship of trust and to protect the student's confidence. Like other educational personnel, interpreters understand the need to work in the child's best interest, and are deeply reluctant to discuss students' personal problems with the classroom teacher.

Many interpreters report being asked why their students were absent, whether they had done their homework, and other personal matters. An interpreter placed in this uncomfortable position should offer to interpret between teacher and student, letting the teacher ask questions and the student respond.

Why Can't You Interpret That?

Teachers working with mainstream classes that include students who are both deaf and hearing often presume that the interpreter can translate anything that can be read or spoken. A number of interviewees felt that their interpretive skills might be inadequate to some of the material they were asked to convey; for example, asking teachers to slow down during difficult passages, only to be looked at with impatience for interrupting the class.

To help solve that problem, interpreters suggest that schools might sponsor workshops to give teachers more information about the art of interpretation and the problems and concerns of educational interpreters. That would give interpreters a chance to clarify their own skill levels and discuss potentially difficult situations. Many teachers do not understand that there is no sign for many words, and that it may sometimes be necessary to slow down and let the interpreter catch up.

Many such problems could also be solved by open communication between interpreters and classroom teachers. Educational interpreters are often placed in classrooms without adequate information to provide the best possible service for their deaf clients. When taking a school assignment, an interpreter should ask for copies of textbooks and other classroom materials that will be used, and additional information that might help make interpreting easier and more accurate.

Overall, educational interpreters tended to express dissatisfaction with faculty/staff communication in the schools where they are employed. They suggested that schools might schedule monthly meetings for interpreters and other educational personnel, or include the interpreters in regular faculty meetings. Ongoing communication would help keep interpreters informed of what is happening in the school, and provide information about other factors that might affect their work; for example, any social or emotional problems affecting individual students in their classes.

Who's in Charge Here?

More than half of the educational interpreters in the survey indicated that they usually consulted with teachers of the deaf to solve classroom problems that occur. Others (15 percent) reported that they were able to discuss their concerns with regular education teachers. Two of the interpreters, who reported that they had no designated supervisor; had learned to handle problems themselves. In general, few interpreters were satisfied with the supervision they received. Too often the burden of supervision was assumed by an administrator with little experience in either deafness or interpreting.

Many interviewees suggested that every school district should have a "master" educational interpreter to oversee the needs of classroom interpreters and to serve as liaison among administrators, teachers, and interpreters. Where such a solution is not feasible, the interpreters suggested special training be provided for supervisors, to increase their comfort and competence in this specialized field. Most also expressed a need for regularly scheduled meetings with their supervisors.

The interpreters also noted that little or no attention is given to regular evaluations of their signing skills. Most reported that their only evaluations were written by school principals, few of whom have any sign experience. Those evaluations, therefore, often focused on such matters as dress, conduct, and attendance. Even interpreters whose sign and interpreting skills were routinely evaluated received little or no feedback. They expressed a need for a minimum of two evaluations each year, conducted by a qualified interpreter.

How Can I Grow Professionally?

Many of the educational interpreters we interviewed were unhappy with the quality of in-service training available to them. Too often, the only available workshops have little relevance to the role of the interpreter, and are led by people who are not familiar with that role. Supervisors who are knowledgeable about deafness and interpretation are more likely to arrange meaningful training for school interpreters.

In order for educational interpreters to be fully integrated into the mainstream school setting, they need the support and understanding of the school district and school personnel. They need clear delineation of their responsibilities and greater opportunity for professional growth.

Interpreters are a vital part of the educational team--the surest link between mainstream educators and their deaf and hard of hearing students. Working together on the relatively straightforward solutions to these problems could enhance the school experience for teachers, interpreters, and most importantly, the children they serve. ■

Bibliography

Caccamise, F., "Artificial Vs. Natural Sign Development: A Response to Rasmus and Allen." **Sign Language Studies,** 63, 127-143, 1989.

Cokely, D., "Sign Language Interpreters: A Demographic Survey." **Sign Language Studies,** 32, 261-286, 1989.

Craig, W., & Craig, H., (eds.), Directory of Services for the Deaf, **American Annals of the Deaf,** 136, 1991.

Dahl. C., & Wilcox, S., "Preparing the Educational Interpreter." **American Annals of the Deaf,** 135, 275-278, 1990.

Frisberg, N., **Interpreting: An Introduction.** Silver Spring, MD: Registry of Interpreters for the Deaf, 1986.

Hayes, P.L., **Educational Interpreters for Deaf Students: Their Responsibilities, Problems, and Concerns.** Dissertation: Abstracts International, 1991.

Maximizing the Independence of Deaf-Blind Teenagers

J.J. Venn; F. Wadler

Abstract: The goal of the Independent Living Project for Deaf/Blind Youth, described here, was to maximize the independence of teenagers who were multiply handicapped due to deafness, blindness, and mental retardation. The teenagers had been overprotected and sheltered in their previous environments. Their educational programs had emphasized one-on-one instruction and direct supervision so that few interaction skills or independent work skills were learned. The project included an independent living apartment in which a unique video monitoring system was used for indirect supervision. Skill areas of home management, personal management, social/emotional skills, work skills, and communication skills were emphasized. The teenagers' autonomy increased over the four and one-half years of the project. They learned many daily living and work skills they would not have learned in a more traditional program.

The Independent Living Project for Deaf/Blind Youth at the Florida School for the Deaf and the Blind in St. Augustine was initially funded by the U.S. Office of Special Education and Rehabilitation Services. The goal of the project was to demonstrate the effectiveness of teaching independent living skills to low-functioning, deaf-blind students. To attain this goal a student environment was established to promote independence.

Previously, the students had been enrolled in traditional deaf-blind education programs that afforded little opportunity for them to develop self-sufficiency and autonomy and to learn neccesary skills ranging from home management to work skills. The students were supervised and monitored by a video camera system within a specially designed apartment. Unobtrusive supervising and monitoring techniques were used outside the apartment. Other techniques included providing choice-making opportunities and employing specialized language and communication methods.

Although some students required more time than others to learn independence in daily living, all the students progressed and some of them made dramatic gains. Many of the skills developed in the project could not have been learned in a more traditional setting.

Deaf/blind students

All the students in the project had multiple primary handicaps. These handicaps included but were not limited to deafness, blindness, and severe to profound mental retardation. The students were nonverbal but understood a few basic signs receptively. However, they did not use sign language spontaneously to communicate. Each student had a unique performance profile of depressed intellectual abilities, minimal communication and decision-making skills, and maladaptive behavior.

In their previous environments the students were rarely without direct supervision and at home they had been sheltered and protected. In addition, the combination of deafness, blindness, and mental retardation affected their ability to learn. The result was almost total dependence on others to initiate, continue, or complete even the skills they had acquired. The deaf/blind education programs in which they had been enrolled included very low teacher-pupil ratios and one-to-one instruction, and thus the students had few opportunities to learn group-interaction skills or independent-work skills. Although the students used many skills in the classroom when given one-to-one instruction, they could not use these skills in other environments.

The project goal was to create an environment for the 11 participating students in which they could make choices, interact without direct supervision, and learn how to be independent. Most of the students participated in Phase I of the project, which emphasized developing independent skills in regular deaf/blind classrooms and dormitories. Graduates of Phase I with the highest levels of independent skills moved into the independent living apartment. Four students, two boys and two girls, 16 years and older, were initially selected for Phase II. The other eight students remained in Phase I the first year of the project.

One of the first steps in preparing students for Phase II was to meet with their parents. The parents were supportive of the project goals but had questions about their children's safety and privacy and the coeducational living conditions. The video system answered the need for safety. Grant funds provided optimal staff supervision at all times. The arrangement of the apartment and the placement of the video cameras promoted privacy and ensured adequate supervision; the potential issue of coeducational living was resolved by preventive counseling with both parents and the staff. A procedure for training students on the importance of bedroom privacy was developed. The boys moved in first and were instructed that the girls' bedroom was off limits. They were taken to the door of the girls' room where they were told in sign language, "No, Don't go in," and "Wrong." These instructions were repeated over time until it was clear that the boys understood. When the girls moved in two weeks later they received the same training. The students cooperated on this and other apartment rules and coeducational living was not a problem.

The independent living apartment

The apartment, barrier free and fully furnished, consisted of an eat-in kitchen, a living room, two bathrooms, and two bedrooms. The apartment, designed for four students, was located in a building separate from the dormitory where other deaf-blind students lived. The location afforded easy access to neighborhood stores, which provided opportunities to develop independent travel skills.

Reactions of students

The students' initial reactions after moving into the apartment were confusion, doubt, and low self-confidence. They were not sure what was expected of them and they did not know how to initiate tasks. At first they stood in doorways or in the kitchen waiting for someone to tell them what to do. They had many of the skills necessary to prepare a meal, to clean a room, or to leave for work, but they didn't know when, where, or how to use these skills. Initially, the students were taken through the daily routines and shown each task they were to complete. During this initial training time, the staff always gave each student the opportunity to initiate a routine before giving a prompt or assistance. If assistance were needed, the least amount of assistance, such as a prompt, was given before more intensive assistance was given. Full assistance was given only when all other methods of instruction failed. Although this process took extra time, the students later demonstrated the desire to do things on their own. After the students were used to the apartment and began developing a concept of independence, their reactions changed from confusion and doubt to confidence, assurance, and a desire for more independence.

The video system

The video system was a key element in attaining the goal of maximum independence. The system included two cameras mounted high on the walls in four of the rooms. They were placed and utilized so that all but the most personal of activities could be observed. These cameras were connected to a bank of eight small monitors to view all the rooms simultaneously. A large monitor allowed the staff to view in detail any activity shown on the smaller monitors. Audio capabilities were included for safety. Also, microphones in the ceilings provided audio support to alert staff to emergencies and such night activities as entering and leaving the apartment. All monitors and speakers were located in an adjacent office area, physically removed from the students' living area, yet close enough to allow for quick access for emergency and instructional intervention.

Staff development and training

Staff development and training began with an introduction to the project in which the goals and philosophy of maximizing independence were explained and discussed. Each staff member was shown how to operate the video system: how to switch cameras between the small monitors and the large monitor, how to

adjust the monitors and the audio, how to videotape, and how to cope with other details of the system. The staff practiced operating the system with the help of the coordinator until they felt comfortable doing it by themselves. The next step in training checked the staff's knowledge of the individual goals and skills of each student. The staff determined the skills of each student by reviewing the individual program objectives and collecting daily progress data. Procedures for indirect and direct supervision were regularly reviewed both formally and informally. However, there was not one set procedure for intervention; specific interventions remained individualized, based upon the student's needs.

After everyone became comfortable with the basic procedures and operation, the audio part of the system proved to be more useful than the video. The staff became attuned to listening for such sounds as the opening and closing of doors. The audio was especially useful for security at night.

Another important training effort involved nonproject staff. This included administrators, teachers, and staff in the community agencies that served the students in the project. The goals of the project were shared with nonproject staff in meetings and through written material. Questions about the project were answered during meetings and in follow-up discussions concerning individual students.

After the students moved into the apartment, staff development and training efforts continued, in part through the efforts of project consultants. The primary consultant visited for at least one day a month. This consultant observed and reviewed project activities on a regular basis, assisted in planning, monitored attainment of goals, and helped write and refine the project curricula. Four other consultants, experts in the deaf-blind field, made one-time yearly visits of two or three days each. These consultants conducted in-service training, observed project activities, and met with parents, staff, and school personnel. The consultants made many helpful recommendations for improving project services.

Instructional procedures

Students were introduced to the daily schedule in the first two weeks of residency. The coordinator, teachers, and paraprofessionals remained in the apartment to prompt and assist until each student

had undertaken all the activities and demonstrated familiarity with the routine. Baseline data on each student's current levels of performance were taken during these two weeks. The data consisted of information about the functional skills of each students and which skills could be used independently. *Independence* was defined as consistently performing a task without prompts. The task had to be performed in more than one situation and with different materials to be considered independent.

The daily schedule

The daily schedule was structured, but flexibility in the schedule allowed for choice making and independence. The schedule was as follows:

6:00–8:00 a.m.— Get up, get dressed, prepare breakfast, eat breakfast, and clean up bedrooms and the kitchen

8:00–12:00 p.m.— Go to work at sites on and off campus (job placements varied for each student)

12:00–1:00 p.m.— Come back to the apartment and have lunch (except for those working off campus)

1:00–3:30 p.m.— Go to class in the deaf–blind department on campus

3:30–5:00 p.m.— Engage in recreational and leisure time activities or go shopping for groceries and other items

5:00–7:00 p.m.— Fix dinner, eat the evening meal, and clean up

7:00–bedtime— Engage in structured and unstructured recreation, leisure, and community activities

Reducing direct supervision

After the baselines were established, direct supervision was gradually reduced during the third week. By the fourth week, interaction between students and staff was reduced to safety intervention and assistance with newly introduced tasks. Indirect supervision with the video camera system largely replaced direct supervision.

In the first stages of the program, extended periods of time were required before the students realized that adult prompts to initiate the next activity were not available. For example, one student waited as long as 30 minutes or more before initiating food preparation at lunchtime. She knew where the food was and had the skills to make a sandwich, but she sat at the dinner table waiting for permission to begin. Finally, the student realized she had to make the decision to cook on her own if she was going to eat. Soon the length of time students spent waiting for prompts decreased as they learned to initiate tasks themselves. Additional skills from each student's repertoire of behavior were introduced as the concept of independence emerged. Once the majority of known skills were at an independent level, new skills were presented.

Vocational training

The goal of maximizing independence through reducing direct supervision and other techniques was carried out in all work activities. Shadowing, fading, and task analysis were some of the techniques utilized. *Shadowing* involved supervising on the job site as unobtrusively as possible. *Fading* involved fading assistance in stages as the worker's skill increased.

A specially developed vocational training guide, *The Systematic Approach to Vocational Education (SAVE)* (Wadler, 1983) was also used. The *SAVE* used a task analytic system to measure progress. Each skill was broken down into small steps and each step was taught individually, making difficult tasks easy to learn. The skill areas on the *SAVE* are basic skills (manipulation, sorting, tool function, tool manipulation, weight, and measurement); preparatory employment skills (packaging, clerical, assembly, and janitorial skills); and employee characteristics and performance (independence, production, and generalization).

Another vocational component established on-campus and off-campus work sites. Job placements included the cafeteria, the laundry, and the community-based workshop, as well as mobile crew work. Students learned to leave for work and walk to the job site or wait for a bus independently. Student reactions to the jobs were enthusiastic.

Transition from school to work

The project centered at a residential school in a small city. The students were from other parts of Florida and returned home for vacations and after graduation. Helping students make the transition from school to their home communities was an important part of the project. The project coordinator was responsible for transition activities, including contact with the students' families, the state adult service agency in the student's home district, and the staff of adult service programs. Contacts were made by telephone calls and correspondence, as well as on-site visits. The parents were partners in the transition and had the opportunity to make suggestions and offer direction at all stages of the process; they were advised on how to arrange for adult services, how to complete paperwork for services, and how to explore program alternatives.

Other transition activities included visiting individual agencies to inquire about programs and placement possibilities. Several visits by the coordinator were usually required and were made with the student's parents. This work was difficult and sometimes frustrating because Florida has long waiting lists for program placements for severely handicapped adults. Agency representatives are overworked and, though usually helpful, are not always available to arrange for specific services. Because of the importance and difficulty of transition, a checklist was developed to keep track of each student. The checklist is presented in Table 1.

Instructional techniques

A variety of instructional techniques were needed to meet the specific needs of the students. Several of the most successful techniques are described here.

Language and communication techniques

Sign language was modified for use with deaf–blind students. Since most students were legally blind but not totally blind, signs were presented directly in their visual field. The number of signs presented and the rate of expression was reduced to meet the level of each student. With some students, only one or two signs at a time, presented slowly, was appropriate. Others could be given more signs at an increased rate. The signs were formed in hands of totally blind students. This was a difficult skill to learn and involved many hours of practice.

Contact signs were also used. Contact signs are modifications of regular signs, which are normally signed with one hand. These one-handed signs are changed so that the hand touches another part of the body such as the forearm. For example, student name signs were all two-handed signs. Contact signs are thought to be more concrete and easier for some students to learn.

Materials and methods for blind students

Since most students had some functional vision, techniques designed for low-vision students were usually employed, including large print and large picture materials. Digital clocks with large numbers were used to teach functional time skills. The minute numerals were covered and the students were taught time by the hour. An 8: on the clock meant it was time to go to work, and a 12: meant it was time to go to lunch. As time skills developed, the other digits were uncovered.

Picture charts and picture cards

Charts, rather than signed or written instruction, were utilized as reminders for initiating, continuing, and completing many tasks. For example, charts with photographs of daily housekeeping chores were posted in various rooms in the apartment. A student's name or picture was then placed next to an assigned chore. Assignments were rotated on a regular basis. These charts reduced direct staff intervention and provided instruc-

Table 1. Transition checklist.

Student's name _____

Date liaison activities were initiated _____

Activity	Date(s)[a]
1. Advise parent/guardian of need to begin referral process to Developmental Services	_____
2. Begin referral after parental approval	_____
3. Visit potential placement sites in the home community	_____
4. Go with the parent to the intake interview	_____
5. Parents notify project staff about date of eligibility evaluation so staff can attend evaluation	_____
6. Parents notify project staff about date of habilitation plan conference so staff can attend	_____
7. Parents and project staff establish a communication system to monitor placement progress and share information	_____
8. Finalize graduation/exit activities	_____
9. Provide technical assistance to agencies after placement	_____
10. Conduct other follow-up activities	_____

[a]Comments, notes, and supporting documentation are enclosed in the attached file.

tions and reminders for each student while encouraging independence. Chart use was taught during the period of introduction to the apartment schedule and activities. Additional charts were added as needed. Several students had to make daily visits to the infirmary to receive eye medication or other medicine and, to remind them, a chart with a single hole punch and an index card was placed in their bedrooms. After each trip to the infirmary, the card was punched by the student to indicate that the appointment had been kept.

Student reaction to the use of picture charts and cards was positive. Having a card that could be held or looked at on the wall next to a picture gave the students a feeling of security and accomplishment. The picture card that the students took with them to the infirmary, which was punched after they were given their medicine, was like having a ticket to a movie or a sporting event. The cards and charts were concrete reinforcers that structured activities.

Role-playing techniques
Role-playing techniques were used to teach students to go through difficult experiences, like going to the dentist successfully. Doctor visits were frightening and difficult because of communication and behavior problems. A method of practicing going to the dentist and the doctor was developed to help the students.

The students practiced mock-visiting the dentist and the doctor on a biweekly basis. The teacher took the students in small groups of two or three to the infirmary and had them wait in the office as they would normally do during a real visit. The students were called into the examining room one by one by the nurse but the teacher or another familiar adult awaited them, dressed in the role of the doctor or the dentist. Students practiced sitting in the dental chair, opening their mouths, using a tongue depressor, getting an injection, etc. Not all these things were practiced in one visit. Each student practiced different things depending on his or her tolerance level. Gradually the students became desensitized to the experience and as a result of this concrete role playing, they successfully transferred and generalized their skills to real office visits.

Interaction with nondeaf-blind peers
Deaf students from the school for the deaf on campus were hired to serve as "buddies." The students were referred to the project by teachers from the school for deaf persons and trained before taking on the buddy role. These buddies interacted with the deaf-blind students in such recreational activities as going to the snack bar, playing outside, and relaxing.

Anticipating problems
The staff tried to anticipate problems before they occurred so that they could intervene appropriately. This method was especially important when dealing with misbehavior. The staff learned to watch for signs of impending misbehavior, such as refusal to leave the apartment and to go to school or work (a problem demonstrated by one particular student). In situations such as cooking, supervision was intensified to prevent accidents. Since the students were nonverbal, the signs of impending trouble were not based on verbal language cues but rather on more subtle nonverbal cues such as body language, facial expressions, and nonverbal vocalizations.

Measuring student progress
Before moving into the independent living apartment, each student was evaluated. The *Systematic Approach to Independent Living Skills (SAILS)* (Venn & Wadler, 1985) was used to determine present levels of functioning, intervention priorities, and student progress. The skill areas and some of the specific skills included in the *SAILS* are listed in Table 2. The progress of four of the students (Table 3 and Figures

Table 2. Skill areas included in the *Systematic Approach to Independent Living Skills (SAILS)* Curriculum Guide.

Skill area	Specific skills
Home management	Housekeeping, food preparation, grocery shopping, clothing care, home maintenance, home security, laundry, dishwashing
Personal management	Eating, cooking, general health care, hygiene, grooming, dressing, toileting
Social/emotional skills	Self-awareness, maturity, interpersonal awareness, interaction, initiation, cooperation, leisure time, human sexuality
Work skills	Workshop skills, employability skills, work behaviors
Functional academics	Perception, cognition, money concepts, time concepts, number concepts, measurement skills
Communication	Receptive communication, expressive communication, sign language

Table 3. Progress of four of the students in learning independent skills in percentage of skills mastered.

Percentage of skills mastered[a]:	Pretest	Posttest	Improvement
Home management			
Mary Beth	05	47	42
George	02	38	36
Rhunetta	02	21	19
Royale	03	37	34
Personal Management			
Mary Beth	21	57	36
George	22	48	26
Rhunetta	26	40	14
Royale	28	49	31
Social skills			
Mary Beth	12	15	03
George	17	17	03
Rhunetta	21	20	− 01
Royale	21	38	17
Work skills			
Mary Beth	31	55	24
George	47	61	14
Rhunetta	14	22	08
Royale	55	65	10
Academic skills			
Mary Beth	06	06	00
George	03	03	00
Rhunetta	06	06	00
Royale	03	05	02

[a]The percentage of skills mastered is the number of skills performed at the independent level divided by the total number of skills in each area of the project curriculum guide (SAILS).

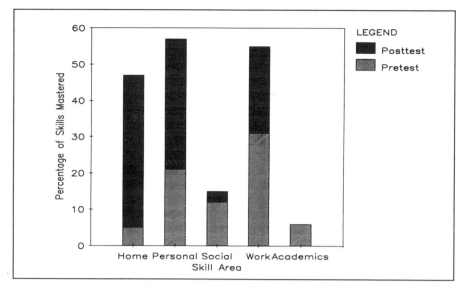

Figure 1. Independent skills mastered by Mary Beth.

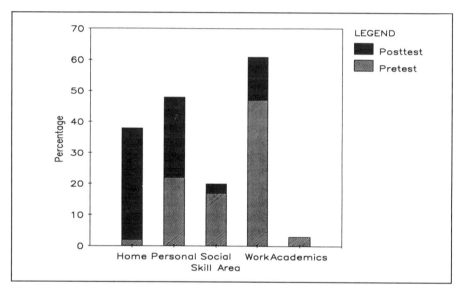

Figure 2. Independent skills mastered by George.

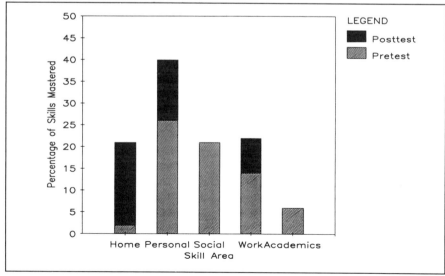

Figure 3. Independent skills mastered by Rhunetta.

1 through 4) is shown in five of the areas measured by the *SAILS:* home management, personal management, social–emotional skills, work skills, and functional academics.

The daily instructional procedure involved collecting progress data on the level at which target skills were being performed. Target skills were individualized based upon the needs, interests, and skill levels of each student. The *SAILS* system included a procedure for identifying intervention priorities for each student and translating those priorities into short- and long-term objectives in the Individual Educational Plan (IEP) and into daily lessons.

Daily student progress data were collected for all the targeted skill areas using the *SAILS*, and individual programs were reviewed and updated every nine weeks. The percentage of independent skills was determined by dividing the number of items passed at an independent level in an area by the total number of items in that area. The pretest percentages were obtained just before the students moved into the apartment. The posttest percentages show the progress made after two years in the apartment. These four students were selected because they were the first students to move into the apartment. Progress data in the area of communication skills are not reported because the communication section was added to the curriculum after the original baseline data were collected.

Meaningful progress was seen in three areas: home management, personal management, and work skills. Little progress was made in social–emotional skills and functional academics. Overall, the largest gains were in home management. The students may have progressed more rapidly in this area due to their experiences in the independent living apartment. However, the extent to which conclusions can be drawn is limited due to the small sample size and the constraints of program evaluation data.

Summary

The project, which lasted four and one-half years, ended in 1987. Many of the project activities have been continued and expanded as part of the regular deaf-blind program at the school. Project acitivies have also been used with other multiply handicapped students at the school.

A total of 11 students participated in the project. Eight of them lived in the apartment at various times. Three of the

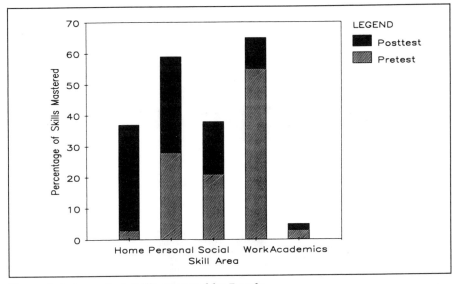

Figure 4. Independent skills mastered by Royale.

students are still enrolled in school, but the others have graduated. Of the eight students who graduated, two have not yet been placed in any type of program or job. The other six young adults are working in the following settings: two in work activities centers, three in a mobile work crew, and one in a competitive job in the community. The members of the mobile crew and the person in competitive employment are receiving assistance from job coaches as part of supported employment programs. In terms of residential services, four of those who graduated are living in group homes in the community. The other four are living at home and are on waiting lists for residential programs.

The results of this project show the effectiveness of maximizing the independence of deaf-blind teenagers. Although some students required more time than others to learn independence in daily living, all the students progressed and some made dramatic gains. Many of the skills developed in the independent living project could not have been learned

in a more traditional setting. These results are consistent with the conclusions of others (Pumpian, West, & Shepard, 1988; Snell & Browder, 1987; Thurman, Meddock, & DuCetti, 1985) and demonstrate the positive effects of environmental modification on the behavior of persons with severe handicaps.

The classic method of teaching deaf-blind persons relies almost exclusively on one-to-one instruction and teaches dependence rather than independence. New methods like video monitoring need to be developed to provide more opportunities for students to learn independence and self-initiation. The methodology of teaching independent living is currently being developed (Budde & Bachelder, 1987). These skills are particularly important for students as they make the transition from school to adult life (Knowlton & Clark, 1987). This project demonstrated how less restrictive educational programs can help deaf-blind students prepare for this transition by learning to be independent.

References

Budde, J.F. & Bachelder, J.L. (1987). Independent living: The concept, model, and methodology. *The Journal of the Association for Persons with Severe Handicaps,* **11**, 240–245.

Knowlton, H. & Clark, G. (1987). Transition issues for the 1990s. *Exceptional Children,* **53**, 562–563.

Pumpian, I., West, E., & Shepard, H. (1988). Vocational education of persons with severe handicaps. In R. Gaylord-Ross (ed.). *Vocational education of persons with handicaps.* Mountain View, CA: Mayfield Publishing Company.

Snell, M.E. & Browder, D.M. (1987). Domestic and community skills. In M.E. Snell (ed.). *Systematic instruction of persons with severe handicaps (3rd Ed.).* Columbus, OH: Charles E. Merrill Publishing Company.

Thurman, K., Meddock, T., & DuCetti, J. (1985). Effects of environmental modification on the behavior of persons with severe handicaps. *The Journal of the Association for Persons with Severe Handicaps,* **10**, 157–163.

Venn, J. & Wadler, F. (1985). *Systematic approach to independent living skills (SAILS).* St. Augustine, FL: The Florida School for the Deaf and the Blind.

Wadler, F. (1983). *Systematic approach to vocational education (SAVE).* St. Augustine, FL: The Florida School for the Deaf and the Blind.

John J. Venn, Ph.D., program director and associate professor, Special Education, College of Education and Human Services, University of North Florida, 4567 St. Johns Bluff Road, South, Jacksonville, FL 32216 and primary consultant for Independent Living Project for Deaf/Blind Teenagers. Frank Wadler, M.A., director of the Transition Project for Deaf/Blind Students, Florida School for the Deaf and Blind, P.O. Box 1209, St. Augustine, Florida, and coordinator of the Independent Living Project for Deaf/Blind Teenagers.

A Local Team Approach

Jane M. Everson

Transition team meeting to discuss postsecondary options.

Transition. Throughout much of the 1980s this word has spurred numerous federal- and state-initiated projects, journal articles, conferences, "how to" manuals, and state legislative mandates. Along the way there has also been a great deal of discussion, resistance, and accusation among educators, school administrators, and adult service providers. Documented unemployment rates of 50% to 75% for postsecondary youth with disabilities (e.g., Hasazi, Gordon, & Roe, 1985) have been met with cries of "It's not my role to find jobs for students!" and "They aren't ready for work when they leave

the public school system!" Suggestions for individualized transition plan (ITP) development (e.g., Wehman, Moon, Everson, Wood, & Barcus, 1988) have been met with similar cries—"It's just more paperwork!"

As we enter the 1990s, frustrated local professionals such as special and vocational educators, vocational rehabilitation counselors, case managers, adult service providers, and parents have begun to isolate common issues that frequently serve as barriers to transition implementation (DeStefano, 1989). In a recent interagency transition training

workshop provided to 13 localities across the state of Virginia (Everson, Wehman, & Bass, 1989), seven issues emerged as needing priority attention: lack of transportation; lack of funds; lack of parent participation; lack of employment opportunities; lack of accurate data; lack of postsecondary education opportunities; and lack of residential services. The issues identified by these 13 localities are not surprising. In fact, they mirror issues that are consistently identified in professional literature, state reports, and teachers' lounge discussions. What *is* surprising is that they are not exclusive to transition practices. Instead, they are general human service issues that describe transition programs, supported employment programs, vocational education programs, vocational rehabilitation programs, and so on.

The Team Approach

As we enter the 1990s, we are increasingly beginning to define transition as "an interagency planning and implementation process that takes place at the local level and that makes available new residential and employment opportunities for youth with disabilities" (Wehman et al., 1988, p. 50). This type of definition focuses our attention away from interagency and interdisciplinary territorial issues and toward cooperative and rational program planning efforts to address these issues (Everson & Moon, 1990).

Interagency and interdisciplinary team planning is not a new concept in human services. It has been discussed at length elsewhere in the literature (e.g., Bellamy, Rhodes, Mank, & Albin, 1988; Elder & Magrab, 1980; Everson & Moon, 1990; Wehman et al., 1988). Until recently, however, team transition planning has been more discussed than implemented. Recently, numerous localities have begun to tackle transition issues using a local interagency team approach. Minnesota, for example, has enacted state legislation mandating the development of local transition planning teams, and Virginia, Louisiana, and New York have funded several projects to train local teams in planning transition efforts. Local transition planning can and is working in these localities because of interagency and interdisciplinary team planning.

Roles of Professionals and Parents

The key to successful transition planning and implementation is participation by *all* key personnel and parents. "Why should I be involved?" and "What is my role?" are two legitimate concerns of local professionals and parents. Although the final answers vary from locality to locality and must ultimately be decided by teams in the individual localities, suggested roles of professionals, parents and students follow:

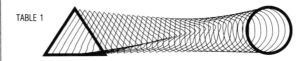

TABLE 1

Using a Local Team Approach to Cooperatively Plan and Implement Transition Practices

1. Generate team definition of transition for the locality.
2. Establish long-term goal for team to implement definition.
3. Brainstorm local needs or issues.
4. Prioritize three to four local needs or issues.
5. Brainstorm resources for each need or issue.
6. Rewrite each need or issue as an objective.
7. Rewrite resources as activities for each objective.
8. Assign timelines and team members responsible for each activity.

Special Education

- Prepare students for adult opportunities by providing functional and community-relevant curricula.
- Provide comprehensive assessment information.
- Conduct local follow-up studies of graduates.
- Initiate transition planning by coordinating and organizing ITP formats and schedules.
- Ensure involvement of key agencies, disciplines, students, and parents.
- Coordinate implementation and evaluation of ITP's.
- Participate in local interagency planning efforts.

Vocational Rehabilitation

- Consult with ITP teams and attend ITP meetings as requested.
- Assist with job placement and training, referrals, vocational assessment, and other postsecondary services for students.
- Participate in local interagency planning efforts.

Vocational Education

- Provide occupational preparation and specific skill instruction for students.
- Conduct vocational assessments.
- Assist with job placement, job instruction, and follow-along referrals.
- Participate in local interagency planning efforts.

Parents/Students

- Attend ITP meetings and voice concerns and preferences in order to focus the team's planning.

- Advocate for desired outcomes and services.
- Participate in local interagency planning efforts.

Addressing Local Needs

The seven issues identified by the 13 local teams in Virginia and the issues described by Moon and Diambra, Hill, and Getzel in this Special Focus section all can be addressed by interagency team planning. Use of a local team approach to cooperatively address pressing local transition issues has been described in detail elsewhere (e.g., Everson & Moon, 1990; Wehman et al., 1988) and is summarized in Table 1.

This approach was used with the Virginia localities. Three of the most common issues they generated can serve as examples of local team planning here.

Lack of Transportation

Lack of transportation options is a real concern in many localities. Both rural localities with no public transportation options and urban localities with limited routes and inaccessible vehicles face tremendous barriers to transition planning. Lack of transportation is often voiced as a reason for not implementing community-based instructional programs and for not making job placements. During the resource brainstorming step outlined below, the 13 Virginia teams identified 10 potential transportation resources that might be used for community-based instruction and job placement.

1. School buses.
2. County vehicles.
3. Car dealer leases at "fleet prices."

4. U.S. Department of Transportation UMPTA funds.
5. Plans for Achieving Self-Sufficiency (PASS).
6. Carpools.
7. Volunteers.
8. "Fee for services" contracts with community providers.
9. Social Security Impairment Related Work Expenses (IRWE).
10. Contracts with taxi companies.

The resources generated by these teams reflect individual team members' experiences, knowledge, and creativity. Any one individual working alone would have had a difficult time generating all of these resources, but working as a team enhanced the number and quality of potential resources for addressing transportation issues.

Choosing from these 10 resources, several teams were able to write objectives and identify activities and timelines for addressing local transportation needs.

Lack of Funding

Unlike transportation facilities, funding opportunities often do exist in a locality, but individual team members may be frustrated in their attempts to secure new monies or access existing monies. Using the process described in Table 1, the 13 Virginia teams identified potential funding resources that might be used for funding new and expanded programs.
1. Plans for Achieving Self-Sufficiency (PASS).
2. Small Business Administration (SBA).
3. Private foundations.
4. United Way.
5. Churches.
6. Carl D. Perkins Vocational Education funds.
7. Job Training Partnership Act (JTPA) funds.
8. Federal/state RFP's from education, developmental disabilities, or vocational rehabilitation.
9. "Fee for services" agreements with business.
10. Interagency funding coalitions.

The 10 potential resources included resources for new program start-up and existing program expansion as well as opportunities for reallocating monies already available in the localities. From this list of resources, several teams were able to write objectives and identify activities and timelines for addressing funding issues.

Lack of Parent Participation

Although most professionals, parent resource centers, and "how to" manuals encourage and emphasize parent involvement in transition planning, the amount and quality of participation are still frequently frustrating, both to parents and professionals. One Virginia locality used the process described in Table 1 to turn the need to overcome a lack of parent participation into a manageable objective for the upcoming school year.

Objective: To increase parent participation in the school vocational training, transition planning, and supported employment programs during the 1989–1990 school year, the local team will target a group of parents for team planning and training.

Activities to Achieve Objective:
1. Identify a parent or parents to participate as a member of the local team.
2. Survey parents' needs, desires, and expectations.
3. Provide a series of parent information workshops on current and future programs.
4. Organize a parent support group.
5. Encourage parent representation in local advocacy groups.
6. Develop a parent networking system (e.g., newsletter, parent-to-parent program).
7. Define roles parents may play in providing job development and transportation assistance.
8. Define roles for parents to play in ITP meetings.

The eight activities identified by this team, when completed with timelines and responsible personnel, will enable the team to reduce their frustration at lack of parent participation by taking an active team approach to addressing the issue.

Conclusion

Transition planning for the 1990s has evolved from simple suggestions for ITP development and student follow-up studies to complex suggestions for long-range local program planning. Viewed in this way, transition planning is not the sole responsibility of one agency or discipline. Instead, comprehensive transition planning requires a commitment from key education and adult service representatives at a local level to problem-solve and address local issues. The resources and strategies suggested in this article are not intended to solve every lo-

cality's transition planning problems. Instead, they are presented as examples of the creativity, resources, and commitment that can be generated when local professionals and parents engage in a cooperative and rational problem-solving approach. The resources listed here and in the other articles in this Special Focus section are suggested to help local professionals and parents begin the process.

Resources

Bellamy, G. T., Rhodes, L. W., Mank, D. M., & Albin, J. M. (1988). *Supported employment. A community implementation guide.* Baltimore: Paul H. Brookes Publishing Co.

DeStefano, L. (1989). Facilitating the transition from school to adult life for youth with disabilities. In W. E. Kiernan & R. L. Schalock (Eds.), *Economics, industry and disability: A look ahead* (pp. 162–177). Baltimore: Paul H. Brookes Publishing Co.

Elder, J. O., & Magrab, P. R. (1980). *Coordinating services to handicapped children. A handbook for interagency collaboration.* Baltimore: Paul H. Brookes Publishing Co.

Everson, J. M., & Moon, M. S. (1987). Professional and parent roles and responsibilities in the transition process. *Journal of the Association for Persons with Severe Handicaps, 12*, 87–95.

Everson, J. M., & Moon, M. S. (1990). Developing community program planning and service delivery teams. In F. Rusch (Ed.), *Supported employment: Models, methods, and issues* (pp. 381–394). Sycamore, IL: Sycamore Publishing Co.

Everson, J. M., Wehman, P., & Bass, T. (1989). *Final report on inservice training workshop for local interagency teams in Virginia.* Unpublished report. Richmond, VA: Virginia Commonwealth University, Rehabilitation Research Training Center and Virginia Department of Rehabilitative Services.

Hasazi, S. B., Gordon, L. R., & Roe, C. A. (1985). Factors associated with the employment status of handicapped youth exiting high school from 1979–1983. *Exceptional Children, 51*(6), 455–469.

La Mar, K., & Rosenberg, B. (1988). *Synthesis of individual transition plans: Format and process.* Sacramento: Education Transition Center, Resources in Special Education. (Available for purchase $20.00: Resources in Special Education, 650 University Avenue, Room 201, Sacramento, CA, 95825.)

Wehman, P., Moon, M. S., Everson, J. M., Wood, W., T. & Barcus, J. M. (1988). *Transition from school to work. New challenges for youth with severe disabilities.* Baltimore: Paul H. Brookes Publishing Co.

Jane M. Everson (CEC Chapter #248) is Project Director, Technical Assistance Center (TAC), Helen Keller National Center (HKNC), Sands Point, NY.

Supported Employment for Persons with Deaf-Blindness and Mental Retardation

S.L. Griffin; J. Lowry

Abstract: This article distinguished particular members of the deaf-blind population as needing additional support to secure and maintain employment. Supported employment is examined and offered as an appropriate vehicle for providing this needed support. The currently held models of supported employment are described in detail as they pertain to this population, and the individual placement model is highlighted as perhaps the best choice for many persons with deaf-blindness. Finally, issues surrounding supported employment are provided and examined to raise questions for further exploration.

Although the unemployment rate in the United States is decreasing, most disabled Americans are not benefiting from this labor market expansion; approximately two-thirds of all disabled Americans between the ages of 16 and 64 are not working (Harris & Associates, 1986). Of the one-third of disabled Americans who are working, 25 percent hold full-time jobs, whereas 10 percent hold half-time jobs.

These figures are even more sobering when one considers the severely disabled segment of the disabled working population. From 50 to 75 percent of this population is unemployed (United States Commission on Civil Rights, 1983). For individuals who are considered to be employed, many are earning only a fraction of what their nondisabled peers earn. For mentally retarded persons with deaf-blindness, an estimated 20,000+ population, there are few employment opportunities, and these are low in quality.

For persons whose disability is not considered to be severe, the type of employment that they might pursue is limited only by the type and amount of supports that would allow them to work. For persons whose disability is considered to be severe, employment options are far

The development of this article was supported in part by a Cooperative Agreement #H133B80052 from the National Institute on Disability and Rehabilitation Research. The opinions expressed in this article are solely those of the authors, and no official endorsement by NIDRR or OSERS should be inferred.

more limited. Entry level jobs such as clerical and service positions are typical for individuals fortunate enough to find work (Harris & Associates, 1986). As a matter of fact, Johnston and Packer (1987) of the Hudson Institute indicate that the twenty-first century will see employment growth only within the service industry, but it is expected that these new service positions will be technologically advanced and require high skill levels. For individuals who are less fortunate and who do not find employment through conventional means or through some form of supported employment, segregated working environments, such as sheltered workshops or work activity centers, may be provided. Of the approximately 100,000 individuals in these services, 60,000 earn wages; however, these wages average $1.00 per day (Jackson & Associates, 1985).

Sheltered services, such as those mentioned above, are limited in their ability to provide the least restrictive environment for severely disabled persons. However, most such individuals are not able to secure employment through conventional methods. There is an obvious gap between securing employment with little or no assistance and securing employment through a non-community–based service. Supported employment programs, which provide whatever supports are necessary for a severely disabled individual to secure and retain employment, offer a closure to this gap in support provision.

The purpose of this article is to determine which members of the deaf-blind population need additional support to secure and retain employment; to offer supported employment as an appropriate vehicle for this support; to review the supported employment models and practices in terms of serving this population; and finally, to raise additional issues for further exploration.

The concept of supported employment

Definition

Supported employment is defined as "competitive work in an integrated work setting with an ongoing support service for individuals with severe handicaps for whom competitive employment (1) has not traditionally occurred or (2) has been interrupted or intermittent as a result of severe handicap; or (3) traditional employment for individuals with chronic mental illness." (*Federal Register*, 1987). The term *work* as used in this definition refers to employment in a community setting in which the individual has contact with nondisabled peers who are not paid caregivers. The individual must work at least 20 hours a week (averaged during pay periods) and must earn commensurate wages.

Up to this point in examining the definitions, we could extrapolate the quality characteristics of an individual placement made through traditional time-limited placement services as well as those made through supported employment. Supported employment, however, differs from traditional placement services in that it offers daily support through a variety of avenues beyond the time limits of traditional vocational rehabilitation placements. Supported employment provides ongoing support services at least twice monthly to the working individual for as long as that individual wishes to work (*Federal Register,* 1987).

Persons who can benefit from supported employment

Because of the nature of the ongoing assessment and advocacy seen in supported employment, such a program can be too restrictive for some individuals. Therefore, some individuals with a disability may not be good candidates for supported employment. Vocational rehabilitation, however, has traditionally included many disabilities in its category, *severe disability*. The newest regulations indicate that supported employment may be the appropriate option for persons who have disabling conditions that range from severe physical disabilities, such as cerebral palsy and paraplegia, to mental disabilities that range from a learning disability to severe or profound mental retardation (Federal Register, 1987). The federal guidelines also state that the determination of a severe disability may also be a result of a combination of the 27 + categories of handicapping conditions. Included within this definition are the disabilities of deafness and blindness.

Severe handicaps is newly defined as meaning a handicapped individual (1) "who has a severe physical or mental disability that seriously limits one or more functional capacities (mobility, communication, self-care, self-direction, interpersonal skills, work tolerance, or work skills) in terms of employability; (2) whose vocational rehabilitation can be expected to require multiple vocational rehabilitation services over an extended period of time; and (3) who has one or more physical or mental disabilities. . ." (Federal Register, 1987).

Persons with deaf-blindness as an appropriate population
Lockett and Rudolph (1980) have stated that perhaps the foremost misconception about individuals who are considered deaf-blind concerns Helen Keller as an appropriate symbol of emotional, social, and vocational accomplishments. The misconception is that, given proper services, *all* individuals can approximate Helen Keller's achievements. In fact, as the result of the rubella epidemic of the early 1960s, approximately two-thirds of this deaf-blind population are believed to have "middle trainable" to "educable" mental retardation (Lockett & Rudolph, 1980).

When one considers what experts, such as Robert J. Smithdas and Myra Taff-Watson, in the field of deaf-blindness have written in terms of the severity of the disability of deaf-blindness, it would be difficult to consider many individuals who are deaf-blind as not suited for some form of supported employment services. Smithdas has often written of the isolation and loneliness that inviduals with deaf-blindness feel because of their difficulties with communication and mobility (Smithdas, 1980).

The second misconception is that all persons who are considered to be deaf-blind and mentally retarded can gain employment through typical vocational rehabilitation services, such as work adjustment, counseling, and competitive

placement. One estimate indicates that 95 percent of the rubella deaf-blind individuals will have special needs that cannot be addressed through current traditional rehabilitation methods (Lockett & Rudolph, 1980). Supported employment, through concerted efforts of several community agencies, may be a cost-effective employment solution for many deaf-blind individuals. Since each case is different, the type and degree of support necessary through supported employment will vary. The remainder of this article will focus on the current popular services delivery models as well as the components common to all the models. The individual placement model will be further examined as one of the least restrictive options available.

Supported employment service delivery models
The extent and type of support given to the individual worker depends, in part, on the type of model considered. Currently, four types of supported employment are nationally recognized as models (Rhodes & Valenta, 1985; Mank, Rhodes, & Bellamy, 1986; Wehman, 1981). These models are the individual placement model (or supported competitive employment), the enclave in industry model, the mobile work crew model, and the small business or entrepreneurial model.

The individual placement model is the only model in which one individual is typically placed in a particular job site. The enclave, mobile crew, and small business models are all group options that allow for up to eight individuals to be placed in the same setting.

The small business approach
The small business approach to supported employment can serve up to eight disabled individuals, as well as workers without handicapping conditions, in a community-based business establishment that is operated by a human services provider or a private entrepreneur. The business may be a prime manufacturer of goods or may do subcontract work for a prime manufacturer. The most widely recognized small business venture of this kind is the benchwork model, which was first organized by the Specialized Training Program. This business is a subcontract group that specializes in small electronics assembly (RRTC, STP Newsletter, 1985). The small business model is particularly effective in providing employment and intensive training to the most severely disabled persons who traditionally would

not be accepted even into a sheltered workshop because of their low productivity and inappropriate social skills (Moon & Griffin, 1988). This model is also effective for persons who have limited self-care skills.

Workers employed within this option are typically paid piece-rate wages, based on their productivity. Wages paid will vary by the type and number of contracts and the efficiency of training. Prospective implementors of supported employment through this option will need to address two questions: (1) Is this most restrictive model really necessary for the individuals who need service? and (2) Will the community be able to support a new small business in whatever industry is chosen (Moon & Griffin, 1988). In either instance, the business must have two goals: 1) to make money and 2) to provide employment and training for individuals with severe disabilities.

The mobile crew approach
The mobile crew approach to supported employment can also serve up to eight individuals. As with typical crews that predominantly employ nondisabled workers, this model proposes that the business operate out of a van and hold several contracts. Typical trades for a mobile crew include lawn maintenance, janitorial work, farm work, and landscaping. Mobile crews can also prosper within a rural area, where transportation is scarce and work exists outside of an industrial setting for those individuals who can travel to the place where the work is (Mank et al., 1986).

A crew can operate out of a not-for-profit human services agency or it can operate out of a small business. As with the small business approach, service providers utilizing this model operate both to make money and to provide employment for persons with severe disabilities. Also like the small business approach, mobile crews may, and are encouraged to, also employ nondisabled workers.

This approach can be utilized for persons with varying degrees of disability. However, since most of the work requires fair mobility and strength, this option may not be open to individuals who are lacking in these areas. The mobile crew option can effect more integration than the small business approach because the crew can travel about the community. However, integration in this, or any model, will vary by type of work. Many professionals who learn about the mobile crew option of supported employment say, "This isn't anything new!" They are correct; the mobile crew approach has been around for a long time, but over the years, the concept has become more formalized to achieve integrated work in a community setting.

The enclave in industry approach
The enclave in industry approach differs from the mobile crew approach and the small business approach in that only one contract is pursued per group of disabled workers. A group of up to eight severely disabled individuals are matched to a job or a set of jobs within one company. The service provider, along with the company representative, may determine how payment will be made to the enclave employee. The company may choose to put each worker on the payroll or the service provider may choose to contract with the company for wages.

The enclave concept originated from the Specialized Training Program in Oregon with an enclave known as Trillum at Physio Control (Rhodes & Valenta, 1985). Many professionals within the field of supported employment consider the enclave approach to be a suitable alternative for more severely disabled individuals who require more supervision than individual placements can offer (Moon & Griffin, 1988). The opportunity for integration exists either within the actual work station or within the context of breaks, lunch, and travel arrangements.

The individual placement model
The individual placement model (also known as supported competitive employment and the supported work model) differs from the previously described models in that typically only one individual is placed at an employment site (Wehman & Kregel, 1985; Wehman, 1981). One potential worker is matched with a position and supports are provided to ensure that the worker can retain his or her job. It is assumed that, over time, the type and amount of assistance or supports can be reduced to allow the individual the maximum amount of freedom within his or her position, yet follow-along support is a permanent feature (Moon & Griffin, 1988).

This model has five primary components, as do the other models discussed. The components include:
- Job development
- Consumer assessment
- Job placement
- Job-site training
- Ongoing assessment and follow-along

These key components will be further discussed within the context of serving individuals with deaf-blindness and mental retardation in the next section.

Summary of service delivery models
The four options described within this section are well-researched models. However, depending upon the community, the economic environment, the demand, and especially the individuals being served, these models will vary from program to program, although certain factors within each model must always be met. These factors are summarized in Table 1.

The individual placement model for persons with deaf-blindness and mental retardation
This model utilizes the services of an employment specialist (a job coach or a job trainer). This individual systematically places and trains a worker in a community job and provides as much support through follow-along as necessary (Griffin & Moon, 1988; Mank et al., 1986; Wehman, 1981; Wehman & Kregel, 1985; Moon, Goodall, Barcus, & Brooke, 1985).

The phases of the individual placement model, mentioned above, are delineated below, with particular emphasis on the role of the employment specialist and application to the worker.

Job development
Job development and worker assessment are typically done simultaneously to ensure an appropriate match between the potential worker's abilities, interest, aptitudes, and transportation needs and the employer's needs and requirements (Moon et al., 1986). This process begins when the employment specialist surveys the community to determine the labor market.

Once an interested employer is identified, the employment specialist sets up an interview to provide the employer with more information and to examine the company and the job more carefully. Once a specific job has been identified, the employment specialist conducts a job analysis of the work environment. It is critical that the job is analyzed adequately to better ensure that the employee keeps the job, once he or she is employed.

An employment specialist wishing to place an individual with deaf-blindness and mental retardation will want to pay particular attention to the types of transportation available to get to the job site; the environment in terms of mobility from work station to work station; the potential for creating an effective communication system within the workplace (e. g., the cues available to assist the individual in moving from task to task); and finally, the employer's willingness to mesh his or her communication system with that of the new worker. These details can be discovered through assessing employee turnover, talking with workers on the job, examining the work environment, and observing the work being done. This type of job development can be time-consuming, but the time is well spent when the critical elements for job retention are accurately determined.

Worker assessment
Job development must occur simultaneously with worker assessment. Assessment performed through (1) studying employee records, (2) gathering information through interviews, and (3) obtaining behavioral assessment information, should provide enough quality information to assist the employment specialist in making a good job/worker match

---

Table 1. Key features of supported employment.*

1. *Employment:* The primary focus of supported employment programs is to provide employment for persons with severe disabilities. Employment is considered to consist of regular wages, regular working conditions, and job security.

2. *Ongoing Support:* The focus of supported employment programs is to provide support necessary for an individual to obtain and retain a job, rather than to assist him or her to obtain a job, only.

3. *Jobs Rather Than Services:* The emphasis on these programs is to concentrate on creating work opportunities rather than to provide skills training services, only.

4. *Full Participation:* No individual who is considered severely disabled is excluded as a candidate for supported employment. Ongoing support will be adjusted on an individual basis so that all persons can participate.

5. *Social Integration:* Contact and relationships are encouraged through supported employment with peers who are *not* paid caregivers. Integration can occur through work interactions, during breaks and lunch, or through participation in nonwork activities.

6. *Variety and Flexibility:* Supported employment makes possible programs to provide varying degrees of employment options for their customers.

*Adapted from the RRTC/STP Newsletter on Supported Employment, Vol. 2, No. 2, 1986.

(Moon et al., 1986). By the time the mentally retarded individual with deaf-blindness is old enough to work, he or she has accumulated many formal records. Typical records include recent medical and physiological test results, school records that include attendance and interest information, vocational aptitude test results and/or skill performance charts, and finally, evaluations from past employers, if available.

In addition to examining formal records, the employment specialist will want to talk to key persons in the prospective worker's life: his or her parents, teachers, vocational training personnel, and past employers, if any. The information gathered through these interviews, as well as data gathered from observing the individual work (if possible), should allow the employment specialist to examine the critical skills that the individual has to offer. Information gathered through this type of process can be effectively recorded in a similar fashion as is the information obtained concerning potential employment positions (Barcus, Brooke, Inge, Moon, & Goodall, 1987). Critical questions such as what areas of town the individual has transportation access to; what amount of vision or hearing the individual has; how many tasks can the individual perform in sequence; what types of cues and reinforcement does the individual respond well to; and how much family support does the individual have concerning getting a job must be addressed before placement can occur (Moon et al., 1986).

Job placement
Job placement can proceed when the information concerning an individual's abilities matches the information concerning a potential job opening. This matching process has been referred to as the job/worker compatibility analysis (Moon et al., 1986). Typically, a match must occur on such issues as: Does the individual have transportation to and from the job site? Are the working hours agreeable to both the individual and his or her family? Will the employer/coworkers be comfortable with the communication process the individual uses? Are the job tasks challenging, yet not beyond the individual's potential capabilities?

Once the employment specialist and the individual have agreed upon a particular job, the future employee and employer will be introduced, and the individual will go through a formal job

Table 2. Communication methods.*

For use with deaf persons	For use with blind persons	For use with deaf-blind persons
Manual alphabet	Braille	Tell-A-Touch machine
Finger-spelling	Low-vision aids	Telebraille
Sign language	Braille time-telling devices	Large print telecommunication devices for the deaf
Gestures	Residual speech/hearing	Perkins Brailler

*Adapted from Yarnell, 1976; Nelipovich & Naegele, 1985; Smithdas, 1980.

interview. The employment specialist plays an active role in this interview process, both to assist the prospective employee and to model appropriate ways for the individual to interact with the employer (Moon & Griffin, 1988). Once the individual is hired, the employment specialist coordinates transportation, social security, and other ancillary services prior to first-day activities.

Job-site training
Job-site training involves direct systematic instruction of tasks to be done and such related skills as communication, transportation, work-appropriate behavior, and appropriate down-time behavior (Moon et al., 1986; Moon & Griffin, 1988). Critical to job-site training with this population will be the establishment of a communication system and the development of a cueing system. Nelipovich and Naegele (1985) stress the need for the trainer to be skilled in the communication system the worker is comfortable with, otherwise substantial training in work or social skills cannot occur. Table 2 cites communication methods the employment specialist may need.

Once the worker has acquired 100 percent of the critical skills of the task analysis and most of the noncritical skills, the employment specialist can formally begin to decrease his or her assistance. Typically, assistance has been slowly decreasing very early on in the placement. Building coworker advocates and transferring supervision to the employer are useful methods of such "fading."

Barcus et al. (1987) have identified three phases of job-site training: (1) job orientation and assessment, which typically last two to four weeks; (2) initial training and skill acquisition, which may last four to eight weeks; and (3) stabilization and fading, which typically last two to four weeks. The amount of time the employment specialist stays at the job site will vary with the severity of the worker's disability and the complexity of the job.

Ongoing assessment and follow-along
Perhaps the most important differen-

tiating feature between traditional sheltered placement and supported employment is the long-term, follow-along component. Supported employment can offer support to the individual on a twice-monthly basis for as long as the individual retains his or her job. Additionally, Nelipovich and Naegele (1985) strongly suggest that this population will require more intensive and more frequent follow-up than current traditional placement services can provide. The employment specialist/worker/employer relationship of continuous assessment of the worker's performance, transportation needs, and support and social needs, in terms of the employer's needs, is perhaps the most important reason for the high retention rate for workers involved in supported employment.

Issues surrounding supported employment for persons who are deaf-blind, and mentally retarded

Employment specialist competencies
Throughout this article, the importance of communication in placing the mentally retarded individual with deaf-blindness has been stressed. With supported employment, the employment specialist is perhaps the key to the success of the models. Competency areas for effective employment specialists who work with these persons can be divided into three categories (1) communication skills, (2) general knowledge, and (3) technical skills, relative to deaf-blindness. Because deaf-blindness is such a devastating disability, persons working with this population must be cognizant of special communication needs and adaptive aids and devices and have an overall understanding of the effects this disability can have on a person's life.

An employment specialist who works primarily with this population must be more than competent in the communication methods. Nelipovich and Naegele (1985) have indicated that without effective communication throughout the rehabilitation process, the individual might feel defeated and segregated and become over-dependent on significant others.

The employment specialist must also be knowledgeable in most areas of deaf-blindness. Since many of the individuals who would be good candidates for supported employment are deaf-blind due to rubella and have many medical problems, the employment specialist should have information in the areas of sight, hearing, and cardiac function.

The trainer should also be adept in such technical skills as training hand-over-hand, assessing job sites and making needed job modifications, training through systematic instruction, and implementing behavior modification programs. The trainer, in conjunction with a vocational rehabilitation counselor, an orientation and mobility specialist, and a rehabilitation teacher, can create a support system.

Supported employment is not a radical change in services
Supported employment should not be considered a radical change in the type of overall vocational rehabilitation services available. Supported employment simply further establishes the long-recognized needs for integration, community-based training, and intensive and long-term support for individuals who may not have any of these benefits without this type of program. For many years, professionals in the area of disability placed individuals, although they realized that these people would not remain employed much beyond the vocational rehabilitation closure point.

Supported employment is not a restrictive service
Robert Smithdas (1980) has remarked that all individuals with deaf blindness will need long-term support to be independent. The support should be nonpaternalistic and provide direction to the individual; it should not be life-long supervision. Supported employment holds these ideals as a foundation for providing employment services. Supported employment, implemented correctly, provides *only* the amount of support necessary for the individual to succeed on the job.

We know that not all individuals will benefit from supported employment. In fact, some adults with deaf-blindness would be severely limited by these services, whereas other deaf-blind adults may lack the family support necessary to be thus served. According to Harrell and Curry (1987), some federal funds are being pulled from such traditional placement services as sheltered employment, work adjustment, and competitive placement and directed toward supported employment. We tend to believe that as the support needs of persons with deaf-blindness become more diversified, funding streams will be forced to follow.

Funding of support employment
Should supported employment be implemented within the deaf-blind community as it is for other disability groups, there will be less emphasis on federal grant money and more on local and state funds. The key to utilizing existing funds is a sharing of funds over several separate agencies (RRTC Staff, 1987).

With particular regard to the deaf-blind population, initial service dollars may be provided through vocational rehabilitation purchase-of-service agreements, whereas long-term follow-along funds may be provided through block grants or hourly fees from organizations that typically provide ongoing funds for the service agency.

Supported employment may be initially more expensive than other employment options; however, costs decrease as the individual continues working. The key to success for supported employment is cooperation between the short-term funding agency, the provider, the long-term funding agency, and the worker.

References
Barcus, M., Brooke, V., Inge, K., Moon, S., & Goodall, P. (1987). *An instructional guide for training on a job site: A supported employment resource*. Richmond, VA: Commonwealth University, Rehabilitation Research and Training Center.

Federal Register. (1987). Part 4: Department of Education, Office of Special Education and Rehabilitative Services, 34CRF, Part 363. The State Supported Employment Services Program, final regulations, 52 (157), 30547.

Harrell, R. & Curry, S. (1987). Services to blind and visually impaired children and adults: Who is responsible? *Journal of Visual Impairment & Blindness*, October, 1987, 368–376.

Harris, L. & Associates (1986). *The ICD Survey of Disabled Americans: Bringing disabled Americans into the mainstream*. New York: ICD-International Center for the Disabled in cooperation with the National Council on the Handicapped.

Jackson & Associates (1985). *National Leadership Institute on supported employment*. Olympia, WA: Jackson & Assoc.

Johnston, W.B. & Packer, A.E. (1987). *Workforce 2000: Work and workers in the twenty-first century*, pp viii–xxvii. Indianapolis, IN: Hudson Institute.

Lockett, T. & Rudolph, J. (1980). Deaf-blind children with maternal rubella: Implications for adult services. *American Annals for the Deaf*, November, 1980, 1002–1006.

Mank, D.M., Rhodes, L.E., & Bellamy, G.T. (1986). Four supported employment alternatives. In W.E. Kiernan, & J.A. Stark (eds.). *Pathways to employment for adults with developmental disabilities*, pp. 139–155. Baltimore, MD: Paul H. Brookes Publishing Co.

Moon, S., Goodall, P., Barcus, M., & Brooke, V. (eds.) (1986). *The supported work model of competitive employment for citizens with severe handicaps: A guide for job trainers* (rev. ed.). Richmond, VA: Virginia Commonwealth University, Rehabilitation Research and Training Center.

Moon, S. & Griffin, S., (1988). Supported employment service delivery models. In P. Wehman & S. Moon (eds.), *Vocational Rehabilitation and Supported Employment*, pp. 17–30. Baltimore, MD: Paul H. Brookes Publishing Co.

Nelipovich, M. & Naegele, L. (1985). The rehabilitation process for persons who are deaf and blind. *Journal of Visual Impairment & Blindness*, March, 1985.

RRTC Staff (1987). *Funding supported employment*, Vol. 4(1). Richmond, VA: Rehabilitation Research and Training Center.

Rhodes, L.E. & Valenta, L. (1985). Industry-based supported employment: An enclave approach. *Journal of the Association for Persons with Severe Handicaps*, 10, 12–20.

Smithdas, R.J. (1980). Reflections of a deaf-blind adult. *American Annals for the Deaf*, Vol. 125 (8) 1015–1018.

Staff, Rehabilitation, Research, and Training Center, & the Specialized Training Program (1986). *Perspectives on Supported Employment*, Vol. 2 (2). Richmond, VA: Rehabilitation, Research and Training Center.

Stuckless, E.R. (1980). Preparing for the rubella client of the eighties, 50–60.

Trybus, R.J., Karchmer, M.A., Kerstetter, P.O., & Hicks, W. (1980). The demographics of deafness resulting from maternal rubella, *American Annals for the Deaf*, November, 1980, 1002–1006.

United States Commission on Civil Rights (1983). *Attitudes toward the handicapped*. Washington, DC: U.S. Government Printing Office.

Wehman, P., (1981). *Competitive employment: New horizons for severely disabled individuals*. Baltimore, MD: Paul H. Brookes Publishing Co.

Wehman, P. & Kregel, J. (1985). A supported work approach to competitive employment of individuals with moderate and severe handicaps. *Journal of the Association for Persons with Severe Handicaps*, 10, 3–11.

Susan Lehmann Griffin, M.S., training associate, Rehabilitation Research and Training Center, School of Education, Virginia Commonwealth University, V.C.U. Box 2011, Richmond VA 23284–2011; Jacqueline Lowry, M.S., deaf-blind specialist, Virginia Department for the Visually Handicapped, 397 Azalea Avenue, Richmond, VA 23227.

Annotated Bibliography

PRINT MATERIALS

Access to Mass Transit for Blind and Visually Impaired Travelers, M. Uslan, A. Peck, W. Wiener, and A. Stern (Eds.), 1990.

Adaptive Play for Special Needs Children, C. R. Musselwhite, 1986.

Advances in Cognition, Education and Deafness, D. Martin (Ed.), 1991.

American Sign Language: A Comprehensive Dictionary, M. L. A. Sternberg, 1981.

American Sign Language: A Teacher's Resource Text on Curriculum, Methods and Evaluation, D. Cokely and C. Baker-Shenk, 1980.

The American Sign Language Phrase Book, Videotape Series, L. Fant, 1988.

Analyzing the Communication Environment (A.C.E.): An Inventory of Ways to Encourage Communication in Functional Activities, C. Rowland and P. Schweigert, 1993.

Assessment of Hearing-Impaired People, F. R. Zieziula, 1986.

Assessment of Vision and Hearing of Deaf-Blind Persons, L. Hyvärinen, L. Gimble, and M. Sorri, 1990.

Audiology: The Fundamentals, F. H. Bess and L. E. Humes, 1990.

Auditory Assessment and Program Manual for Severely Handicapped Deaf-Blind Students, L. Goetz, B. Utley, K. Gee, M. Baldwin, and W. Sailor, 1982.

Augmentative and Alternative Communication Systems for Persons with Moderate and Severe Disabilities, D. Baumgart, J. Johnson, and E. Helmstetter, 1990.

Augmentative Communication for Children with Deaf-Blindness: Guidelines for Decision-Making, C. Cress, P. Mathy-Laikko, and J. Angelo, 1989.

A Basic Course in Manual Communication, T. J. O'Rourke, 1970.

Beyond Arm's Reach: Enhancing Distance Vision, A.J. Smith and L.M. O'Donnell, 1992.

Beyond Tracking: Enhancing Vision Development from Birth to One Year of Age, M. Hanson, 1988.

The Biology of Hearing and Deafness, R. Harrison, 1988.

The Book of Name Signs: Naming in American Sign Language, S. Supalla, 1992.

Can't Your Child See? A Guide for Parents of Visually Impaired Children (2nd ed.), E. P. Scott, J. E. Jan, and R. D. Freeman, 1985.

No author has been indicated for titles in this list for which authorship is not clearly identified. Entries in the annotated bibliography that follows this list have been alphabetized by author. The designation "NA" has been assigned to titles when authorship is not indicated, and these titles may be found under that designation in the bibliography itself.

The Carolina Curriculum for Infants and Toddlers with Special Needs (2nd ed.), N. M. Johnson-Martin, K. G. Jens, S. M. Attermeier, and B. J. Hacker, 1991.

The Carolina Curriculum for Preschoolers with Special Needs, N. M. Johnson-Martin, S. M. Attermeier, and B. Hacker, 1990.

CHARGE Syndrome: A Booklet for Families, M. A. Hefner, J. W. Thelin, S. L. H. Davenport, and J. A. Mitchell, 1988.

Children with Disabilities: A Medical Primer (3rd ed.), M. L. Batshaw and Y. M. Perret, 1992.

Choosing Options and Accommodations for Children (COACH): A Guide to Planning Inclusive Education, M. Giangreco, C. Cloninger, and V. Iverson, 1992.

Collaboration in the Schools: An Inservice and Preservice Curriculum for Teachers, Support Staff, and Administrators, J. West, L. Idol, and G. Cannon, 1989.

Communication Development in Young Children with Deaf-Blindness: Literature Review, M. Bullis and G. Fielding (Eds.), 1988.

Communication in Sign Language: A Series of Lessons for Beginners, Y. Clark and T. Clark, 1986.

Communication Programming for Persons with Severe Handicaps, C. R. Musselwhite and K. W. St. Louis, 1988.

Communication Skills for Visually Impaired Learners, R. Harley, M. Truan, and L. Sanford, 1987.

Community-Based Curriculum: Instructional Strategies for Students with Severe Handicaps, M. A. Falvey (Ed.), 1986.

A Complete Guide to Communication with Deaf-Blind Persons, L. Kates and J. D. Schein, 1980.

The Comprehending Hand, L. Nielsen, 1991.

Coping with the Multi-Handicapped Hearing Impaired, H. T. Prickett and E. Duncan (Eds.), 1988.

The Deaf-Blind Baby: A Programme of Care, P. Freeman, 1985.

Deaf-Blind Infants and Children: A Developmental Guide, J. M. McInnes and J. A. Treffry, 1982.

Deaf Students and the School-to-Work Transition, T. E. Allen, B. W. Rawlings, and A. N. Schildroth, 1989.

Developing Cognition in Young Hearing Impaired Children, S. Watkins, 1983.

Developing Consistent and Effective Total Communication in the Home, S. Watkins, 1982.

Developing Sign Communication with the Multi-handicapped Sensory Impaired Child, S. Watkins, 1985.

Dimensions: Visually Impaired Persons with Multiple Disabilities, J. Erin (Ed.), 1989.

The Early Communication Process Using Microswitch Technology, C. Rowland and P. Schweigert, 1994.

Early Language Intervention (2nd ed.), L. McCormick and R. L. Schiefelbusch, 1990.

Educating Children with Multiple Disabilities: A Transdisciplinary Approach, F. P. Orelove and D. Sobsey, 1991.

Educating the Deaf: Psychology, Principles and Practices (3rd ed.), D. F. Moores, 1987.

Educational and Developmental Aspects of Deafness, D. Moores and K. P. Meadow-Orlans, 1990.

Education for Severely Handicapped Hearing Impaired Students, D. W. Naiman (Ed.), 1980.

Enhancing Nonsymbolic Communication Interactions among Learners with Severe Disabilities, E. Siegel-Causey and D. Guess, 1989.

Eyes, Hands, Voices: Communication Issues among Deaf People, M. D. Garretson (Ed.), 1990.

First Steps: A Handbook for Teaching Young Children Who Are Visually Impaired, Blind Children's Center, 1993.

Foundations of Education for Blind and Visually Handicapped Children and Youth: Theory and Practice, G. Scholl (Ed.), 1986.

Foundations of Orientation and Mobility, R. Welsh and B. Blasch, 1980.

Functional Living Skills for Moderately and Severely Handicapped Individuals, P. Wehman, A. Renzaglia, and P. Bates, 1985.

GA and SK Etiquette: Guidelines for Telecommunications in the Deaf Community, S. T. Cagle and K. M. Cagle, 1991.

Gallaudet Survival Guide to Signing, L. Lane, 1990.

Guidelines and Games for Teaching Efficient Braille Reading, M. R. Olson, 1981.

Guidelines for Video Store Participation in the SKI*HI Home Total Communication Video Program, SKI*HI Institute, 1986.

Hearing-Impaired Children and Youth with Developmental Disabilities: An Interdisciplinary Foundation for Service, E. Cherow, N. Matkin, and R. Trybus (Eds.), 1985.

Hearing Impairments in Young Children, A. Boothroyd, 1988.

Hearing in Children (4th ed.), J. L. Northern and M. P. Downs, 1991.

HELP at Home: Hawaii Early Learning Profile—Activity Sheets for Parents, S. Parks (Ed.), 1991.

HELP: Hawaii Early Learning Profile Activity Guide, S. Furono, K. A. O'Reilly, C. M. Hosaka, T. T. Inatsuka, T. Allman, and B. Zeisloft, 1985.

How to Thrive, Not Just Survive: A Guide to Developing Independent Life Skills for Blind and Visually Impaired Children and Youths, R. Swallow and K. Huebner (Eds.), 1987.

IMPACT: A Functional Curriculum Handbook for Students with Moderate to Severe Disabilities, R. Neel and F. Billingsley, 1989.

Implementing Augmentative and Alternative Communication: Strategies for Learners with Severe Disabilities, J. Reichle, J. York, and J. Sigafoos, 1991.

Independence Without Sight or Sound, D. Sauerburger, 1993.

Innovative Program Design for Individuals with Dual Sensory Impairments, L. Goetz, D. Guess, and K. Stremel-Campbell (Eds.), 1987.

The INSITE Model: Home Intervention for Infant, Toddler, and Preschool Aged Multihandicapped Sensory Impaired Children, S. Watkins, 1989.

Interpreting and Transliterating for Persons Who Are Deaf-Blind, K. Raistrick, 1988.

Itinerant Teaching: Tricks of the Trade for Teachers of Blind and Visually Impaired Students, J. Olmstead, 1991.

John Tracy Clinic Correspondence Learning Program for Parents of Young Deaf-Blind Children, John Tracy Clinic, 1990.

Just Enough to Know Better: A Braille Primer, E. Curran, 1988.

Kids in Action: Developing Body Awareness in Young Children, P. J. Gilroy, 1986.

Kids in Motion: An Early Childhood Movement Education Program, P. J. Gilroy, 1985.

Language Learning Practices with Deaf Children, P. McAnally, S. Rose, and S. Quigley, 1987.

Living Skills Inventories: For Individuals with Deaf-Blindness, FIND, 1990.

Low Vision: A Resource Guide with Adaptations for Students with Visual Impairments, N. Levack, 1991.

Manual Communication: Implications for Education, H. Bornstein (Ed.), 1990.

Movement and Fundamental Motor Skills for Sensory Deprived Children, L. Kratz, L. Tutt, and D. Black, 1987.

Neurodevelopmental Strategies for Managing Communication Disorders in Children with Severe Motor Dysfunction, M. Langley and L. Lombardino (Eds.), 1991.

New Programmed Instruction in Braille, S. Ashcroft, F. Henderson, L. Sanford, and A. Koenig, 1991.

Observing and Enhancing Communication Skills in Children with Multisensory Impairments, C. Rowland, P. Schweigert, K. Stremel, and Utah State University, 1992.

One Step at a Time: A Manual for Families of Children with Hearing and Vision Impairments, S. Bolton, 1990.

The Oregon Project for Visually Impaired and Blind Preschool Children (5th ed.), S. Anderson, S. Boigon, and K. Davis, 1991.

An Orientation and Mobility Primer for Families and Young Children, B. Dodson-Burke and E. W. Hill, 1989.

Parenting Preschoolers: Suggestions for Raising Young Blind and Visually Impaired Children, K. Ferrell, 1984.

Parents and Visually Impaired Infants (PAVI), D. Chen, C. T. Friedman, and G. Calvello, 1990.

Perkins Activity and Resource Guide, K. Heydt, M. J. Clark, C. Cushman, S. Edwards, and M. Allon, 1992.

Persons Handicapped by Rubella—Victors and Victims: A Follow-Up Study, J. Van Dijk, 1991.

Pigeon-Birds and Rhyming Words: The Role of Parents in Language Learning, N. Baron, 1990.

Play Activities for Young Children with Sensory Impairments, J. Rich, E. Rich, R. Fewell, A. Schlater, and P. Vadasy, 1983.

Preschool Orientation and Mobility Screening, B. Dodson-Burke and E. W. Hill, 1989.

Preschool Vision Stimulation: It's More Than a Flashlight! L. Harrell and N. Akeson, 1987.

Pre-Sign Language Motor Skills, M. D. Klein, 1988.

Proceedings of the National Symposium on Children and Youth Who Are Deaf-Blind, J. W. Reiman and P. A. Johnson (Eds.), 1993.

Program Guidelines for Individuals Who Are Deaf-Blind, California State Department of Education, 1990.

Reach Out and Teach: Meeting the Training Needs of Parents of Visually and Multiply Handicapped Young Children, K. Ferrell, 1985.

Research on the Communication Development of Young Children with Deaf-Blindness, M. Bullis (Ed.), 1989.

A Resource Manual for Understanding and Interacting with Infants, Toddlers and Preschool Age Children with Deaf-Blindness, 1993.

Sensory Assessment Manual, P. J. Cress, 1989.

Sensory Integration and the Child, A. J. Ayres, 1979.

Sign and Culture: A Reader for Students of American Sign Language, W. C. Stokoe (Ed.), 1980.

Signing Naturally: Level 1, C. Smith, E. M. Lentz, and K. Mikos, 1988.

Signing Naturally: Level 2, E. M. Lentz, K. Mikos, and C. Smith, 1989.

Sign Language for the Family, S. Watkins, 1989.

Sign Language Interpreters in the Public Schools, Sign Media and Madonna University, 1991.

Sign Language Research: Theoretical Issues, C. Lucas (Ed.), 1990.

Sign Me Fine: Experiencing American Sign Language, L. Greene and E. Dicker, 1989.

SKI*HI Home Total Communication Videotape Program Instruction Booklet, SKI*HI Institute, 1986.

The SKI*HI Model: Programming for Hearing Impaired Infants through Home Intervention, T. Clark and S. Watkins, 1985.

The Syracuse Community-referenced Curriculum Guide for Students with Moderate and Severe Disabilities, A. Ford, R. Schnorr, L. Meyer, L. Davern, J. Black, and P. Dempsey (Eds.), 1989.

Tactile Graphics, P. K. Edman, 1992.

Tangible Symbol Systems: Symbolic Communication for Individuals with Multisensory Impairments, C. Rowland and P. Schweigert, 1990.

The Teachability of Language, M. Rice and R. Schiefelbusch (Eds.), 1989.

A Teacher's Guide to the Special Educational Needs of Blind and Visually Handicapped Children, S. S. Mangold (Ed.), 1982.

Teaching Age-Appropriate Purposeful Skills: An Orientation & Mobility Curriculum for Students with Visual Impairments, R. Pogrund et al, 1993.

Teaching Conversation Skills to Individuals with Severe Disabilities with a Communication Book Adaptation: Instructional Handbook, P. Hunt, M. Alwell, and L. Goetz, undated.

Teaching Expressive and Receptive Language to Students with Moderate and Severe Handicaps, L. Makohon and H. D. Fredericks (Eds.), 1985.

The Teaching of Braille Reading, R. Harley, F. Henderson, and M. Truan, 1979.

Teaching Reading to Deaf Children, B. Hart, 1978.

TEEM: A Manual to Support the Transition of Young Children with Special Needs and Their Families from Preschool into Kindergarten and Other Regular Education Environments, J. Ross-Allen and M. Conn-Powers, 1991.

Theoretical Issues in Sign Language Research, S. Fischer and P. Siple (Eds.), 1990.

They Grow in Silence: Understanding Deaf Children and Adults, E. Mindel and M. Vernon, 1987.

Transition for Persons with Deaf-Blindness and Other Profound Handicaps: State of the Art, A. Covert and H. D. Fredericks, 1987.

Understanding Deafness Socially, P. Higgins and J. Nash (Eds.), 1987.

Understanding Low Vision, R. Jose (Ed.), 1983.

Usher's Syndrome: What It Is, How to Cope, and How to Help, E. Duncan, H. Prickett, D. Finkelstein, M. Vernon, and T. Hollingsworth, 1988.

Value-Based Services for Young Adults with Deaf-Blindness, A. M. Covert and T. S. Carr, 1988.

A Vision Guide for Teachers of Multi-handicapped or Deaf-Blind Children, M. Efron and B. Reilly Duboff, 1990.

Vision in Children: Normal and Abnormal, L. Hyvärinen, 1988.

Visuals to Accompany the Delivery of SKI*HI Home Communication Program: Aural-Oral/Total Communication, SKI*HI Institute, undated.

When You Have a Visually Handicapped Child in Your Classroom: Suggestions for Teachers (2nd ed.), I. Torres and A. L. Corn, 1990.

Working with Students Who Have Dual Sensory Impairments and Cognitive Disabilities: A Handbook for Special Education Teachers and Related Services Personnel, C. R. Gothelf, C. H. Rikhye, and R. K. Silberman, 1988.

You and Your Hearing-Impaired Child: A Self-Instructional Guide for Parents, J. Adams, 1988.

AUDIOVISUAL MATERIALS

American Sign Language: A Teacher's Resource Text on Curriculum, Methods, and Evaluation, D. Cokely and C. Baker-Shenk, 1980.

The American Sign Language Phrase Book, Videotape Series, L. Fant, 1988.

Analyzing the Communication Environment (A.C.E.): An Inventory of Ways to Encourage Communication in Functional Activities, C. Rowland and P. Schweigert, 1993.

Bringing Out the Best: Encouraging Expressive Communication in Children with Multiple Handicaps, E. Cooley and G. Singer, 1989.

Children with Motor Impairments: Part 1, SKI*HI Institute, 1987.

Children with Motor Impairments: Part 2, SKI*HI Institute, 1987.

Deaf-Blind Communication and Community: 1. Overview and Interaction. 2. Getting Involved—A Conversation, T. Smith, 1992.

Deaf-Blindness: Connecting through Communication, Canadian National Institute for the Blind, 1990.

Deaf-Blindness: Freedom through Intervention, Canadian National Institute for the Blind, 1991.

The Early Communication Process Using Microswitch Technology, C. Rowland and P. Schweigert, 1994.

Fingerspelling: Expressive and Receptive Fluency, J. L. Groode, 1992.

Fingerspelling Practice Tapes (Proper Nouns, Geographic Locations, Fingerspelled Loan Signs, and Miscellaneous Items), 1991.

Getting in Touch: Communicating with a Child Who Is Deaf-Blind, E. Cooley, 1987.

Helping Your Child Learn, South Dakota Department of Education and Cultural Affairs, 1992.

An Introduction to American Deaf Culture, M. J. Bienvenu and B. Colonomos, 1986 and 1988.

Introduction to Tactile Communication for Children Who Are Deaf-Blind, 1993.

An Introduction to the Deaf Community, 1993.

Observing and Enhancing Communication Skills in Children with Multisensory Impairments, C. Rowland, P. Schweigert, K. Stremel, and Utah State University, 1992.

Parent Sign Series, 1988.

Partners in Language, 1993.

Playing the Crucial Role in Your Child's Development, 1985.

Reach Out and Teach: Meeting the Training Needs of Parents of Visually and Multiply Handicapped Young Children, K. Ferrell, 1985.

Signing Naturally: Level 1, C. Smith, E. M. Lentz, and K. Mikos, 1988.

Signing Naturally: Level 2, E. M. Lentz, K. Mikos, and C. Smith, 1989.

Sign Language Interpreters in the Public Schools, Sign Media and Madonna University, 1991.

SKI*HI Coactive Sign System, SKI*HI Institute, 1991.

SKI*HI Slide/Tape Programs, SKI*HI Institute, undated.

SKI*HI Total Communication Videotape Program, SKI*HI Institute, 1986.

Tangible Symbol Systems: Symbolic Communication for Individuals with Multisensory Impairments, C. Rowland and P. Schweigert, 1990.

Using Tactile Interactive Conversational Signing with Children Who Are Deaf-Blind, 1993.

Using Tactile Signals and Cues with Children Who Are Deaf-Blind, 1993.

Using Your TTY/TDD (rev. ed.), 1993.

Within Reach: Getting to Know People Who Are Deaf-Blind, P. Brush and M. Otos, 1987.

Author: Adams, J.

Title: *You and Your Hearing-Impaired Child: A Self-Instructional Guide for Parents*

Date: 1988

Publisher: Gallaudet University Press
800 Florida Avenue, NE, Washington, DC 20002

ISBN: 0-930323-40-8

Cost: $10.00

Format: Softcover book, 142 pp.

Subject: Families, deafness and hearing impairments

Summary: A self-instructional guide for parents of children with hearing impairments. The topics include the psychosocial impact of hearing impairments, the development of skills, principles to live and learn by, and activities. A concise discussion of communication modes and agencies is also presented.

Author: Allen, T. E., Rawlings, B. W., and Schildroth, A. N.

Title: *Deaf Students and the School-to-Work Transition*

Date: 1989

Publisher: Paul H. Brookes Publishing Co.
P.O. Box 10624, Baltimore, MD 21285-0624

ISBN: 1-55766-020-4

Cost: $23.00

Format: Softcover book, 272 pp.

Subject: Deafness and hearing impairments, transition, families, communication

Summary: A handbook that discusses transition issues for students who are deaf. Laws, regulations, service-provision factors, and the need for interagency cooperation are detailed. Family involvement in the process is emphasized.

Author: Anderson, S., Boigon, S., and Davis, K.

Title: *The Oregon Project for Visually Impaired and Blind Preschool Children (rev. ed.)*

Date: 1991 (5th ed.)

Publisher:	Jackson Education Service District 101 North Grape Street, Medford, OR 97501
ISBN:	NA
Cost:	$119.00
Format:	Three-ring binder, 490 pp.; spiral-bound skills-checklist booklet, 80 pp.
Subject:	Blindness and low vision, early intervention, communication, motor development
Summary:	A curriculum for early intervention with young children who have visual impairments. Information and activities are included for vital life-skills areas: cognitive, language, social, and motor development; self-help skills; and compensatory skills development. Forms and a checklist can be reproduced to document a student's progress.

Author:	Ashcroft, S., Henderson, F., Sanford, L., and Koenig, A.
Title:	*New Programmed Instruction in Braille*
Date:	1991
Publisher:	SCALARS Publishing P.O. Box 158123, Nashville, TN 37215
ISBN:	NA
Cost:	$45.00
Format:	Spiral-bound book, 374 pp.
Subject:	Blindness and low vision, communication, education, braille
Summary:	A self-instructional guide for parents, families, and service providers who are involved in the education of children who are blind or visually impaired. The topics include the history of braille; the braille literary code; numerals, punctuation, and composition signs; and braille symbols for contractions and abbreviations. The appendixes contain a braille proficiency self-test and a checklist of problem words.

Author:	Ayres, A. J.
Title:	*Sensory Integration and the Child*
Date:	1979

Publisher:	Sensory Integration International
	1402 Cravens Avenue, Torrance, CA 90501-1728
ISBN:	0-87424-158-8
Cost:	$20.00
Format:	Softcover book, 191 pp.
Subject:	Motor development, sensory integration, disabilities
Summary:	A basic text on how the brain handles sensory information and on dysfunction that results from neurological disabilities. Visual and auditory perception and integration of information are explained, and therapy principles are outlined. Some children function as deaf-blind as a result of neurological trauma, and this information gives teachers more understanding of these students' needs.

Author:	Baron, N.
Title:	*Pigeon-Birds and Rhyming Words: The Role of Parents in Language Learning*
Date:	1990
Publisher:	Center for Applied Linguistics
	Prentice-Hall, Englewood Cliffs, NJ 07632
ISBN:	013-662875-3
Cost:	$19.00
Format:	Softcover book, 136 pp.
Subject:	Families, communication, early intervention
Summary:	A guide to increasing language-based interaction between parents and young children. The roles of language acquisition and cultural factors are considered, as are numerous patterns of interaction between mothers and young children. The lengthy reference list cites additional sources of information on the topic.

Author:	Batshaw, M. L., and Perret, Y. M.
Title:	*Children with Disabilities: A Medical Primer (3rd ed.)*
Date:	1992
Publisher:	Paul H. Brookes Publishing Co.
	P.O. Box 10624, Baltimore, MD 21285-0624
ISBN:	1-55766-102-2

Cost:	$29.00
Format:	Softcover book, 688 pp.
Subject:	Disabilities, families, medical information
Summary:	Medical information about embryology, lifetime growth, and disabilities. System development is explained from a biological viewpoint. Specific sections on vision, hearing, and cognitive and motor differences in development are included. Major disability areas are outlined, and ideas for working with families are presented.

Author:	Baumgart, D., Johnson, J., and Helmstetter, E.
Title:	*Augmentative and Alternative Communication Systems for Persons with Moderate and Severe Disabilities*
Date:	1990
Publisher:	Paul H. Brookes Publishing Co. P.O. Box 10624, Baltimore, MD 21285-0624
ISBN:	1-55766-049-2
Cost:	$22.00
Format:	Softcover book, 254 pp.
Subject:	Augmentative communication, severe disabilities, education
Summary:	A comprehensive text covering augmentative and alternative communication that presents guidelines and suggestions for selecting and designing systems for individual users. Many sections address issues that are unique to children of preschool and elementary age, including the assessment of visual factors, hand preferences, and language skills.

Author:	Bess, F. H., and Humes, L. E.
Title:	*Audiology: The Fundamentals*
Date:	1990
Publisher:	Williams & Wilkins 428 East Preston Street, Baltimore, MD 21202
ISBN:	0-683-00619-3
Cost:	$39.00

Format:	Hardcover book, 242 pp.
Subject:	Deafness and hearing impairments, assessment, audiology
Summary:	A basic textbook on clinical audiology and assessment of hearing loss that defines terms and discusses common procedures for measuring hearing acuity. Includes a section on hearing loss and problems with the auditory system, with some common syndromes described.

Author:	Blind Children's Center
Title:	*First Steps: A Handbook for Teaching Young Children Who Are Visually Impaired*
Date:	1993
Publisher:	Blind Children's Center 4120 Marathon Street, Los Angeles, CA 90029
ISBN:	NA
Cost:	$19.95
Format:	Softcover book, 224 pp.
Subject:	Blindness and low vision, early intervention, communication
Summary:	Basic information on and concepts of early childhood development and vision; technical aspects of speech and language acquisition, sensorimotor integration, and motor development; and program areas of behavior management, orientation and mobility, and self-help skills. Final chapter addresses design of individualized educational plans and individualized family service plans.

Author:	Bolton, S.
Title:	*One Step at a Time: A Manual for Families of Children with Hearing and Vision Impairments*
Date:	1990
Publisher:	Teaching Research 345 North Monmouth Avenue, Monmouth, OR 97361
ISBN:	NA
Cost:	$10.00
Format:	Booklet, 38 pp.
Subject:	Families, deaf-blindness, early intervention

Summary: A manual for families that presents specific guidelines and strategies for communication, feeding and eating, play, self-care skills, toilet training, bedtime routines, and motor development. Many photographs are integrated into the text. A resource section lists useful toys and provides information on hearing aids, eyeglasses, and financial assistance.

Author:	Boothroyd, A.
Title:	*Hearing Impairments in Young Children*
Date:	1988
Publisher:	Alexander Graham Bell Association for the Deaf 3701 Volta Place, Washington, DC 20007
ISBN:	0-56372-013-2
Cost:	$20.00
Format:	Softcover book, 239 pp.
Subject:	Deafness and hearing impairments, early intervention
Summary:	A description of hearing impairments and their consequences in children from birth to age 5. The author explores the techniques of minimizing these problems through hearing aids, audiological management, and education of parents. The oral method is emphasized.

Author:	Bornstein, H. (Ed.)
Title:	*Manual Communication: Implications for Education*
Date:	1990
Publisher:	Gallaudet University Press 800 Florida Avenue, NE , Washington, DC 20002
ISBN:	0-930323-57-2
Cost:	$34.95
Format:	Hardcover book, 197 pp.
Subject:	Sign language, deafness and hearing impairments, education
Summary:	Views by supporters of both "manual" (sign language) and "oral" (speech, speechreading, and auditory training) communication modes about which is most appropriate in instructional settings. American Sign Language as a primary language and several English-based systems are

considered, including Signing Exact English, Signed English, and Cued Speech.

Author:	Bullis, M. (Ed.)
Title:	*Research on the Communication Development of Young Children with Deaf-Blindness*
Date:	1989
Publisher:	Teaching Research 345 North Monmouth Avenue, Monmouth, OR 97361
ISBN:	NA
Cost:	$10.00
Format:	Softcover book, 160 pp.
Subject:	Communication, education, deaf-blindness
Summary:	Seven chapters covering topics related to research on the development of communication and on deaf-blindness. The topics include vision assessment, use of microswitch technology, communication opportunities in classrooms, strategies for facilitating nonsymbolic communication, the use of tactile augmentative communication devices, play, and evaluation of a training program to enhance social interactions.

Author:	Bullis, M., and Fielding, G. (Eds.)
Title:	*Communication Development in Young Children with Deaf-Blindness: Literature Review*
Date:	1988
Publisher:	Teaching Research 345 North Monmouth Avenue, Monmouth, OR 97361
ISBN:	NA
Cost:	$8.00
Format:	Softcover book, 261 pp.
Subject:	Deaf-blindness, early intervention, communication, education
Summary:	A 10-chapter overview, written by noted specialists on topics related to the development of communication in young children who are deaf-blind. The topics include assessment (of communication, vision, and hearing), tactile communication, nonsymbolic communication, moth-

er-child interactions, play, emergent language, contingency intervention, and augmentative communication systems.

Author:	Cagle, S. T., and Cagle, K. M.
Title:	*GA and SK Etiquette: Guidelines for Telecommunications in the Deaf Community*
Date:	1991
Publisher:	Gallaudet University Press 800 Florida Avenue, NE, Washington, DC 20002
ISBN:	0-9614621-7-5
Cost:	$8.95
Format:	Spiral-bound booklet, 53 pp.
Subject:	Deafness and hearing impairments, communication, transition, technology
Summary:	Tips and explanations for using a TTY/TDD effectively. Basic abbreviations and procedures are covered, as well as guidelines for proper manners when communicating via TTY/TDD.

Author:	California State Department of Education
Title:	*Program Guidelines for Individuals Who Are Deaf-Blind*
Date:	1990
Publisher:	California State Department of Education 721 Capitol Mall, P.O. Box 944272, Sacramento, CA 94244-2720
ISBN:	NA
Cost:	$6.00
Format:	Booklet, 83 pp.
Subject:	Deaf-blindness, education
Summary:	Guidelines that were developed to serve as a model for providing high-quality, cost-effective education within the requirements of California state and federal laws to students who are deaf-blind. Chapters cover identifying individuals who are deaf-blind and their unique educational needs, assessing unique educational needs, providing instruction and services, and organizing and supporting instruction and services. Appendixes contain a guide for

self-review, resources for technical assistance, and an inventory of assessment tools for use with students who have severe multiple disabilities.

Author:	Chen, D., Friedman, C. T., and Calvello, G.
Title:	*Parents and Visually Impaired Infants (PAVI)*
Date:	1990
Publisher:	American Printing House for the Blind P.O. Box 6085, Louisville, KY 40206-0085
ISBN:	NA
Cost:	Binder, $26.00; companion booklet, $2.25
Format:	Three-ring binder with 11 module booklets, 5–25 pp. each Companion booklet, *Learning Together: A Parent Guide to Socially Based Routines for Visually Impaired Infants,* 44 pp.
Subject:	Blindness and low vision, families, early intervention
Summary:	A kit with booklets on topics related to working with parents of children with visual impairments. Topics include parents' assessment of children's needs, observation procedures, vision and hearing information, assessing how children interact with objects (including for play), and working with parents.

Author:	Cherow, E., Matkin, N., and Trybus, R. (Eds.)
Title:	*Hearing-Impaired Children and Youth with Developmental Disabilities: An Interdisciplinary Foundation for Service*
Date:	1985
Publisher:	Gallaudet University Press 800 Florida Avenue, NE, Washington, DC 20002
ISBN:	0-913580-97-X
Cost:	$30.00
Format:	Hardcover book, 394 pp.
Subject:	Deafness and hearing impairments, multiple disabilities, education
Summary:	A 20-chapter textbook that discusses the provision of services to persons who are hearing impaired and have developmental disabilities and their families. The topics

include interdisciplinary teamwork, intervention with families, the pediatrician's role, assessment, curriculum planning, augmentative communication, and stress management. Basic definitions, references, and lists of agencies are also presented.

Author:	Clark, T., and Watkins, S.
Title:	*The SKI*HI Model: Programming for Hearing Impaired Infants through Home Intervention*
Date:	1985
Publisher:	HOPE, Inc. 809 North 800 East, Logan, UT 84321
ISBN:	NA
Cost:	Binders, $35.00; scale, $5.00; pamphlets, $7.00; test forms, 60 cents each
Format:	Three-ring binders, 647 pp., plus optional scale, instructional pamphlets, and flip charts
Subject:	Deafness and hearing impairments, communication, families
Summary:	A comprehensive home-intervention strategy for educators working with parents and young children who are deaf. The topics include the parents' readiness, psycho-emotional support, home visits, home programs for the use of hearing aids, auditory training, and the stimulation of communication.

Author:	Clark, Y., and Clark, T.
Title:	*Communication in Sign Language: A Series of Lessons for Beginners*
Date:	1986
Publisher:	HOPE, Inc. 809 North 800 East, Logan, UT 84321
ISBN:	NA
Cost:	$15.00
Format:	Softcover book, 140 pp.
Subject:	Sign language, communication, families
Summary:	A booklet on the development of sign-language communication by young children that includes line drawings

and written descriptions of signs, arranged by category. A comprehensive resource section lists agencies and sources of information.

Author:	Cokely, D., and Baker-Shenk, C.
Title:	*American Sign Language: A Teacher's Resource Text on Curriculum, Methods, and Evaluation*
Date:	1980
Publisher:	Sign Media Burtonsville Commerce Center, 4020 Blackburn Lane, Burtonsville, MD 20866
ISBN:	0-930323-85-8 (book)
Cost:	Book, $16.95; videotape, $34.95; set, $44.95
Format:	Softcover book, 187 pp.; videotape, 60 min.
Subject:	Sign language, communication, deafness and hearing impairments
Summary:	A teacher's guide for developing and implementing an instructional program in American Sign Language that emphasizes second language learning and teaching methods. The videotape shows examples of instructional activities.

Author:	Covert, A., and Fredericks, H. D.
Title:	*Transition for Persons with Deaf-Blindness and Other Profound Handicaps: State of the Art*
Date:	1987
Publisher:	Teaching Research 345 North Monmouth Avenue, Monmouth, OR 97361
ISBN:	0-944232-00-0
Cost:	$10.00
Format:	Softcover book, 163 pp.
Subject:	Transition, deaf-blindness, severe disabilities
Summary:	A discussion of transition and issues related to the delivery of community-based services for people who are deaf-blind. The topics include residential factors, vocational considerations, leisure and social interests, and health.

Author:	Covert, A. M., and Carr, T. S.
Title:	*Value-Based Services for Young Adults with Deaf-Blindness*

Date: 1988

Publisher: Helen Keller National Center for Deaf-Blind Youths and Adults
Technical Assistance Center, 111 Middle Neck Road, Sands Point, NY 11050

ISBN: NA

Cost: Free (limited quantities)

Format: Softcover book, 107 pp.

Subject: Transition, deaf-blindness

Summary: A collection of papers by content specialists, service providers, parents, and individuals who are deaf-blind that presents definitions, tips and strategies for dealing with the transitional needs of individuals who are deaf-blind, and ways to achieve community integration.

Author: Cress, C., Mathy-Laikko, P., and Angelo, J.

Title: *Augmentative Communication for Children with Deaf-Blindness: Guidelines for Decision-Making*

Date: 1989

Publisher: Teaching Research
345 North Monmouth Avenue, Monmouth, OR 97361

ISBN: NA

Cost: $10.00

Format: Booklet, 59 pp.

Subject: Augmentative communication, education, multiple disabilities

Summary: A manual for developing augmentative communication systems that features a flow chart that documents the decision-making process for developing systems. It presents information on 29 products and guidelines for the assessment of motor skills related to communication. The appendix contains definitions of specific communication systems, modes, and aids.

Author: Cress, P. J.

Title: *Sensory Assessment Manual*

Date: 1989

Publisher:	Teaching Research 345 North Monmouth Avenue, Monmouth, OR 97361
ISBN:	NA
Cost:	$10.00
Format:	Booklet, 21 pp.
Subject:	Assessment, education, deaf-blindness
Summary:	A summary of information on the ongoing sensory assessment of children who are deaf-blind that explains specific visual and auditory assessment procedures, including the evaluation of visual reflexes, visual fields, ocular motility, and visual acuity.

Author:	Curran, E.
Title:	*Just Enough to Know Better: A Braille Primer*
Date:	1988
Publisher:	National Braille Press 88 St. Stephen Street, Boston, MA 02115
ISBN:	0-939173-15-8
Cost:	$13.00
Format:	Softcover book, 128 pp.
Subject:	Blindness and low vision, communication, braille, families
Summary:	An easy-to-use resource for sighted individuals to learn to read braille that provides concise explanations of the basics of literary braille, including the braille alphabet, punctuation, contractions, short-form words, and special symbols. The lessons are sequenced in nine self-study exercises. A set of braille alphabet flashcards is included.

Author:	Dodson-Burke, B., and Hill, E. W.
Title:	*An Orientation and Mobility Primer for Families and Young Children*
Date:	1989
Publisher:	American Foundation for the Blind 15 West 16th Street, New York, NY 10011
ISBN:	0-89128-157-6
Cost:	$9.00
Format:	Softcover book, 48 pp.

Subject:	Motor development, orientation and mobility
Summary:	Practical information on sensory training, concept development, motor development, and orientation skills. Contains a glossary of commonly used terms and a compilation of resources.
Author:	Dodson-Burke, B., and Hill, E. W.
Title:	*Preschool Orientation and Mobility Screening*
Date:	1989
Publisher:	Association for Education and Rehabilitation of the Blind and Visually Impaired 206 North Washington Street, Suite 320 Alexandria, VA 22314
ISBN:	NA
Cost:	$20.00
Format:	Booklet, 28 pp.
Subject:	Orientation and mobility, early intervention, motor development
Summary:	An assessment tool for orientation and mobility instructors to use with students from birth to five years who are visually impaired and who may have additional physical, sensory, or cognitive impairments. Divided into two sections, one for younger children who are not ambulatory and the other for those who are mobile, the assessment covers background information, gross motor skills, visual functioning, auditory skills, tactile skills, and body image/exploratory behavior. Directions for administration are included.
Author:	Duncan, E., Prickett, H., Finkelstein, D., Vernon, M., and Hollingsworth, T.
Title:	*Usher's Syndrome: What It Is, How to Cope, and How to Help*
Date:	1988
Publisher:	Charles C Thomas 2600 South First Street, Springfield, IL 62794-9265
ISBN:	0-398-05481-9
Cost:	$28.00

Format:	Hardcover book, 93 pp.
Subject:	Deafness and hearing impairments, medical information, blindness and low vision, deaf-blindness
Summary:	A resource for individuals who have Usher's syndrome, their families, and service providers that includes interviews with individuals who have Usher's syndrome, medical aspects, how to communicate the diagnosis, psychological adjustment, educational concerns, and employment and vocational rehabilitation.

Author:	Edman, P. K.
Title:	*Tactile Graphics*
Date:	1992
Publisher:	American Foundation for the Blind 15 West 16th Street, New York, NY 10011
ISBN:	0-89128-194-0
Cost:	$80.00
Format:	Hardcover book, 544 pp.
Subject:	Education, blindness and low vision, tactile materials
Summary:	A guide for creating tactile information for use by people who are blind. Covered are step-by-step instructions for educators, rehabilitators, graphic artists, and museum and business personnel, as well as employers. Individual chapters are devoted to preparing and producing tactile maps, pictures, charts, and graphs, as well as displays for persons with low vision.

Author:	Efron, M., and Reilly Duboff, B.
Title:	*A Vision Guide for Teachers of Multi-handicapped or Deaf-Blind Children*
Date:	1990
Publisher:	North Carolina Department of Public Instruction 116 West Edenton Street, Raleigh, NC 27603-1712
ISBN:	NA
Cost:	$3.00
Format:	Booklet, 72 pp.
Subject:	Deaf-blindness, education

Summary: A guide for instructing children who have multiple disabilities or are deaf-blind that includes a detailed informal assessment for evaluating visual sensation, visual-motor activity, and visual perception; practical information on techniques and materials for improving visual functioning; and definitions of common visual problems for children who have multiple disabilities or are deaf-blind.

Author: Erin, J. (Ed.)

Title: *Dimensions: Visually Impaired Persons with Multiple Disabilities*

Date: 1989

Publisher: American Foundation for the Blind
15 West 16th Street, New York, NY 10011

ISBN: 0-89128-163-0

Cost: $15.00

Format: Softcover book, 107 pp.

Subject: Blindness, deaf-blindness, multiple disabilities, severe disabilities, education, communication

Summary: Twenty-one articles from the *Journal of Visual Impairment & Blindness* that address assessment techniques, a team approach to diagnosis, a multidisciplinary approach to intervention, pragmatic information on the development of language skills, play skills and communicative competence, functional vision screening and stimulation studies, behavioral treatment procedures, adaptive mobility techniques, community group homes, and community-based programs for young adults.

Author: Falvey, M. A. (Ed.)

Title: *Community-Based Curriculum: Instructional Strategies for Students with Severe Handicaps*

Date: 1986

Publisher: Paul H. Brookes Publishing Co.
P.O. Box 10624, Baltimore, MD 21285-0624

ISBN: 1-55766-023-9

Cost: $31.00

Format: Softcover book, 372 pp.

Subject: Education, severe disabilities

Summary: Strategies for developing and implementing educational programs for individuals with severe handicaps. Topics include assessment strategies, instructional strategies, community skills, domestic skills, recreational skills, employment skills, and functional academic skills. Integration issues and strategies are also discussed.

Author: Ferrell, K.

Title: *Parenting Preschoolers: Suggestions for Raising Young Blind and Visually Impaired Children*

Date: 1984

Publisher: American Foundation for the Blind
15 West 16th Street, New York, NY 10011

ISBN: 0-89128-998-4

Cost: Bulk orders of 25 copies, $30.00

Format: Booklet, 28 pp.

Subject: Early intervention, blindness and low vision, families

Summary: Answers to the most frequent questions asked by parents who have just learned that their children have vision problems. Topics include what to expect if a child is visually impaired, where to get help, and how to choose an early childhood program. Basic definitions, references, and lists of agencies are also presented.

Author: Ferrell, K.

Title: *Reach Out and Teach: Meeting the Training Needs of Parents of Visually and Multiply Handicapped Young Children*

Date: 1985

Publisher: American Foundation for the Blind
15 West 16th Street, New York, NY 10011

ISBN: 0-89128-208-4

Cost: Parents' handbook and reachbook set, $40.00; slide-videotape and manual set, $175.00

Format: Parents' handbook, spiral-bound, 272 pp.
Reachbook, spiral-bound, 176 pp.

Slide-videotape presentation, 105 min.

Teacher's manual, 103 pp.

Subject: Families, early intervention, blindness and low vision

Summary: A two-volume set consisting of a handbook and a workbook for parents. It provides background information and step-by-step training techniques to facilitate motor and cognitive development. The parents' handbook details activities; the reachbook allows parents to log their child's responses to exercises, to enter information, and to keep records. A slide-videotape presentation and a teacher's manual are also available.

Author: FIND

Title: *Living Skills Inventories: For Individuals with Deaf-Blindness*

Date: 1990

Publisher: FIND
119 North 4th Street, Suite 302 D,
Minneapolis, MN 55401

ISBN: 0-9626896-0-2

Cost: $30.00

Format: Booklet, 85 pp.

Subject: Transition, education, deaf-blindness

Summary: Inventory forms to measure levels of functioning in eight areas—communication, adaptive equipment, personal care, money management, food and nutrition, home-apartment care, community resources, and physical fitness—that can be used as checklists for assessments, especially for transition-aged individuals.

Author: Fischer, S., and Siple, P. (Eds.)

Title: *Theoretical Issues in Sign Language Research*

Date: 1990

Publisher: University of Chicago Press
1130 South Langley Avenue, Chicago, IL 60628

ISBN: 0-226-25150-0

Cost: $125.00 (two-volume set)

Format: Hardcover book, two volumes, 338 pp. and 314 pp.

Subject: Sign language

Summary: A two-volume book on research on sign language, primarily American Sign Language. Visual attention and communication of hearing mothers with deaf children is explained. The effects of using speech and sign language together are explored.

Author: Ford, A., Schnorr, R., Meyer, L., Davern, L., Black, J., and Dempsey, P. (Eds.)

Title: *The Syracuse Community-referenced Curriculum Guide for Students with Moderate and Severe Disabilities*

Date: 1989

Publisher: Paul H. Brookes Publishing Co.
P.O. Box 10624, Baltimore, MD 21285-0624

ISBN: 1-55766-027-1

Cost: $47.00

Format: Spiral-bound book, 416 pp.

Subject: Severe disabilities, education

Summary: A functional curriculum guide for teachers of students from kindergarten age to 21 years with moderate to severe disabilities. Information about community living and functional academic domains, as well as adaptations for specific local needs, is included; skills for specific areas and sample forms to use with individual program designs are presented.

Author: Freeman, P.

Title: *The Deaf-blind Baby: A Programme of Care*

Date: 1985

Publisher: William Heinemann Medical Books
23 Bedford Square, London, WC1B 3HH, England

ISBN: 0-433-10906-8

Cost: $29.95

Format: Softcover book, 152 pp.

Subject: Deaf-blindness, early intervention, families

Summary: An essential explanation of the effects of deaf-blindness on early development. A sequential program is outlined

for interaction that will support learning. Suggestions for activities and important areas to adapt are included.

Author:	Furono, S., O'Reilly, K. A., Hosaka, C. M., Inatsuka, T. T., Allman, T., and Zeisloft, B.
Title:	*HELP: Hawaii Early Learning Profile Activity Guide*
Date:	1985
Publisher:	VORT Corporation P.O. Box 60132, Palo Alto, CA 94306
ISBN:	NA
Cost:	Book, $19.95; checklist-pamphlet, $2.95
Format:	Softcover book, 190 pp.; checklist-pamphlet, 18 pp.
Subject:	Early intervention, families, education
Summary:	An activity guide for the expected behaviors and skills of infants and toddlers from birth through 36 months. Areas that can be developed and assessed include language and cognitive development, gross and fine motor development, and social-emotional and self-help skills. The HELP checklist-pamphlet lists 685 developmental skills/behaviors.

Author:	Garretson, M. D. (Ed.)
Title:	*Eyes, Hands, Voices:* *Communication Issues among Deaf People*
Date:	1990
Publisher:	National Association of the Deaf 814 Thayer Avenue, Silver Spring, MD 20910
ISBN:	0011-72x
Cost:	$20.00
Format:	Softcover book, 137 pp.
Subject:	Communication, sign language, culture, deafness and hearing impairments
Summary:	A collection of 29 articles on a variety of communication issues for individuals who are deaf, including American Sign Language, ethics, lipreading, employment, citizenship, and bilingualism.

Author:	Giangreco, M., Cloninger, C., and Iverson, V.
Title:	*Choosing Options and Accommodations for Children (COACH): A Guide to Planning Inclusive Education*
Date:	1992
Publisher:	Paul H. Brookes Publishing Co. P.O. Box 10624, Baltimore, MD 21285-0624
ISBN:	1-55766-106-5
Cost:	$29.00
Format:	Softcover book, 192 pp.
Subject:	Education, severe disabilities, multiple disabilities
Summary:	A manual to help you through the practical assessment and planning process that includes comprehensive instructions and easy-to-follow forms to identify the content of a student's educational program, incorporate the program into a general educational setting, and pursue family-valued outcomes.

Author:	Gilroy, P. J.
Title:	*Kids in Action: Developing Body Awareness in Young Children*
Date:	1986
Publisher:	Communication Skill Builders 3830 East Bellevue, P.O. Box 42050-E91, Tucson, AZ 85733
ISBN:	0-88450-960-5
Cost:	$12.95
Format:	Booklet, 76 pp.
Subject:	Motor development
Summary:	A movement program for young children that is designed to increase their body awareness, help them control their bodies as they manipulate objects, relate to the space around them, and move cooperatively with others. Monthly goals and weekly objectives accompany 36 lessons, including warm-up activities, suggested materials, organization of the classroom, and structured activities, as well as lyrics and notes.

Author:	Gilroy, P. J.
Title:	*Kids in Motion: An Early Childhood Movement Education Program*
Date:	1985
Publisher:	Communication Skill Builders 3830 East Bellevue, P.O. Box 42050-E91, Tucson, AZ 85733
ISBN:	0-88450-923-0
Cost:	$12.95
Format:	Booklet, 73 pp.
Subject:	Motor development
Summary:	A movement program for young children in the classroom or during individual instruction that is designed to increase their body awareness, awareness of self, and awareness of other people and objects, as well as balance, flexibility, cooperative behavior, controlled patterned movement, and increased control of small objects. Program objectives are accompanied by 36 lessons that include warm-up activities, teaching materials, class organization, and structured activities.

Author:	Goetz, L., Guess, D., and Stremel-Campbell, K. (Eds.)
Title:	*Innovative Program Design for Individuals with Dual Sensory Impairments*
Date:	1987
Publisher:	Paul H. Brookes Publishing Co. P.O. Box 10624, Baltimore, MD 21285-0624
ISBN:	0-933716-84-2
Cost:	$30.00
Format:	Softcover book, 366 pp.
Subject:	Deaf-blindness, communication, education
Summary:	An overview of programming for students who are deaf-blind that covers the assessment of residual sight and hearing, orientation and mobility skills, functional living skills, and the use of natural cues and prompting sequences to develop communication.

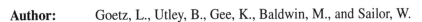

Author:	Goetz, L., Utley, B., Gee, K., Baldwin, M., and Sailor, W.
Title:	*Auditory Assessment and Program Manual for Severely Handicapped Deaf-Blind Students*
Date:	1982
Publisher:	TASH 11201 Greenwood Avenue North, Seattle, WA 98133
ISBN:	NA
Cost:	$5.00
Format:	Booklet, 50 pp.
Subject:	Deafness and hearing impairments, audiology, assessment, deaf-blindness
Summary:	A manual for teachers and other service providers that offers basic information about hearing and audiological assessments, including strategies for preparing hard-to-test students for audiometric testing, designing functional auditory skills programs, reading audiograms, and the care of hearing aids.

Author:	Gothelf, C. R., Rikhye, C. H., and Silberman, R. K.
Title:	*Working with Students Who Have Dual Sensory Impairments and Cognitive Disabilities: A Handbook for Special Education Teachers and Related Services Personnel*
Date:	1988
Publisher:	New York State Education Department Office for Education of Children with Handicapping Conditions, Title VI-C, Albany, NY
ERIC:	ED297-506 (Note: This publication should be obtained from ERIC, an educational database, using this ED number. To access ERIC, contact: Council for Exceptional Children, 1920 Association Drive, Reston, VA 22091.)
Cost:	$10.00
Format:	Photocopied pamphlet, 97 pp.
Subject:	Communication, orientation and mobility, deaf-blindness, education
Summary:	An overview of assessment, principles of communication, orientation and mobility, classroom environments, and

curriculum for students who are deaf-blind and have multiple impairments.

Author:	Greene, L., and Dicker, E.
Title:	*Sign Me Fine: Experiencing American Sign Language*
Date:	1989
Publisher:	Kendall Green Publications Gallaudet University Press, 800 Florida Avenue, NE, Washington, DC 20002
ISBN:	0-930323-76-9
Cost:	$6.00
Format:	Softcover book, 110 pp.
Subject:	Sign language, communication, deafness and hearing impairments
Summary:	A comprehensive introduction to the structures and use of American Sign Language (ASL). Topics include a brief history of ASL, ASL grammar, and silent speech. The book features photographs and line drawings, as well as games, recreational activities, poems, and songs.

Author:	Hanson, M.
Title:	*Beyond Tracking: Enhancing Vision Development from Birth to One Year of Age*
Date:	1988
Publisher:	Vision Unlimited P.O. Box 1591, Bridgeview, IL 60455
ISBN:	NA
Cost:	$8.00
Format:	Booklet, 48 pp.
Subject:	Blindness and low vision, early intervention
Summary:	A guide for early intervention specialists and parents on the early development and assessment of vision, including activities to stimulate the development of vision.

Author:	Harley, R., Henderson, F., and Truan, M.
Title:	*The Teaching of Braille Reading*

Date:	1979
Publisher:	Charles C Thomas 2600 South First Street, Springfield, IL 62794-9265
ISBN:	0-398-03836-8
Cost:	$31.00
Format:	Hardcover book, 187 pp.
Subject:	Braille, education, communication, blindness and low vision
Summary:	A book that presents basic information on reading and using braille, discusses braille reading in relation to other aspects of child development, reviews research and identifies areas that may be difficult for braille readers, offers strategies for identifying braille reading readiness, describes approaches to reading instruction and building tactual perception and word-identification skills, and suggests appropriate materials and ways to adapt materials for designing individualized reading programs.
Author:	Harley, R., Truan, M., and Sanford, L.
Title:	*Communication Skills for Visually Impaired Learners*
Date:	1987
Publisher:	Charles C Thomas 2600 South First Street, Springfield, IL 62794-9265
ISBN:	0-398-05362-0
Cost:	$48.00
Format:	Hardcover book, 346 pp.
Subject:	Blindness and low vision, communication
Summary:	A 12-chapter overview of communication skills for visually impaired learners. Topics include historical perspectives, assessment, teaching techniques, writing skills, use of technology, and instructional materials and games. Appendixes feature a sight vocabulary list, behavioral objectives, a word-identification mastery guide for grades K–6, and a checklist for the mechanics of braille reading.
Author:	Harrell, L., and Akeson, N.
Title:	*Preschool Vision Stimulation: It's More Than a Flashlight!*

Date:	1987
Publisher:	American Foundation for the Blind 15 West 16th Street, New York, NY 10011
ISBN:	0-89128-136-3
Cost:	$9.00
Format:	Softcover book, 60 pp.
Subject:	Blindness and low vision, early intervention
Summary:	A review of sensory development from infancy to age 4 that demonstrates procedures for early vision stimulation with the aid of photographs and illustrations and presents step-by-step charts on the sequence of visual development, variables in the low-vision profile, how to stimulate the use of vision, low vision considerations, and objectives. A glossary, resource list, and recommended reading list are also included.

Author:	Harrison, R.
Title:	*The Biology of Hearing and Deafness*
Date:	1988
Publisher:	Charles C Thomas 2600 South First Street, Springfield, IL 62794-9265
ISBN:	0-398-05432-0
Cost:	$85.00
Format:	Hardcover book, 432 pp.
Subject:	Deafness and hearing impairments, medical information
Summary:	A comprehensive medical reference about the ear and the process of hearing that discusses issues related to hearing loss, including acoustical trauma, ototoxic poisoning, hearing loss owing to aging, and profound deafness.

Author:	Hart, B.
Title:	*Teaching Reading to Deaf Children*
Date:	1978
Publisher:	Alexander Graham Bell Association for the Deaf 3417 Volta Place, NW, Washington, DC 20007
ISBN:	0-88200-117-5
Cost:	$15.95

Format:	Softcover book, 232 pp.
Subject:	Education, communication, deafness and hearing impairments
Summary:	Specific tips and strategies for teaching reading to students who are deaf and have never heard spoken English. Strong emphasis on using illustrations (primarily visual, but with potential for adaptation to tactile forms) to teach reading. This is one of the few available specific resources for reading instruction for students who are deaf or deaf-blind.
Author:	Hefner, M. A., Thelin, J. W., Davenport, S. L. H., and Mitchell, J. A.
Title:	*CHARGE Syndrome: A Booklet for Families*
Date:	1988
Publisher:	Quota Club 2004 Parkade Boulevard, Columbia, MO 65202
ISBN:	NA
Cost:	$1.50
Format:	Booklet, 48 pp.
Subject:	Deaf-blindness, families, medical information
Summary:	Concise and useful information on CHARGE syndrome. Defines the features of the syndrome and provides a glossary of associated medical terms with easily understandable explanations and related photographs. The booklet lists other resources on CHARGE syndrome available from the Quota Club, as well as additional recommended organizations and publications.
Author:	Heydt, K., Clark, M. J., Cushman, C., Edwards, S., and Allon, M.
Title:	*Perkins Activity and Resource Guide*
Date:	1992
Publisher:	Perkins School for the Blind Public Relations and Publications, 175 North Beacon Street, Watertown, MA 02172
ISBN:	NA
Cost:	$65.00 (two-volume set)

Format:	Set of two three-ring binders, with audiocassettes, 1,000 pp.
Subject:	Deaf-blindness, education, technology
Summary:	A curriculum guide that addresses topics such as adaptive technology, leisure activities, sensory integration, vocational training, and social development. Activities, resources, instructional strategies, and information about these areas are included.

Author:	Higgins, P., and Nash, J. (Eds.)
Title:	*Understanding Deafness Socially*
Date:	1987
Publisher:	Charles C Thomas 2600 South First Street, Springfield, IL 62794-9265
ISBN:	0-398-05300-6
Cost:	$37.00
Format:	Hardcover book, 196 pp.
Subject:	Deafness and hearing impairments (culture)
Summary:	A presentation of the cultural perspective of deafness and individuals in the deaf community that explains communication factors that are important and common to members of the deaf community and discusses such controversial issues as American Sign Language and Signed English.

Author:	Hunt, P., Alwell, M., and Goetz, L.
Title:	*Teaching Conversation Skills to Individuals with Severe Disabilities with a Communication Book Adaptation: Instructional Handbook*
Date:	Undated
Publisher:	Dr. Pam Hunt Department of Special Education, San Francisco State University, 1600 Holloway Avenue, San Francisco, CA 94132
ISBN:	NA
Cost:	$10.00
Format:	Booklet, 54 pp.

Subject: Augmentative communication, severe disabilities

Summary: An instructional tool for an augmentative communication adaptation. Teaching strategies, explanations of use, and a description of students who can use the adaptation effectively are included. Appendixes show actual pages from communication books, partner training scripts, and instructional data-recording forms.

Author: Hyvärinen, L.

Title: *Vision in Children: Normal and Abnormal*

Date: 1988

Publisher: Canadian Deaf-Blind and Rubella Association
747 Second Avenue East, Suite 4, Owen Sound, Ontario, N4K 2G9, Canada

ISBN: 0-921434-00-6

Cost: $5.00 (Canadian dollars)

Format: Booklet, 63 pp.

Subject: Blindness and low vision, early intervention

Summary: A concise discussion of issues related to early visual behavior and impairment. Contains practical information for the enhancement of visual development of young children, including those with multiple disabilities.

Author: Hyvärinen, L., Gimble, L., and Sorri, M.

Title: *Assessment of Vision and Hearing of Deaf-Blind Persons*

Date: 1990

Publisher: Royal Victorian Institute for the Blind
333 Burwood Highway, Burwood, Victoria, 3125, Australia

ISBN: 0-949390-11-9

Cost: $16.00 plus $5.00 shipping

Format: Booklet, 67 pp.

Subject: Communication, assessment, audiology, deaf-blindness

Summary: Guidelines for service providers on auditory and visual assessments of individuals who are deaf-blind. Specific topics include using an interpreter for the assessment, how to communicate information to the individual who is deaf-blind, and how to work with students who have multiple disabilities.

Author:	Johnson-Martin, N. M., Attermeier, S. M., and Hacker, B.
Title:	*The Carolina Curriculum for Preschoolers with Special Needs*
Date:	1990
Publisher:	Paul H. Brookes Publishing Co. P.O. Box 10624, Baltimore, MD 21285-0624
ISBN:	1-55766-032-8 (spiral-bound book) 1-55766-039-5 (assessment log)
Cost:	Book, $34.00; assessment log, $20.00
Format:	Spiral-bound book, 352 pp.; assessment log, 28 pp.
Subject:	Early intervention, communication, motor development, education, families
Summary:	Assessment and intervention strategies for preschool children who are "at risk" or have mild to moderate disabilities. The five major areas of development (cognitive development, communication, and social, gross motor, and fine motor development) are subdivided into 25 more specific areas. Group and individual activities are included with assessment information and sample forms to use in preschool instructional settings.

Author:	Johnson-Martin, N. M., Jens, K. G., Attermeier, S. M., and Hacker, B. J.
Title:	*The Carolina Curriculum for Infants and Toddlers with Special Needs (2nd ed.)*
Date:	1991
Publisher:	Paul H. Brookes Publishing Co. P.O. Box 10624, Baltimore, MD 21285-0624
ISBN:	1-55766-074-3
Cost:	$40.00
Format:	Spiral-bound book, 384 pp.
Subject:	Early intervention, communication, motor development, education, families
Summary:	Approaches to assessment and intervention with infants and toddlers. Includes evaluation and instruction activities

and concepts for five major areas of child development: cognitive development, communication, and social, fine motor, and gross motor skills. Adaptations for children with visual, hearing, and motor impairments are described for many activities. Accompanying volumes include forms that can be used to design individual programs.

Author:	John Tracy Clinic
Title:	*John Tracy Clinic Correspondence Learning Program for Parents of Young Deaf-Blind Children*
Date:	1990
Publisher:	John Tracy Clinic 806 West Adams Boulevard, Los Angeles, CA 90007
ISBN:	NA
Cost:	$18.00
Format:	Softcover book, 490 pp.
Subject:	Deaf-blindness, families, early intervention
Summary:	Twelve lessons for parents of children and youths who are deaf-blind that contain information on general development, communication (including basic signs), what to expect, and activities. Each lesson is cross-referenced to a sequence of "Learning Steps" at the back of the text that provide additional information on gross motor development, fine motor development, eating, sleeping, dressing, toilet training, and personal hygiene.

Author:	Jose, R. (Ed.)
Title:	*Understanding Low Vision*
Date:	1983
Publisher:	American Foundation for the Blind 15 West 16th Street, New York, NY 10011
ISBN:	0-89128-119-3
Cost:	$40.00
Format:	Hardcover book, 560 pp.
Subject:	Blindness and low vision
Summary:	A 20-chapter overview of trends in the provision of care for persons with low vision that includes information on understanding the effects of low vision (or the loss of

vision) on functioning, learning, and psychosocial status and descriptions of professional services. Special sections contain reports, technical materials, questionnaires, charts, resources, and selected references.

Author:	Kates, L., and Schein, J. D.
Title:	*A Complete Guide to Communication with Deaf-Blind Persons*
Date:	1980
Publisher:	National Association of the Deaf 814 Thayer Avenue, Silver Spring, MD 20910
ISBN:	0-913072-40-0
Cost:	$4.95
Format:	Softcover book, 108 pp.
Subject:	Communication, deaf-blindness, sign language
Summary:	A comprehensive guide to a variety of communication modes, systems, and devices for individuals who are deaf-blind. Includes photographs and illustrations to demonstrate use. Divided categorically by sense used: hearing (including speech and amplification devices), vision (including sign language and low vision magnification devices), and touch (including tactile manual communication methods and tactile low- and high-tech devices).

Author:	Klein, M. D.
Title:	*Pre-Sign Language Motor Skills*
Date:	1988
Publisher:	Communication Skill Builders 3830 East Bellevue, P.O. Box 42050, Tucson, AZ 85733
ISBN:	0-88450-821-8
Cost:	$23.00
Format:	Softcover book, 104 pp.
Subject:	Sign language, motor development, early intervention, severe disabilities, families
Summary:	A workbook for families and service providers that explains motor development and its effects on the ability to execute sign language. Examples and activities are presented to use in motor skill development for students who

are deaf, including those who are deaf-blind and/or have multiple disabilities, to prepare them for communication with signs.

Author:	Kratz, L., Tutt, L., and Black, D.
Title:	*Movement and Fundamental Motor Skills for Sensory Deprived Children*
Date:	1987
Publisher:	Charles C Thomas 2600 South First Street, Springfield, IL 62794-9265
ISBN:	0-398-05392-8
Cost:	$25.50
Format:	Hardcover book, 74 pp.
Subject:	Motor development, deaf-blindness, education
Summary:	A discussion of how to plan and teach fundamental motor skills to children who are deaf-blind that covers early movement training for infants and young children, developmental theories, the development of motor skills, evaluation scales for fundamental motor skills, and a specific plan for teaching motor skills at home.

Author:	Lane, L.
Title:	*Gallaudet Survival Guide to Signing*
Date:	1990
Publisher:	Gallaudet University Press 800 Florida Avenue, NE, Washington, DC 20002
ISBN:	0-923323-67-X
Cost:	$5.00
Format:	Softcover book, 203 pp.
Subject:	Sign language, deafness and hearing impairments, communication
Summary:	A reference presenting a basic vocabulary of some 500 common signs in alphabetical order, each with a written description and line drawing illustrating how the sign is produced. The introduction includes seven concise suggestions for beginners and five frequently used handshapes in addition to manual alphabet handshapes.

Author:	Langley, M., and Lombardino, L. (Eds.)
Title:	*Neurodevelopmental Strategies for Managing Communication Disorders in Children with Severe Motor Dysfunction*
Date:	1991
Publisher:	Pro-Ed 8700 Shoal Creek Boulevard, Austin, TX 78758
ISBN:	0-89079-422-7
Cost:	$29.00
Format:	Hardcover book, 342 pp.
Subject:	Multiple disabilities, motor development
Summary:	A synthesis of knowledge and practice in the area of communication intervention for children with severe motor dysfunction (presented in the context of the neurodevelopmental treatment model). Topics include communication and oral-motor development; the development of cognitive, social, and symbolic skills; and alternative-augmentative modes of communication production. Discussions of prespeech assessment and treatment strategies, alternate feeding methods, and sensory preparation of oral-motor development are accompanied by illustrations.

Author:	Lentz, E. M., Mikos, K., and Smith, C.
Title:	*Signing Naturally: Level 2*
Date:	1989
Publisher:	Dawn Sign Press 9080-A Activity Road, San Diego, CA 92126
ISBN:	0-915035-08-1 (curriculum guide) 0-915035-11-4 (student's workbook)
Cost:	Teacher's set, $69.00; student's set, 59.95
Format:	Teacher's curriculum guide, spiral-bound book, 228 pp. Student's workbook, spiral-bound book, 178 pp. Accompanying set of three videotapes: first tape, 34 min.; second and third tapes, 120 min. each
Subject:	Sign language, communication, deafness and hearing impairments
Summary:	A comprehensive American Sign Language instructional curriculum, advanced level, that is a continuation of level

one work. Includes practice activities on videotape and reproducible worksheets.

Author:	Levack, N.
Title:	*Low Vision: A Resource Guide with Adaptations for Students with Visual Impairments*
Date:	1991
Publisher:	Texas School for the Blind and Visually Impaired 1100 West 45th Street, Austin, TX 78756-3494
ISBN:	1-880366-04-5
Cost:	$10.00
Format:	Spiral-bound book, 280 pp.
Subject:	Blindness and low vision, education, medical information
Summary:	Practical information on formal and functional assessments, instructional strategies and adaptations, the effects of physical conditions and sensory systems on vision, and the psychosocial implications of visual impairment developed by teachers for teachers. The chapter on 50 medical conditions and diseases discusses physical characteristics, medical treatment, causes, possible effects on vision, adaptations, and educational considerations.

Author:	Lucas, C. (Ed.)
Title:	*Sign Language Research: Theoretical Issues*
Date:	1990
Publisher:	Gallaudet University Press 800 Florida Avenue, NE, Washington, DC 20002
ISBN:	0-930323-58-0
Cost:	$50.00
Format:	Hardcover book, 384 pp.
Subject:	Sign language, deafness and hearing impairments, communication
Summary:	A compilation of papers presented at a 1988 forum by specialists in linguistics, interpreting, education of students who are deaf, psychology, and cognition that emphasize that sign language is a true language, comparable to spoken language, with a unique grammar and syntax, and that focus on the sociological-cultural perspectives of sign language.

Author:	Makohon, L., and Fredericks, H. D. (Eds.)
Title:	*Teaching Expressive and Receptive Language to Students with Moderate and Severe Handicaps*
Date:	1985
Publisher:	Pro-Ed
	8700 Shoal Creek Boulevard, Austin, TX 78758
ISBN:	0-936104-68-6
Cost:	$34.00
Format:	Spiral-bound book, 210 pp.
Subject:	Communication, severe disabilities, education
Summary:	Information on learning theory, assessments, and procedures for developing language skills in young children, including developmental skill lists with record-keeping forms and strategies to use with individual students.

Author:	Mangold, S. S. (Ed.)
Title:	*A Teacher's Guide to the Special Educational Needs of Blind and Visually Handicapped Children*
Date:	1982
Publisher:	American Foundation for the Blind
	15 West 16th Street, New York, NY 10011
ISBN:	0-89128-108-8
Cost:	$15.00
Format:	Softcover book, 164 pp.
Subject:	Blindness and low vision, education
Summary:	A multidisciplinary approach to the education of students who are blind or visually impaired, with each chapter focusing on a unique educational need: teaching reading via braille, concept development, communication curriculum, functional vision, nonacademic skills, orientation to low vision needs, sexuality, nurturing high self-esteem, art, science, and aural reading skills.

Author:	Martin, D. (Ed.)
Title:	*Advances in Cognition, Education and Deafness*
Date:	1991

Publisher:	Gallaudet University Press
	800 Florida Avenue, NE, Washington, DC 20002
ISBN:	0-930323-79-3
Cost:	$35.00
Format:	Hardcover book, 447 pp.
Subject:	Deafness and hearing impairments, education, cognitive development
Summary:	Summaries of presentations from an international forum on cognition and deafness that emphasize that people who are deaf and rely on vision for communication and cognitive development form concepts about the world differently, yet appropriately, and that discount earlier notions that visual language is inferior and that deafness prevents abstract thinking.

Author:	McAnally, P., Rose, S., and Quigley, S.
Title:	*Language Learning Practices with Deaf Children*
Date:	1987
ISBN:	0-316-55343-3
Publisher:	College-Hill Press
	Little, Brown & Co., 34 Beacon Street,
	Boston, MA 02108
Cost:	$31.00
Format:	Hardcover book, 238 pp.
Subject:	Communication, deafness and hearing impairments, education
Summary:	An explanation of typical language development processes and how language can be developed when auditory information is distorted or not useful. A natural language approach to instruction and strategies for the early development of language are stressed.

Author:	McCormick, L., and Schiefelbusch, R. L.
Title:	*Early Language Intervention (2nd ed.)*
Date:	1990
Publisher:	Charles E. Merrill Publishing Co.
	860 Taylor Station Road, Blacklick, OH 43004

ISBN:	0-675-21194-8
Cost:	$39.75
Format:	Hardcover book, 480 pp.
Subject:	Communication, early childhood intervention
Summary:	Introductory information on language-acquisition processes and intervention strategies. Differences in development associated with various disabilities are explained. Design of an intervention program is outlined, and techniques are suggested. Assessment information is included for specific areas.

Author:	McInnes, J. M., and Treffry, J. A.
Title:	*Deaf-Blind Infants and Children: A Developmental Guide*
Date:	1982
Publisher:	University of Toronto Press 5201 Dufferin, North York, Ontario, M3H 5T8, Canada
ISBN:	0-8020-2415-7
Cost:	$17.95 (U.S. dollars)
Format:	Softcover book, 284 pp.
Subject:	Deaf-blindness, communication, early intervention, education
Summary:	An essential reference on the development of children who are deaf-blind. Outlines the effects of deaf-blindness on development and instructional methods and adaptations to support growth and development for these students. Both general and specific suggestions are presented, including sample activities for some areas.

Author:	Mindel, E., and Vernon M.
Title:	*They Grow in Silence:* *Understanding Deaf Children and Adults*
Date:	1987
Publisher:	College-Hill Press Little, Brown & Co., 34 Beacon Street, Boston, MA 02108
ISBN:	0-316-57422-8
Cost:	$28.00

Format:	Softcover book, 204 pp.
Subject:	Deafness and hearing impairments, education, families
Summary:	A discussion of the differences and overall effects on families with a member who is deaf that presents basic concepts of deafness, psychological-emotional issues, language development, and education.

Author:	Moores, D., and Meadow-Orlans, K. P.
Title:	*Educational and Developmental Aspects of Deafness*
Date:	1990
Publisher:	Gallaudet University Press 800 Florida Avenue, NE, Washington, DC 20002
ISBN:	0-930323-52-1
Cost:	$40.00
Format:	Hardcover book, 451 pp.
Subject:	Deafness and hearing impairments, education, families
Summary:	A comprehensive overview of recent directions in the education of children who are deaf, including instruction for cognitive and language development.

Author:	Moores, D. F.
Title:	*Educating the Deaf:* *Psychology, Principles and Practices (3rd ed.)*
Date:	1987
Publisher:	Gallaudet University Press 800 Florida Avenue, NE, Washington, DC 20002
ISBN:	0-395-35781-0
Cost:	$47.95
Format:	Hardcover book, 383 pp.
Subject:	Deafness and hearing impairments, education
Summary:	An overview of education for students who are deaf, with basic information on the history of the field and current practices. Sections also cover causes of deafness, including common etiologies and syndromes; deafness with multiple disabilities, including blindness; effects on families with a member who is deaf; cognitive development and mental health with deafness; early intervention; and

communication methods and modes of instruction. Some information on postsecondary options is given, but the emphasis is on elementary and secondary education.

Author:	Musselwhite, C. R.
Title:	*Adaptive Play for Special Needs Children*
Date:	1986
Publisher:	College-Hill Press Little, Brown & Co., 34 Beacon Street, Boston, MA 02108
ISBN:	0-316-59213-7
Cost:	$27.00
Format:	Softcover book, 249 pp.
Subject:	Communication, education, early intervention, severe disabilities
Summary:	An overview of how play is adapted and used to serve the needs of children with disabilities that covers the function of adapted play, making play materials, developing adaptive play strategies for communicative goals, and resources for adaptive play programs at home and in school.

Author:	Musselwhite, C. R., and St. Louis, K. W.
Title:	*Communication Programming for Persons with Severe Handicaps*
Date:	1988
Publisher:	College-Hill Press Little, Brown & Co., 34 Beacon Street, Boston, MA 02108
ISBN:	0-316-59216-1
Cost:	$28.00
Format:	Softcover book, 395 pp.
Subject:	Severe disabilities, communication, augmentative communication
Summary:	Discussion of a wide variety of special populations and their unique communication needs, an overview of issues and augmentative communication systems, and a list of additional resources.

Author:	NA
Title:	*A Resource Manual for Understanding and Interacting with Infants, Toddlers and Preschool Age Children with Deaf-Blindness*
Date:	1993
Publisher:	HOPE, Inc. 809 North 800 East, Logan, UT 84321
ISBN:	NA
Cost:	$50.00
Format:	Softcover book, 546 pp.
Subject:	Deaf-blindness, early intervention, communication, motor development
Summary:	A training guide with easy-to-read information on topics related to working with very young children who are deaf-blind. Topics include auditory training, use of functional vision, communication, daily care, motor skills, orientation and mobility, working with medically fragile children, and other program areas. Also contains program activities related to the specific topics and a section on available resources.

Author:	Naiman, D. W. (Ed.)
Title:	*Education for Severely Handicapped Hearing Impaired Students*
Date:	1980
Publisher:	National Association of the Deaf 814 Thayer Avenue, Silver Spring, MD 20910
ISBN:	0-913072-34-6
Cost:	$4.00
Format:	Booklet, 84 pp.
Subject:	Deafness and hearing impairments, multiple disabilities, education
Summary:	A discussion of the programming needs of students who are deaf and have multiple disabilities and how educators can work with parents of these students.

Author:	Neel, R., and Billingsley, F.
Title:	*IMPACT: A Functional Curriculum Handbook for Students with Moderate to Severe Disabilities*
Date:	1989
Publisher:	Paul H. Brookes Publishing Co. P.O. Box 10624, Baltimore, MD 21285-0624
ISBN:	1-55766-026-3
Cost:	$28.00
Format:	Softcover book, 199 pp.
Subject:	Education, severe disabilities
Summary:	Practical methods for integrating traditional services into a functional curriculum for students with mental disabilities, such as autism and moderate-to-severe mental retardation, including a design for an individualized curriculum, ecological inventories, and forms used for data collection and planning.

Author:	Nielsen, L.
Title:	*The Comprehending Hand*
Date:	1991
Publisher:	Socialstyrelsen Postboxs 2555, 2100 Copenhagen, Denmark
ISBN:	87-503-6790-9
Cost:	$9.00
Format:	Booklet, 60 pp.
Subject:	Blindness and low vision, multiple disabilities, education, families
Summary:	Information and suggestions for activities and objects that educators and parents can use to develop tactile skills in young children who are visually impaired and have multiple handicaps.

Author:	Northern, J. L., and Downs, M. P.
Title:	*Hearing in Children (4th ed.)*
Date:	1991
Publisher:	Williams & Wilkins 428 East Preston Street, Baltimore, MD 21202

ISBN:	0-683-06574-2
Cost:	$49.00
Format:	Hardcover book, 418 pp.
Subject:	Deafness and hearing impairments, assessment, audiology
Summary:	A widely used text and reference on hearing loss and deafness in infants, toddlers, children, and youths. Multicultural references describe ear diseases specific to Native American children (Indian and Eskimo). The development of hearing skills is outlined. Issues in auditory assessment and management, including amplification, for children are discussed. A 20-page appendix describes syndromes and etiologies, with additional details about multiple disabilities.

Author:	Olmstead, J.
Title:	*Itinerant Teaching: Tricks of the Trade for Teachers of Blind and Visually Impaired Students*
Date:	1991
Publisher:	American Foundation for the Blind 15 West 16th Street, New York, NY 10011
ISBN:	0-89128-190-8
Cost:	$19.00
Format:	Softcover book, 136 pp.
Subject:	Blindness and low vision, education
Summary:	A guide to itinerant teaching of students with visual impairments that includes 30 sample letters and forms; photographs; an index; resource sections on sources of information, materials, and equipment; a classification system for materials; and a bibliography.

Author:	Olson, M. R.
Title:	*Guidelines and Games for Teaching Efficient Braille Reading*
Date:	1981
Publisher:	American Foundation for the Blind 15 West 16th Street, New York, NY 10011
ISBN:	0-89128-105-3

Cost:	$16.95
Format:	Softcover book, 109 pp.
Subject:	Braille, education, blindness and low vision
Summary:	A resource book of games and activities to build reading readiness for braille and to support the development of strong reading skills in braille. Specific examples are given, with illustrations of activities, and resources are included.

Author:	Orelove, F. P., and Sobsey, D.
Title:	*Educating Children with Multiple Disabilities: A Transdisciplinary Approach*
Date:	1991
Publisher:	Paul H. Brookes Publishing Co. P.O. Box 10624, Baltimore, MD 21285-0624
ISBN:	1-55766-077-8
Cost:	$29.00
Format:	Softcover book, 481 pp.
Subject:	Education, severe disabilities
Summary:	A guide to planning and implementing curricula for children with severe disabilities who have motor or sensory impairments. It addresses combining the transdisciplinary team model with an array of assessment, intervention, and evaluation techniques and covers such topics as sensory impairments, developing instructional adaptations, mealtime skills, and self-care skills.

Author:	O'Rourke, T. J.
Title:	*A Basic Course in Manual Communication*
Date:	1970
Publisher:	National Association of the Deaf 814 Thayer Avenue, Silver Spring, MD 20910
ISBN:	0-913072-01-X
Cost:	$9.95
Format:	Softcover book, 158 pp.
Subject:	Sign language, communication, deafness and hearing impairments

Summary: A widely used resource for learning sign language. Signs are covered in lessons 1–45, with practice sentences and additional-resources sections that include bibliographies of other sign language materials. Each lesson has a central theme, for example, pronouns or categories of similar adjectives, and may include additional signs to supplement practice routines. Line drawings indicate how signs are to be made.

Author: Parks, S. (Ed.)

Title: *HELP at Home: Hawaii Early Learning Profile— Activity Sheets for Parents*

Date: 1991

Publisher: VORT Corporation
P.O. Box 60132, Palo Alto, CA 94306

ISBN: 0-89718-096-8

Cost: $64.95

Format: Three-ring binder, 550 pp.

Subject: Early intervention, families, education

Summary: An activity guide for parents on expected behaviors and skills for infants and toddlers from birth through 36 months. Areas that can be stimulated with specific activities include language and cognitive development, gross and fine motor development, and social-emotional and self-help skills.

Author: Pogrund, R., Healy, G., Jones, K., Levack, N., Martin-Curry, S., Martinez, C., Marz, J., Roberson-Smith, B., and Vrba, A.

Title: *Teaching Age-Appropriate Purposeful Skills: An Orientation & Mobility Curriculum for Students with Visual Impairments*

Date: 1993

Publisher: Texas School for the Blind and Visually Impaired
1100 West 45th Street, Austin, Texas 78756-3494

ISBN: 1-880366-10-X

Cost: Curriculum with evaluation booklet, $40.00; evaluation booklet, $7.50

Format:	Softcover book, spiral bound, 364 pp.
	Softcover booklet, 100 pp.
Subject:	Orientation and mobility, blindness and low vision
Summary:	A comprehensive orientation and mobility (O&M) assessment and curriculum for students ages 3 to 21. Strategies are provided for students who are blind or have low vision and are appropriate for students who also have other disabilities including deaf-blindness, orthopedic impairments, other health impairments, and developmental delays. Covers teaching O&M in such environments as the home, residential and commercial areas, and public transportation. Appendixes include screening and assessment resources for infants. Glossary, resource list, and references are also included.

Author:	Prickett, H. T., and Duncan, E. (Eds.)
Title:	*Coping with the Multi-Handicapped Hearing Impaired*
Date:	1988
Publisher:	Charles C Thomas
	2600 South First Street, Springfield, IL 62794-9265
ISBN:	0-398-05412-6
Cost:	$24.00
Format:	Hardcover book, 80 pp.
Subject:	Deafness and hearing impairments, multiple disabilities, education
Summary:	Examples of specific programs and activities for students who are deaf and have multiple disabilities, including deafness and autism, deafness and physical disabilities, and deafness and cognitive impairments.

Author:	Raistrick, K.
Title:	*Interpreting and Transliterating for Persons Who Are Deaf-Blind*
Date:	1988
Publisher:	Illinois Department of Rehabilitation Services
	Division of Services for the Hearing Impaired, 623 East Adams, P.O. Box 19429, Springfield, IL 62794-9429
ISBN:	NA

Cost:	Free (limited quantities)
Format:	Pamphlet, 24 pp.
Subject:	Interpreting, communication, deaf-blindness
Summary:	A compact source of basic information for individuals who interpret for people who are deaf-blind, including practical considerations; unique factors; and tactile, aural, and visual modes of communication.

Author:	Reichle, J., York, J., and Sigafoos, J.
Title:	*Implementing Augmentative and Alternative Communication: Strategies for Learners with Severe Disabilities*
Date:	1991
Publisher:	Paul H. Brookes Publishing Co. P.O. Box 10624, Baltimore, MD 21285-0624
ISBN:	1-55766-044-1
Cost:	$46.00
Format:	Softcover book, 320 pp.
Subject:	Augmentative communication, severe disabilities, education
Summary:	Comprehensive information on developing augmentative, primarily graphic, communication systems, including strategies for ecological inventories, initial communicative intents, requesting and rejecting repertoires, communicative exchanges, and replacing excessive behavior with communicative repertoires.

Author:	Reiman, J. W., and Johnson, P. A. (Eds.)
Title:	*Proceedings of the National Symposium on Children and Youth Who Are Deaf-Blind*
Date:	1993
Publisher:	Teaching Research 345 North Monmouth Avenue, Monmouth, OR 97361
ISBN:	NA
Cost:	$15.00
Format:	Softcover book, 240 pp. (also available on disk in WordPerfect 5.1 or ASCII)

Subject: Deaf-blindness, education

Summary: Invited papers and recommendations from focus groups at a national symposium held in December 1992. Issues included are personnel preparation, early intervention for students who are deaf-blind, family services, demographics, psychosocial and educational services, independent living, and adult services.

Author: Rice, M., and Schiefelbusch, R. (Eds.)

Title: *The Teachability of Language*

Date: 1989

Publisher: Paul H. Brookes Publishing Co.
P.O. Box 10624, Baltimore, MD 21285-0624

ISBN: 1-55766-011-5

Cost: $39.00

Format: Hardcover book, 370 pp.

Subject: Communication, education

Summary: A collection of articles on various topics related to the acquisition of language and constraints on the development of language.

Author: Rich, J., Rich, E., Fewell, R., Schlater, A., and Vadasy, P.

Title: *Play Activities for Young Children with Sensory Impairments*

Date: 1983

Publisher: Teaching Research
345 North Monmouth Avenue, Monmouth, OR 97361

ISBN: NA

Cost: $10.00

Format: Pamphlet, 20 pp.

Subject: Early intervention, deaf-blindness, education

Summary: Descriptions of play activities to promote communication by young children who are blind or visually impaired, deaf or hearing impaired, or deaf-blind.

Author: Ross-Allen, J., and Conn-Powers, M.

Title: *TEEM: A Manual to Support the Transition of Young Children with Special Needs and Their Families from Preschool into Kindergarten and Other Regular Education Environments*

Date: 1991

Publisher: Center for Developmental Disabilities University Affiliated Program of Vermont, University of Vermont, 499C Waterman Building, Burlington, VT 05405

ISBN: NA

Cost: Free (limited quantities)

Format: Booklet, 50 pp.

Subject: Education, transition, disabilities

Summary: Information about the transition to various levels of schooling, such as from preschool to elementary school, and forms for achieving such transitions, with timelines and directions for planning transitional activities.

Author: Rowland, C., and Schweigert, P.

Title: *Analyzing the Communication Environment (A.C.E.): An Inventory of Ways to Encourage Communication in Functional Activities*

Format: Softcover book. For details, see entry under Audiovisual Materials.

Author: Rowland, C., and Schweigert, P.

Title: *The Early Communication Process Using Microswitch Technology*

Format: Softcover book. For details, see entry under Audiovisual Materials.

Author: Rowland, C., and Schweigert, P.

Title: *Tangible Symbol Systems: Symbolic Communication for Individuals with Multisensory Impairments*

Format: Booklet. For details, see entry under Audiovisual Materials.

Author: Rowland, C., Schweigert, P., Stremel, K., and Utah State University

Title: *Observing and Enhancing Communication Skills in Children with Multisensory Impairments*

Format: Softcover book. For details, see entry under Audiovisual Materials.

Author: Sauerburger, D.

Title: *Independence Without Sight or Sound*

Date: 1993

Publisher: American Foundation for the Blind
15 West 16th Street, New York, NY 10011

ISBN: 0-89128-246-7

Cost: $35.00

Format: Softcover book, 420 pp. (also available in braille)

Subject: Communication, orientation and mobility, deaf-blindness, transition

Summary: Methods and techniques for teaching orientation and mobility to people who are deaf-blind, including numerous practical applications and examples for teachers. The emphasis is on instruction for daily living needs.

Author: Scholl, G. (Ed.)

Title: *Foundations of Education for Blind and Visually Handicapped Children and Youth: Theory and Practice*

Date: 1986

Publisher: American Foundation for the Blind
15 West 16th Street, New York, NY 10011

ISBN: 0-89128-124-X (hardcover book)
0-89128-181-9 (audiocassette)

Cost: $50.00 (hardcover book or audiocassette)

Format: Hardcover book, 528 pp. (also available on six audiotapes, approximately 360 min. each)

Subject: Blindness and low vision, education

Summary: A basic reference that provides a comprehensive overview of educational theory and practice with students who are blind or visually impaired from preschool through high school. Major sections cover the history of education, growth and development, educational theory, components of a high-quality educational program, low vision and visual efficiency, severe multiple handicaps, psychoeducational assessment, resources, media and technology, social skills, curricular adaptations, and the transition to adulthood.

Author:	Scott, E. P., Jan, J. E., and Freeman, R. D.
Title:	*Can't Your Child See? A Guide for Parents of Visually Impaired Children (2nd ed.)*
Date:	1985
Publisher:	Pro-Ed 8700 Shoal Creek Boulevard, Austin, TX 78758
ISBN:	0-936104-56-2
Cost:	$22.00
Format:	Softcover book, 248 pp.
Subject:	Blindness and low vision, early intervention, families
Summary:	A volume for families with children who are visually impaired. Early development and types of vision loss are described, including multiple disabilities. Suggestions for how the family can help the child adapt and learn at home are included, as is a section on education and future planning.

Author:	Siegel-Causey, E., and Guess, D.
Title:	*Enhancing Nonsymbolic Communication Interactions Among Learners with Severe Disabilities*
Date:	1989
Publisher:	Paul H. Brookes Publishing Co. P.O. Box 10624, Baltimore, MD 21285-0624
ISBN:	1-55766-019-0
Cost:	$28.00
Format:	Softcover book, 208 pp.
Subject:	Communication, augmentative communication, education
Summary:	An overview of nonsymbolic communication interactions and instructional guidelines for enhancing nonsymbolic interaction in five areas: (1) developing nurturing relation-

ships, (2) enhancing sensitivity to nonsymbolic communication, (3) increasing opportunities for communication,
(4) sequencing experiences in a predictable order, and (5)
utilizing movement within natural interactions. The final
section presents hypothetical studies detailing the practice
of various strategies and procedures.

Author:	Sign Media and Madonna University
Title:	*Sign Language Interpreters in the Public Schools*
Format:	Five pamphlets and two resource lists. For details, see entry under Audiovisual Materials.

Author:	SKI*HI Institute
Title:	*Guidelines for Video Store Participation in the SKI*HI Home Total Communication Video Program*
Date:	1986
Publisher:	HOPE, Inc. 809 North 800 East, Logan, UT 84321
ISBN:	NA
Cost:	Free
Format:	Pamphlet, 18 pp.
Subject:	Deafness and hearing impairments, sign language
Summary:	An explanation of how parents can work with local video stores to make the SKI*HI videotape program on sign language available for rental.

Author:	SKI*HI Institute
Title:	*SKI*HI Home Total Communication Videotape Program Instruction Booklet*
Date:	1986
Publisher:	HOPE, Inc. 809 North 800 East, Logan, UT 84321
ISBN:	NA
Cost:	Free
Format:	Booklet, 42 pp.
Subject:	Deafness, hearing impairments, sign language

Summary: A guide to the 20 videotapes in the SKI*HI program series on home-based teaching of sign language to children who are deaf. Lesson formats are explained, the research that supported the development of the lessons is described, and users are shown how the taped lessons fit into the overall SKI*HI program. An index lists signs that are demonstrated in alphabetical order and tells in which lessons (on which tapes) they may be found.

Author: SKI*HI Institute

Title: *Visuals to Accompany the Delivery of SKI*HI Home Communication Program: Aural-Oral/Total Communication*

Date: Undated

Publisher: HOPE, Inc.
809 North 800 East, Logan, UT 84321

ISBN: NA

Cost: $37.00

Format: Spiral-bound easel booklet, 18 pp.

Subject: Communication, deafness and hearing impairment, early intervention

Summary: Visuals that parent-infant program specialists can use to help parents communicate with their infants and young children and promote the development of language skills using auditory information, speech and speech reading, and total communication.

Author: Smith, A.J. and O'Donnell, L.M.

Title: *Beyond Arm's Reach: Enhancing Distance Vision*

Date: 1992

Publisher: Pennsylvania College of Optometry Press
1200 West Godfrey Street, Philadelphia, PA 19141

ISBN: NA

Cost: $27.00

Format: Softcover book, 184 pp.

Subject: Blindness and low vision, education

Summary: A series of 45 lessons designed to maximize the distance visual efficiency of students with low vision who have light projection or gross object or form perception. The lesssons can be applied to students who are multiply impaired. Includes strategies for teaching visual perception and movement through the environment, covering position, distance, and depth cues and how to increase experiential knowledge through visual exploration in different environments. Appendixes, references, and resources are also included.

Author:	Smith, C., Lentz, E. M., and Mikos, K.
Title:	*Signing Naturally: Level 1*
Date:	1988
Publisher:	Dawn Sign Press 9080-A Activity Road, San Diego, CA 92126
ISBN:	0-915035-07-3 (curriculum guide) 0-915035-10-3 (student's workbook)
Cost:	Teacher's set, $69.00; student's set, $33.95
Format:	Teacher's curriculum guide, spiral-bound book, 308 pp. Student's workbook, 88 pp. Accompanying videotape: for teachers, 22 min.; for students, 118 min.
Subject:	Sign language, communication, deafness and hearing impairments
Summary:	A comprehensive American Sign Language program that emphasizes a functional approach. Includes practice activities on videotape and reproducible activity worksheets.

Author:	Sternberg, M. L. A.
Title:	*American Sign Language: A Comprehensive Dictionary*
Date:	1981
Publisher:	Harper & Row 10 East 53rd Street, New York, NY 10022
ISBN:	0-06-014097-6
Cost:	$65.00
Format:	Hardcover book, 1,132 pp.
Subject:	Sign language, communication, deafness and hearing impairments
Summary:	An essential reference tool with the most comprehensive

sign vocabulary in print: 8,000 line drawings of signs with definitions. Entries are presented alphabetically, according to written English translation/interpretation, with task analysis of sign production that includes hand-shape and movements needed. Regional variations in signs are included.

(Note: An abridged version of this dictionary, entitled *American Sign Language Concise Dictionary,* with 2,000 signs illustrated, is available for $8.00 in paperback from Gallaudet University Bookstore, 800 Florida Avenue, NE, Washington, DC 20002.)

Author:	Stokoe, W. C. (Ed.)
Title:	*Sign and Culture: A Reader for Students of American Sign Language*
Date:	1980
Publisher:	Sign Media Burtonsville Commerce Center, 4020 Blackburn Lane, Burtonsville, MD 20866
ISBN:	0-932130-07-0
Cost:	$18.95
Format:	Softcover book, 375 pp.
Subject:	Sign language, communication, deafness and hearing impairments (culture)
Summary:	Seventeen contributed works that constitute an essential text on American Sign Language and deaf culture. The concept of a "sign language" is defined and is compared to that of spoken languages. How sign languages are learned and used is explained, and how sign languages are basic to the culture of individuals who are deaf is discussed.

Author:	Supalla, S.
Title:	*The Book of Name Signs: Naming in American Sign Language*
Date:	1992
Publisher:	Dawn Sign Press 9080-A Activity Road, San Diego, CA 92126
ISBN:	0-915035-30-8

Cost:	$12.95
Format:	Softcover book, 112 pp.
Subject:	Sign language, communication, deafness and visual impairments (culture)
Summary:	A deaf-studies resource book that describes the process of how name signs are assigned to individuals in American Sign Language and discusses the rules of formation and use.

Author:	Swallow, R., and Huebner, K. (Eds.)
Title:	*How to Thrive, Not Just Survive: A Guide to Developing Independent Life Skills for Blind and Visually Impaired Children and Youths*
Date:	1987
Publisher:	American Foundation for the Blind 15 West 16th Street, New York, NY 10011
ISBN:	0-89128-148-7
Cost:	$13.00
Format:	Softcover book, 104 pp.
Subject:	Blindness and low vision, education
Summary:	Guidelines and sequential strategies for helping children who are blind or visually impaired develop and apply skills that are necessary for socialization, orientation and mobility, and leisure-time and recreational activities. The topics include eating, toileting, dressing, motor development, using landmarks as clues, personal hygiene and grooming, selecting of clothing, self-esteem, managing household tasks, communication, and low-vision devices.

Author:	Torres, I., and Corn, A. L.
Title:	*When You Have a Visually Handicapped Child in Your Classroom: Suggestions for Teachers (2nd ed.)*
Date:	1990
Publisher:	American Foundation for the Blind 15 West 16th Street, New York, NY 10011
ISBN:	0-89128-175-4
Cost:	Bulk orders only: 25 copies, $85.00

Format:	Booklet, 48 pp.
Subject:	Education, blindness and low vision
Summary:	Information for integrating students with visual impairments into regular classrooms. Topics covered include helping students feel comfortable, orienting students to their classrooms and school, understanding special devices, and working with the resource room. Explains concepts related to blindness and low vision.

Author:	Uslan, M., Peck, A., Wiener, W., and Stern, A. (Eds.)
Title:	*Access to Mass Transit for Blind and Visually Impaired Travelers*
Date:	1990
Publisher:	American Foundation for the Blind 15 West 16th Street, New York, NY 10011
ISBN:	0-89128-166-5
Cost:	$22.00
Format:	Softcover book, 191 pp.
Subject:	Orientation and mobility, transition
Summary:	A handbook on the use of public transportation by persons who are blind or visually impaired that includes a step-by-step program for using orientation and mobility techniques in rapid rail systems; a three-pronged plan for soliciting travel information; and a glossary, resource list, and bibliography.

Author:	van Dijk, J.
Title:	*Persons Handicapped by Rubella—Victors and Victims: A Follow-Up Study*
Date:	1991
Publisher:	Taylor and Francis 1900 Frost Road, Suite 101, Bristol, PA 19007
ISBN:	90-265-1128-0
Cost:	$36.00
Format:	Softcover book, 180 pp.
Subject:	Deaf-blindness, education

Summary: A report on the findings of a 1988 reassessment of a sub-sample of persons who are deaf-blind who had been assessed in 1976 that describes the current status of the "rubella problem" and details the original and follow-up studies, the subjects, and educational strategies for these individuals.

Author:	Watkins, S.
Title:	*Developing Cognition in Young Hearing Impaired Children*
Date:	1983
Publisher:	HOPE, Inc. 809 North 800 East, Logan, UT 84321
ISBN:	NA
Cost:	$11.00
Format:	Softcover book, 122 pp.
Subject:	Communication, education, cognitive development
Summary:	Information that will help service providers guide parent training about concept development, including how hearing loss affects the development of concepts and the understanding of symbols so that parents can make adaptations to promote development. Other SKI*HI program materials complement this information.

Author:	Watkins, S.
Title:	*Developing Consistent and Effective Total Communication in the Home*
Date:	1982
Publisher:	HOPE, Inc. 809 North 800 East, Logan, UT 84321
ISBN:	NA
Cost:	$14.00
Format:	Softcover book, 153 pp.
Subject:	Communication, sign language, deafness and hearing impairments
Summary:	A monograph intended for service providers who are familiar with sign language to train parents of infants and toddlers in total communication. It includes an outline of

the program, illustrations of a few handshapes and signs, and a list of supplementary sign language text. Other SKI*HI program materials complement this monograph.

Author:	Watkins, S.
Title:	*Developing Sign Communication with the Multi-handi-capped Sensory Impaired Child*
Date:	1985
Publisher:	HOPE, Inc. 809 North 800 East, Logan, UT 84321
ISBN:	NA
Cost:	$14.00
Format:	Booklet, 68 pp.
Subject:	Sign language, communication, deaf-blindness
Summary:	Part of the INSITE Communication Program—a home intervention program for infants and young children who are deaf-blind and have multiple handicaps—that includes signs organized into categories relevant to home life and photographs that illustrate three levels of signing: natural gestures, coactive signs, and interactive signs.

Author:	Watkins, S. (Ed.)
Title:	*The INSITE Model:* *Home Intervention for Infant, Toddler, and Preschool* *Aged Multihandicapped Sensory Impaired Children*
Date:	1989
Publisher:	HOPE, Inc. 809 North 800 East, Logan, UT 84321
ISBN:	NA
Cost:	$90.00 (two-volume set)
Format:	Two three-ring binders, 400 pp. each volume
Subject:	Deaf-blindness, early intervention, families
Summary:	A home-based programming curriculum. The first volume contains an overview of the INSITE model and information for parent advisers who work in home-intervention programs. Topics include the child with multiple disabilities and sensory impairments; determining family needs;

providing family support; and planning, delivering, and assessing programs. The second part of Volume 1 and the entire second volume contain the actual home-instruction lessons in five program areas: communication, hearing, vision, cognition, and motor impairment.

Author:	Watkins, S.
Title:	*Sign Language for the Family*
Date:	1989
Publisher:	HOPE, Inc.
	809 North 800 East, Logan, UT 84321
ISBN:	NA
Cost:	$21.00
Format:	Softcover book, 227 pp.
Subject:	Families, sign language
Summary:	Designed to accompany the SKI*HI Total Communication Videotapes, this book follows the same 60-lesson sequence. Each lesson includes a list of signs, practice sentences, suggested home activities and games, and pictures and descriptions of the signs that focus on daily living activities.

Author:	Wehman, P., Renzaglia, A., and Bates, P.
Title:	*Functional Living Skills for Moderately and Severely Handicapped Individuals*
Date:	1985
Publisher:	Pro-Ed
	8700 Shoal Creek Boulevard, Austin, TX 78758
ISBN:	0-936104-49-X
Cost:	$29.00
Format:	Softcover book, 281 pp.
Subject:	Moderate and severe disabilities, education
Summary:	Guidelines for functional programming that consider age appropriateness and community-based skills, review the characteristics of individuals with moderate and severe disabilities (primarily cognitive), and outline programs that will maximize independence.

Author: Welsh, R., and Blasch, B.

Title: *Foundations of Orientation and Mobility*

Date: 1980

Publisher: American Foundation for the Blind
15 West 16th Street, New York, NY 10011

ISBN: 0-89128-093-6

Cost: $40.00

Format: Hardcover book, 662 pp.

Subject: Orientation and mobility

Summary: A basic, comprehensive textbook that presents the origins, history, and principles of orientation and mobility (O&M). The topics include perception and locomotion; audition; tactile sensation; low vision; concept development; orientation aids and mobility devices; adaptations for teaching O&M to individuals with orthopedic impairments, diabetes, cerebral palsy, and cognitive impairments; environmental modifications; and administrative aspects of providing O&M services in educational and rehabilitation settings.

Author: West, J., Idol, L., and Cannon, G.

Title: *Collaboration in the Schools: An Inservice and Preservice Curriculum for Teachers, Support Staff, and Administrators*

Date: 1989

Publisher: Pro-Ed
8700 Shoal Creek Boulevard, Austin, TX 78758

ISBN: NA

Cost: Learner's book, $17.00; trainer's manual, $83.00

Format: Learner's book, softcover, 283 pp.; trainer's manual, softcover, 306 pp.

Subject: Education, families, disabilities

Summary: A teacher-training curriculum that addresses skills in communication, interaction, and problem solving as a member of an educational team.

Author:	Zieziula, F. R.
Title:	*Assessment of Hearing-Impaired People*
Date:	1986
Publisher:	Gallaudet University Press 800 Florida Avenue, NE, Washington, DC 20002
ISBN:	0-913580-80-5
Cost:	$14.00
Format:	Softcover book, 128 pp.
Subject:	Assessment, transition, deafness and hearing impairments
Summary:	A compilation of information about the problems of assessing people who are hearing impaired that includes explanations of assessment issues and lists of appropriate instruments and resources.

Author:	Bienvenu, M. J., and Colonomos, B.
Title:	*An Introduction to American Deaf Culture*
Date:	1986 and 1988
Publisher:	Sign Media Burtonsville Commerce Center, 4020 Blackburn Lane, Burtonsville, MD 20866
ISBN:	NA
Cost:	$49.95 (each), $229.95 (set) (Workbooks are available at $7.95 each)
Format:	Set of five videotapes, 38–55 min. each
Subject:	Deafness and hearing impairments (culture), sign language
Summary:	An overview of the unique cultural aspects of the deaf community that emphasizes the visual aspects of culture and interaction. Five basic topics are covered: rules of social interaction, values, language and traditions, group norms, and identity.

Author:	Brush, P., and Otos, M.
Title:	*Within Reach: Getting to Know People Who Are Deaf-Blind*
Date:	1987
Publisher:	Teaching Research 345 North Monmouth Avenue, Monmouth, OR 97361
ISBN:	NA
Cost:	$10.00
Format:	Videotape, 25 min.
Subject:	Deaf-blindness, education
Summary:	A videotape that presents an overview of individuals who are deaf-blind and have a wide range of disabilities and discusses their basic educational needs. The topics include communication needs, teaching techniques, home and community settings, and technology.

Author:	Canadian National Institute for the Blind
Title:	*Deaf-Blindness: Connecting through Communication*

Date:	1990
Publisher:	Canadian National Institute for the Blind 1929 Bayview Avenue, Toronto, Ontario, M4G 3E8, Canada
ISBN:	NA
Cost:	$40.00 (Canadian dollars) plus $5.00 shipping
Format:	Videotape (open captioned), 15 min.
Subject:	Deaf-blindness, communication, transition
Summary:	An overview of deaf-blindness that presents basic information; highlights individuals with advanced skills; and demonstrates several communication modes, including braille, TeleBraille, large-print telephone adaptations, two-hand Canadian manual fingerspelling, tactile American Sign Language, print-on-palm, and closed-circuit television reading devices.

Author:	Canadian National Institute for the Blind
Title:	*Deaf-Blindness: Freedom through Intervention*
Date:	1991
Publisher:	Canadian National Institute for the Blind 1929 Bayview Avenue, Toronto, Ontario, M4G 3E8, Canada
ISBN:	NA
Cost:	$40.00 (Canadian dollars) plus $5.00 shipping
Format:	Videotape (open captioned), 8 min.
Subject:	Deaf-blindness, communication, transition
Summary:	A brief overview of "intervention," a Canadian concept for the provision of support services to persons who are deaf-blind. Intervention includes interpreting and providing assistance for travel, reading mail, personal business, and other daily living activities.

Author:	Cokely, D., and Baker-Shenk, C.
Title:	*American Sign Language: A Teacher's Resource Text on Curriculum, Methods, and Evaluation*
Format:	Videotape. For details, see entry under Print Materials.

Author:	Cooley, E.
Title:	*Getting in Touch: Communicating with a Child Who Is Deaf-Blind*
Date:	1987
Publisher:	Research Press Department 118, P.O. Box 3177, Champaign, IL 61821
ISBN:	NA
Cost:	$150.00
Format:	Videotape, 30 min.
Subject:	Deaf-blindness, communication
Summary:	An introduction to basic communication concepts for children and youths who are deaf-blind, including guidelines on how to initiate, conduct, and facilitate smooth communication; information on basic modes of communication, touch cues, object cues, and formal language (spoken and signed); and general concepts for teaching children who are deaf-blind.

Author:	Cooley, E., and Singer, G.
Title:	*Bringing Out the Best: Encouraging Expressive Communication in Children with Multiple Handicaps*
Date:	1989
Publisher:	Research Press Department 118, P.O. Box 3177, Champaign, IL 61821
ISBN:	NA
Cost:	$150.00
Format:	Videotape, 24 min.
Subject:	Communication, multiple disabilities
Summary:	Specific techniques for teaching expressive communication skills to children and youths, including methods on interrupting routines, responding to protest, and shaping the environment, and strategies to help children generalize these skills.

Author:	Fant, L.
Title:	*The American Sign Language Phrase Book, Videotape Series*

Date:	1988
Publisher:	Sign Media Burtonsville Commerce Center, 4020 Blackburn Lane, Burtonsville, MD 20866
ISBN:	0-8092-5507-3 (manual)
Cost:	Videotapes, $59.95 (each); manual, $14.95. Three tapes and one manual, $169.95.
Format:	Set of three videotapes, 60 min. each; softcover manual, 346 pp.
Subject:	Sign language, communication, deafness and hearing impairments
Summary:	Tapes and manual covering basic phrases in American Sign Language for daily interaction. Phrases include such daily topics as social expressions, health, weather, family, school, food, clothing, recreation, travel, and religion.

Author:	Ferrell, K.
Title:	*Reach Out and Teach: Meeting the Training Needs of Parents of Visually and Multiply Handicapped Young Children*
Format:	Slide-videotape presentation. For details, see entry under Print Materials.

Author:	Groode, J. L.
Title:	*Fingerspelling: Expressive and Receptive Fluency*
Date:	1992
Publisher:	Dawn Sign Press 9080 Activity Road, Suite A, San Diego, CA 92126
ISBN:	0-915035-13-8 (booklet)
Cost:	$39.95
Format:	Videotape, 120 min.; instructional booklet, 24 pp.
Subject:	Sign language, communication, deafness
Summary:	An in-depth discussion of fingerspelling, with opportunities to practice reading and expressive fingerspelling. Facts about fingerspelling, special techniques, and strategies are presented.

Author: Lentz, E. M., Mikos, K., and Smith, C.

Title: *Signing Naturally: Level 2*

Format: Set of three videotapes. For details, see entry under Print Materials.

Author: NA

Title: *Fingerspelling Practice Tapes (Proper Nouns, Geographic Locations, Fingerspelled Loan Signs, and Miscellaneous Items)*

Date: 1991

Publisher: Sign Media
Burtonsville Commerce Center, 4020 Blackburn Lane, Burtonsville, MD 20866

ISBN: NA

Cost: $59.95 (each), $199.95 (set)

Format: Set of four videotapes, 60 min. each

Subject: Sign language, communication, deafness and hearing impairments

Summary: Practice tapes for improving fingerspelling, both for expressive and receptive skills. Specific kinds of finger-spelled words are covered. Of special interest are "finger-spelled loan signs," for which fingerspelled words that may actually have signs are used in a quasi-sign mode, for emphasis or a specific communication task.

Author: NA

Title: *Introduction to Tactile Communication for Children Who Are Deaf-Blind*

Date: 1993

Publisher: HOPE, Inc.
809 North 800 East, Logan, UT 84321

ISBN: NA

Cost: $25.00

Format: Videotape, 60 min.

Subject: Communication, deaf-blindness

Summary: A description of how to interact with a person who is deaf-blind and how to recognize various means of communication. Includes suggestions to help children gain access to new people, places, and events. Also guides users in selecting materials from SKI*HI Institute's videotape series on tactile communication with children who are deaf-blind.

Author:	NA
Title:	*An Introduction to the Deaf Community*
Date:	1993
Publisher:	Sign Media Burtonsville Commerce Center, 4020 Blackburn Lane, Burtonsville, MD 20866
ISBN:	NA
Cost:	$29.95
Format:	Videotape (open captioned), 30 min.
Subject:	Deafness and hearing impairments (culture), sign language
Summary:	An overview of the deaf community in the United States. Cultural factors, rather than medical perspectives, are emphasized, and resource organizations are discussed.

Author:	NA
Title:	*Parent Sign Series*
Date:	1988
Publisher:	Sign Media Burtonsville Commerce Center, 4020 Blackburn Lane, Burtonsville, MD 20866
ISBN:	NA
Cost:	$29.95 (each), $264.95 (set)
Format:	Set of 10 videotapes, 60 min. each
Subject:	Families, sign language, deafness and hearing impairments, communication
Summary:	Instructional videotapes for parents of deaf children who wish to learn sign language. Emphasis is on everyday family interactions and activities, with such topics as waking up and getting dressed, the grocery store, and an afternoon at the park.

Author: NA

Title: *Partners in Language*

Date: 1993

Publisher: Helen Keller National Center
Communications Department, 111 Middle Neck Road,
Sands Point, NY 11050

ISBN: NA

Cost: $35.00 plus $2.00 shipping

Format: Videotape, 28 min., and accompanying listing
of resources

Subject: Deaf-blindness, communication, education

Summary: A videotape that shows how communication training is
provided to staff members working with clients who are
deaf-blind. A case-study format is used, and all the
methods and strategies used are summarized.

Author: NA

Title: *Playing the Crucial Role in Your Child's Development*

Date: 1985

Publisher: American Printing House for the Blind
P.O. Box 6085, Louisville, KY 40206

ISBN: NA

Cost: $20.00

Format: Videotape, 10 min. (converted from a slide-tape format)

Subject: Blindness and low vision, early intervention, families

Summary: Suggestions for parents of activities that provide sensory
stimulation to young children with visual impairments.

Author: NA

Title: *Using Tactile Interactive Conversational Signing
with Children Who Are Deaf-Blind*

Date: 1993

Publisher: HOPE, Inc.
809 North 800 East, Logan, UT 84321

ISBN: NA

Cost: $150.00 (set)

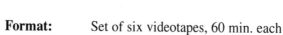

Format:	Set of six videotapes, 60 min. each
Subject:	Communication, deaf-blindness
Summary:	Part of the SKI*HI videotape series on tactile communication. Topics addressed include conversational interaction, moving from coactive to interactive signing, conveying emotion and meaning through tactile signs, and interpreting for individuals who are deaf-blind. Demonstrates tactile signing and features nationally known deaf-blind individuals.

Author:	NA
Title:	*Using Tactile Signals and Cues with Children Who Are Deaf-Blind*
Date:	1993
Publisher:	HOPE, Inc. 809 North 800 East, Logan, UT 84321
ISBN:	NA
Cost:	$200.00 (set)
Format:	Set of four videotapes, 60 min. each
Subject:	Communication, deaf-blindness
Summary:	Part of the SKI*HI videotape series on tactile communication. Topics include encouraging interaction, selecting signals, using signals in daily routines, responding to signals, and choosing strategies and activities to encourage communication.

Author:	NA
Title:	*Using Your TTY/TDD (rev. ed.)*
Date:	1993
Publisher:	Sign Media Burtonsville Commerce Center, 4020 Blackburn Lane, Burtonsville, MD 20866
ISBN:	NA
Cost:	$34.95
Format:	Videotape, 30 min.
Subject:	Deafness and hearing impairments, communication, transition, technology

Summary: An overview of the basic use of and etiquette for telephoning by TTY/TDD that can be used to train staff members and other new TTY users. Includes an 8" x 5" tips card to keep near the TTY.

Author: Rowland, C., and Schweigert, P.

Title: *Analyzing the Communication Environment (A.C.E.): An Inventory of Ways to Encourage Communication in Functional Activities*

Date: 1993

Publisher: Communication Skill Builders
3830 East Bellevue, Tucson, AZ 85733

ISBN: 0-88450-011-X (book)

Cost: $99.00

Format: Videotape, 90 min.; softcover book, 80 pp.

Subject: Communication, severe disabilities

Summary: An ecological inventory for assessing the communication value of specific functional activities and an overview of ways to increase the communication value of programs. Emphasizes practical strategies to promote communication using naturally occurring cues.

Author: Rowland, C., and Schweigert, P.

Title: *The Early Communication Process Using Microswitch Technology*

Date: 1994

Publisher: Communication Skill Builders
3830 East Bellevue, Tucson, AZ 85733

ISBN: 0-88450-008-X (book)

Cost: $99.00

Format: Videotape, 90 min.; softcover book, 102 pp.

Subject: Communication, severe disabilities

Summary: Systematic strategies for using microswitches to encourage intentional communication in children with severe sensory, orthopedic, and cognitive disabilities.

Author:	Rowland, C., and Schweigert, P.
Title:	*Tangible Symbol Systems: Symbolic Communication for Individuals with Multisensory Impairments*
Date:	1990
Publisher:	Communication Skill Builders 3830 East Bellevue, Tucson, AZ 85733
ISBN:	0-88450-462-X (manual)
Cost:	Videotape, $70.00; manual, $17.00
Format:	Videotape, 60 min.; manual, booklet, 61 pp.
Subject:	Augmentative communication, severe disabilities, deaf-blindness
Summary:	A videotape and manual describing and illustrating how to teach tactile symbols for receptive and expressive communication to students who are unable to use traditional spoken or sign language communication. Topics include vocabulary development and expansion, structured communication opportunities, and the use of tangible symbols in communication for everyday activities.

Author:	Rowland, C., Schweigert, P., Stremel, K., and Utah State University
Title:	*Observing and Enhancing Communication Skills in Children with Multisensory Impairments*
Date:	1992
Publisher:	Communication Skill Builders 3830 East Bellevue, Tucson, AZ 85733
ISBN:	0-88450-589-8 (book)
Cost:	$175.00 (set)
Format:	Set of two videotapes, 60 min. each; softcover book, 122 pp.
Subject:	Communication, deaf-blindness, severe disabilities
Summary:	Communication modes and intents that may be used by young children with multisensory impairments. Shows how to conduct observations, how to respond to communication, and how to provide opportunities to communicate.

Author:	Sign Media and Madonna University
Title:	*Sign Language Interpreters in the Public Schools*
Date:	1991
Publisher:	Sign Media Burtonsville Commerce Center, 4020 Blackburn Lane, Burtonsville, MD 20866
ISBN:	NA
Cost:	$299.95 (set)
Format:	Set of three videotapes, 60 min. each, and five accompanying print pamphlets and two resource lists, approximately 10 pp. each
Subject:	Sign language, education, deafness and hearing impairments, interpreting
Summary:	An in-service informational kit with three specific videotapes that assist with educational interpreting (elementary and secondary). Specific areas addressed are administrative issues in public elementary and secondary settings, educators' issues in using interpreters, and issues of educational interpreters themselves.

Author:	SKI*HI Institute
Title:	*Children with Motor Impairments: Part 1* *Children with Motor Impairments: Part 2*
Date:	1987
Publisher:	HOPE, Inc. 809 North 800 East, Logan, UT 84321
ISBN:	NA
Cost:	$30.00 each
Format:	Set of two videotapes, 60 min. each
Subject:	Motor development, early intervention
Summary:	Two videotapes that show a therapist working directly with a family, explaining the basic types of motor impairments—spastic cerebral palsy, athetosis/ataxia, and hypotonia (low tone), among others—and demonstrate techniques for a variety of activities: bathing, feeding, dressing, sitting, carrying, and general positioning.

Author:	SKI*HI Institute
Title:	*SKI*HI Coactive Sign System*
Date:	1991
Publisher:	HOPE, Inc. 809 North 800 East, Logan, UT 84321
ISBN:	NA
Cost:	$125.00 (set)
Format:	Set of nine videotapes, 20–30 min. each
Subject:	Deaf-blindness, communication, early intervention
Summary:	A home-intervention series showing American Sign Language signs arranged categorically with modifications and tips for interaction. Each lesson is cross-referenced to other supporting material in the series. The material is not captioned.

Author:	SKI*HI Institute
Title:	*SKI*HI Slide/Tape Programs*
Date:	Undated
Publisher:	HOPE, Inc. 809 North 800 East, Logan, UT 84321
ISBN:	NA
Cost:	$175.00
Format:	Videotape, approximately 30 min. (converted from slide-tape program)
Subject:	Deafness and hearing impairments, early intervention, communication
Summary:	A combination of five slide-tape presentations about home intervention programming that includes several components, among them hearing aids and auditory use and communication issues for children with hearing impairments, and that demonstrates how home intervenors can use the visuals in a flip-chart format.

Author:	SKI*HI Institute
Title:	*SKI*HI Total Communication Videotape Program*
Date:	1986

Publisher:	HOPE, Inc. 809 North 800 East, Logan, UT 84321
ISBN:	NA
Cost:	$225.00 (set)
Format:	Set of 20 videotapes, 25–30 min. each
Subject:	Sign language, families, early intervention
Summary:	An introduction to signs for the SEE system and basic signs (generally American Sign Language or Signed English) related to early childhood activities and experiences. The first tape explains how the entire series should be used and introduces basic family signs. The series is not captioned, and some of the signs may not be used in every part of the country.
Author:	Smith, C., Lentz, E. M., and Mikos, K.
Title:	*Signing Naturally: Level 1*
Format:	Videotape. For details, see entry under Print Materials.
Author:	Smith, T.
Title:	*Deaf-Blind Communication and Community:* 1: *Overview and Interaction* 2: *Getting Involved—A Conversation*
Date:	1992
Publisher:	Sign Media Burtonsville Commerce Center, 4020 Blackburn Lane, Burtonsville, MD 20866
ISBN:	NA
Cost:	Tape 1, $59.95; Tape 2, $79.95; both, $109.95
Format:	Set of two videotapes, 40 min. and 90 min.
Subject:	Sign language, deaf-blindness, communication
Summary:	An overview of how various visual impairments seem to individuals who have them; explains various factors in deaf-blindness, especially for communication and mobility. Tips for beginning with communication are given. Tape on conversation explains communication factors in more depth.

Author:	South Dakota Department of Education and Cultural Affairs
Title:	*Helping Your Child Learn*
Date:	1992
Publisher:	Walkervision Video
P.O. Box 930182, Verona, WI 53593-0182
ISBN:	NA
Cost:	$35.00 (per tape), $85.00 (set)
Format:	Set of three videotapes, 30 min. each
Subject:	Families, education, deaf-blindness
Summary:	A three-volume series of videotapes, filmed in the homes of 25 families of children who have significant vision and hearing impairments, as well as other disabilities. Volume 1 addresses teaching in natural settings and at naturally occurring times, helping children express themselves more appropriately, and enhancing play skills. Volume 2 shows how to break down learning tasks into manageable steps, the importance of including choices in daily routines, and hints for teaching dressing skills. Volume 3 shows successful teaching strategies, how to adapt activities to ensure participation and success, and teaching mealtime skills.